Rosalind Miles is the author of twenty-three books of fiction and non-fiction, including the internationally acclaimed *The Women's History of the World*. Translated into over forty languages, it became a top-ten bestseller in the UK and the US. She holds a number of degrees, and her doctoral work at the Shakespeare Institute led to the international best-selling historical novel, *I, Elizabeth*, the story of Queen Elizabeth I in her own words. Her varied career also includes teaching, serving as a magistrate, broadcasting and award-winning journalism. She is a Fellow of the Royal Society of Arts, Honorary Fellow of the University of Kent, a founder member of the International Women's Forum UK, the Women's Equality Party and a founder contributor of *The Literary Review*, *Working Woman UK* and *Prospect* Magazine. She lives in Hertfordshire with her husband, the historian, Robin Cross.

GIVE US FREEDOM

The Women Who Revolutionised the Modern World

ROSALIND MILES

virago

VIRAGO

First published as *Rebel Women* in Great Britain in 2020 by Virago Press
This paperback edition published in 2021 by Virago Press

1 3 5 7 9 10 8 6 4 2

A CIP catalogue record for this book
is available from the British Library.

ISBN 978-0-349-00608-6

Typeset in Bembo by M Rules
Printed and bound in Great Britain by
Clays Ltd, Elcograf S.p.A.

Papers used by Virago are from well-managed forests
and other responsible sources.

Virago Press
An imprint of
Little, Brown Book Group
Carmelite House
50 Victoria Embankment
London EC4Y 0DZ

An Hachette UK Company
www.hachette.co.uk

www.virago.co.uk

For all the women of the world
who are making their own history

CONTENTS

4 The Longest March

FOREWORD

Who was the all-time top goal scorer in the Football World Cup? None other than the aptly named quicksilver forward of the Brazilian women's team, Marta Vieira da Silva, who is changing history and making it anew. When I was a girl we never played football, and never thought we could. It was only one of the many ways that horizons were narrowing for girls at the same time as they were expanding for boys, a situation that was not expected to change.

As a child, I cannot remember when I realised that to most people, girls were less important than boys. Expecting a baby, I discovered that all pregnant women were called 'Mother' by the medical staff. Leaving college and trying to get a job, I was routinely asked, 'You've got a wonderful husband and two lovely children, what are you compensating for?'

Events like these are less likely to happen now that women have begun rebelling against their long-established role as adjuncts to the lives of men and children, and have emerged as strong and significant in their own right. This striking and exhilarating change has been the work of the women we celebrate in this book, even as we share the rewards of their determination and pluck. Rebel women have spent the last two hundred years thinking the unthinkable, dreaming of change, and making it come true. A female premier? A female president? A female pope? *Why not?*

It has been a thrilling task to track the stories of these extraordinary women who are no longer voices singing in the wilderness like the change-makers of former times, but have banded together to re-make our world. The freedom they have won for women has been in an unofficial alliance with other groups, including good men, when liberating girls from the narrow demands of compulsory wife-and-motherhood has allowed boys too to choose a different path. The Women's Movement has grown up and come of age in the same era as the wider LGBT+ community, Black Lives Matter, anti-racist protests and calls for diversity, all creating a more inclusive and a better society for us all.

Such a wide canvas had to be selective and I had to leave out so many of my own heroines that I can only apologise if I have omitted yours. I aimed to achieve a balance between those who are household names and the many women who are less well-known, in the hope of encouraging readers to follow their trail, and that of all the others who have been lost to us and gone unnoticed by the history books. I accept that readers may find this account concentrates heavily on the western world, but I do not present it as definitive. Liberating women is a work in progress. I want this to be a story that inspires others to take the history of women further and higher in our emergence from centuries in the shadows to the broad light of day.

Some readers may feel that this is not 'real' history, because like my previous *Women's History of the World*, published in America as *Who Cooked the Last Supper?*, it makes no pretence to the traditional historical fiction of impartiality. Others might feel that it is unfair to men. I can only make the same defence that I made then, echoing the pioneer women's historian Mary Ritter Beard, who faced the same charges and made this robust response: 'There is sure to be an over-emphasis in places, but my apology is that when conditions have been long weighted too much on one side, it is necessary to bear down heavily on the other.'

In the twenty-first century we are looking forward to a world that offers a myriad of opportunities to follow in the footsteps of my rebel women. These are the lamplighters who have gone before to show us the way, and we must not let them down. Let us not rest till all of us are free.

Rosalind Miles

I

Turning The Wheel

As I sat watching Everyman at the Charterhouse, I said to myself Why not Everywoman?

GEORGE BERNARD SHAW

CHAPTER 1

RIGHTS – FOR WOMEN?

Bliss was it in that dawn to be alive.

WILLIAM WORDSWORTH

So you think revolutions can be made with rosewater?

SÉBASTIEN-ROCH NICOLAS DE CHAMFORT

The position of women in the [civil rights]
movement is prone.

STOKELY CARMICHAEL

Prone, said the man.

Was she face down that day, or face up? Staring into the basket of blood-soaked severed heads where her own would shortly drop, or strapped to the board on her back, looking up at the blade as it fell?

It was the French Revolution, the dawning of the modern age. For women, it promised the best and swiftly delivered the worst. This forty-five-year old met her death with her thick black hair hacked off in clumps to bare her neck for the blade, the common treatment for condemned women including the Queen, Marie Antoinette. When so many were killed that the cobbles of Paris were sticky with their blood, most women died unknown and unnamed. But this guillotine on this dank day of 3 November 1793 sliced through the neck and silenced the brain of one of the most original thinkers of the time, Olympe de Gouges.

Her last moments were recorded by an anonymous Parisian:

> Yesterday, at seven o'clock in the evening, a most extraordinary person called Olympe de Gouges who held the imposing title of woman of letters, was taken to the scaffold . . .
>
> She approached the scaffold with a calm and serene expression on her face, and forced the guillotine's furies, which had driven her to this place of torture, to admit that such courage and beauty had never been seen before . . . That woman . . . had thrown herself in the Revolution, body and soul. But having quickly perceived how atrocious the system adopted by the Jacobins was, she chose to retrace her steps. She attempted to unmask the villains through the literary productions which she had printed and put up. They never forgave her, and she paid for her carelessness with her head.

The reason for the death of de Gouges lay in the slogan that set out the aims of the Revolution: *Liberté, Égalité, Fraternité.* Under this banner the revolutionaries rising up against the monarchy paraded their wares, promising citizenship, comradeship and freedom from tyranny, all three on offer for the first time in French history. But any hopes the women of France might have entertained of liberty or equality were soon crushed. One by one they had to face the reality every revolution delivers sooner or later, that when freedom is given out, women are not in the queue. Both liberty and equality are restricted to, and controlled by, the universal fraternity of men.

From sea to shining sea

That hard truth had been forced down the throats of the women of America only fourteen years earlier, when the War of Independence broke out in 1775. This eight-year conflict, a crucial forerunner to the French Revolution, saw many rebel women fighting on the front line alongside men. They died like men too, either in battle or from combat diseases like typhoid fever or infected wounds. The 'she-souldier' Deborah Sampson, who enlisted in the 4th Massachusetts Regiment at the age of twenty-one, showed the courage that made the nation when she dug out a musket ball lodged in her groin with her pen-knife and sewed up the wound afterwards, all without benefit of anaesthetic.

A few of these female patriots fought as women, especially if they had a husband or brother at their side. But most found it expedient to disguise themselves as men, whatever the risk of discovery. In the ranks, Sampson – who adopted the alias of Robert Shirtliff – was teased for her lack of facial hair and nicknamed 'Molly', a slang term for a gay or effeminate male. Undeterred, she proved her worth not only in battle but as the leader of dangerous reconnaissance expeditions, scouting targets for attack so important that they were chosen by the commander-in-chief of the army, George Washington himself. She was only discovered during an epidemic of camp fever, when she was too ill to resist the army doctor's examination, but her valour was recognised. Honourably discharged in October 1783, Sampson married, had three children, and later became the only woman soldier of the Continental Army to be granted a full military pension. Another world first was achieved by her widowed husband when he petitioned for spousal rights to Sampson's pension after her death in 1867 – and won.

In the American Civil War of 1861–5, an Illinois-born mother of three, Frances Clalin Clayton, was one of a number of women who signed up for active service disguised as men. Enlisting as 'Jack Williams', she joined the Union Army with her husband, and fought side by side with him until he was killed, then reportedly stepped over his body to continue fighting. Like Deborah Sampson, Clayton lived to see her war service recognised and to be honoured as a veteran.

Were these the first steps towards equality?

Shoulder to shoulder, bolder and bolder, women fighting side by side with men, *yes*!

But women's rights as a political aim?

Hell, no!

Revolutions only succeed because they win women's support by offering the promise of inclusion into the brave new world where men and women make common cause and go forward together. Yet however sincerely intended, this promise vanishes when women actively engage in the struggle. During the Revolution, American women discovered what the French women were shortly to learn: that whatever their courage and endurance, they were all working for men, in a system run by men, for the cause of men. To question the cause was to betray it, so they were never able to single out their own interests as women, and to fight for that cause and that alone.

Look no further than the closing lines of 'America the Beautiful', the patriotic ode to manhood of 1893 written by the writer, professor and activist Katharine Lee Bates for proof:

America! America!
God shed his grace on thee

And crown thy good with brotherhood
From sea to shining sea!

Yes, brotherhood, or *fraternité*, as the French had it. It's that happy lad Frater Familias, every girl's brother playing Junior to good ol' Pater Familias in the family hierarchy, in training for the top job from birth. Who could deny that young Junior's god, 'Brotherhood', had to be protected in order to ensure his succession?

Revolution the great engine

The American Revolution ended the King of England's rule and founded the American republic on 3 September 1783 with the Treaty of Paris. Where one revolution ended, another began. Less than six years later, also in Paris, the people of France embarked on their own struggle to overthrow their monarchy and set up a republic.

For French women, the omens were good. The American Revolution had been a male military campaign in which the women who participated largely passed as men and served under male command. By direct contrast, the women of France began and led the spontaneous uprising that sparked the French Revolution, and throughout the struggle women equalled or even outdid the men. They had every reason to believe that the freedom they were fighting for would be theirs on equal terms with men.

And for a brief shining moment the women of Paris were indeed a vital part of that new dawn, if not the dawn itself. That occurred when a raging mob stormed the Bastille on 14 July 1789, a date now recognised as the start of hostilities between the monarchy and the *sans-culottes*, persons too poor to have pants. In the heroic story that ran around the world, a woman dressed as an Amazon led the attack on the Bastille, the most dreaded symbol of the King's power. According to the pamphlets pumped out by the royalist press, this rebel commander was a twenty-six-year-old Belgian, Théroigne de Méricourt.

Tall, strong-featured, wild-haired and with more than a hint of a squint, de Méricourt cut a striking figure as she plunged into the life of revolutionary Paris, striding around town in a man's riding clothes and sporting a large hat with a flamboyantly phallic plume. De Méricourt had arrived in town just two months earlier, escaping a rackety past that included a spell as a courtesan, a failed attempt to become an opera singer, and a series of disastrous love affairs. Her last was a hopeless passion for the world-famous Italian male soprano and professional charmer Giusto Fernando Tenducci, at fifty-two exactly twice her age but still floridly handsome, with heavy-lidded eyes, quizzical eyebrows and a luscious mouth. Regrettably, Tenducci was both a married man and a castrato, and had no love for her. When she left him, crushed and humiliated by yet another defeat, Paris offered her the chance to reinvent herself and to start again.

She seized it with both hands, beginning with her name. Born Anne-Josèphe Terwagne in the small town of Marcourt in the Southern Netherlands, she changed 'Terwagne' into '*Théroigne*' and 'Marcourt' into '*Méricourt*', then tossed in *de*, the patronymic of French aristocrats, to imply social significance. Reborn, she threw herself into the revolutionary ferment gripping the French capital. By November 1789, her activities had drawn the fire of the royalist pamphleteers, who portrayed her as the hideously ugly 'war chief' of the Revolution.

They also painted her as 'the patriots' whore', a prostitute so prolific that she was supposed to have had sex with every one of the 576 members of the newly formed National Assembly – which meant that since her arrival in May she would have had to entertain ninety-six men a month, or at least three a day, every day. Who better, then, than this 'harlot' to be identified as the man-hating Amazon who had brought about the Fall of the Bastille and overseen the live dismemberment of the commander of the garrison, along with many other casualties and deaths?

It was all too good to be true, and so it proved. De Méricourt was not even in the city at the time but out at Versailles, where she was closely following the debates of the National Assembly. But why let the facts interfere with a good story? Women were indeed crucial to the uprising, and three months later in the heart of the city an unknown market woman, mad with hunger, obsessively pounding a drum and screaming 'No bread! No bread!' triggered the first and one of the most decisive events of the Revolution, the Women's March on Versailles of 5 October 1789.

The starvation that had gripped the poor of Paris that summer fell more heavily on the women than on the men, because they generally fed their families before themselves. Every hungry woman in Paris that day felt the same hollow drum beating in her own empty belly, and they rallied to the call. 'Women were in the forward ranks of our revolution,' the historian François Mignet wrote. 'We should not be surprised at this, they suffered more.' Fishwives and stall-holders, shop girls, sex workers and the women of the neighbourhood, respectable *bourgeoises* and even *femmes à chapeau*, the wealthy and well-dressed, all swarmed into the city clamouring for action, and the march began.

Fishwives to the fore

Few things are more fearsome than a female mob, as the Ancient Greeks could have told the *ancien régime*. On that day in October 1789, their numbers swelling by the minute and every one of them frantic for relief, for change, for *food*, thousands of women set out from Paris for Versailles, where the King, the Queen, the royal family and all their key officials were in residence. Seventeen miles on foot in the pouring rain was a long way to go for starving women, marching from the city centre to the gilded palace of Marie Antoinette and Louis XVI. They were led, bullied and beaten on when necessary, by the famously foul-mouthed fishwives of Paris shouting, 'The old order? *We don't give a fuck for your order!*', hoping, when they got there, that they could catch and gut a royal flounder or two.

For the famished rebels, there were to be no loaves or fishes that day. But nor was there any miracle on hand to save the fat and fated creatures in Versailles: their goose was cooked. The next day, the leaders of the mob forced the royal party to go back to Paris, a decision Louis XVI had neither taken nor agreed. That one act of subjecting the King to the women's demands, the crowning achievement of their march, foreshadowed the overthrow of the monarchy. It also put paid for ever to any French king's unquestioned right to rule, previously held to be both natural and divine. The will of the people – female people in this case – had succeeded in reversing history, theology and the very concept of authority to create a new order in which the citizen, not the monarch, held sovereign power.

What a march that was! And what a day for the women who took part! For the first time in their lives they tasted power, and with it the promise of freedom and equality as a reality, not merely as a slogan. This was the true revolution, the world turned upside down, when as powerless women they confronted the King and Queen in their palace at Versailles and brought them down. As the news spread, Paris became a magnet for rebellious women of all nations whose experience of life had left them ready for radical change.

Sisters in arms

This theme of reinvention runs through the stories of all the leading women of the revolution, every one in search of an identity, a new life, and a means to throw off the chains of the past. Almost all had suffered at the hands of a string of abusive men, ranging from absent or alcoholic fathers to calculating and callous seducers, and they came to Paris with a furious determination to seize the day, every day. Among them was the multi-lingual, multi-talented Dutch-born Etta Palm d'Aelders. Pinging round Europe from lover to lover after a failed marriage, Etta found her feet, her voice and her vocation in Paris when she arrived in 1773 at the age of thirty. There she parlayed her day job as a spy for the Dutch and her night job as a courtesan to the rich and famous into the role of a political hostess, and her salon attracted powerful men like the brilliant physician and political journalist Jean-Paul Marat, then cresting the wave as a leader of the Revolution.

But who needed salons? In those days, you only had to leave the house to come across a debate, a public meeting, a riot or a demonstration of some sort, as the monarchy lost its grip on the masses and with it the struggle to suppress that most vital of freedoms, the freedom of speech. In 1790 Etta joined the newly formed Fraternal Society of Patriots of Both Sexes, a political club remarkable for allowing women to take an active role in its meetings and discussions, and even to hold office, though not that of President. But it soon became clear that female voices could never be freely heard in a mixed environment. Rebel women responded by forming an estimated thirty political clubs of their own.

In 1791 Etta founded one of them herself, the Patriotic and Charitable Society of the Women Friends of Truth. Considerably more radical was the Society of Revolutionary Republican Women, formed in May 1793, while another group founded in the same year, the Republican Revolutionary Women Citizens' Club, was simply called *Le Club*. Whatever their names, these gatherings provided women with a unique opportunity to argue about the issues of the moment and to thrash out political solutions free from male interference or control.

Meeting several times a week, sometimes every day and every night, they created places of safety in which women could, above all, challenge the dictates of the men. As these clubs evolved, printing presses were brought in to turn the main themes of the debates into pamphlets that could be distributed, hot off the press, the following day. In those crowded, candlelit attics and damp, smoky cellars, rebel women seized the sudden, spangled moment to claim personal autonomy, the right to think and act for themselves.

Many years ahead of the great mantra of modern feminism, for these women the personal was indeed political. But their focus on themselves as women was far more political than personal. They saw the women of France serving the Revolution by shaping, directing and fighting for the infinitely precious but still pathetically fragile republic. Along with that, they were fighting for themselves. If the Revolution overthrew the King as a figure of unlawful authority, they argued, how could men continue to rule their wives with the same undisputed and unregulated power? Only if women were free from the tyranny of the 'masculine monarchy' could they take their place as equals in the new republic and live out its ideals.

For the deceptively demure but sublimely belligerent twenty-six-year-old Pauline Léon, a former chocolate-maker, the situation called for action, not argument. More than a century before Mao Zedong declared that 'Political power grows out of the barrel of a gun', Léon argued that freedom and full citizenship for women lay in the right to bear arms. In March 1791, with France facing the threat of invasion from both Austria and Prussia, she organised 319 women to petition the National Assembly for the right to form an all-female National Guard to defend Paris and themselves.

A battalion of women?

What next?

Léon's petition was refused.

But the intense political debate went on.

Égalité, mesdames?

In this wild and whirling firmament, Olympe de Gouges came up with a claim that was to prove more revolutionary than many of the movements traditionally recognised as a revolution. When every voice around her in the political assemblies, clubs and cafés was loudly proclaiming the inalienable rights of man, and women's attempts to align themselves with the new freedoms were decried or dismissed, she reasoned *why*? Why were women considered unworthy of the rights available to men? Alone at her desk in the watches of the night, after a day of activity in revolutionary Paris, she set herself to tease out the history of women's inferiority, and to attack the tyranny of the men who proclaimed it. In doing so, she gave birth to one of the most radical proposals in the history of the world: no less than the idea that *women should be fully and freely equal to men.*

Who was this rebel woman who wanted to change the world with a vision so advanced that over two hundred years later not one country, state or nation has achieved it, yet in essence a concept so simple that a child could understand? Born Marie Gouze in the deep south-west of France in 1748, she grew up believing that she was not the daughter of her mother's husband, the crude peasant butcher Pierre Gouze, but the bye-blow of a local nobleman famed in the Languedoc as a prolific dramatist, poet and essayist, the Marquis de Pompignan. Her claim against

him was unsurprisingly dismissed by the Marquis in a humiliating public declaration, and at the age of seventeen Marie was
forced into marriage with Louis-Yves Aubry, a much older man
she utterly despised.

Soon pregnant, she gave birth to a son, Pierre, in 1766, and
four months later, in the depths of winter and at a time of
raging floods, her husband died. The next year her luck turned
again when she found a rich young lover in Jacques Biétrix de
Rozières. His wealthy family would not allow him to marry the
low-born Marie, but he paid for her lodgings when she followed
him to Paris with Pierre some time before 1770.

And who was she now?

Not 'the Widow Aubry', the label she had been forced to bear
for the last four years: she flatly refused any further connection
with the husband she never pretended to mourn. Nor did she
ever style herself 'Madame Biétrix de Rozières'. Little is known
of her connection with her lover in Paris but although he supported her generously for the rest of her life, she would never
marry again. She was single, she was independent, and to make
a new life she needed a new name. As a re-branding exercise,
every element of the name she chose speaks volumes about the
life she intended to carve out in the capital.

First came '*Olympe*', chosen for her Olympian ideals and
hopes, but intriguingly also the name of the mother she had
left behind. Then came the aristocratic '*de*' to elevate her status,
a paradoxical choice for a revolutionary but perhaps reassert-
ing her claim to be the daughter of the literary aristocrat de
Pompignan. Finally she changed Gouze to '*Gouges*', dropping
the tell-tale 'z' of her native *langue d'oc* in favour of something
more French-sounding, soothing and grand. And there she was,
the rough provincial Marie Gouze now every inch the smart
Parisienne Olympe de Gouges, from her handmade silk shoes
to the roots of her fashionably powdered hair.

In Paris, Olympe was immediately noticed for the 'radiance' of her dark Occitan beauty, but even more for her vivacity and wit. 'She spoke a lot and at great length,' recalled the actor A.-J. Fleury in his *Mémoires* of 1847, indicating that she had no fear of her new-found audience of city sophisticates, and clearly enjoyed being the centre of attention. 'Lively, with a keen eye and ear and a good memory,' he continued, 'she boasted of her sharp wording and ingenious repartee, and rightly so.' Supremely, even annoyingly, confident she clearly was, but Fleury also remembered her as 'generous, kind, compassionate, humane'. Free at last to be herself, Olympe de Gouges now emerged as a prolific writer, confidently turning out over sixty essays, novels, plays and political pamphlets during her Paris years.

If her energy was prodigious, her range was equally remarkable. One play of 1788, *L'Esclavage des Noirs* ('The Slavery of Negroes'), mounted a strong attack on the slave trade, making de Gouges among the earliest to identify and defend what had yet to be recognised as 'human rights' applying to all, and not merely to the assorted and disputed 'rights of man'. From 1789, she was welcomed into the salon of Sophie de Condorcet, a famously good-hearted proto-feminist who made a point of including other women among her guests, and whose husband publicly called for civic rights for women and argued that they should have the vote. There de Gouges rubbed shoulders with like-minded radicals including the writer and polymath Pierre Beaumarchais, the Scottish 'Father of Economics' Adam Smith and the American Envoy to France – and future President – Thomas Jefferson.

When the Bastille fell in 1789 and the Paris of the 1790s became the revolutionary hotspot of the world, Olympe de Gouges was poised for action and passionate to engage. On the verge of her forties, with her son off her hands making his way as a soldier, she refreshed her image by dropping seven years from her age and plunged headlong into the fiery furnace of debate and action. Meeting, marching, speaking, writing, she drove herself day and night in the service of the cause.

A for effort, B for back in your box

The effort was stupendous, the work exceptional, but how was it received? Despite widespread public admiration for the exploits of individual women, the tide was swiftly and strongly turning against them as the Revolution drew to a close. Among those raising his voice to reassert women's natural subjection to men was that great lover of women and all-round Mr Nice Guy, the Marquis de Sade. 'Our so-called chivalry,' he explained in his novel *Juliette* (1798), 'derives from the fear of witches that once plagued our ignorant ancestors. Their terror was transmuted ... into respect ... but such respect is fundamentally unnatural, since Nature nowhere gives a single instance of it. The natural inferiority of women to men is universally evident, and nothing intrinsic to the female sex naturally inspires respect.'

It is beyond satire that a man who spent his life inflicting violence and sexual torture on women could consider himself superior to anyone, but de Sade never wavered in his utter contempt for the female sex. In another of history's little jokes, the malevolent Marquis was a member of the National Convention in April 1793, when Pauline Léon, that long-standing advocate of women's right to bear arms, brought up the question again. Two years earlier her attempt to secure permission to form an all-female fighting force to defend Paris had failed. With France now at war against both Austria and Prussia, Léon tried once more to establish a woman's right to fight for the Republic, and for themselves. Her action spectacularly backfired. The members of the National Convention, desk-generals to a man, banned women in perpetuity from bearing arms or serving in the army in any role. No prizes for guessing which way de Sade cast his vote.

Like Théroigne de Méricourt and other prominent women of the time, Olympe de Gouges supported Léon's claim for women to be granted the right to use force, either in civic defence or in action against an enemy, allowing them to play an active and militant role in the new citizenship. But with her luminous, wide-ranging intelligence and depth of understanding, de Gouges saw that this was not a single-issue struggle. What was the key to it all, the one over-arching, organising factor that would unite and incorporate all women's hopes and demands? And should not that be the site of the struggle, and the sole aim of female revolutionaries?

Pondering these issues, de Gouges wrote the piece for which she is still remembered, her declaration of 'The Rights of Woman and of the Female Citizen' (*Les Droits de la Femme et de la Citoyenne*). Produced in 1791, this was a bold, even reckless response to the French Revolutionary Council's 1789 *Declaration des Droits de l'Homme et du Citoyen*, its 'Declaration of the Rights of Man', or more accurately, '*the* Man, the *Male*'. As to 'the Citizen', the masculine noun '*Citoyen*' once again meant the male only, which placed all law, all social organisation, all occupation and all control in the hands of men.

With little formal education, still less any legal training, de Gouges nevertheless saw that any change had to begin by recognising that female inferiority was not natural, but enforced. Men made themselves superior by suppressing women, by treating them as unequal and denying them equality at every turn. This system was not accidental but structural, and it deformed women's lives. It had created a rock-solid and enduring injustice that now demanded a new and total revolution in which the law, the constitution, the culture and the world itself had to change if women were to be free.

In an age electric with hope, the Revolution seemed the perfect time for renewal, offering an unrepeatable opportunity to reshape the world in a more female-friendly form. External change promoted self-examination and self-development, and the Revolution gave women a unique chance to change themselves and their former beliefs. That change, powered from within, was an essential precursor to identifying and re-shaping the external structures that held women back. Each individual right counted for little by itself, without the one fundamental right from which all others derived: equality. Women were equal to men, and they would no longer be relegated to a lower status. By using the term '*La Citoyenne*', de Gouges created a vision of the future for the whole of the female sex in a newly invented ideal of a civic community, without the domination of men as law-makers, husbands, priests or kings: a republic of equals.

Alas, de Gouges had committed the unpardonable offence of daring to challenge the most sacred tenets of the French Revolution, its founding ideals of liberty, equality and, above all, the cherished fraternity. How could this slogan be true, she wrote furiously, when men claimed all three in the name of universal humanity, and then reserved all the benefits for themselves? 'Woman is born free and remains equal to man in rights,' she declaimed in her passionate and persuasive polemic. 'Women, wake up … recognise your rights! Oh women, women, when will you cease to be blind? What advantages have you gathered in the Revolution? A scorn more marked, a disdain more conspicuous … Whatever the barriers set up against you, it is in your power to overcome them; you only have to want it!'

You only have to want it

A rallying cry for women that rings down the ages and remains a clarion call today. Want it and it can be yours, freedom, equality, the right to live your life in the way you choose: a resonant challenge in any age, but fighting talk in 1791 and far too radical for the Revolution's leaders, eager to promote ragged-arsed men, the *sans-culottes*, but pitiless when it came to the female of the species. Ten thousand years of patriarchy with its blessed endowment of command and control, not to mention every man's own personal sense of superiority and full entitlement to the prerogative of the penis: imagine all that stitched up in the women's claim to equality and then ditched in that same instant.

You can see why the men got annoyed. No power-holder ever gave up power without a fight, and having only just torn their own flimsy shreds of authority from the hands of the King, the Church and the state, the male revolutionaries were in no mind to take such an angry rebuke from a woman. To some, de Gouges foretold her own fate when she wrote that if a woman committed a capital offence, the state demanded that she died on equal terms with men: how could it then refuse her the right to live on equal terms as well? Why should not women live as men lived, shaping the state and the law with action and debate? As long as every female had 'the right to mount the scaffold', de Gouges declared, then 'she should have the right equally to mount the public platform as well'. In other words, all ideas of freedom were hollow and meaningless unless women were granted the rights that would make them equal with men.

Rights for women?

Female equality?

Women making policy, women arguing and debating terms like men, women fighting to bear arms like Pauline Léon's proposed brigade of Amazons clamouring for weapons and spoiling for a fight? All these raised a far deeper question: *whose revolution is it anyway?*

For the men who had brought about the French Revolution and now ruled the roost, from the fiery orator Georges-Jacques Danton to the ice-cold lawyer Maximilien Robespierre, there was only one answer to this. So what if the women of France had marched with them and even ahead of them, had fought and died with them from the start? The Revolution was men's business, and always would be. The agonising years of struggle and suffering had so far failed to get the republic onto a firm footing, taken up as the men were with the ongoing battle to free the nation from the sclerotic grip of the past, the old order which so stubbornly refused to die. And now the women were up in arms, demanding their half of the spoils of a war not yet won?

The members of the governing National Convention were left with two stark choices, both equally problematic:

- To redefine citizenship to include women as full members, thereby admitting them to government.
- To deny the demands for equality, to crush women in politics and prevent further agitation.

There could be only one outcome.

And how to deal with the woman who had raised the cry for equality, who had dared to make the most outlandish and revolutionary claim of them all, Olympe de Gouges? Among those who saw the best and the worst of these times, none had succeeded in containing its contradictions as brilliantly as she did. A convinced republican, she nevertheless argued against the execution of Louis XVI, because she opposed the death penalty as barbaric and inhumane. An opponent of royal tyranny and colonial slavery, she stood out against the elected revolutionary government on the grounds that its over-zealous judgements and paranoid regulations rendered it no better than the monarchy, which had made slaves of one and all.

More dangerously, however, she refused to doff her cap to the men in charge. In all her wide-ranging and confrontational polemics like the 'Urgent Notice to the Convention' and 'The National Pact', Olympe analysed and attacked without fear or favour. Nor would she tolerate sexist discrimination. 'Let's not talk about my sex,' she instructed her readers. 'Women are just as capable of generosity and heroism, the Revolution has proved it so on many occasions [and] until something is done to elevate women's minds, and until men become open-minded enough to seriously deal with the glory of women, the State can never prosper.'

In May 1793, de Gouges heard that her son had been wounded in battle. Fearing for his life, she raced to Touraine where Pierre lived with his wife and baby son. There she learned that the young man had recovered enough to travel to Paris in search of a commission to further his career. Away from the capital, she felt the peace of the countryside so deeply that she bought herself a nearby thatched cottage. She seems to have been planning to use the *chaumière* to be closer to her family, and as a refuge from the increasingly dangerous atmosphere in the city. But there was little chance of that.

As the revolutionary fervour intensified in Paris, de Gouges was arrested and imprisoned in July. By September, the monomaniacal Robespierre was the most powerful man in France. He and his supporters pushed through laws that gave them sweeping new powers to authorise arrest on any suspicion, however slight, closely followed by death without trial. October brought the guillotining of Marie Antoinette, a public spectacle that reignited republican fury and heightened tensions in the capital. On 30 October the National Convention issued a decree excluding women from all political activity. Their clubs were closed down, their leaders arrested and their debates banned, to put an end to women's active citizenship and their participation in the Revolution. The women were proscribed as a threat to the fledgling republic and its leaders, and as an abomination of nature repulsive to all. 'Impudent women who want to turn themselves into men, don't you have enough already?' spluttered Pierre Chaumette, the president of the Paris Revolutionary Council. He thought it horrible – unnatural – for a woman to want to become a man. And as the childbearers of the world, they were also a danger to the future of the human race – monsters, in fact.

This October decree sealed the political death of the women of France even as the Revolution was gearing up to bring about their civic and legal deaths with equally harsh repression. The new regulation was also intended to control the volatile Paris mob, the still-starving, still-savage *sans-culottes*, now infamous for sadistic murders and impromptu lynchings. 'Let us be terrible,' Georges-Jacques Danton declared, 'in order to stop the people from being so.' In truth, the Revolution had been terrible for some time, as the members of the viciously divided Convention lost control of themselves and one another, and could see no way of resolving their political conflicts other than by destroying their opponents. Robespierre succeeded in turning the full force of his political party against the moderates, the group with which de Gouges allied herself. By the end of the month, twenty-nine of his opponents had been guillotined and he was unassailable. This phase of the Revolution, a bloodbath of random accusations and summary executions became known as the Reign of Terror, or simply 'the Terror'.

A time to speak out?

Even before the Terror was launched and thousands were guillotined for small transgressions or none, de Gouges was under arrest and in danger of her life. To her, this was no reason to stop her blistering onslaughts on the failings of the men running – and ruining – the republic. To most observers, however, she was tweaking the devil by his tail. From prison, she responded with another broadside, *Les Trois Urnes, ou le Salut de la Patrie* ('The Three Urns, or the Safety of the Mother Country'). In this she proposed that the people be given a choice of three different forms of government: a single republic, a federal system, or a constitutional monarchy.

Given that one of the major aims of the Revolution, if not its single most important act, had been the destruction of the monarchy, any proposal to restore it in any form could only be seen as a betrayal. Olympe had already argued against the execution of the King, even offering to defend him at his trial. Now, by suggesting the restoration of the monarchy, she could be branded as a full-blown royalist and counter-revolutionary, either of which would ensure her death.

Olympe still had one chance to save herself. Sent to an open prison from which she could easily have escaped, she chose to stay in Paris publishing her prison diary and protesting her innocence. She finally faced the Revolutionary Tribunal on 2 November 1793, where, ironically, she was denied a lawyer on the grounds that a woman of her ability was able to defend herself. Under the name 'the Widow Aubry', which she had rejected decades ago, she was charged with attacking the republic and the sovereignty of the people, with seeking to re-establish the monarchy, and with 'calumniating and spewing out bile' against the revolutionary leaders.

Alone and undefended, Olympe refused to betray her beliefs.

Asked to recant her attack on the leaders of the Revolution, she refused: they were all ambitious men simply out for themselves, not for France. As to undermining the Revolution, she told the Tribunal, she had ruined herself in the great cause. 'I am a woman, I fear death,' she concluded, 'but I have nothing to confess.' Her plea of innocence was dismissed and the judges found her guilty. Her crime had been to attack the male right to power, or at least the man in power. A newspaper report of the verdict also indicates her other major offence:

> Olympe de Gouges, born with an exalted imagination, believed her delusions were inspired by nature. She wanted to be a statesman: it would seem that the law has punished this plotter for having forgotten the virtues suitable to her own sex.

A time to die

Now de Gouges was granted the only equality women enjoyed on the same terms as men: the right to be killed by the state. Condemned to die, she tried to buy time by claiming to be pregnant, but a medical examination the same afternoon exposed the pitiful falsehood. That night she composed a last letter to her son, declaring her innocence and insisting that her only fault lay in her uncritical devotion to the Revolution, which left her exposed to the 'unmuzzled tigers' who destroyed all opposition. Predictably, the letter never reached him. And so to the guillotine. With one last cry of defiance, *'Enfants de la patrie, vous vengerez ma mort!'* ('Children of the mother country, you will avenge my death!'), Olympe de Gouges was tied to the board and beheaded, face up or face down.

Five days later another woman labelled an enemy of the Republic, Madame Roland, was sent to the guillotine accused of treason and of engaging in politics as a woman. At the foot of the scaffold in the Place de la Revolution, she caught sight of the statue of Liberty and cried out against the politicians who had perverted the Revolution's noblest ideal for their own corrupt purposes: '*Oh Liberté, que de crimes on commet en ton nom!*' ('Oh Liberty, what crimes are committed in your name!') Roland's *cri de cœur* has lost none of its power since her death. Bloody purges by despotic regimes, trials without the right of defence or appeal, and murky actions of opaque and unaccountable secret services have proliferated in the twentieth century. And every one of these would claim that they were valiantly defending the liberty of the homeland as they saw it.

Roland's death put an end to the brief and brilliant blaze of women banding together to create their own political agenda. The consolidation of everyday power in the hands of men meant that women were denied any chance of building on the unity they had briefly enjoyed when they came together in political protest and action. Now they had no choice but to operate within the man-made structures of the new republic that iron-ically they had helped to create. With her explicit declaration that women were fully equal to men, Olympe de Gouges had mounted a direct attack on the principle of male supremacy, and she was exterminated. For the rebel women of France, the hopes of freedom dimmed as the Revolution came to an end. It fell to an Englishwoman to pick up the flickering torch and rekindle the flame.

'That hyena in petticoats'

The high-minded bluestocking, only interested in her books, is one version of womanhood. The ardent romantic, hungry for love and reckless in the pursuit of it, lives her life at the opposite extreme. Writer, philosopher, enthusiast and visionary,

Mary Wollstonecraft was both. This rare combination of the intellectual and emotional gave her work a unique power and bite, and her attacks on privilege and injustice can still sting.

A hyena then, was she?

This famous insult was bestowed on Wollstonecraft by the aesthete and writer Horace Walpole, high priest of the Gothic Revival in eighteenth-century England and a gentleman of famous refinement and style, as this shows. It was only one of many random brickbats and violent onslaughts that clouded Wollstonecraft's life and shaped her political philosophy. Raised in the chaos of a violent home with a brutal alcoholic father and at the age of nineteen subject to the genteel purgatory of employment as a 'companion to a lady', Mary Wollstonecraft developed a keen interest in gender relations, made all the sharper by her own experience.

Like Olympe de Gouges, Wollstonecraft quarrelled bitterly with the idea of inherited power as enshrined in the monarchy, the aristocracy and the Church. Learning French, she eagerly followed events across the Channel, and composed her 1790 pamphlet *A Vindication of The Rights of Men* in response to an essay defending France's *ancien régime* by the deeply conservative Anglo-Irish MP Edmund Burke. Wollstonecraft's riposte vigorously upheld the republic and its revolutionary ideals, and mounted a no-holds-barred attack on traditional privilege with all its inherent cruelties, such as slavery – another link with de Gouges. Arguing that every man had the right to be judged on his own merits as an individual and not by his specific race, caste or class, she came to see that the same principle should apply to women too.

The reception of Wollstonecraft's pamphlet was an immediate validation of her ideas. Published anonymously, the first edition sold out in three weeks. When the second came out in Mary's name, it was greeted with a storm of mockery and hostility. In

France, the highly influential politician Charles Talleyrand, one of the co-authors of the revolutionary *Declaration of the Rights of Man*, presented a plan of public education to the National Assembly, which should include all classes of men, but not women, who only needed a 'domestic education' in the 'calm and seclusion' of 'the paternal home'. To Wollstonecraft, already sick of girls being raised to be soft and silly to appeal to men, Talleyrand's wholesale dismissal of women was intolerable. It proved to be the catalyst for the creation of her most important work, *A Vindication of the Rights of Woman*.

As Mary already knew, women everywhere were treated like tame animals, fit only for the domestic ménage. How to change this? Writing at white-hot speed as her publisher snatched each sheet from under her flying pen and rushed it to the press, Mary thought and fought her way into a deeper level of understanding, one that very few of her contemporaries were ready to accept. She propounded the radical concept that both men and women were subject to the essentially and totally gendered nature of every aspect of personal, social, political and public life. But men were expected and encouraged to explore all that the world had to offer and to make something of themselves. Women were not, and so the male always remained first, while the female was deliberately held back and then despised for her limitations.

A Vindication of the Rights of Woman: with Strictures on Political and Moral Subjects, to give it its formal title, came out in London in January 1792. Powerful and pugnacious, in revolt against everything lauded as female or feminine, it vehemently demanded that every woman deserved an education on equal terms with any man. Women are not born to be domestic pets, matrimonial property or ornamental trophies for fathers and husbands, but could all be true companions to their partners if they were treated as human beings with the same basic needs.

Instead they are subjected to a wide-ranging set of double standards, with all their energies funnelled into emotional displays
and phoney parades of weak-minded 'sentimentalism' in place
of intellectual activity. The behaviour this produced only served
to confirm the essential brainlessness and lack of reason of the
female, in itself enough to justify their relegation to perpetual
inferiority.

Smart women, foolish choices

Social, political, philosophical, educational, matrimonial,
behavioural: scratching away from dawn to dusk about wom-
en's rights under the constant pressure of daily events and
a shortage of cash, Mary's frantic mind ranged over every
dimension of women's lives except one, the sexual. Rising
thirty-three at a time when the age of consent for a female in
England was still a flexible twelve as it had been since 1275,
Mary had always made taking care of her mother and younger
sisters her priority, as well as maintaining strong connections
to her women friends. With a wife-battering wastrel of a father
as another deterrent, she had every reason to resist the allure
of men and marriage.

But Aphrodite, as the Ancient Greeks say, will not be scorned.
Soon after the publication of the *Vindication*, Mary fell madly
in love with the fifty-one-year-old Swiss artist Henry Fuseli,
well-known in London as the creator of startling other-worldly
images of heaven and hell. These were to prove the twin poles
of the relationship that followed. Fuseli had not long married
one of his models, the young Sophia Rawlins, and unsurprisingly she reacted with maximum prejudice to Mary's passion for
her husband, not least to Mary's poignantly naive notion that the
two women could agree to share the great man. The ensuing
fight, which Sophia won hands down, was a total *dégringolade*

for Mary. Defeated, rejected and heart-sick, that December she fled London for France.

Arriving in Paris, Wollstonecraft lost no time in making contact with other British expatriates, most notably the remarkable Welshwoman and sprightly Francophile Helen Maria Williams, another free-thinker and religious dissenter. Williams welcomed Wollstonecraft to her salon where she also hosted the likes of Tom Paine, whose own two works on the doctrine of the Rights of Man had book-ended Wollstonecraft's, appearing in March 1791 and February 1792. Think of it: mixing with fellow philosophers and intellectuals during that winter of 1792 in *la Ville Lumière*, the City of Light, less than a year after de Gouges had brought out her *Declaration des Droits de Femme et de la Citoyenne*, Wollstonecraft had found a promising new base indeed.

But in early 1793 Wollstonecraft met the all-American twenty-two carat hustler, world-class twister and sex bandit Gilbert Imlay, and by September she was pregnant with his child. Often romantically described as an 'adventurer', Imlay had served in the army during the War of Independence, an experience he felt entitled him to the rank of captain, a title he flourished all his life. The 'captain' then ran through a series of grandiose but failed land ventures in Kentucky, and fled to France under a mountain of debt. By 1793, although a bankrupt and fugitive from the law, Imlay had established himself in Paris as the diplomatic representative of the United States, while simultaneously aiding the British in maintaining naval blockades against France. This shameless crook was to be the second *amour fou* of our author's life. The inexperienced and virginal Wollstonecraft idealised Imlay and indeed the idea of love so much that she never really knew him – but who ever knows a con man, even himself?

In May 1794, the union seemed to be sealed when she gave

birth to Imlay's daughter and enjoyed a few weeks of family life, writing joyfully to friends about her baby and the new father. But Imlay was bad dad material. As the pace of events in Paris picked up once the Terror got under way, Imlay turned to the well-established French principle of *sauve qui peut* (every man for himself). And when *Madame La Guillotine* sang all day and into the night and not a soul was safe, the heartless, hopeless partner, provider and parent abandoned Wollstonecraft and his child, and slipped away to England.

As a woman alone and an enemy foreigner too, Wollstonecraft sought the safety of the American Embassy, where Imlay had falsely registered her as his wife in the springtime of their love, then followed him back to England, arriving in April 1795. There she found the love-skunk ensconced with another woman, and tried twice to kill herself. Pulled from the Thames on the second attempt, she bitterly attacked her unknown saviour, insisting that suicide was her only rational solution because her life was at an end. But a London acquaintance who admired her writing, the writer and philosopher William Godwin, had other ideas. When she recovered, Wollstonecraft was blessed at the age of thirty-seven with a late-flowering love, one that finally brought her the equal and devoted partnership she had always craved. Pregnant by the end of 1796, she married Godwin in March 1797.

Godwin's daughter, named Mary after her mother and destined to become the great writer Mary Shelley, was born on 30 August. Ten days later, in the grip of raging septicaemia following a ruptured placenta, Mary Wollstonecraft died a dreadful death, her brilliant, restless intellect cut off before its time. What if she had lived? The *Vindication of the Rights of Woman*, subsequently attacked for its lack of structure and chaotic emotionalism, was never intended to be her last word. Encouraged by Godwin, she had planned a more considered and analytical follow-up, but her death put paid to that. Olympe de Gouges perished unlamented and almost unknown outside her revolutionary world, ensuring that her *Declaration*, a pamphlet written in French, was consigned to the scrap-heap of history for centuries to come. Wollstonecraft's work similarly suffered a short eclipse after she died.

The new century was born and baptised in revolutionary blood. But for women, two revolutions, the American in the new world and the French in the old, had failed.

The moral of this story is that women cannot carry out a revolution for women within a revolution led by men. Interpreted as a revolution *against* men, it cannot be tolerated and must be put down. Which throws up another hard truth: that men make the rules, and seemingly only men can break them. So the women of the American Revolution got nowhere with their modest petitions for some inclusion in that brave new star-spangled world. Olympe de Gouges likewise failed to convince the French, women and men alike, and her name was for decades almost buried under the sands of time.

More and more of the same was to come. All these revolutions, all these attempts to build a better society, all these assemblies of free-thinkers and enlightened minds sincerely believing that they were promoting freedom and equality, *all stopped short of sexual equality* – equality for women on the same terms as men.

But the more women were excluded and expelled, suppressed and silenced, gagged and guillotined, the more the *ideal* woman, the *idea* of woman, blossomed and grew. Both before and after the Revolution, women were suppressed as subjects in their own lives, only to be exalted as objects of men's untroubled admiration and desire.

Now who is this lovely creature scampering half-naked over the barricades against a stormy sky, her bare breasts bulging so

Liberty leading the people – Marianne in action by Eugène Delacroix.

freely and fetchingly as she goes? Enter the iconic 'Marianne', the poster girl of revolution, and Paris's Playmate of the First Republic, far too busy raising the *Tricolore* and leading the attack to realise that a serious wardrobe malfunction had left her with her bosoms hanging out. What about the bullets, let alone the cold? Deft handiwork, no, to replace real-life active, troublesome and vocal older women like de Gouges with a one-dimensional soft-porn image of a young female beauty radiating faith and unconflicted loyalty, frozen for ever in silence and slow time? And there Marianne was to remain, an object of male mythology and voyeuristic fantasy, never the star of her own story or a subject in her own right.

The men are in control, and Fantasy Woman rules alone as the heroine of the Revolution: was this to be the enduring legacy of a century and more of revolutions, when every revolution left men more free and women where they were before, if not worse?

Don't even think it.

Women's fight for freedom had only just begun.

And the loss of de Gouges and Wollstonecraft was not the end, but the end of the beginning of one of the longest and greatest revolutions the world was yet to know.

CHAPTER 2

NEW WORLDS AND OLD WAYS

The conduct of the women during the half year has been good, with a few exceptions ... The crimes are of an ordinary character ... viz. drunkenness, insolence and obscene language.

REPORT ON THE CONVICT WOMEN TRANSPORTED FROM BRITAIN TO AUSTRALIA

Nature intended women to be our slaves.

NAPOLEON BONAPARTE

The process of industrialisation is necessarily painful.

E. P. THOMPSON

Fairy tales favour the number three for its power to suggest that life offers more than a choice between only two options. Things will turn out all right in the end: *third time lucky!* And three factors ensured that the cause of women continued to spread and grow in the century following the age of revolution:

- Women were changing the world.
- The world was changing for women.
- Women were changing too.

When Mary Wollstonecraft died, the book she had planned to follow the *Vindication* died with her. But the idea of women's rights and her powerful plea for female equality were up and running, and making their way round the globe. In England, those known to have read Wollstonecraft include figures such as George Eliot, who compared her with the pioneering American writer, reformer and feminist Margaret Fuller in an essay of 1855. That great leader of women's suffrage, Millicent Garrett Fawcett, wrote the introduction to a centenary edition of *The Rights of Woman* in 1892, placing Wollstonecraft solidly at the head and heart of the struggle for the vote.

In America, Wollstonecraft found a new readership already primed to take on new and revolutionary ideas. As early as 1798, the aspiring author Charles Brockden Brown was inspired by Wollstonecraft to publish *Alcuin: A Dialogue on the Rights of Women*, which spread the word among his admirers, including Edgar Allan Poe, Nathaniel Hawthorne, Henry Wadsworth Longfellow and many others. Fast-forward another century and the redoubtable Emma Rauschenbusch-Clough, an American Baptist missionary working in India, was awarded a doctorate from the University of Berne for her thesis 'A Study of Mary Wollstonecraft and the Rights of Woman'.

And the world itself was opening up to women in unimaginable ways. When Australia was 'discovered' by Europeans and excitedly hailed as *terra nullius*, a land that belonged to nobody, this strange and splendid island had been home to countless inhabitants pursuing their traditional way of life for an estimated seventy thousand years. For the incomers arriving on the First Fleet in 1788 bearing the trauma of transportation with its life sentence of dislocation, loss and suffering, their new world offered some hope of survival and recovery, even of ownership and prosperity as time went by. But the eleven ships of the fleet with their 1480 men, women and children on board brought a very different future for the indigenous people of Australia.

At first, while the men were generally suspicious of the newcomers and often hostile, some of the women were ready to help. One young woman of the Eora nation called Patyegarang, aged about fifteen, was among the first to break the language barrier dividing the residents from the colonists. Over a period of time, she taught the local language to a lieutenant of the First Fleet, the scholarly and sympathetic William Dawes.

Patyegarang seems to have stayed with the twenty-six-year-old Dawes in his hut, with the inevitable suggestion that she may have been his lover. These extracts from his notebooks recording her words and phrases, as well as her sweetly formal name for him, 'Mr D', suggest a relationship like that of a teacher or respected elder rather than a bedfellow:

> *Taríadyaou*: 'I made a mistake in speaking.' This Patye said
>   after she had desired me to take away the blanket
>   when she meant the candle.
> PATYEGARANG: *Nyímuŋ candle Mr D.* 'Put out the candle Mr D.'
> DAWES: *Mínyin bial naŋadyími?* 'Why don't you sleep?'
> PATYEGARANG: *Kandúlin.* 'Because of the candle.'

Sexual or not, whatever passed between Patyegarang and Dawes bore fruit. They created the first written record of what he called 'the Aboriginal Language of Sydney'. Far more than a dictionary, it included reflections on grammar and syntax, and colourful examples of local expressions like 'the stink of pus in a sore', as well as many different words to describe the natural world such as *bōkbōk* (owl), *boóroodoo* (louse), *co_ing* (the sun), and *yan_nă_dah* (the moon). This ground-breaking work ended when Dawes was ordered back to England for insubordination after refusing to take part in a punitive raid on the local inhabitants in 1791. His later life and career in the Navy, including his unsuccessful attempts to get back to Australia (and to Patyegarang?) are all on record, though nothing more is known of Patyegarang's life.

The story of Patyegarang is unique, but her spirit was not. The women of the Eora, a revelation to the European immigrants, risked their lives every day to provide their communities with fish, their main source of food. Taking to the sea in bark canoes described by the British naval officers as no more than 'contemptible skiffs', they crested the waves of a surf heavy enough to horrify even the grizzled old British sea-dogs watching from the shore, each woman carrying her hand-woven fishing lines, her knives and hunting spears, and any of her children too young to be left behind.

Eora fisherwomen at sea with their on-board fire, cooking their catch to feed their families. Note the male eating (*centre*) and the lactating mother (*right*), still working her fishing line with a baby at her breast.

Singing together and keeping time as they rowed, fishing all the year round whatever the weather, by day and by night, these sea-wives crossed and re-crossed the coastal waters of Sydney's coves and bays with the confidence born of generations of experience. Chief among them was the small but formidable Barangaroo, believed by the colonists to be around forty years old and therefore about twelve years older than her second husband, the young warrior leader Bennelong. While other men hung back or attacked the Europeans, Bennelong cooperated with them, apparently won over by their offers of exotic food like bread and beef, and the new-found transports of delight afforded by alcohol.

Proud and hot-tempered, Barangaroo strongly opposed her husband's collaboration with the colonists, and furiously defied his often violent attempts to make her adopt their standards. At an encounter in 1790 with a party of men of the First Fleet, the marine officer Watkin Tench noted Barangaroo's disgust when Bennelong tried to force her to drink wine. Tench also watched as she shrugged off a petticoat which one of the other Eora women had put on her, and 'stood armed *cap-a-pee* [from head to foot] in nakedness'. That was her everyday appearance, according to the Australian historian Grace Karskens: 'all she ever wore was a slim bone through her nose'.

Barangaroo clashed with her young husband again in 1791, when she became pregnant with his child. Bennelong wanted her to have the baby in the Governor's house, while the Governor insisted that the colony's rough-and-ready hospital was the only choice. Her own woman to the last, Barangaroo spurned both options and took refuge in the bush, where she gave birth alone. Some days later she died, and Bennelong cremated her body. Her baby, a little girl, did not survive being handed over to a wet nurse drawn from among the convict women, and was buried with her mother's ashes.

So ended the life of one of the most remarkable women of Australia's First Nations, who shrewdly foresaw and tenaciously opposed the colonists' encroachment on her people's traditional way of life. Before the Europeans arrived, the vital work of the fisherwomen in ensuring the food supply placed them at the heart of their communities. But now, when one ship could net a thousand fish in one sweep, the women's expertise became a thing of the past almost overnight, and without it they dwindled into secondary importance. The shape of things to come was also clear when the Governor of the colony, Captain Arthur Phillip, presented Bennelong and his warriors with the extravagant gift of forty salmon, more than the men could eat.

To Barangaroo and many others, the newcomers were not settlers but destroyers, whose seizure of their territory precipitated a downward spiral of abuse. Their age-old belief that the land belonged to everyone and so could never be owned or sold, was overwhelmed by incomers who believed the exact opposite. As the colony grew, the women found that even their gender was eliminated when they were classed by the English as 'blackfellas' the same as their men. Some white masters treated their 'gins' – abori-*gin*-al female workers/chattels/slaves – not only as a lower form of human being, but as a lower form of animal, using them worse than their horses or dogs with savage floggings and slicing their buttocks for meat when food was scarce.

Despite these outrages and many more, including a variety of government attempts to tackle 'the aboriginal problem' by phasing them out of European society, women's courage and endurance lived on through the centuries. The 1931 story of three young girls, Molly, Daisy and Gracie, who were taken from their families as children for training as domestic servants and relocated in a government settlement many miles away, shows an almost superhuman resourcefulness. Led by the oldest, Molly, then aged about fourteen and armed only with the knowledge that their home town, Jigalong, lay somewhere along the rabbit-proof fence that divides Western Australia from north to south, they escaped and followed it all the way back on foot, a journey of almost a thousand miles.

The women who survived all this were at least familiar with the harsh terrain of the world that had been theirs since the dawn of time. For some of the convicts, especially the men, predominantly poor city dwellers with no knowledge of agriculture, to be dumped on the shores of Australia or Van Diemen's Land with a few spades and shovels and some bags of rotting grain proved to be almost as dismal a prospect as the hanging they had escaped in England. Their previous criminal experience lay far behind them and if they had a trade, as a cooper for instance or a tiler, there was little call for it in this wilderness.

In every era, women commit far fewer crimes than men, and women were outnumbered by the male convicts on the First Fleet by about eight to one. But as the British authorities well knew, a settlement of men could only ever be a garrison, never a community. The classic female skills – baking and brewing, tending and mending, sewing, sowing and growing, bearing children – were all essential if a desolate penal outpost of some 150,000 desperate and dangerous men was ever to be turned into a viable colony. And for the men who served out their sentence and chose to stay on as free Australians, a good number of women had to be available as wives.

Back in Britain, trial judges were therefore instructed to 'feed the female famine' by sentencing women to transportation wherever possible, especially if they were 'of breeding age'. The judiciary responded with enthusiasm to this patriotic call. In the century that followed the launch of the First Fleet until transportation was abolished in 1868, a total of around twenty-five thousand women were transported, often for petty offences or none. In the early nineteenth century, a London servant girl borrowed her mistress's fine kid gloves one Sunday, in the hope of catching the eye of a handsome young man at her church as she held her hands up to pray. Back at the house, her mistress caught her slipping the gloves back into their box and had her arrested for theft, a capital crime that brought down trial, conviction and transportation upon the girl's head, to the agony of her mother, who never saw her again. Under English law, theft is an act 'with intention permanently to deprive', so the maid had committed no crime. This was only one of the wrongful convictions women received simply because they were female.

Women changing the world

'No, no – surely not! My God – not more of those damned whores!' was the anguished cry of one officer of the First Fleet, Lieutenant Ralph Clark, when he saw the first female-only convict transport ship sailing into Sydney Harbour in 1790. In fact, not one of the women was transported for prostitution, because that was never a capital (and therefore transportable) offence. But whatever their history, once they had escaped death by hanging, they were trapped in the tiny ships of the day along with male convicts, the sailors in charge of the boat, and the soldiers in charge of them all. During the four-month voyage to Australia in those cockleshell cockpits, they were completely at the mercy of men who saw them as fair game. Finding a male protector or bargaining for sex could mean the difference between survival and another threat of the death they thought they had left behind.

But survive most of them did, to build the new country that was now their home. Eighty-two-year-old Dorothy Handland, a London dealer in old clothes and the oldest woman known to be transported, was a rare returner, sailing back to England in 1794 when she had served out her seven-year sentence. Most chose to stay on in the colony, creating lives they could never have had in the old country. At eleven years of age, the London street-sweeper Mary Wade was sentenced to hang for stealing the clothes of a younger girl, then reprieved and transported in 1790. She was the youngest known female transport, and lived to raise twenty-one children. Her descendants numbered three hundred by the time she died in 1859.

Another Mary, the astounding wife and widow Reibey, transported at fourteen for stealing a horse while masquerading as a boy (*how else was she to ride it?*), was married at seventeen to a free settler, and helped to populate the colony with seven little Australians. She also became a phenomenally successful businesswoman, expanding the trading company she began with her husband in Sydney as far as India and China, and becoming a great landowner and shipowner along the way.

These women were making the new world in the course of re-making themselves. Mary Reibey became a pillar of the community, so trusted and respected that in 1817 the first bank in Australia, the Bank of New South Wales, was opened in her house. Strangely, she never lost her regard for the country that had transported her, returning to her home village in England in her later years to display her wealth and power. She also sent two of her grandsons to Eton and Oxford, where, ironically, they would receive the same education as the judge who sent her away. A million miles away from the teenage horse rustler, the respectable Mary Reibey is now honoured on the Australian twenty-dollar banknote as a key figure in the foundation of trade, commerce and banking in her adopted country. *And good on her!* as the Aussies say.

Women changing too

The hard lives that most of the women had endured before being transported stood them in good stead on their arrival when they were sent to the so-called 'Female Factory' in Parramatta, outside Sydney. This dreadful institution combined the functions of a reformatory, a workhouse and a prison, but it also served as a form of hiring fair, where any man who was either a free settler or a freed convict could claim a woman to work for him. By the authority of the Governor of New South Wales, the women were offered to men in search of a female worker of any sort, and they had no power to refuse.

The status of the women was so low, and this system so open to abuse, that the majority of men took it for granted that the women's sexual services were part of the deal. As the number of female transports increased, some of the male 'employers' became notorious for swinging by the Female Factories to pick up a fresh sex slave to replace the last season's 'maid' or 'cook'. The women not chosen stayed on in the Factory to endure life in the equivalent of a labour camp, working inhuman hours to make everything from gunpowder to straitjackets, fed on prison slops and guarded by soldiers who were not above using them sexually themselves. The women who 'refused service' to the men who took them ostensibly for housework were sent back to the Factory to serve sentences of hard labour, picking oakum or breaking rocks.

Yet against these often desperate odds, the physical courage and mental strength of many of the convict women were not crushed. Whatever punishments they faced – being placed in irons, committed to solitary confinement on bread and water, or whipped – they fought back with might and main. Five serious riots rocked the Parramatta Female Factory between 1827 and 1843, and on occasion it took guards armed with fixed bayonets to bring the 'amazonian *banditti*' under control. Particularly detested was the punishment of head-shaving, designed not only to humiliate the offender but to mark her out as a troublemaker for months or years to come: this triggered one of the worst revolts in 1833. Indeed, the extreme conditions the women endured only strengthened their determination to resist.

And their urge to transgress. Swearing was the norm, along with wild ribaldry and obscenity, and the women delighted in belting out filthy songs to outrage any listeners, while their raucous behaviour often spilled over into drunken, uproarious rampages that their guards struggled to subdue. The day-to-day treatment of the inmates built a strong sense of solidarity, and when the authorities tried to single out the ringleaders for punishment, the entire group was known to chant as one, '*we are all alike, we are all alike*'.

This was certainly true of what was, fundamentally speaking, one of the rudest, crudest, most sporting and most disrespectful of all our heroines' high jinks. At the Cascades Female Factory in Van Diemen's Land in 1838, the women were on church parade for the island's governor and his entourage, awaiting a sermon by the Reverend William Bedford, a celebrated moral crusader known as 'Holy Willie' for his remarkable odour of sanctity. Quite unexpectedly, as the priest later reported,

the three hundred women turned right around and at one impulse pulled up their clothes showing their naked posteriors which they simultaneously smacked with their hands making a loud and not very musical noise. This was the work of a moment, and although constables, warders etc. were there in plenty, yet three hundred women could not well be all arrested and tried for such an offence, and when all did the same act the ringleaders could not be picked out.

The spectacle of a heaving sea of some six hundred buttocks doubling as percussion instruments astonished and offended the Governor and his men but refreshingly, the ladies in the governor's group thought it was hilarious.

A new world against the old

To grasp the struggle rebel women everywhere had to face at this time, we must remember that there was *nowhere in the world where women were free.* Not a single soul could tell of any country, any institution, any community, where women were not subject to men. To believe in and to follow the example of Olympe de Gouges and Mary Wollstonecraft meant accepting that everything good people had been brought up to understand about men and women was at best a profound delusion, and at worst one great lie.

Could a woman imagine that she was equal to a man? That she too could work, think and decide, organise her life, buy property and use it to house the children she could bear and support alone? Could women demand rights of their own, independent of men?

Who could answer that?

Sara Coleridge, married to the English poet, worked her way through his erratic transports over each new field of dreams, learning to survive his frequent absences, his use of opium and the resulting lack of money. This she bore along with four of his children, whom she not only raised but had *delivered* entirely alone. Yet Coleridge still felt free to tell her that 'in sex, acquirements, and in the quantity and quality of natural endowments whether of Feeling, or of Intellect, you are The Inferior'.

He was not unique in this view. A deep belief in the essential, God-given and eternal superiority of the male is carved into the story of the human race. But it was not always so. Before the triumph of the phallus, a wealth of evidence suggests that the early idea of power was female, not male, a historical reality all but lost today. Who now remembers that the world's first known poet was a woman, Enheduanna of Sumeria, in the south of modern Iraq around 2300 BCE? Who knows that Enheduanna was also the first known priest, indeed the chief priest of Sumeria? Who knows that the world's earliest surviving religious text – Enheduanna's hymn in praise of Sumeria's god, 'The Exaltation of Innana' – was composed by a woman? And that the deity Innana was female too?

In one highly charged carving from about 2000 BCE, Innana is shown displaying her power over the natural world. Flashing a leg as toned as any Olympic athlete and flaring her double set of divine wings, she dominates the snarling lion underfoot, attended by the goddess Ninshubur, her deputy and wing-woman. From images like this, from goddess figurines like the Venus of Willendorf, from temple carvings, and grave goods, archaeologists estimate that humans believed God was a woman for between twenty-five and fifty thousand years. Encountering her temples, statues, shrines and votive offerings from Ireland to Asia Minor and from Africa to the borders of modern day Poland and Ukraine in the course of their empire-building, the Romans called her *Magna Mater*, 'the Great Mother'. To our ancestors, the divinity of the female sprang partly from the moon-linked menstruation of every earthly woman, her ability to bleed spontaneously without injury, illness, infection or death, and then to heal herself equally mysteriously of this brief, cyclical, invisible and inexplicable wound.

The forty-plus weeks (nine calendar months or more) of a woman's gestation meant that to our prehistoric forebears, there was no apparent link between the act of sex and the birth of a child. It seemed that women gave birth out of their own bodies, without the involvement of men. Women were therefore credited with the most divine power of all: the ability to create new life.

When the world's early men and women first began to understand that the male played a vital role in creating life, this dawning realisation was to overthrow the thought patterns of thousands of years. The conclusive discovery of biological paternity was the world's first and greatest revolution, and it brought an upheaval whose consequences are with us still. It cannot be dated with any certainty since it is likely to have reached different groups at different times, as our ancestors emerged from the centuries of magic thought and learned to make connections and, above all, to *count*. But it was known by the time of Aristotle, some two thousand years after Enheduanna. Once it was recognised that the male carried in his body the seeds of generation, men became the true source of life, and the female lost her singular power of creation and with it, her power in the world. 'The male semen cooks and shapes the menstrual blood into a new human being,' Aristotle explained. 'The woman is merely the passive incubator of his seed.'

Nearer my god to Thee

In this binary opposition dating back to Ancient Greece, the female was no more than a receptacle, foreshadowing many of the disputes about the nature and function of women that were to come. But interestingly, the very era that propagated the idea of women's inferiority also produced some of the world's most arresting, enduring and powerful images of women in art, sculpture, poetry and, above all, drama. Playwrights created female choruses behind central female characters ranging from the innocent Iphigenia to the spine-chilling child-killer Medea.

Isn't he lovely, shooting at the sky? And look! He can fly! ... though he struggles to walk ... A selection of the numerous Ancient Greek and Roman phalluses.

The phallus took centre stage. He was now to be adored and worshipped as the divine source of life in all his many forms, and sacred in each one.

The Ancient World also produced numerous women of awesome mental superiority. The mathematician and philosopher Pythagoras always had female pupils, one of whom reportedly became his wife, the superstar Theano.

Ready at the back there?

Here she is in full flow:

I have learned that many of the Greeks believe Pythagoras said all things are generated from number. The very assertion poses a difficulty: how can things which do not exist even be conceived to generate? But he did not say that all things come to be from number; rather, in accordance with number – on the grounds that order in the primary sense is in number, and it is by participation in order that a first and a second and the rest sequentially are assigned to things which are counted.

Got that?
On we go.

Let there be light

The belief in female inferiority was not simply a notion that might have gone the way of other unsustainable concepts like the long-lasting conviction that the earth was flat. It became an organisational principle that dominated every earthly structure: marriage, the family, property, land, the Church, the military and the professions. Men had to own and control everything, because women were simply incapable of what was required. They were born that way, just as men were born to cater to their disabilities.

Fast-forward to the early nineteenth century when this dark and age-old misconception received a boost, ironically enough from what became known as the Enlightenment, a movement that began in Europe the century before. A massive upsurge of intellectual, philosophical and scientific enquiry, it aimed to replace faith with reason, sweeping away the outmoded ideas of the past that had held the people down. Both the leaders of the French Revolution and the War of Independence drew ideas and inspiration from its discussions of freedom and equality, as did Olympe de Gouges and Mary Wollstonecraft. But the light it shed turned out to be both partial and predictable, for reasons that were not far to seek.

The writer, philosopher and fervent atheist Denis Diderot,

a crucial figure in the Enlightenment, summed up his visceral hatred of the Establishment in his blood-thirsty battle cry, 'Man will never be free till the last king is strangled with the entrails of the last priest!' Hailed as 'the Father of the Enlightenment', Diderot was the author of its core text, the massive *Encyclopédie* written and edited with the help of others such as Jean-Jacques Rousseau. Published between 1751 and 1772, the encyclopaedia was explicitly designed '*to change the way people think*', and despite ferocious opposition from the authorities it repeatedly challenged and frequently overthrew the established beliefs of centuries. Reason, logic, free thought and free enquiry were now the order of the day, not the delusion, deception and dogma of all religions, but especially, Diderot believed, of Christianity.

Like much of history, the Enlightenment has traditionally been presented as a boys' club. In fact the two giants of the movement, Diderot and Rousseau, only got to know one another in the salon of Louise d'Épinay, where women mingled freely with men and debated with them on equal terms. Madame d'Épinay was herself a regular house-guest of Voltaire and the extraordinarily brilliant physicist Émilie du Châtelet, his lover, whose work on heat, light and energy anticipated a great deal of future research, and who identified a number of errors in the *Principia Mathematica* of the great Isaac Newton, no less.

Of all the women involved in the Enlightenment, one of the most active was the mighty Russian Empress Catherine the Great. As intellectually voracious as she was sexually frisky, she enthusiastically embraced its ideas and experimented with applying them to her government. In her thirty-four-year reign, the canny Catherine established Russia as a leading European power. She fostered free thinking, promoted art and culture, and established the first higher education institution for women in Russia. Most notably, she supported Diderot against the savage and sustained persecution he suffered from both Church and state, and offered him sanctuary at her court to complete his great work.

The new European thinkers placed a high value on rebelling against established patterns of belief. 'Dare to know!' trumpeted Immanuel Kant in 1784, in his seminal essay 'An Answer to the Question: What Is Enlightenment?': *'Have the courage to use your own reason!'* Following Kant, Diderot, Rousseau and the other leading lights of the Age of Light used their reason to conclude that every individual possessed fundamental rights and freedoms, regardless of class, creed, country or colour.

But not of gender. Women were far too useful as a group to be allowed any individuality, argued the egregious Rousseau in his 1762 treatise *Émile, or On Education*. How could society run smoothly without their services? It was the only logical solution to the problems of daily life, *non*? Constant suppression of females from childhood was the key, he declared, otherwise 'men would be tyrannised by women ... for given the ease with which women arouse men's senses, men would finally be their victims'. Women had to learn their place and be confined to a domestic role, setting men free to manage the public sphere. As a result, he directed, act with reason: 'Always justify the burdens you impose upon girls, but impose them anyway.'

Great thinker though he was, Rousseau seems never to have thought that women and girls could think too, and think for themselves. When they did, why would they accept this pack-horse proposition making them the beasts of burden, while men took on the heavy man-work of hanging out with other men, thinking and drinking (*excuse me, debating the issues of the day*) which always took more drinking and more thinking about more drinking and thinking before they could sort out the way things ought to be?

Worlds changing, women changing themselves and changing

the new worlds where they found themselves: all this took place when the Western world was alive with the excitement of the new order, when all things seemed possible. But despite all the women involved, the Enlightenment only concerned itself with enlightening men, and the Age of Reason had reasoned out of existence any idea that women might have reason too. And the new men who came to power in France once the Revolution was over had far from new ideas. On the contrary, as the world leaped, staggered, stumbled and tumbled into the modern age, they set out to restore and indeed increase women's subjection to men. In one of history's many ironies, the men who had killed a king for his despotic power over their lives saw no contradiction in inflicting the same treatment on their women by making themselves despots at home and abroad.

Consider the works of the mighty . . .

And now, *mes amis*, please welcome one of the greatest and most significant woman-haters of the world, Napoleon Bonaparte. As a great and mighty loser, his one abiding success was a hand-crafted piece of misogyny so solidly enshrined in the law that bears his name that it survived for two hundred years after its inception and may well endure for two hundred more.

But every great loser was a winner at the start. Flaming like a comet over Europe, the soldier from Corsica known as *le petit caporal* (the little corporal) burst onto the scene in Paris in 1793, the year Olympe de Gouges was put to death. He made his name by turning cannon fire on poorly armed royal troops, a wholesale slaughter he airily dismissed as 'giving them a whiff of grapeshot'. He then consolidated his battlefield successes to seize power in 1799 with a brilliant blend of military genius and political acumen. By 1811, he had carved out an empire of some seventy million souls, and crowned his triumph by having himself exalted as Emperor, bedecked in ermine, silk and crimson velvet, silver, gold and diamonds, a riot of bling that set the style for later tinpot dictators worldwide.

From there, the only way was down. Napoleon's ill-conceived invasion of Russia in 1812 led to the destruction of his *Grande Armée*, and eventually brought about his spectacular defeat at the Battle of Waterloo in 1815. He ended his days marooned on the barren rock called St Helena in the South Atlantic Ocean, one of the most remote places on earth. For a man who had triumphed as a war leader, king and emperor, it was a bitter banishment. From there he vented his rage and frustration against the world, as in this outburst to his loyal aide-de-camp Gaspard Gourgaud, in a letter of 1817:

> Nature intended women to be our slaves ... They belong to us, just as a tree which bears fruit belongs to the gardener. What a mad idea to demand equality for women! ... Women are nothing but machines for producing children.

So far, so bigoted. But the massive power that the coarse Corse had wielded before his fall gave this attitude enormous significance in the lives of women of many lands. Historians agree that Napoleon's greatest gift to the emerging modern world was the legal system he introduced, the Code Napoléon of 1804. Drawn up by senior jurists working from his instructions, it won praise from the start for its clear and cogent response to the basic demands of the Revolution:

- Equality before the law.
- Freedom of religion.
- No promotion based on hereditary privilege.
- Open competition for positions of authority.

BUT –

'Never forget that all men would be tyrants if they could,' Abigail Adams had warned her husband, the US President John Adams, in 1776. *Equality before the law?* Men only, it seemed. In truth, Napoleon made it his life's work to create a new legal role for men as the 'head of the household', to extend the power of men over women, and to buttress it with all the force of law. The Code set down in detail, item by item, the right of men to possess and control women. In so doing, it also revoked freedoms women had enjoyed for centuries under the royal regime, such as the right to come and go as they pleased, to handle money or inherit property, or even to run a lowly whelk stall like the famous fishwives of the Revolution. From 1804, not one of these actions and many more besides could legally be undertaken by women without their husband's express permission.

'The wife is obliged'

Forward into the past it was, then, for the females of France and its colonies. Married women in particular traded their birthright as freeborn singletons and sold their souls for the trick-or-treat promise of the happiness and security of marriage. Most women of that time, if not all, were steeped in religion and deeply believed that if they had sex without the Church ritual of marriage, they would burn in hell. How many of them realised that simply by marrying they were signing up to a lifetime ban on even going out to buy food at the market unless their husbands agreed? That from the moment they made their vows they were henceforth compelled to obey their husbands in *everything*? Especially anything to do with money or property, access to either of which might have given them their freedom from their legal slave owners (*sorry, their rightful masters, their loving and protective husbands*). Oh, and by the way, if they were caught in adultery they faced the death sentence, a penalty that did not apply to men?

Napoleon's system of law, now regarded not only as his personal bequest to the world but as the only lasting outcome of the French Revolution apart from the Republic itself, was based on one simple and reassuring notion: women belong to men, and are put on earth purely for men's use and comfort. Rolled out to every corner of the French Empire, the Code Napoléon spread from Italy to Poland and beyond. To this day, it remains the backbone of the law in much of Europe, and became the model for the law throughout most of the colonies and territories ever held by France. These included the state of Louisiana, which France had sold to the Americans in the famous Louisiana Purchase of 1803. The Code also heavily influenced the laws of modern Canada in the French Province of Québec.

With a military and political reach stretching from Spain to Egypt, from Russia to the United States, Napoleon achieved no less that the creation of a new world order. The Code set down deep roots in the French national psyche and social life, and was to cost French women dear. If you doubt that, fast-forward a hundred and fifty years. Trailing way behind other countries, France did not give its women the vote until 1944: contrast this with New Zealand and Australia over half a century earlier. Not until 1965 did French women win the right to take a job or to enter a profession without the express permission of their husbands.

As late as 1970, French men were still clinging on to their legal status as the head of the family, with all the rights, controls and potential for abuse contingent on that. More ominously, twenty-first-century observers have noted the numbers of Middle Eastern and African governments reaching for modernisation and Europeanisation who have found the Napoleonic Code remarkably harmonious with their cultural and religious beliefs, the insistence on the supremacy of the male, for instance, plus confining women to the house, and requiring them to obtain permission for everyday activities such as going to work.

So the dear old Code Napoléon proved its value as an instrument for enslaving women time and again. Even in the modern world, it proved to be the gift that kept on giving.

Thank you, Mr Malaparte.

The march of the machines

'The Revolution is over!' Napoleon famously announced when he seized power in the deftly plotted coup of 1799. He was wrong about that, too. For still they came throughout the nineteenth century, revolutions in politics, revolutions in thought, revolutions in the relations between the races, between the sexes, all reverberating round the globe.

Could any of them change the world for women?

Yes, indeed!

The female of the species was of particular interest to the leaders of the Industrial Revolution, when steam and fire power, originally harnessed in Britain, furnished Europe and America with factories small and large, producing a wider variety of goods than the world had ever seen. Women began to be seen as consumers with the mass production of delightful and tempting objects designed to appeal to the female heart like fine china, glittering trinkets, and fabrics with patterns never seen before, like the tempting teardrop paisley motif coming all the way from Persia.

Add to that the freedom to move beyond the place where you were born, a right to roam that had been against the law of England for centuries – *what a thrill!* Every horizon expanded with the advent of omnibuses, trams and the train. Almost everything leaped forward with lightning, even frightening, speed, as postal services and the telegraph combined to streamline communications, and modern banking systems evolved to handle the cascades of cash pouring into each advancing nation's coffers from all round the world.

Dark and satanic

The gains were great, but the losses were terrible. William Blake was not alone in dreading the forward march of the 'dark satanic mills' over 'England's green and pleasant land', gobbling up fields and woods, turning villages into towns and towns into cities where the poor huddled together and all too often starved to death in stinking, teeming tenements, along with their extended family of rats, mice, lice, ticks and fleas.

Outside the home, the normal working day began at 5 a.m. and ran until 8 p.m., and at peak times workers would begin at 3 a.m. and work until 10 p.m. without extra pay. Women and children turned up with the men at first light to grapple with huge, deafening and dangerous machines, while mines, furnaces and factories all produced conditions of suffocating heat in which no one was permitted to drink water without permission on pain of a fine. In his stark satire of 1911, 'The Secret of the Machines', Rudyard Kipling imagined the machines gloating over the workers as if they were their prisoners in danger of a savage beating or death:

> We can neither love nor pity nor forgive.
>   If you make a slip in handling us you die!
> We are greater than the Peoples or the Kings—
>   Be humble, as you crawl beneath our rods!

Machines en masse inevitably meant factory organisation of labour, with rigid segregation of workers along gender lines. Women and men who had previously worked in or near their home with their children around them were now separated, and although men and women both suffered, the women came out worse. The female home worker anywhere could manage her time as she chose, and run her paid work in with her unpaid 'women's work'. Spinning or weaving, she could always move around when her back was aching, and change her baby if her nose told her it was time. She could step outside to tend the patch where she grew beans and peas, get the pot on the fire to feed the family, and at home she was free to relieve herself whenever she liked – often a dire necessity in the days of multiple child-bearing and consequent rearrangement of the waterworks.

It is easy to romanticise the pre-industrial cottage-based life which was often desperately hard, but it did give a woman more control. Now she worked much the same hours – twelve, fourteen, even twenty a day – but most of them in relentless servitude, facing the same crippling routine from dawn till dusk. No longer at hand, her children were all working too. 'Children are taken down [the mine] as soon as they can crawl,' was the bleak observation of William Jenkins, the under-agent of the Gelligaer Colliery in Glamorgan, South Wales, in 1842. Our woman worker's girls, generally regarded as more responsible and biddable than her boys, could be scraping a handful of pence from the age of three. Certainly the girls could be earning by the time they reached the age of five, when their little bodies made them the perfect size to work as trap-operators in the smallest of the coal tunnels of the mine shafts.

Another grievous loss for women workers in the Industrial Revolution was any long-lasting or regular contact with the natural world and with the hallowed rhythms of the seasons, a factor now regarded as a critical component of mental health. In the pre-industrial universe, a woman's life revolved around Easter for sowing, Michaelmas for gathering and harvest home, and Christmas for making mincemeat from the dried apples and salted meat she had set aside for this treat. Every parish had its own rituals, feeding deep spiritual needs and re-affirming the comforting customs of the past. Well dressing, raising the maypole, beating the bounds: all these customs withered under the tyranny of the new factory regimes designed to wring every drop of time and effort out of the workforce, with no thought of the human cost, to their men and children, as well as to the women themselves.

Spin, Jenny, spin

Of all the machinery that came into its own at this time, the stand-out creation was the Spinning Jenny. This simple horizontal frame patented in 1770 by James Hargreaves, employed eight spindles for spinning wool or cotton into thread. As the technology progressed, the Jenny's eight spindles rose to eighty and eventually to a hundred and twenty, and once established 'she' spread rapidly throughout the Western world. On this machine each spindle could do the work of one 'spinster', a woman who earned her living by spinning, so a single factory worker could replace up to a hundred home workers and more. It thus became the icon of the Industrial Revolution and the ultimate symbol of how machine power could replace the work of women, rendering a lifetime of their skills and experience redundant at a stroke.

In changes as radical as these, men were displaced too. But when machines replaced human labour, men were in charge. Now our working woman found herself not only married to the machine but under the cosh of the factory overseer, a man empowered to dish out the beatings and fines deemed necessary to keep the workers' noses to the grindstone. In England, the woman worker standing at a Spinning Jenny for up to fourteen hours instead of sitting at a spinning wheel could find that visits to 'the necessary', the factory privy, were strictly rationed and not allowed without the overseer's permission. Whether menstruating, pregnant, perinatal, lactating, menopausal or suffering what that era called 'the flux', she could also be fined if she lingered in the lavatory too long. For all this, she was earning less than the pay of the lowliest male. And when she got home, she still had all 'her' domestic work to do, unless her man was prepared to lift a dishcloth or lend a hand with the chores.

Not surprisingly, the increase in productivity brought about by the machines exerted a top-down pressure on women and girls still hand-working in the traditional way. The grievous factory hours became standard practice even for those employed in private businesses. This child seamstress is speaking to one of the Parliamentary Commissioners of the British Children's Employment Commission in February of 1841, when the UK government began to take notice of the human cost of the march of the machines:

> The common hours of business are from 8 a.m. till 11 p.m. in the winters; in the summer from 6 or half-past 6 a.m. til 12 at night. During the fashionable season, that is from April til the latter end of July, it frequently happens that the ordinary hours are greatly exceeded: if there is a drawing-room or grand fête, or mourning to be made. It often happens that the work goes on for 20 hours out of the 24, occasionally all night. Every season, in at least half the houses of business, it happens that the young persons occasionally work 20 hours out of the 24 twice or thrice a week.

Snapshots of children like these, frozen in time, foreshadow their lives as women that lay ahead: grinding labour, lifelong poverty, multiple childbirth, unaffordable illness and early death. The misery of women's work in the mills, furnaces and factories is still vividly alive in the official records of the time, with every accident, every fine, every failure, every blow recorded in painful detail. Here is the voice of Catherine Hughes, no longer deemed a child at fourteen years of age, who worked in a South Wales blast furnace performing what the Parliamentary Commissioner for South Wales, Robert Hugh Franks, described in 1842 as 'heavy and fatiguing work':

> [I] carry water on the hill for the men who char the coal for the blast furnaces; I work seven days and seven nights; less work on Sundays, 12 to 13 hours on other periods ... [She knows] twelve pennies in a shilling; five fingers on each hand; six days in the week; cannot say how many months in the year [but knows] a month contains more days than a week.

'Run over'/'Fell down'/'Killed'

Unsurprisingly, accidents were frequent and often fatal, recorded by the overseers with a terse indifference that suggested they were everyday occurrences in the collieries and mines:

> **Mary Price** outdoor girl fell asleep and fell on the rail. Tram ran over her and broke her leg.
> **Ann Jenkins** aged 12 fell down pit. Killed.
> **Henrietta Franklin** aged 11 crushed by horse and tram. Not killed.

By a rare coincidence, Henrietta Franklin's (or Frankland's – spellings vary) own account of the accident survives. She was a 'drammer', crawling on hands and knees with a leather strap round her waist and a chain between her legs to pull a cart loaded with coal through waterlogged passages on average little higher than her undeveloped haunches. Despite her injury, note the present tense – the crippled child still saw herself as a worker, only 'laid idle' for a while:

> When well I draw the drams [carts], which contain four to five cwt. of coal, from the heads to the main roads; I make forty-eight to fifty journeys ... The mine is wet where we work, as the water passes through the roof, and the workings are only thirty to thirty-three inches high. I have been laid idle two months, as a horse fell upon me and the cart passed over me and crushed my inside; no ribs were broken, but the pain was very great and continues still.

Like the mine owners, factory bosses too were swift to exploit very young girls, regardless of the danger posed by the powerful machines.

The young machine operators regularly lost fingers, toes, hands or arms, and death was never far away. John Brown,

Child worker in a textile mill. Note that the machines have no safety guards and she has no shoes.

a British journalist working on an article about child labour, recorded this account by the textile worker Robert Blincoe, who had himself lost a finger to a machine when he began in the cotton mill at the age of seven. Still, he counted himself lucky in comparison with this nine-year-old in an accident he had seen in 1822:

A girl named Mary Richards ... not quite ten years of age, attended a drawing frame ... It happened one evening, when her apron was caught by the shaft. In an instant the poor girl was drawn by an irresistible force and dashed on the floor. She uttered the most heart-rending shrieks! Blincoe ran towards her ... He saw her whirled round and round with the shaft – he heard the bones of her arms, legs, thighs, etc. successively snap asunder, crushed, seemingly, to atoms, as the machinery whirled her round, and drew tighter and tighter her body within the works ... at last, her mangled body was jammed in so fast, between the shafts and the floor, that ... it stopped the main shaft. When she was extricated, every bone was found broken – her head dreadfully crushed. She was carried off quite lifeless.

And for all this, girls from the age of three and women of any age were paid between one-third and two-thirds of what men took home. In general this wage discrepancy was contrived and maintained to protect the higher-earning occupations of men. Women were not allowed to work as 'mule spinners', operating a complex machine that produced a superior yarn, because the early trade unions banned men from training them. In other cases, the mental superiority of the male was assumed, so schoolmasters were always paid more than schoolmistresses, whatever their level of learning.

Mainly, however, women were paid less because of the fixed

belief that women and their children were supported by their men, and therefore did not need a living wage of their own. This concept of the male 'breadwinner', as enshrined in the Code Napoléon, was particularly hard on widows, orphans and single women, but all women were judged by their gender, and paid accordingly. The disparity was obvious. But the work had to go on. This was *progress*. Who could argue with that?

Many could and did. Influential men of the middle and upper classes were at first disbelieving and then appalled when they learned that pregnant women mine-workers were giving birth in the basket winching them back to the surface, because even in labour they did not dare to miss their shift.

All we need is a few good men

And there were more than a few. As one of the administrators of the Poor Law in Leeds, the MP Michael Sadler had seen for himself the often desperate distress of the labouring masses, particularly the exhausted children who 'droop and sicken, and, in many cases, become cripples and die, before they reach their prime'. Introducing a bill in March 1832 to restrict hours of working to ten hours a day for anyone under eighteen, Sadler won the support of the Yorkshire mill owner and moderniser John Wood, who ran the most successful wool-spinning business in Britain. Against his own financial interests, Wood donated the eye-popping sum of forty thousand pounds to fund the fight for the ten-hour day.

When Sadler lost his seat in Parliament later that year, Wood recruited the young MP Lord Ashley, later the 7th Earl of Shaftesbury, to push through Sadler's ten-hour restriction on labour, to ban any child under ten from employment in mines or collieries, and to prevent any woman or girl under fifteen from working underground. Ashley's concerns for the poor and vulnerable included factory workers, 'climbing boys' (chimney sweeps) and 'ragged schools', providing education for the very poorest. The efforts of this great man set countless women, their men and their children free from unregulated employment, inhuman working hours, and the ever-present danger of death.

And the pace of change was increasing everywhere. The new worlds of Australia and America had both accepted many thousands of migrants and convicts, a proud but problematic bunch of old world refuseniks, goodniks and badniks, and it was a potent mix. As the old world was turning, the new world was churning with people, plans and projects dying to be born. Women had undergone enormous changes in that time. More were to come. And with every one would come new trials, bringing new setbacks and defeats for sure, but above all creating new chances for women, new horizons for girls, and new hope for all.

CHAPTER 3

ALL CHANGE

We Abolition Women are turning the world
upside down.

ANGELINA GRIMKÉ

The greatest revolution the world has yet seen.

The Times, AUGUST 1853

Tess was no insignificant creature to toy with and
dismiss; but a woman living her precious life – a life
which, to herself who endured or enjoyed it, possessed as
great a dimension as the life of the mightiest to himself.

THOMAS HARDY

Change?

It could and it did.

Everything changes and nothing stands still, said Heracleitus, introducing his most famous philosophical proposition, the theory of universal flux. Change, argued the old sage, is the fundamental, eternal and prime motor of the universe, the only constant on which we can rely, and it should not be resisted. A fundamental re-adjustment in the relationship between the sexes occurred in the nineteenth century, when a handful of women took up the claim to freedom and raised it to a higher plane.

Talking of freedom . . .

Industrialisation had stormed its way round the globe and battered significant parts of it into a different shape. But for many, the wind of change that swept through Europe and America then on to the wider world, never came. What of the women and girls of the countries where female hands of all colours but white grew all the world's tea, coffee and cotton, and picked it and packed it too, but never processed it nor profited from it – and where the most brutal forms of agricultural labour remained their only way of life?

With a certain shift of perspective, women in the non-industrialised nations whose traditional crafts could not be mechanised or monetised could be called luckier than their sisters who were suffering the worst excesses of industrial labour. Perhaps some were. Millions were not. Countless women in Africa lost their freedom, their ancient way of life and even the right to remain safe in their own homes when their bodies became the commodity that could be bought and sold, not merely the products of their labour.

As the transatlantic slave trade picked up speed in the eighteenth century to supply the labour-hungry New World, women were at first safer than their men, whose size and strength made them more attractive as labourers. Alas, the slave owners swiftly figured out that female labour could be exploited in two ways. A young woman could work in the fields and she could also produce children to be sold for ready cash, so very soon women and girls became targets too.

Losing their family, their kin, their country when they were taken – this was only the beginning. Black men had to labour for the white master by day; women also had to lie with him at night. Day in, day out sexual harassment of the owners and overseers was part of their lives. And a mother may have had many children, but never a family she could call her own.

How did the women react to all this? Here is Harriet Jacobs, who escaped from her plantation in 1853: 'God gave me a soul that burned for freedom and a heart nerved with determination to suffer even unto death in pursuit of it!' Harriet was literate, lucky, and extremely brave. Most were not. They could not write and did not dare to speak. To resurrect slave women's stories from the graveyard of the past is to give life to millions on millions of silenced female voices.

Sally Hemings was first seen in 1790 as a fourteen-year-old girl escorting her master's small daughter from Virginia to Paris, where he was serving as the American envoy to France. The master was Thomas Jefferson, one of the giants of the American Revolution and soon to become the third President of the United States. Hemings was remembered by a fellow slave, Isaac Jefferson, in 1847 as 'mighty near white ... very handsome, long straight hair down her back'. In Paris, Hemings was young, beautiful, and at Jefferson's beck and call. Jefferson was a widower, a man of power and accustomed to command. Although a slave-owner, he was also a lifelong campaigner against the slave trade.

A relationship began between Jefferson and Hemings that lasted until his death in 1826. Jefferson never publicly acknowledged Hemings, though she lived in his house and bore him seven children. But the story broke in 1802 as a red-hot international scandal, involving as it did presidential misconduct and the betrayal of the republic's ideals, extramarital sex and the much-feared 'miscegenation', sexual intercourse considered to be 'interbreeding' between two individuals of different races, particularly black and white. Many flatly refused to believe that the great man could have brought himself to have sex with a 'mulatto' woman, a person of mixed parentage, part white and part black, even after DNA testing of descendants in 1998 proved it beyond doubt. Others excused it on the grounds that Jefferson's late wife had made him promise never to marry again, so he was forced to use a female slave for natural sexual relief. Jefferson treated Sally well, we are told without a shred of evidence one way or another, a convenient blank that has allowed some pure-hearted souls to paint the relationship as a thirty-seven-year love affair.

The American historian and Harvard professor Annette Gordon-Reed has some sympathy with the love angle, insisting that not every relationship between a black female slave and her white master should be seen as rape:

Rape and the threat of it blighted the lives of countless enslaved women. At the same time, some black women and white men did form bonds quite different in character than from those resulting from sexual coercion. No social system can ever stamp out all the constitutive aspects of the human character. Heterosexual men and women thrown together in intimate circumstances will become attracted to one another.

For some critics, there was also the question of the thirty-year age gap. However, in almost every era up to the twenty-first century, Hemings would not have been seen as an underage victim. The law-makers of many lands had for centuries fixed the age of consent for females at around twelve or thirteen, and relationships with girls as young as this were accepted as legal. The girl destined to become Queen Elizabeth in 1558 was only thirteen when the thirty-eight-year-old adventurer Sir Thomas Seymour regularly surprised her naked in her bed and romped with her behind the curtains, with the encouragement of her waiting gentlewoman. Shakespeare-lovers also generally overlook the fact that in one of the world's greatest love stories, the heroine Juliet is only thirteen.

And Sally must be credited with a will of her own. In 1873, two years after she died, her oldest son, Madison, informed a journalist that in 1791 his mother, pregnant in Paris at the age of fifteen, realised that there was no legal slavery in France and told Jefferson that she would not go back to America with him. Doubtless aware that he could never enforce US laws of slave ownership overseas, Jefferson struck what Madison called 'a treaty' with Sally, asking her to stay on in his household as his 'concubine', offering her a settled status as his live-in sexual partner and unofficial wife. If she accepted, he would give her his 'solemn pledge' that he would free her – their – children from slavery when they were adults.

Hemings clearly agreed. She not only returned to the United States and stayed with Jefferson for the next thirty-six years, but also bore him six more children, three of whom died in infancy. Holding her tongue for almost four decades, she won her freedom after Jefferson died, and lived to see her four surviving children set free and doing well. In the Deep South, one drop of black blood made any individual, however pale-skinned, a 'negro', and the so-called 'one-drop rule' was to become law in no fewer than ten states between 1910 and 1931. Despite this, Hemings's three younger children all broke through the rigid 'colour bar' and moved without difficulty into 'white' society and lived to know a better life than their mother's.

Hemings was lucky that her rebellion against her master turned out as it did. Women in slavery often found ways to rebel, but the outcome was usually poor for the rank and file. In May 1836, two years after slavery had nominally been abolished in Jamaica, four enslaved women were brought before the stipendiary magistrate for refusing to work in the fields. As mothers of young children they were protesting the action of a new overseer, who had suddenly withdrawn the long-established privilege of maternity that exempted them from the hard and dangerous labour of cutting sugar cane. The punishments for their 'insolence' escalated from seven days' solitary confinement in the house of correction to fourteen days of the same, this time with two spells on the treadmill every day. Add to these penalties the misery of being separated from their children and therefore unable to breastfeed, throw in hours on the treadmill with painfully engorged and leaking breasts in the Caribbean heat, and their defiance looks courageous indeed.

Countless other slave women endured their lives without ever knuckling under to accept the state of 'natural servitude' that their white owners insisted was their divine lot. Harriet Tubman rebelled as an individual when she succeeded in escaping from her Maryland plantation in 1849. From there she went on to become an important 'conductor' on the Underground Railroad, a secret route with a network of safe houses for runaways, and returned nineteen times to lead over three hundred slaves to freedom in Canada. 'I was the conductor on the Underground Railroad for eight years,' she recalled, 'and I can say what most conductors can't, I never run my train off the track and I never lost a passenger.' Those who joined the group already knew too much about the operation to be allowed to get off the 'train', and any faint-hearts thinking of turning back would feel the barrel of Tubman's gun against the side of their neck as she spelled out the choice they had: 'You'll be free, or *you'll die a slave!*'

Credit where it's due

Enslavement had been a part of human society time out of mind. But the political revolutions of the nineteenth century forced a general questioning of established assumptions. In Britain, the movement to ban the slave trade began as early as 1783, a campaign in which women were prominently involved. Among them was the Irish Quaker Mary Birkett Card, who had written a lengthy 'Poem on the African Slave Trade' when she was only seventeen, addressed 'to her own sex'. Acting together, she argued, all her 'sisters' had the power to end the suffering of the slaves by refusing to buy sugar, molasses and rum, since turning a blind eye to the human cost of these luxuries made women guilty of their own brand of cruelty too.

Many felt the same. In 1852, a forty-year-old white teacher from Connecticut published a book destined to be not only the best-selling novel of the nineteenth century but also its second biggest seller after the Bible. *Uncle Tom's Cabin* lost favour as the struggle against slavery progressed, and its author, Harriet Beecher Stowe, has been depicted as a racist for her creation of characters like the warm black Mammy, the 'piccaninny' Topsy, and above all the faithful slave of the novel's title. All were later rejected as demeaning stereotypes, but in her lifetime Stowe was a courageous and convinced abolitionist, and her radical approach in the novel, giving dignity to her black characters, exposed the true horrors of slavery.

The international success of *Uncle Tom's Cabin* is also credited with winning vital support for the North at the start of the American Civil War, when her portrayal of plantation life was set against the blind resistance of the South to any suggestion of setting their slaves free. One man recognised the pivotal role played by Harriet Beecher Stowe in awakening the world to the evils of slavery. Meeting her in 1862, the newly elected President Lincoln reportedly greeted Harriet Beecher Stowe with the observation, 'So this is the little lady who started this great war.'

'We abolition women . . . '

Stowe undoubtedly helped to turn the tide of popular opinion against slavery in America, but she did not do it alone. Many strong and determined women were active in the struggle, and by the 1830s, female anti-slavery associations had sprung up all over the United States. Particularly powerful was the testimony of freed slaves like this passionate declaration by the black activist Sojourner Truth:

That man over there says women need to be helped into carriages and lifted over ditches, and to have the best place everywhere. Nobody ever helps me into carriages, and lifted over ditches, and over mud-puddles, or gives me any best place! And ain't I a woman? Look at me! Look at my arm! I have ploughed and planted and gathered into barns, and no man could head me! And ain't I a woman? I could work as much and eat as much as a man – when I could get it – and bear the lash as well. And ain't I a woman? I have borne thirteen children, and seen most of all sold off to slavery, and when I cried out with my mother's grief, none but Jesus heard me! And ain't I a woman?

Equally notable and way ahead of the rest of the activists were the Grimké sisters, Sarah and Angelina. The daughters of a powerful South Carolina judge who upheld the subordination of women as strongly as he defended his ownership of slaves, they had plenty to rebel against. Moving to Philadelphia as adults in search of a more liberal environment, they joined the local Quaker community and set to work to end slavery by writing and speaking, earning their place in history as the only white women of the American South to commit themselves wholeheartedly to work for the campaign for abolition, serving as officials of the American Anti-Slavery Society. The older sister, Sarah, was quieter than Angelina but if anything more determined, and they worked together to drive their message home.

Sojourner Truth (*left*) and Harriet Tubman, seen here a world away from the sufferings of slavery and the dangers they faced in the fight against it.

Their courage was astonishing in an era when rabid bigotry, racial hatred and violence could fall on those who even questioned slavery. In 1836 Angelina published a fearless and fiery appeal to all Southern women to speak out against slavery and to sign up to the abolitionist cause. The sisters then received a letter from their church raging that they had brought 'shame and dishonor' on themselves, inflicted a 'permanent injury' on devout Christians, and condemned waverers to 'degeneracy and ruin'. Above all, frothed the church fathers, how dare they as women speak in 'promiscuous assemblies' and 'say publicly' what they thought? What gave them the right to address mixed groups of both men and women in the way men did?

Sarah's counterblast to this outburst of fire and brimstone conveys a stinging put-down of its own. She began by condemning a letter 'which aims to tear from woman her dearest rights, & substitute the paltry privilege of leaning upon the fallen creature [Man], instead of the strong arm of the Almighty God. We believe,' she went on, 'that the Lord will help us to endure the opposition, contumely & scorn which will be cast upon womanhood, & that he will make us more than conquerors ... If it is right for thee, dear brother, to lecture to promiscuous assemblies, it is right for us to do the same.'

She ended on a magnanimous note, confident that she had won the day:

> *As far as we are concerned, we are entirely willing that thou*
> *shouldst 'say publicly' any thing thou wishes,*
> *THY SISTER IN THE BONDS OF THE GOSPEL,*
> *Sarah M. Grimké*

Further attempts at squelching the sisters invariably failed. A spell-binding orator, Angelina regularly stirred up large audiences, and her final public speech in 1848 ended in violent uproar when protesters stoned the venue and showered the audience with shards of broken glass. That was the last event to be held at the Pennsylvania Hall in Philadelphia: after the gathering, the mob burned it to the ground. And like Olympe de Gouges, Sarah and Angelina were not only fighting for themselves and other women. Here is Angelina writing in 1837:

> What man or woman of common sense now doubts the intellectual capacity of colored people? Who does not know, that with all our efforts as a nation to crush and annihilate the mind of this portion of our race, we have never yet been able to do it?

Only connect

Olympe de Gouges had made the link between the oppression of slaves and that of women in her play *L'Esclavage des Noirs*. More than fifty years later the Grimké sisters likewise understood that both slaves and women had rights that were *human* rights, on a par with those of men. To the sisters, the connection was obvious. 'Women ought to feel a peculiar sympathy in the colored man's wrong,' Angelina observed, 'for, like him, she has been accused of mental inferiority, and denied the privileges of a liberal education.' Sarah was equally confident. 'I am persuaded that the rights of woman, like the rights of slaves,' she wrote in 1837, 'need only be examined to be understood and asserted.' She returned to this theme in another letter that year:

> Men and women were CREATED EQUAL; they were both moral and accountable beings, and whatever is *right* for a man to do, is *right* for woman.

Other abolitionists took longer to make the link between the plight of slaves and their own. The truth of it was painfully borne in on the newly married American Elizabeth Cady Stanton, when she attended the 1840 World Anti-Slavery Congress in London. On arrival with her husband Henry Brewster Stanton, another passionate anti-slavery campaigner, Stanton discovered that she was one of a small group of seven other women, all attending as she was by invitation from the organisers to their local anti-slavery organisations in the United States.

Somehow it did not seem to have occurred to the London committee that any of the delegates could be women. When the party arrived at the venue, the women were rudely rebuffed at the door. When they insisted on entering, they were banished to a curtained-off visitors' gallery where they could neither see nor take part in the convention, but had to listen to the organisers justifying their exclusion on the grounds that as women, they were 'constitutionally unfit for public and business meetings'.

Constitutionally unfit ... insulted and refused entry to the meeting ... segregated and set apart from those in authority ... relegated to a cramped and comfortless place that demonstrated their inferiority ... persons of no status ...

Was that the moment when the women began to make the connection between their situation and that of slavery? Were they not effectively subjugated by a system that denied them votes and kept them under the control of men in the legal status of a child? The gulf between the black woman's grim and gruelling life of labour on the plantation and that of the white lady living in the lap of luxury in the great colonial mansion was a chasm of incomprehension that many could not bridge. But for the women in London, the doors of perception were blown off their hinges when they were denied entry to the World Anti-Slavery Congress, and they never looked back.

They fought their case, of course. The inspirational Quaker preacher Lucretia Mott took the lead in pressing for inclusion, vigorously supported by Elizabeth Cady Stanton, and the two struck up an instant rapport when they discovered that they had both read Mary Wollstonecraft. Mott later recalled that meeting with Stanton as the vital spark which inspired them to organise a meeting on women's rights. Was it necessary, some questioned, because the concept of man included woman, and the rights of man were already enshrined in the United States Constitution? But despite opposition, the Seneca Falls Convention – the first women's rights meeting in the world – took place in July 1848. Elizabeth Cady Stanton took on the daunting task of writing the keynote document, the declaration of the rights of women that would be debated, and hopefully ratified, by a vote of the attendees. Where was she to start?

Stanton's brainwave was to base the manifesto on the country's revered Declaration of Independence, with its rousing assertion that 'all men are created equal', and who could argue with that? She began with an all-out attack on this cherished foundation: 'The history of mankind is a history of repeated injuries and usurpation on the part of man toward woman, having in direct object the establishment of an absolute tyranny over her.' Male tyranny, she asserted, took many forms:

- Women were not allowed to vote.
- They were forced to submit to laws they had no part in enacting or voting on.
- If they married, they were 'in the eye of the law, civilly dead'.
- They were prevented from owning any property, even the money they earned.
- The law gave men power to beat women and to keep them locked up.
- Divorce laws were framed to give men every advantage over women.
- Women were denied entry to any college.
- Women were excluded from most 'profitable employments' and 'all the avenues to wealth and distinction'.
- Men claimed the right to rule women's lives as if they were God.

And perhaps the heaviest charge against man came last:

- 'He has endeavored, in every way that he could, to destroy her confidence in her own powers, to lessen her self-respect, and to make her willing to lead a dependent and abject life.'

Every item on Stanton's list of grievances was highly contentious. But the most difficult of all proved to be her assertion that it was the duty of women to work to win the vote. This would of course involve them in politics, and the high-minded Mott feared that women drawn into that corrupt milieu would inevitably be corrupted too. But Stanton, the daughter of a judge, had studied law in her father's office and convinced Mott that women had to get into politics because the power to make the laws was the only right through which all other rights could be secured. The motion was passed.

At the end of the Convention, sixty-eight women and thirty-two men signed the Declaration of Rights and Sentiments, around a third of the some three hundred who attended. The event was a great success and inspired others all over America and beyond, one only two weeks later when a group of attendees decided to hold their own Women's Rights Conference

The Seneca Falls Convention became the model for all women-led gatherings, like this suffrage meeting. Note the passionate conviction of the speaker, the packed audience, and the men and women seated together in the kind of 'promiscuous assembly' previously taboo.

in their home town of Rochester, near to Seneca Falls. Mott and Stanton were persuaded to stay on in the area to support the event, and support they did. The conference president later admitted that the fear of stepping out of her female role to address a mixed audience had made her so nervous that she could hardly speak. But 'at the close of the first session,' she recalled, 'Lucretia Mott came forward, folded me tenderly in her arms and thanked me for presiding ... When I found that my labors were finished, my strength seemed to leave me and I cried like a baby.'

That trembling taboo-breaker, Abigail Bush, is now honoured as the first woman to preside over a public meeting of both men and women in the US. In October 1850, the first National Woman's Rights Convention met in Worcester, Massachusetts, drawing over a thousand attendees from eleven different states, and had a substantial input from men, both as speakers and organisers. The following year, the Women's Rights Convention held in Akron, Ohio, similarly attracted a high turnout, and growing support from men. 'The women are coming up, blessed be God,' declared Sojourner Truth in her speech to the convention, 'and a few of the men are coming up with them.'

Cometh the hour, cometh the women ...

All through the excitement of these conventions, the work went on. The prime movers now were two powerful women whose interlocking skills made their campaign for women one of the most sophisticated of the day. Den mother and later the mother of seven children too, was the warm but no-nonsense Elizabeth Cady Stanton. Pack leader was the scholarly and austere single-ton Susan B. Anthony. They met by chance on a street corner in Seneca Falls, New York, three years after the Women's Rights

Convention of 1848, introduced by the fellow-activist Amelia Bloomer, who knew them both.

From this random encounter sprang a deep lifelong friendship and professional partnership like no other. Stanton had begun by campaigning against slavery, Anthony by crusading against alcohol and advocating prohibition. They formed an immediate compact to promote the cause of women, and wherever they lived for the rest of their lives, Stanton always kept a room in her house for Anthony, so that the work could carry on. Those who knew them agreed that Stanton was the ideas woman, writing the pamphlets, declarations and speeches, while Anthony organised the meetings and parades, and brought the cause to life in the outside world. Stanton's husband said, 'Susan stirred the puddings, Elizabeth stirred up Susan, and then Susan stirs up the world!' Stanton herself commented drily, 'I forged the thunderbolts, she fired them.' Add to this dynamic duo another woman of power, Lucy Stone, and a picture emerges of a formidable alliance whose time had come.

Stone had been educated at Oberlin College in Ohio, the first institute of higher education in the United States to accept black students in 1835, and the first to go co-educational two years later. She maintained the trailblazing tradition of her alma mater by becoming the first Massachusetts woman to get a degree, and – like Stanton – among the first to refuse to change her name on marriage, or to promise to 'obey' her husband afterwards. Both Stanton and Anthony were immediately struck by the radiance and strength of Stone's personality, a gift that won over men and women at public meetings. Variously called 'the Morning Star' and 'the heart and soul of the women's rights movement', Stone was also nicknamed 'the Orator' for the spellbinding power of her speeches and the beauty of her voice, with its uniquely pure, silvery and bell-like tone.

Stanton, no mean speaker herself, hailed Stone as 'the first person by whom the heart of the American public was deeply stirred on the woman question'. But sentiment was not enough. When Stanton and Anthony founded a radical feminist newspaper in 1869 and called it *Revolution*, there was no doubt about the change they sought. Anthony's battle slogan for the new publication has never been bettered:

> Men, their rights and nothing more.
> Women, their rights and nothing less.

Slaves' rights or women's rights?

In 1848, Elizabeth Cady Stanton had persuaded the Seneca Falls Convention that all other rights for women were meaningless unless they won the right to vote. Over the next twenty years, the campaign for women's suffrage gained momentum, and women who had been heavily involved in the abolitionist movement now faced a competition for their time, energy and cash between the two causes.

It was a hard choice, since the battle to end slavery was far from won. Many felt that the anti-slavery struggle was the nobler cause, especially in the eyes of God who had ordained the subordination of women, but not of men. Those who favoured the campaign for women's rights were often accused of betraying the abolitionists, and tempers ran high. Speaking at an Anti-Slavery Society meeting in Boston in 1851, Lucy Stone was reproved by the presiding official for linking the misery of slavery with the lifelong thrall of 'enchained womanhood'. Rounding on him, Stone declared, 'I was a woman before I was an abolitionist. I must speak for women.'

Stone's sense that the women's battle was the one most in need of their full fighting force was borne out. In 1865 the 13th amendment abolished slavery in the United States. Then, in 1868 and 1870, the 14th and 15th amendments granted voting rights, citizenship and equality under the law to 'all persons born or naturalized in the United States', regardless of 'race, color, or previous condition of servitude'.

But *not regardless of gender.*

Defining the new rights, the 14th amendment pronounced that the right to vote was not to be denied 'to any of the male inhabitants ... being twenty-one years of age'. By introducing the word 'male' into the Constitution, the government had officially made women non-persons by law. All over the country, they protested by entering voting stations and trying to cast a vote, although there were none to be had. Among them were Sarah and Angelina Grimké, older now than in their glory days but no less fierce and fiery when roused. In March 1870, they led a suffrage squad of forty-two Massachusetts women to try to cast a vote in a town election in Lexington, where the first shot was fired in another historic struggle for independence, the Revolutionary War. But even the Grimkés were roughly turned away.

Yet the cause surged on. Was the good old territory of Wyoming aware that it was making history as the first place in the world to grant women full suffrage in 1868, followed by the territory of Utah a year later? Neither was yet a state of the Union, but a powerful precedent was set. And these were not bloodless victories, since any advancement for women was met with strong resistance and often violent opposition. Even the mildest of men had a vested interest in the legal, political, social and personal control of women, which gave them a status and centrality they were reluctant to forgo.

Against our sex . . .

Predictably, men like these were not the only opponents of women's freedom and progress. Many women also accepted without question men's 'natural' superiority, and strongly resisted any challenge to the lives they had built around men's dominance and the accommodations they had had to make in response to it. The US anti-suffrage movement began in 1871, when nineteen women petitioned Congress to ban votes for women, the first organised anti-suffrage activity by women against women. Similar groups sprouted up, with three principal objections:

- Involving women in public activity would destroy the family unit, and take women away from their 'rightful sphere', the home.
- Women should not be allowed to vote because they lacked the capacity to make informed judgements, and their inclusion would weaken the electorate.
- And, last but not least, it was against God's will, as He had ordained women to be inferior to men, to submit to men's will and to obey them all their lives.

I know, I know.
But they believed it, and defended it all the more fiercely when their blind faith was challenged by reasoned argument.

In Britain, the formal debate on women's rights had launched as early as 1825 with the publication of 'An Appeal of One Half the Human Race, Women, Against the Pretensions of the Other Half, Men, to Retain Them in Political, and Thence in Civil and Domestic Slavery: In Reply to Mr Mill's Celebrated Article on Government'. The author, William Thompson, a philosopher and social reformer, described the Appeal as the 'joint property' of himself and Anna Wheeler. Educated at home, Irish-born Wheeler had found her way to fighting the cause of women by reading Mary Wollstonecraft. Like so many others, she came to the struggle the hard way, when a romantic youthful marriage (she was fifteen when she married a rich and captivating lad of nineteen) left her shackled for the next twelve years to a drunken thug. Unsurprisingly, then, she was not convinced by the 'Celebrated Article' of 'Mr Mill'.

This was a piece published by the Scots philosopher James Mill, stating that women did not need the vote. The interests of women were necessarily bound up with those of their fathers or husbands, who of course could always be trusted to safeguard them. It's fun to be able to record that James Mill was the father of the great reformer John Stuart Mill, who later threw himself into promoting women's interests, and in particular, the vote.

Votes for women!

The first petition for female suffrage in the UK, a pamphlet written by a wealthy Yorkshire woman, Mary Smith, was presented at Westminster in 1832 by the radical MP Henry 'Orator' Hunt. In it, Smith 'stated that she paid taxes and therefore did not see why she should not have a share in the election of a Representative; she also stated that women were liable to all the punishments of the law, not excepting death, and ought to have a voice in the making of them'. We can hear the echoes here of arguments circulating for at least fifty years from the American Revolution ('No Taxation without Representation!') and from Olympe de Gouges ('the right to mount the scaffold' should permit women 'to lay claim to the speaker's platform as well'). This petition was received by the Honourable Members of the House of Commons, commentators noted, with 'coarse jokes' and 'very beastly rib- aldry', which Hunt deftly handled to ensure that the petition was at least printed and distributed for discussion, no mean feat in the 'noble House', with its time-hallowed traditions of howling down the opposition like wild dogs baying the moon.

This was in the August of 1832, two months after 'the Mother of Parliaments' passed the ironically named Great Reform Act, which for the first time defined all voters as 'male'. No reform for women there, then, as the Act specifically withdrew the voting rights that some women of property or position – women like the disgruntled Mary Smith – had held for centuries. This explicit exclusion worked wonders in provoking women to rebel. In the following decades, support for women's suffrage gathered strength throughout the country, with many local associations springing up in scattered boroughs and previously sleepy country towns.

In 1866, the first formal petition for female suffrage, signed by 1499 eminent women including the likes of Florence Nightingale, was presented to Parliament by John Stuart Mill. That same year nineteen-year-old Millicent Garrett, sister of the first British female doctor, Elizabeth Garrett Anderson, became the secretary of the London Society for Women's Suffrage. This all happened after her sister took Millicent to meet the great Emily Davies, later co-founder of Girton College, Cambridge. 'It is quite clear what has to be done,' Emily briskly informed Elizabeth. 'I must devote myself to securing higher education, while you open the medical profession to women. After these things are done, we must see about getting the vote.' She turned to Millicent: 'You are younger than we are, Millie, so you must attend to that.' Infinitely patient, highly intelligent and hard- working, Millicent obeyed her instructions to the letter.

We are not amused

It is a supreme irony that the one woman in the world who had the power to advance the cause of women was opposed to the very idea of it. The small but significant Victoria Regina, less than five foot in height but 'Her Majesty Victoria, by the Grace of God, of the United Kingdom of Great Britain and Ireland Queen, Defender of the Faith, Empress of India', abandoned the centuries-old British tradition of royal neutrality in state affairs to mount a public attack on equality for women, and on anyone who had any hand in it.

Not for the first time, the baffled Queen was way behind the times. In fairness to the pitifully uneducated Victoria, her long reign, her limited understanding and her reactionary bias meant that new thinking left her far behind. When she came to the throne in 1837, the Brontë sisters were writing by candlelight and travelling by stage coach. When she died sixty-four years later, the world had steam trains and telegrams, electricity and gas, and her favourite nephew, Kaiser Wilhelm II, King of Prussia and Emperor of Germany, a keen if erratic moderniser, had already embarked on what became known as the 'New Course' of government, now thought to have led to the outbreak of the First World War. Mary Wollstonecraft's work, with its avowed intent to turn the world upside down, had rolled around the world from America to China without apparently reaching Kensington Palace, where Victoria grew up. In addition, the first debate on votes for women – when Orator Hunt presented Mary Smith's petition – took place in Parliament in August 1832, when she was thirteen and already heir presumptive to the throne. It is a tribute to the exceptionally rigid and intellectually stifling regime of her widowed mother, the Duchess of Kent, that the young Victoria grew up in ignorance of most of this.

It is against this background that we should see the splut-
tering rage of Queen Victoria when she burst out in 1870
against what had become a considerable movement. Here is
the pint-sized potentate writing to her trusted courtier Sir
Theodore Martin:

> The Queen is most anxious to enlist every one who can
> speak or write to join in checking this mad, wicked folly of
> 'Woman's Rights', with all its attendant horrors, on which
> her poor feeble sex is bent, forgetting every sense of wom-
> anly feeling and propriety. Lady [Amberley] ought to get a
> *good whipping*.

And there was more:

> It is a subject which makes the Queen so furious that she
> cannot contain herself. God created men and women differ-
> ent: – then let them remain each in their own position ...
> Woman will become the most hateful, heathen and disgust-
> ing of human beings were she allowed to 'unsex' herself, and
> where would be the protection which man was intended to
> give the weaker sex?

The flames of the Queen's anger were fanned by her then
Prime Minister, William Gladstone, who took time off from
his nocturnal pastime of hobnobbing with prostitutes (*rescuing
fallen women, surely?*) to support Victoria's keen desire to keep
other women in their place. Another supporter was her favourite
among her Prime Ministers, Benjamin Disraeli, whose skill in
manipulating the needy and limited 'widow of Windsor' knew
no bounds.

Oh, and the wicked Lady Amberley?

Born into one high-class left-leaning family and marrying

into another, both she and her husband favoured *all* rights for women, beginning with the vote, equal pay for equal work, and equal opportunities of higher education and entry to the professions. Katharine Russell, to give the viscountess her name, was a formidable free-thinker, and the Articles of Women's Rights she composed in 1871 are striking in their modernity:

- education for girls
- entry to university and to the professions
- the right to own property
- guaranteed guardianship to widows of their own children
- the vote
- equal opportunity of employment
- no legal subordination in marriage
- and equal pay for equal work.

And Victoria hated her why? Because Amberley was a rebel against everything she ought to uphold, the social order of God and Man. Born into the aristocracy, she chose her gender above her class when she joined a suffrage association and began to work for the cause. Her speech in the early summer of 1870 at the Mechanics Institute in Stroud, darkest Gloucestershire, was ridiculed in the press, but at the end of the meeting twelve volunteers came forward to form a local branch of the Women's Suffragist Association. To Victoria, Amberley was a class traitor and deserved all she got.

Fortunately, history was on the side of the maverick in this struggle, not the queen in her castle, and slowly, slowly, the idea of rights for women gained ground. By the mid-nineteenth century no force on earth could turn the swelling tide. Now that the ideas not only of freedom but of *women's freedom*, not just rights for men but *human rights for women* were working their way round the world, the cause surged on like

an underground river, breaking the surface in many unexpected places.

Slow boat in China

A vivid example of this arose in the unlikely setting of China,
known for an autocracy so absolute that freedom even for men
was still a distant dream. From 1850 to 1864, the country was
torn apart by a civil war of such hideous savagery that estimates
of the dead range from twenty to seventy million. Widely
regarded as the most destructive conflict of the nineteenth century, the Taiping Rebellion was also described by *The Times* in
August 1853 as 'the greatest revolution the world has yet seen'.
Its visionary leader saw that the modernisation of agriculture,
mass industrialisation and a complete overhaul of the five-
thousand-year-old system of government were all vital to the
progress of the country, and long overdue. Astonishingly, he
also promised to bring equality between the sexes, potentially
a revolution of equal magnitude.

How did this come about? The bright son of a poor farming
family, thirty-six-year-old Hong Xiuchuan failed the exami-
nations of the Imperial Civil Service not once but four times
despite twenty years of study – quite easily done when less
than one per cent of candidates ever succeeded. After a severe
breakdown, he saw himself reborn as the Chinese Son of God,
Christ's younger brother divinely ordained to relieve the plight
of women. There was no shortage of opportunity there. From
the Han dynasty at the start of the second century BCE, laws
promoted men not only as the head of the family but as the
family itself, with kinship traced entirely through the male line.
A woman only existed in relation to her nearest male relatives,
subject to her father and brothers, to her husband and his father,
and finally to her sons, however old she became.

As a result, Chinese women were never people but property, owned first by the family they were born into, then by the family of their husband when they were traded as a bride. On a literal and a littoral level too, they did not exist, since female names were never recorded on the family tree. They lived their lives as slaves and were beaten for any failure, however slight. These controls were not only legal and cultural, but physical. One of the key texts of Confucianism, the Book of Rites, stated that only men should live in the public parts of a house. When not working, women were to be kept in the window-less inner rooms, confined to cramped and insanitary quarters where they could not mix with outsiders, or be seen. Women of higher status might enjoy better conditions, but could never fully overcome their misfortune of birth.

Hong Xiuchuan came to power in 1853 when a series of military victories led to the capture of Nanking and allowed him to set up the capital of his 'Heavenly Kingdom' there. Among his first acts was to order that women were to be freed from their traditional house arrest. They were not only allowed but encouraged to take part in the war, to fight alongside men and to organise into women-only battalions trained to a high level of discipline and effectiveness.

Lotus women

To make this possible, the Taiping chief announced a total ban on the ancient custom of foot-binding, in which a girl's feet were systematically broken, bone by bone, then re-shaped with tight binding to create the tiny foot deemed an ideal of femininity. After this, the feet had to be re-broken and re-bound as long as the girl was growing, causing repeated infections and constant pain – even gangrene that could result in death. The perfect foot, called the 'Golden Lotus', was less than ten centimetres long. Anything bigger was rated as a 'Silver' or an 'Iron Lotus', although both were still a savage reduction of the size of a normal foot.

This baroque form of child abuse began in court circles, spread widely through society, and was practised for centuries. What was the purpose of subjecting girls to a lifetime of torture? The standard explanation is that it sent out a clear signal of wealth and status, by indicating that the family had no need for the labour the young female could provide, since she would not be able to move freely about the house, let alone work in the fields. As a mark of distinction and refinement, it was also intended to ensure a good marriage for the girl by appealing to a better class of suitor, and putting her out of reach of the local yokels.

For men, the 'Lotus Women' were also a focus of intense erotic fantasy and desire. The crippled feet resulted in a trembling, tottering way of walking known as 'the Lotus gait', and because the woman had to work hard to maintain her balance even with some assistance, the effort was erroneously believed to bulk up the muscles in the vagina, pelvis and thighs, making sex more enjoyable for the male partner. Sex manuals from the Qing Dynasty also describe a number of ways the male could use the 'three-inch golden lilies' for pleasure. The foot itself, comments Jan Ryan, who studied Chinese migrant families, was 'viewed as a sexual organ, and possibly the most forbidden zone', because it was 'round like a breast' and 'small like a mouth'. Ryan describes the love play called 'Eating the Golden Lotus', when 'a man would insert a woman's naked foot into his mouth and chew on it vigorously. This was considered the pinnacle of erotic pleasure.'

At the start of his revolution Hong Xiuchuan had no desire to protect such traditional privileges of men. His followers were therefore forbidden the customary male prerogatives of polygamy, concubines and prostitutes, not to mention opium, gambling, tobacco and alcohol. Alas, the women of China soon learned that there was to be no revolution for them. As Hong Xiuchuan and his army ravaged China until his death in 1864, he and his commanders kept not one but bundles of concubines, and were too busy fighting and killing their enemies and each other to implement a single one of their female-friendly policies.

So, in China, the freedom and equality thing for women just didn't happen, as it hadn't in America and France.

But the women soldiered on.

And the idea spread again.

Rebel women everywhere

Paris, long considered the avant-garde capital of Europe, and not only by the French, played host in 1878 to the world's first International Congress of Women. In the following years and into the new century, similar meetings were held in London, Berlin, Amsterdam, Toronto and Stockholm. As the 'mad, wicked folly' of women's rights built up an increasingly powerful head of steam, the men in charge could no longer pretend it was all hot air, and began to take action. In 1915, with the world at war and the Netherlands neutral, a congress was arranged in the Hague. The French and Russian women were banned by their governments from attending on the grounds of national security, while the 180 members of the British delegation were all denied passports. Twenty-four were then made available, but only to women approved by the Home Secretary. When the delegates were finally due to take the ferry to the conference, the Admiralty closed the North Sea to all shipping. As always the heavy-handed use of *force majeure* only strengthened the cause.

And as the power-holders tended to forget, women were always there to notice such manoeuvres, because *women were everywhere*: twelve hundred of them from over a dozen countries including Germany and the USA succeeded in attending the congress at the Hague. As the nineteenth century unfolded, the Industrial Revolution was just one of the earthquakes that shook the modern world. Political upheavals generated a series of revolutions, from the ideological to the technological, and in every one, a woman was involved at some level. On 24 May 1844, Samuel F. B. Morse sent the first telegram from Washington to Baltimore, while in 1848 Karl Marx and Friedrich Engels published *The Communist Manifesto*, and all these men relied on the women around them in some way.

Morse's helper was eighteen-year-old Annie Ellsworth. She worked at the US Patent Office with her father, who had championed Morse's invention from the start. At Morse's invitation, she was the originator of the first words ever transmitted, 'What Hath God Wrought?' Morse himself was at pains to credit Annie for her part in his historic achievement, enshrining her name in his own hand across the top of the paper tape with the dots and dashes of Morse code.

Annie Ellsworth gave Morse four words. The brave and big-souled Jenny Marx gave husband Karl a lifetime of mind-boggling devotion, ranging from tireless cooperation with his writing to pawning her jewels to keep the family afloat. Her strong dedication to him and to his work has been overshadowed by the importance attached to his friend, co-author and *éminence grise*, Friedrich Engels. But there is no denying the massive debt that Marx, Engels and the ideological juggernaut of Marxism all owe to her. It is heart-wrenching to consider Marx's posthumous success in contrast with the starvation-level poverty the couple and their children endured. With today's royalties, Marx could have founded his own political party, or at least kept more than three of his seven children alive. But then, as Jenny is supposed to have observed, 'I wish that dear Karl could have spent more time acquiring capital instead of merely writing about it.'

Behind every great man, as they say, is a good woman. In Marx's case, there were two. Writing in German, Marx had no access to the all-important Anglo-American world of ideas. That gap was filled by the resourceful Scot Helen Macfarlane, who translated *The Communist Manifesto* into English in 1850. Born in the same year as Emily Brontë, Macfarlane could not have led a more different life from the Yorkshire recluse. A radical socialist, feminist, Chartist and philosopher, the highly educated Macfarlane was present at the revolution in Vienna that brought down the Habsburg Empire in 1848, and loved every minute of it. As she recalled the events:

the most joyful of all spectacles possible in these times is the one ... I enjoyed extremely at Vienna, in March 1848 – i.e. 'an universal tumbling of impostors' – For it amounts to this, that men are determined to live no longer in lies ... And how do men come to perceive that the old social forms are worn out and useless? By the advent of a new Idea.

New ideas were stirring throughout Europe and beyond, and ever-growing numbers of women were stirring with them, beginning to take possession of their lives and to question the paths laid out for them from birth. Above all, they were coming to rebel against the inflexible social dogma that men come first, and that their own hopes and ambitions, their interests and inclinations, must take second place.

And so it changed, and the change flowed on. It was to prove a long and winding river with many shallows, diversions and dangers, but there was to be no stopping it now. Rights, freedoms, opportunities, possibilities, all beckoned, however distantly, for those who would reach out, seize the moment and take their chance.

2

One Way Pendulum

A farce in a new dimension.

N. F. SIMPSON

CHAPTER 4

WOMEN WHO DARED

Disobedience, in the eyes of any one who has
read history, is man's original virtue. It is through
disobedience that progress has been made, through
disobedience and through rebellion.

OSCAR WILDE

Well-behaved women seldom make history.

LAUREL THATCHER ULRICH

A ship in port is safe, but that is not what ships are for.
Sail out to sea and do new things.

REAR ADMIRAL 'AMAZING' GRACE HOPPER

One Way Pendulum: A Farce in a New Dimension – the title of N. F.
Simpson's hit play of 1959 sums up both the exhilarating progress
women made in the nineteenth century and the reaction to it.
The pendulum of history may swing back against women, but
with every forward movement it travels a little farther in women's favour. Women make progress in times of change, when the

old certainties break down and create cracks and fissures in the monoliths they previously could never hope to penetrate.

Change and chance, then, bringing hopes and possibilities and distant, dazzling dreams – who would pursue them? Who would dare? As the century unfolded, there were more and more women of adventure, bold souls like the Austrian explorer Ida Pfeiffer, who became the first European known to have survived a visit to the Patak cannibals of Indonesia. Fending off the understandable alarm of her sons, she made a virtue of the fact that she was beginning her travels at the age of forty-five. No one would dream of eating her, she reassured them, because she was far too old and tough. A century of revolutions inspired many other women like Pfeiffer to strike out in new directions wherever they could be found.

Here be adventures . . .

Other spirited women found their natural home in untamed pockets of the globe like the Wild West of the young US of A. This was to prove particularly hospitable to any number of red-blooded runaways and roaring girls who simply blew female modesty to the winds and lived their lives with the freedom of men. In the early days of the American frontier, the daredevil horsewoman and army scout Martha Jane Cannary wore men's clothes for safety as well as convenience, and earned the nickname 'Calamity Jane' by warning any men who messed with her that they were '*Courtin' calamity!*' With that established, 'I was at all times with the men when there was excitement and adventures to be had,' she said, proudly recalling an overland trek from Missouri to Montana in 1865. 'I was considered a remarkable good shot and a fearless rider for a girl of my age.'

Doesn't that sound a lot more fun than the home life of the young girl condemned to 'sit on a cushion and sew a fine seam', even if that meant she would be rewarded with the 'strawber-ries, sugar and cream' promised in the nursery rhyme? The American sharpshooter Annie 'Get Your Gun' Oakley travelled the world with a hair-raising repertoire of terrifying tricks, including knocking the ash off a cigarette held in her husband's mouth with a single shot. 'Little Miss Sure Shot', as she was billed, entranced the crowned heads of Europe and despite seri-ous injuries in road and train accidents never missed a shot. Still a sure-shot in her sixties, Oakley taught other women to shoot, and proposed putting together a team of female sharpshooters to fight for the United States in time of war. Shooting should be a normal part of women's lives as it was for men, she remarked. 'I would like to see every woman know how to handle [guns] as naturally as they know how to handle babies.' She supported numerous charities caring for orphans and young women strug-gling to get a start in life, both with hefty donations and also by performing her celebrated act without charge, a guaranteed fund-raiser that always drew the crowds.

Circus life carried clear risks for Annie: her repertoire included taking pot shots at various targets while standing on the back of a cantering horse. But as daring goes, few could match the Italian high-wire artiste Maria Spelterini. Born into the circus, Spelterini discovered her gift for rope-walking at around the age of three, and from her father's big top in Italy, she toured as far as Russia, completing death-defying feats like crossing the River Neva in St Petersburg without any kind of harness or safety net. Her *pièce de résistance* came in 1876, on the border between Canada and America, when she became the first and only woman to walk a tightrope over Niagara Gorge.

With her rich Mediterranean looks and womanly body ('buxom' and 'about 150 lbs' as the newspapers admiringly recorded), Spelterini won admirers wherever she went, per-forming in a saucy hat, a bright red tunic showing off her legs and a vivid green bodice tightly corseting her waist (*how did she breathe?*). That summer in Niagara, she walked the tightrope across the gorge, then returned, stepping backwards. She crossed with her feet in baskets, with her head in a bag, and with her wrists and ankles manacled, though not all at the same time. In a lifetime of performing terrifyingly dangerous stunts, Spelterini's uncanny skill never failed her, and she died peacefully in her bed. If you ever feel your own nerve failing, think of Spelterini and tell yourself, '*Whatever this is, it's not Niagara Falls!*'

Maria Spelterini in action on 8 July 1876, four days after her first crossing. Note the baskets on her feet, the suspension bridge jam-packed with spectators, and Niagara Falls in the background.

Who dares wins

Is this so new? Girls and women were involved in circus per-
formances and public entertainments from time out of mind. A
fresco of about 1400 BCE from the Palace of Knossos in Crete
shows the fearsome sport of bull-leaping, with two athletic
female figures at the head and tail of the charging animal, apparently working as the thrower and catcher for the male acrobat
vaulting over the bull's back. But women traditionally played
decorative or supporting roles, adding a little spangle to the saw-
dust to bring the punters in. Now, for the first time, Spelterini
and her strong and daring sisters could become star attractions
in their own right during this women's century of change and
chance: check out the ground-breaking aerial acrobat Leona
Dare, tiger tamer Mabel Stark and Antoinette Concello, billed
as 'the greatest woman flyer of all time', all of whom, give or
take a mishap like accidentally killing a male partner as befell
the aerialist Dare, carved out substantial careers.

These women put paid to the notion of female frailty at the
same time as the women's movement was beginning to mount
a serious challenge to the idea that women were weaker than
men. Spelterini was hailed as striking a blow for women's equality because she repeated the Niagara crossing first performed
nearly twenty years earlier by a man, the French rope-walker
known as 'Blondin', Jean-François Gravelet. Spelterini's iron
nerve was a powerful counterbalance to the regular charge of
female hysteria, while 'the Woman of Steel', Bavarian-born
Katie Brumbach, earned that title in her adolescence. The queen
of women weightlifters, Brumbach could balance her 165lb
husband and their baby on one arm. She sealed her reputation
by raising 300lbs above her head to defeat the world-famous
Prussian strongman Eugene Sandow in a weightlifting contest.

To ensure that no one ever forgot her outstanding victory

over the man now recognised as the father of powerlifting, Brumbach changed her stage name to a feminine form of Sandow and billed herself as 'Sandwina' for the rest of her career. A similar strength and growing self-confidence was evident throughout the Western world as women began moving for themselves and making progress over the whole range of science and the arts. Poetry, drama, music and dance, fine art and sculpture, all invented by the Ancient Greeks, had given men a head start of two thousand years. But now came an art form open to women on the same terms as men, one as fresh and new as its name, the *novel*.

'By a Lady'

Enter the 'Lady Novelists', stepping into history in their hundreds worldwide, along with Fanny Burney, Jane Austen, Maria Edgeworth and all the other well-loved 'authoresses' of the UK. In the US, Sarah Josepha Hale gave the world the nursery rhyme 'Mary Had a Little Lamb', and dreamed up the country's national Thanksgiving holiday in addition to blazing a trail as one of America's first women novelists, while the expressive Anna Cora Mowatt first broke out at the age of fifteen by eloping with a man almost twice her age, then went on to dazzle New York and London as a journalist, biographer, novelist, playwright and, not least, a leading lady winning acclaim in Shakespearean roles.

Mary Theresa Vidal became Australia's first female novelist in 1845 with her *Tales for the Bush* (a somewhat sanitised account of life in the outback, so real-life bushwhackers said), while the writer Harriet Miller Davidson was so highly regarded that when her husband was appointed a professor of English at the newly created University of Adelaide, the common view was that the post should have gone to his wife. The well-travelled

Mary Anne Barker published a total of twenty-two books, starting in 1870 with *Station Life in New Zealand*, moving on to *A Year's Housekeeping in South Africa* (1880), and ending with her valedictory *Colonial Memories* of 1904.

None, however, had the success Isabella Bird enjoyed with *A Lady's Life in the Rocky Mountains* (1879). In it Bird enthusiastically relates the adventures she had with a 'dear desperado', the attractive, one-eyed 'Rocky Mountain Jim', an escapade the august Royal Geographical Society does not seem to have held against her when they honoured her with the invitation to become their first female Fellow in 1892.

Wherever they were writing, these women had dared to move out of the conventional female role of service and self-sacrifice to pursue their own needs and drives. Dogged by financial insecurity, ill health and bad eyesight as a number of them were, it took a special kind of courage to defy the stifling social expectations of the time and to bear the often brutal discouragement they faced, usually in the family.

This peculiar misery befell the pioneer Fanny Burney not once but twice. To her father, his middle daughter was neither as good looking nor as intelligent as her two sisters, so they were sent to Paris to be educated while she was left at home to teach herself. Her father's second marriage, to a rich but ignorant and bad-tempered widow in 1767 when Fanny was fifteen brought another setback, the dread of her stepmother's disapproval. Within the year the anxious teenager made a bonfire of all her 'scribblings', burning everything she had written, including a full-length novel, for fear that this 'unladylike' activity 'might vex' her stepmother. Happily, the lost girl found herself and tried again. Fanny went on to enjoy great success as a writer, not least with her novel *Camilla* (1796), among whose purchasers was a twenty-one-year-old resident of Steventon Parsonage in Hampshire, one 'Miss J. Austen'.

As the great Jane well knew, a woman attempting any form of writing risked severe censure, social exclusion, a despised old-maidhood and more. Very few at the time, male or female, would have disputed the assumption that a woman's duties were social, matrimonial and domestic, and could not, should not be anything else. When the young Charlotte Brontë wrote for advice to the poet laureate Robert Southey, she was loftily told that 'literature cannot be the business of a woman's life', and referred back to peeling the potatoes and washing the pots and pans. Fortunately Charlotte resisted Southey's advice and beat on into the murky waters of story-telling, that dark and dangerous, ever-beckoning sea.

And what a voyage! Charlotte, Anne and their equally extraordinary and even more original sister Emily, all cruised the wilder shores of love, and their daring is without parallel. What provoked three virgins, the daughters of a parson living quietly in the north country, to create characters like Mr Rochester in *Jane Eyre*, the Heathcliff of *Wuthering Heights* and to some readers the most shocking of them all, the drunken, destructive abuser Arthur Huntingdon in *The Tenant of Wildfell Hall*, every one of them a grim and startling fantasy of a dark and deadly man? How did they spin unvarnished accounts of male brutality and female degradation into romance and love, feeding the fevered imaginations of generations of women to come?

Nineteenth-century critics objected strongly to the throbbing eroticism and sadomasochism of their work. Their contemporary, the prominent British writer Elizabeth Rigby, considered Mr Rochester to be a 'strange brute', dark, surly, sarcastic, and 'of the brigand stamp'. But the heroines of these novels were also spirited, particularly given the age. Who can forget that great line from *Jane Eyre*: 'I do not think, sir, you have a right to command me, merely because you are older than I, or because you have seen more of the world than I have; your claim to superiority depends on the use you have made of your time and experience.'

Jane is shown here as challenging Rochester's 'right to command' and his 'claim to superiority', expressing her defiance of convention and her refusal to be judged as inferior to a man. This is no less than her claim as a woman to the right to control her own existence – to freedom and independence, in fact.

Science, knowledge, power

One woman who achieved that and more was the German-born astronomer Caroline Herschel. Working for the British royal family alongside her brother, Herschel discovered eight comets and fourteen nebulae, besides her other 'discoveries, observations, and laborious calculations', as one of her admirers, the Prussian polymath Alexander von Humboldt, noted in 1846. Granted a salary of fifty pounds a year by George III, and standing only 4 feet 3 inches tall and as feisty as they come, Herschel became the first woman in Britain (and probably in the world) to earn an income for her scientific work, and the first ever to earn a living from astronomy. Herschel's starry career earned her a gold medal from the Royal Astronomical Society in 1828, and she was made an Honorary Member in 1835. Eleven years later, at the age of ninety-six, the tiny watcher of the skies was awarded a golden gong, the highest medal of the Prussian Academy of Sciences, by the king of Prussia himself

Herschel was a pioneer in another important regard too. Clever girls, whatever their gifts, were constantly taught that they must play 'pretty-please' and submit to the men around them to get on. Herschel gloriously defied this age-old formula. Constitutionally cantankerous, uninterested in marriage and so wedded to her work that she once rode thirty miles at night in her middle age from Windsor to the Royal Observatory at Greenwich in order to record a discovery before another astronomer could beat her to it, Herschel met the world unabashed and head on.

Another boundary-buster was the sharp-eyed Mary Anning, who discovered the first known skeleton of the prehistoric marine reptile ichthyosaur when she was only twelve years old. She grew up to become an important palaeontologist working on the Jurassic fossil beds of Lyme Regis in Dorset. When she was twenty-four, she found the first complete relic of the ichthyosaur's larger cousin the plesiosaur, and five years later the first British example of the flying reptiles known as pterosaurs.

Anning was also exceptional for her skill at preserving her fossils and for her readiness to share her work. Her ability was recognised by the leading scholars and collectors of the day, but she never let the weight of academic authority deflect her from an accurate identification, whatever the previous history. Besides the reclamation of so many different fossils, Anning's other major contribution to the scientific understanding of the age of dinosaurs was a re-examination of the importance attached to the so-called 'bezoar stones'. These unique objects, strangely coloured and oddly shaped, had been highly valued for their supposed magical and medicinal properties since they were brought into Europe by Arab traders hundreds of years before. They were as expensive as diamonds or sapphires, and believed to offer a powerful, other-worldly protection to anyone who could afford them. Undazzled by either their reputation or their price, Anning was able to show that these wonders of the world were in fact fossilised faeces, primeval deposits of good old-fashioned dinosaur droppings, and nothing mystical at all.

A new age

Describing the achievements of the astounding Mary Fairfax Somerville, the *London Post* was able to declare that 'a new era had begun'. A well-born Scot, Somerville could not read, write, or add up until the age of ten because her mother saw no point in educating a girl, but she stumbled upon the joys of Euclid's *Principles of Geometry* in the family library (as you do) and began to teach herself. Forbidden to study by her parents after the death of her younger sister was blamed on too much reading, Mary persisted in secret, immersing herself in trigonometry and astronomy and Newton's *Principia Mathematica*.

As she hit her stride, there seemed no limit to what Somerville could do. Famed for combining a strong scholarly discipline with remarkable intellectual daring, in 1842 she predicted the existence of a massive, mysterious, unknown and invisible planet through her mathematical analysis of the movement of the planet Uranus. Following Mary's workings, the French astronomer Urbain Le Verrier and his English counterpart John Couch Adams confirmed the existence of Neptune four years later.

Unlike Caroline Herschel, Somerville was not interested in recognition or fame. Her main focus was always on her work, which she knew she was lucky to be able to pursue. In her memoirs she recalled her father insisting that 'the strain of abstract thought would injure the tender female frame', while her first husband, a naval officer called Samuel Greig, 'had a very low opinion of the capacity of my sex and no interest in science of any kind'. As it turned out, Greig died after only three years of marriage, and Somerville could now risk her 'tender female frame' with a lifetime of scientific work. She also married again very happily and bore four healthy children. In her spare time she became a popular member of the

Edinburgh social set, befriended Sir Walter Scott and supported the women novelists of her day before her death at the ripe old age of ninety-one.

Working at this level while also caring for her husband, family and friends, Somerville somehow made time for teaching too, and one of her pupils was the budding genius Augusta Byron, known as Ada. The only child of the Romantic poet Lord Byron, famous for being 'mad, bad, and dangerous to know', and his equally damaged and damaging wife, Annabella, Ada met her destiny as a mathematician and thinker when Somerville introduced her to Charles Babbage, an equally brilliant professor of mathematics at Cambridge University.

Babbage had created a machine that could add up mechanically, in order to eliminate the human errors in making calculations by hand. It was the world's first computer, and the rest was history. Ada got it immediately. Indeed, its inventor soon realised that the teenage beginner understood Babbage's Analytical Engine, as he called it, better than he did himself, as he acknowledged in his affectionate nickname for her, 'the Queen of Number'.

Number was the name of the game. Ada grasped that the machine could do more than simply add up, and wrote what is now recognised as the world's first computer program. More than that, she had a vision that raw numbers could be made to stand for more than simple quantities, therefore a machine that could manipulate numbers could manipulate anything represented by numbers. Pondering these things, Ada created the first algorithms, and only her death from uterine cancer at the age of thirty-six cut her off from a stellar career in what she called her 'poetical science'. She is one of a minority of women scientists in London to be honoured with a blue plaque: hers in St James's Square states that 'Ada, Countess of Lovelace, pioneer of computing, lived here'.

Light and truth

The world, of course, preferred to see these pioneering academic women and girls as puzzling anomalies or even as sinister abnormalities, and at first only a few followed in their footsteps. Yet entry to higher education had been at the top of the list of women's claims for equality for hundreds of years, and the new revolutionary era gave a vital boost to that. In 1783, a young American student applied for entry to Yale College. Under examination in Latin and Greek by the college president Ezra Stiles himself, the candidate was pronounced fully qualified for admission, and given an immediate diploma of exceptional merit.

Fully qualified, said the man, and he ought to know. The Reverend Doctor Stiles also knew that the aspiring classicist was only twelve years old, but that was no obstacle at a time when universities everywhere admitted boys from as early as ten. Indeed this applicant was suitable for the university in every way, 'except', as the president regretfully recorded, 'in regard to sex'. The young Lucinda Foote did not meet the first and most basic requirement for entry: no male, no Yale.

Unusually, though, Lucinda got her Yale-style education. Stiles stayed in touch, and with the blessing of her family taught her Hebrew and took her through the full course of the college curriculum. Nor did studying ancient languages make her less female or fecund, a fear that has bedevilled the education of girls since the Middle Ages. So far from being made barren by brain-work, Lucinda bore nine children in ten years to the doctor she married in 1790, and enjoyed a long life as a woman widely admired for the breadth of her education and her impressive mental powers. Nearly two hundred years later, in 1969, Yale University finally stood up to those predicting the end of the world if women were admitted as full students, and the sky did not fall in.

Full steam ahead

Yale was not alone. Oxford and Cambridge, true to their monastic and priestly origins, clung to their proud and ancient traditions of fearing, despising and excluding female students for as long as they could. Other universities all over the world, however, began to admit women to study for degrees. Between 1875 and 1880, institutions of higher education in Denmark, Italy, the Netherlands, the United States, Chile, India, Australia, Belgium, Canada and France, as well as the University of London, opened their doors. Female students flocked from far and wide. Three brave pioneers – Anandibai Gopal Joshi from India, Kei Okami from Japan and Sabat Islambooly from Syria – were students at the Women's Medical College of Pennsylvania in 1886. All three went on to complete their medical studies, and each was the first woman from her country to qualify in Western medicine.

England's oldest universities held out for as long as they could. Even with the founding of Girton College at Cambridge in 1869 and Lady Margaret Hall in Oxford nine years later, female students were allowed to complete a course only on the understanding that it would not lead to a degree.

Enter the great Anthony Traill, Provost of Trinity College Dublin, who successfully presided over the admission of women to this college on his appointment in 1904, and now proposed granting any woman who had completed her course at Oxford or Cambridge a degree from Trinity. Why would any woman refuse the chance of a degree from the college founded in 1592 by another dedicated female student and outstanding intellect, Elizabeth I? TCD, as the college is widely known, was the alma mater of immortals like the Restoration playwright William Congreve, the greatest of British satirists Jonathan Swift, and constellations of other stars, as well as later giving a home to women as diverse as singer-songwriter Courtney Love and Mary McAleese, Ireland's second female president. They came by the boatload, of course. Between 1904 and 1907, 720 Oxbridge women, called 'the Steamboat Ladies' for their method of transport, sailed to Dublin to receive degrees. Among them were:

Julia Bell, whose later work on fragile X syndrome was a key step to mapping the human genome.

Philippa Fawcett, daughter of suffrage leader Millicent, who came first in the mathematics Tripos exams at Cambridge, but was not honoured with the traditional title of Senior Wrangler because as a woman, her result could not stand.

Eleanor Rathbone, who would become one of the first woman Members of Parliament, where she spoke out against female genital mutilation in Kenya as early as 1929, and called for free entry to the UK for Jews during the Second World War.

Gertrude Elles, a geologist and palaeontologist, who also trained the pioneering Australian geologists of the next generation, Elizabeth Ripper and the intrepid Dorothy Hill.

These women, however, were luckier than many others. The eldest of the three daughters of the suffragette leader Emmeline Pankhurst graduated from the University of Manchester in 1906 with a first class honours degree in law. But as a woman, Christabel Pankhurst could not get a position as a solicitor or a pupillage at the Inns of Court to become a barrister like her father, and without that could never practise.

La lutte continue!

But the fight goes on, and nowhere more vigorously than in France. The republic established with so much blood, terror and devastation had lasted a mere decade before it was overthrown by Napoleon in 1799. In 1848, another revolution brought in another republic, one that restored two key planks of democracy: the freedom of the press, and the right of public assembly. Among the first to form clubs and associations were the women, bursting to express their discontent with their second-class status, wanting the *égalité* promised so long ago.

The strongest and most radical of these groups were the Vésuviennes, who flourished in the 1850s, a fiery bunch of unmarried and low-paid working-class girls. They took their name from Mount Vesuvius, styling themselves as 'like lava, so long held back that it must at last pour out' and promising that their promotion of equality for women would be 'in no way incendiary, but in all ways regenerating'. Contemporary sketches depicted them wearing military-style hats and carrying out drill under the command of a senior woman who was usually bearing a weapon of some sort. Their mood was uncompromising and their agenda simple:

- Military service for women on the same terms as men.
- The right of women to wear men's dress.
- Legal equality for women with men.
- Complete domestic equality between men and women.

Simple, yes, but so radical that nearly two hundred years later most societies that consider themselves advanced are still working on at least two of the women's four points. Elsewhere, they all have yet to be achieved.

The tactics of the Vésuviennes were as challenging as their

Vésuviennes in their masculine uniform of matching hats and *culottes*, drilling under the command of a leader to demonstrate their two key claims: the right to serve in the military and the right to wear men's clothes.

manifesto, from staging demonstrations in the street to wearing *culottes* in public. The image of young women in *culottes* subsequently became a derogatory shorthand for all Western feminists. The same was true of the 'bloomers' sported by radical feminists after Amelia Bloomer took up the outfit introduced to New England in 1851 by the dress reformer and activist Elizabeth Smith Miller. Of course, it was never just about the leg coverings. Dress reform had been high on many women's agenda for decades. But wherever they appeared, the sight of women in 'bloomers' caused such excitement and provoked so much hostility that both the French and American women had to give up wearing them because the anger they triggered proved too dangerous to the wearer and too damaging to the cause.

The Vésuviennes are so poorly documented that some modern historians have suggested that the whole movement was cooked up by the Paris police to justify attacks on low-class women and sex workers. But its agenda is still remarkably resonant, and kept the flame of action for equality alive until it could once again, like lava, change the landscape.

Backlash, backlash

Inevitably progress was slow and the spirit of reaction strong. The great pendulum of history always swings back to a place of safety before it can swing forward again. In the Mendelssohn family, Fanny was originally rated as more talented than her younger brother Felix by their tutor, the distinguished composer Carl Friedrich Zelter. Hearing Fanny play in 1816 when she was eleven, Zelter raved to his friend the poet Goethe, 'This child is really something special.' At thirteen, Fanny knew all Bach's Preludes by heart, and when she was twenty-six, Zelter paid her his supreme compliment: '*She plays like a man.*'

But she was female. 'Music will perhaps become [Felix's] profession,' her father told her, 'while for you it can and must be only an ornament.' Felix thought the same. Fanny, he opined in 1837, 'has neither inclination nor vocation for authorship. She is too much all that a woman ought to be for this. She regulates her house [as a wife and mother], and neither thinks of the public nor of the musical world, nor even of music at all, until her first duties are fulfilled.'

How did he know? Felix also thought little of publishing Fanny's work as his own. But in 1842, when Queen Victoria played him her favourite of 'his' pieces at Buckingham Palace, the embarrassed composer was forced to admit it had been written by his sister. Happily Fanny does not seem to have taken much notice of all this, and composed over 460 pieces of music.

Boys must be boss

Women lived, suffered, failed or achieved as individuals, but historically they died as a sub-species of the human race. A strong back-swing of the pendulum came towards the end of the nineteenth century, with a global renewal of male domination. In Japan, the new emperor, who came to power in 1867 at the age of fourteen, took the name Meiji, 'Enlightened Rule', promising 'Revolution, renovation, reform and renewal'. But in 1899 the Enlightened One was to introduce laws barring women from succeeding to the throne for the first time in Japanese history.

Before this 'modernisation', eight empresses had ruled Japan, the first, Empress Suiko, as early as the sixth century CE. Others included Empress Genmei in the eighth century, who abdicated in favour of her daughter to keep the power in female hands as a vital check on the hyper-aggressive warlords whose antics all too often plunged the country into civil war. But on the brink of the twentieth century it was goodbye to women in power, and hello to housebound housewives. No more women on the Chrysanthemum Throne. In the Land of the Rising Sun, the son only rises.

Worldwide, this pattern was to repeat itself with disheartening inevitability. Age-old traditions of women rulers were set aside, a process consolidated by the European colonial masters just as systematically as the Roman invaders of the British Isles in the first century CE obliterated Celtic queens like Boudicca. China followed the same path of action against powerful women as the twentieth century loomed. There were to be no more 'Little Lotuses', girls prostituted to the Imperial harem as children, a handful of whom rose to become empresses. The last in this long line was the former concubine who seized power in 1861 and ran China for the next forty-seven years as the Dowager Empress Cixi.

This tiny, terrifying tyrant known as the Dragon Lady ruthlessly eliminated all opposition, favouring public beheadings of high officials to keep their colleagues on their toes, and also to provide entertainment for the populace. As a female autocrat and a dictator never afraid to deal out arbitrary death, Cixi was in a league of her own. But to general bemusement, the blood-soaked despot saw herself as a sister-empress of Queen Victoria, a sentiment that constitutional monarch understandably struggled to share.

The power of change

Unlike Cixi, other ruling queens used their power to stabilise their country and to defend its heritage. Succeeding her husband Radama I as ruler of Madagascar in 1828, Queen Ranaaloana reigned for thirty-three years, adroitly fending off the imperial overtures of both Britain and France during this time. Other female rulers seized the chance to promote reform and to alleviate the many and cruel disadvantages women suffered. When Kaahumanu, a widow of King Kamehameha I, came to the throne of Hawaii in 1819 as regent for the twenty-two-year-old heir King Liholiho, she inherited a court and a country strangled for centuries by a rigid code of behaviour called 'Ai kapu that entrenched the absolute power of the king and the inferiority of women.

'Ai kapu, meaning 'sacred eating', supposedly dated from the birth of the nation, when the Great Father God Wākea planned to keep the Mother God tied up at regular times of the day so that he might have sex with his daughter. Women were therefore banned from sharing the king's food and always ate separately from the men, on pain of death for defying the will of the gods and provoking their revenge. Against all advice, one of the first acts of Queen Kaahumanu was to invite Liholiho to have dinner with her, his mother and her ladies, and a terrified court braced itself for a violent death and the world going up in flames. When all the members of the party were still alive the next morning, *'Ai kapu* withered away.

Last in a line of famous African queens, Zauditu was crowned Empress of Ethiopia in 1917, becoming the first female head of state in an internationally recognised African country and the last empress regnant of the Ethiopian Empire in direct descent from the Queen of Sheba. Outmanoeuvred by Ras Tafari Makonnen, a younger relative who had been appointed to serve as her regent, she then died suddenly and unexpectedly in 1930, leaving him free to seize the throne. Later known as Haile Selassie, self-styled 'King of Kings' and revered as a god on earth by Rastafarians worldwide, the 'Lion of Judah' introduced a new constitution in 1955 that like the 'Enlightenment' of Japan, specifically banned women from holding power.

Is it true what they say about Dixie?

While nations and states moved one way, women could and did choose another. Once the idea of equality for women had spread as far as rural China, the genie was out of the bottle and there was no going back. Individual women had the daring to forge on, especially when bolstered by class, cash and confidence like the astonishing Lady Florence Dixie. Born into the upper echelons of British aristocracy as the daughter of the Marquess of Queensberry, she saw no limits to what she could achieve.

Married at nineteen to Sir Alexander Beaumont Churchill Dixie, she became the first European woman to enter Patagonia only a few weeks after the birth of her second son in 1887. Soon afterwards she covered the First Boer War (1880–1) for the *Morning Post* of London, becoming one of the first women to work as an accredited war correspondent.

In that role, Dixie braved the wrath of the British government by championing the cause of the deposed and imprisoned King Cetshwayo. The ill-fated Zulu king was only one of the many issues she boldly took up, pitching into the debate on Irish Home Rule so powerfully that an attempt was made on her life by outraged but luckily incompetent Irish republicans. But her ever-fizzing and undaunted spirit found its main focus in a wide variety of feminist proposals and actions, most of which have a distinctly modern ring:

- Full emancipation for women, including the vote.
- Equal rights for both sexes in marriage and divorce.
- The first-born child of the British monarch to inherit the throne.
- Women and men to be free to wear clothes currently restricted to the opposite sex.
- Women to play sports, especially football.

Dixie's vision found its most radical expression in her vigorous promotion of football for women. Early female footballers are recorded in ancient documents and illustrations from China to France, but in the modern era football was a game played only by men. In 1895 Dixie founded the British Ladies' Football Club and became its first president. She raised the team, arranged the venues, and managed and funded the fixtures, tours and charity games. Working with the captain, Miss Nettie J. Honeyball, she made only one stipulation, that 'the girls should enter into the spirit of the game with heart and soul'.

Who was Miss Nettie J. Honeyball? No one knows. She has been identified as a Miss Mary Hutson of Dublin, but that gets us little further. Her witty pseudonym was probably a cover for pursuing an activity she felt forced to conceal. Was it from fear of family or social disapproval? And did the name she chose encapsulate a sly dig at netball, a new game for women based on men's basketball but considerably toned down to make it more ladylike and refined? We shall never know.

Whatever Nettie's secret, the women's first match in London drew ten thousand excited spectators, and women's football in Britain grew rapidly in popularity. During the First World War, games attracted crowds of up to sixty thousand and generated large sums of money for charity. Indeed, women's sport was gaining traction across the board. The decision to include women in the second modern Olympic Games in Paris in 1900, gave them entry to the sailing and equestrian events, croquet, golf and tennis. In a field of nearly a thousand male competitors, there were women entrants in all five categories, a total of twenty-two.

The first to strike gold was the American-born Hélène de Pourtalès, crewing in her Swiss husband's yacht, and she won a silver medal too in the race that followed. The British tennis player Charlotte Cooper became the first individual female Olympic champion, winning two golds in Paris. Another noteworthy entrant was the American Margaret Abbott, who won the women's golf tournament with a score of forty-seven over a nine-hole course. Also making history was a fellow competitor, Margaret's mother Mary, who came seventh with a score of sixty-five, making this the only time that a mother and daughter have competed in the same sport in the same event at the same Olympics. Albeit slowly, the success of these athletes opened the door to the increased participation of women and girls in a number of sports, especially when they had a chance to see them in action, as they did with the female footballers.

But by 1921, the all-male Football Association had grown angry at the attention the women were getting, and even angrier that the money they made went to every good cause except the FA's own coffers. Women were henceforth banned from playing football on the grounds that they were 'unsuitable' for the game. Try telling that to star winger Lily Parr, who scored more than a thousand goals in a thirty-one year career, thirty-four of them in her first season when she was only fourteen. Famed for her cannonball kick, she once took a challenge from a professional goalkeeper who swore that she could never get past him, and broke his arm.

Like her footballers, Lady Florence Dixie defied any notions of female incompetence, and equality for women remained her driving force. In 1890 she published *Gloriana, or the Revolution of 1900*, a futuristic novel in which the heroine of the title passes herself off as a man cunningly/punningly named Hector l'Estrange, and gets elected to Parliament. In her portrayal of Hector, Dixie drew heavily on the life of Oscar Wilde. Incarnating Wilde, Dixie flamboyantly displayed her radical, transgressive instincts and her total disdain for male authority, happily bobbing her hair and wearing masculine clothes with never a corset in sight. The photograph opposite was taken for the frontispiece of her novel, published by Henry and Co. in 1890.

Cross-dressing women and unconventional men, Dixie seems to suggest, were more likely to be in sympathy with the cause of women than the rigid 'straights' of either gender. Through the efforts of Hector/Gloriana, women win the right to vote and by 1999, when the book ends, the government of Britain is firmly in female hands.

And rightly so, Dixie argued, since 'Nature has unmistakeably

Faithfully yours.
Florence Dixie.

Hello, sailor!

given to woman a greater brain power ... perceivable in child-hood.' Despite this, she went on:

> ... man deliberately sets himself to stunt that early evidence of mental capacity, by laying down the law that woman's education shall be on a lower level than that of man's ... this procedure is arbitrary and cruel, and false to Nature ... It has been the means of sending to their graves unknown, unknelled, and unnamed, thousands of women whose high intellects have been wasted, and whose powers for good have been paralysed and undeveloped.

By ending her novel in 1999, Dixie made clear her assumption that it would take a century and more for her ambitions for women's advancement to be realised. She saw, as many did not, that other social and political struggles for freedom in the nineteenth century did not help women but rather hindered their cause. The feeling of these movements was often what did women need freedom for? Freedom from what? To do what? And if they got it, what would become of the real work of their lives, their husbands and children? Freedom meant freedom for men, and the women's claim to be included was often regarded as a sideshow, a distraction, a display of feminine pettiness that demeaned and diminished the nobler rights of man.

Dixie's career was undoubtedly extraordinary, but it also demonstrated that even her prodigious courage and conviction were not enough. One woman fighting alone would never change the world. To take on a system, to challenge, let alone to overthrow, the structures of male domination dating back ten thousand years, required more: more women, more effort, more money, more public action and debate – in short, group action.

Rebel women walk

In 1828, a change of ownership in a cotton mill in Dover, New Hampshire, had led to the first all-female strike in America when the women employees found that their pay was to be reduced by five cents a day while the men's remained the same. They also faced instant dismissal if they joined a union or talked to one another at work, to be followed by blacklisting to ensure they would never work again. On top of all this, they could be fined twelve and a half cents for one minute's lateness, which amounted to one third of their payment for the entire day. Four hundred of them walked out, with speeches, banners, placards and parades round the town. The company immediately advertised for five hundred 'better behaved' women, and most of the strikers had to crawl back or starve. Their only victory was the lifting of the no-talking rule.

Nevertheless, in the decades to come women's use of strike action spread across the United States, and as far afield as Sri Lanka. St Petersburg saw a steady stream of often tumultuous protests, after three hundred tobacco workers launched Russia's first all-female industrial action in 1878 by wrecking the factory, then throwing all their tools, work benches and the tobacco itself out into the street. The same tactic was successfully employed by another thirteen hundred of the city's 'cigarette girls' when an attempt was made to cut their wages in 1895. They trashed their workshops so comprehensively that it took one hundred armed police and two fire brigades to subdue them, an outrageous 'pussy riot' a century and more ahead of the Russian rebels who mounted their protests under that that name. In Vienna, the powerfully effective Social Democrat Adelheid Popp organised the first strike of Austrian women in 1893. Popp had started out in a succession of such degrading jobs that she could only see herself as a slave, but she won the fight and secured the textile workers a minimum wage and a ten-hour day.

In London, the 'match-girls' at the Bryant and May factory carried out the first successful strike of UK women in 1888, when they brought production to a standstill and compelled the owners to meet all their demands. Conditions at the factory had long been appalling. The women and girls worked eleven and a half hours a day in the summer and ten in the winter for seven days a week, taking home wages that began at a meagre four shillings a week. Illegal fines and deductions were regularly imposed, the workers having to pay for their own glue and brushes, and losing half a day's pay for being late. They also had to pay the staggeringly high charge of one shilling per worker when Mr Bryant and Mr May decided to raise a statue to the Liberal prime minister William Gladstone in 1832, whatever their political persuasion. In addition, all of them were in danger of developing the horrific 'phossy jaw', a grotesque and foul-smelling facial deformity caused by the phosphorus used to make the match-heads, which usually resulted in brain damage, organ failure and death.

The strike began when the campaigning journalist and women's rights activist Annie Besant, undeterred by her previous brushes with the law, investigated the factory, spoke to some of the workers and exposed their working conditions in her radical newspaper *The Link*. Enraged, Bartholomew Bryant dismissed the story as 'twaddle', threatened to sue Besant and sacked one of the women he suspected of being the ringleader. The others were expected to sign a statement rubbishing Besant's article if they wanted to keep their jobs. Heroically, the entire workforce, all fourteen hundred of them, walked out. Directed by Besant, they picketed, (wo)manned the gates and doors, and shut the place down, they held marches and meetings, they lobbied Parliament and organised a strike fund. Crucially, they generated the kind of adverse publicity that rapidly brought the bosses to the table ready to agree to their demands.

Seen as a ground-breaking episode, this singular triumph is widely celebrated, not least in the 1966 musical *The Matchgirls*. Less well recognised is the impact the women's action had on the emerging labour movement as a whole. Where they led, the men could follow, as the labour leader John Burns exhorted the dockers only a year later in the run-up to the great London Dock strike of 1889: 'Stand shoulder to shoulder! Remember the match-women, who won their fight and formed a union.'

And there you have it, one story among many of women pulling together, women daring to change their lives, making their own history and thereby changing history for men too.

Remember the match-girls . . .

Rebel women finding new lives and new horizons and taking new chances to speak out, to speak directly to the holders of power, and to speak the truths of their own lives. If they could, would the next revolution bring a revolution for women too?

CHAPTER 5

PEARLS BEYOND PRICE

Woman must have her freedom – the fundamental freedom of choosing whether or not she shall be a mother and how many children she will have.

MARGARET SANGER

No one disputes that the bull differs in disposition from the cow, the wild boar from the sow, the stallion from the mare, and . . . the males of the larger apes from the females. Woman seems to differ from man in mental disposition . . .

CHARLES DARWIN

We women suffragists have a great mission – the greatest mission the world has ever known. It is to free half the human race, and through that freedom to save the rest.

EMMELINE PANKHURST

A revolution for women? The nineteenth century was to bring not one turn of the wheel, but two, as progress for women in the West found its focus on the right to contraception, and the right to vote. Winning the vote was seen as the 'queen of rights', the jewel in the crown. Without it, women had no power to choose those who had power over them, the men who made the laws by which they had to live. With it, they could change the laws and the law-makers too, since the right to vote out a representative was just as important as the right to vote one in.

But how could women demonstrate their right to equality when they were at the mercy of their biology? Even if women had been granted the vote, by the time they were twenty-one and old enough to go to the ballot box, all too many were disabled or dead. Even in the twenty-first century, having a baby is still the most life-threatening process any woman can undergo, and even with the benefit of modern medicine there are still pitfalls at every stage. It was essential, then, that women should break the chain binding them to that fate. 'No woman can call herself free who does not own and control her own body,' was the rallying cry of Margaret Sanger, the Irish-American campaigner who became known as the 'Mother of Birth Control'. For women, the right to vote and the right to control their bodies were both pearls beyond price. Both were vitally important and both the personal and public were equally political, but Sanger was clear as to which came first, in a declaration that still resonates today:

Birth control is the first important step woman must take toward the goal of her freedom. It is the first step she must take to be man's equal. It is the first step they must both take toward human emancipation.

And the decision had to be taken by the woman. The battleground was the female body, her body, and only she had the right to determine her body's life. 'Regardless of what man's attitude may be,' Sanger wrote, 'that problem is hers – and before it can be his, it is hers alone. She goes through "the valley of the shadow of death" alone, each time a babe is born. As it is the right neither of man nor the state to coerce her into this ordeal, so it is her right to decide whether she will endure it.'

The first step

And a giant step it was, the start of a revolution in millions of women's lives. As with our other rebel heroines, it came from home truths. Sanger's mother bore eighteen children in twenty-two years of marriage and died at the age of forty-nine: 'You killed her!' she reportedly accused her father at the funeral. The sixth of the eleven who survived, Sanger trained as a nurse, and working in the slums of New York attended a woman she called 'Sadie Sachs', who had dealt with her numerous unwanted pregnancies with increasingly dangerous home abortions. Sanger heard 'Sadie' imploring the doctor for advice on avoiding another pregnancy. *Abstain*, he said. But how was Sadie going to make her man 'abstain'? The next time Sanger was called to the tenement, 'Sadie' was dying in a sea of blood. In a blind rage, Sanger hurled her medical bag against the wall and her life's work began.

Sanger was driven to use her medical knowledge and experience to offer women a better way. In 1912 she began writing a column in the socialist newspaper *The Call* entitled 'What Every Girl Should Know', and two years later started the *Woman Rebel*, a monthly magazine that promoted contraception for women as a right.

The woman rebel

By choosing this bold title for her periodical, Sanger consciously aligned herself with the progressive thinkers of the early twentieth century, but her work was addressing an eternal need. As far back as the ancient Egyptians, every culture records numerous attempts to control reproduction, some hilarious, some lethal, all horrible. Imagine preparing for a night of love, or even a routine connubial copulation, by stuffing your nether cavity with dollops of crocodile dung, as recommended in a papyrus of 1250 BCE.

No?

How about a wedge of rock salt, then?

Or soda ash?

Maybe chalk?

If not, the sages suggested a light snack of monkey's brains washed down with an amusing little glass of vintage urine, boiled horsefly or quicksilver – take your pick. Mercury was much favoured in Japan, although it attacks the blood cells, the ovaries, the heart, the kidneys and the nervous system, and is guaranteed to destroy a foetus *in utero* if it does not kill the mother first.

Men were involved in the search for safety too, but their interest lay in preserving the seed pod, not in blocking the seed, protecting themselves from women, not protecting women from pregnancy. The time-honoured device for this was the sheath, later called the condom, made from animal skin, soft leather or a stiff linen soaked in chemicals strong enough to strip the chrome off a bath chain. The comfort of the woman usually came a distant second to the man's imperative to avoid venereal infection, so a lover who had travelled in the East might have picked up a personal and reusable sperm-catcher hand-carved from translucent tortoiseshell or polished ram's horn. Many and ingenious were the devices designed to ensure that a man could walk away from a spot of jig-a-jig unspotted and unharmed.

Equally ingenious were the experiments of the first movers

and shakers in the modern era. The legendary Giacomo Casanova knew of women using hand-knitted silk discs as a barrier over the neck of the cervix, but mainly relied on inserting half a lemon into his *inamorata* before the action began. *Half a lemon?* Even allowing that lemon juice can serve as a spermicide, didn't it *sting*? Casanova also used condoms, providing hours of fun for boys and girls. It is one of history's better jokes that Casanova, a self-confessed love skunk, compulsive sex addict and moral bankrupt, was on the same side as the most high-minded feminists, radical thinkers, altruistic campaigners and social reformers, all actively defying, as he was, the fearsome punishments for using contraception threatened in this world by the state, and by the Church in the next.

And the idea of birth control was spreading. In Britain, the free-thinker Richard Carlile made history in 1826 when he published a pamphlet detailing the available methods of contraception, specifying *coitus interruptus*, the use of condoms and the insertion of a vaginal sponge. Equally radical was his decision to put this information directly into the hands of women by calling his pamphlet *Every Woman's Book*, and this practical sex manual went on to sell ten thousand copies. More radical still was Carlile's contention that women were naturally, sexually, equal to men. Sex between couples was not the man's to command and demand, he argued, but the right of both men and women, and essential to their health.

Unknown to Carlile but writing only four years later, in 1832, the American family doctor Charles Knowlton composed a booklet for his patients in rural Massachusetts, calling it *The Fruits of Philosophy, or the Private Companion of Young Married People*. In it he outlined the basic facts of conception, and described the technique of vaginal douching as a way of preventing it. But when this limited-edition and essentially innocent leaflet found its way into outside hands, Knowlton was prosecuted, fined, and spent three months in prison with hard labour. Carlile too was imprisoned for publishing *Every Woman's Book*, but released without trial.

All we need is a few good men . . .

Nearly half a century later, two British pioneers of the right to freedom of information re-published *The Fruits of Philosophy* in London. Charles Bradlaugh was a deeply committed activist and reformer, as was Annie Besant, of match-girls fame. They worked together to bring out liberal and radical material, and amid sensational headlines they faced the full wrath of the law. Tried and convicted for obscenity in 1877, they were punished with heavy fines and sentences of six months' imprisonment.

Both were then cleared by the Court of Appeal on the grounds that the prosecution had not demonstrated that there were any obscene words or phrases in the allegedly 'obscene' publication (an understandable omission, since there were none). The scandal was huge, and the publicity wonderful. The booklet was a runaway success, selling around 125,000 copies in the course of the following year. Bradlaugh went on to become an MP and a force for good in the land. Besant was prosecuted as an unfit mother by her estranged husband, and lost custody of her two children.

Rebels to the fore

Once women knew that it was possible to gain control over their fertility, more and more began trying to find out how. In or around New York in the second half of the nineteenth century, there was one pre-eminent port of call, the famous 'female specialist' Madame Restell. At a cost of $20 for poor women and $100 for the rich, Madame dispensed information and advice, and sold pills, potions and powders to 'married females'. For those who could not seek treatment in person, she provided a mail-order service, charging $1 for a box of French Female Monthly Pills (No.1), $3 for the No. 2 ('guaranteed four times as strong as No. 1'), and $5 for a package of Preventative Powder.

In an era when normal menstruation was treated as a malady, Madame aroused little suspicion with her 'Monthly Pills', although they were clearly intended as contraceptives. The picture darkens with the medications she prescribed to 'regulate' the monthly periods of 'ladies laboring under a suspension of their natural illness' (read: *women who were missing their periods and not wanting to be pregnant*), when the true purpose was to re-start the natural cycle by procuring a miscarriage. Madame also ran a back-up service when the drugs failed, providing the last-ditch but usually reliable option of a surgical abortion. If that failed too, or if the abortion had been requested too late, the client could rely on Madame to take care of the delivery, after which the problem could be left with her, to be solved with the help of a well-regarded adoption agency.

Restell was not the only purveyor of personal services to the intimately indisposed females of the rapidly growing metropolis of New York City, but she was by far the most successful, probably because she was not one person, but two. The woman acting as a French-American pharmacist and doctor who had trained as a midwife under her French grandmother, a renowned physician called Restell, was in fact the impoverished English immigrant Ann Trow, a widow with a child to support. Trow's partner and the co-creator of the business and their professional persona, was the well-educated German-American printer and publisher Charles Lohman, already active in a group of radicals and freethinkers committed to spreading ideas of women's rights, family size and population control.

They met, married, then made a trip to Europe, taking in France to give a little French polish to Trow's claims to have qualified there. Back in New York they created 'Madame Restell', who opened for business in 1836. Madame made so much money that the couple began investing in property in the city, and pulled off a sensational coup when they purchased a plot of land on Fifth Avenue earmarked for the palace of the Roman Catholic archbishop, snatching it from under the nose of the man who had previously denounced Restell as a child-killer and an instrument of Satan. On this prime site they built a magnificent four-storey brownstone, and entertained there on a scale so lavish that none of the City Fathers refused their invitations – they just didn't bring their wives along.

Those were the glory days for Trow and Lohman, the peak of their success. When Ann Trow quietly began trading as Madame Restell, inducing a miscarriage was not illegal in New York State. By the time she died forty years later, any form of intervention in the 'natural' cycle of menstruation, ovulation and conception was against the law. Even preventing a pregnancy was now equated with killing a child, and actively performing abortions made Restell a mass murderer in the eyes of the guardians of public morality and of the law. Over the years a number of prosecutions sought to bring her to justice and she became a convicted criminal with a prison record. Sensational press coverage of her trials made her notorious throughout the United States as 'the Wickedest Woman in America', triggering a moral panic about evil in the ascendant and women out of control.

This was largely the work of the moral crusader Anthony Comstock, a former postal inspector who promoted himself to the role of a special agent of the United States Postal Service, licensed to operate with police powers. In a lifetime of persecuting every publication he deemed to be 'lewd' or 'obscene', including anatomical textbooks for medical students, Comstock

THE FEMALE ABORTIONIST.

Trow/Restell pictured as a satanic baby-killer

brought about the destruction of nearly four million pictures and fifteen tons of objectionable books. The Abominable Postman also boasted that he was personally responsible for four thousand arrests, and claimed he drove fifteen people to suicide.

One of them was Madame Restell. In a career spanning more than forty years, she had rebelled against the rule of law, social convention and every expectation of womanhood. She had made a fortune and enjoyed flaunting it, and had survived repeated harassment, arrest and a spell in prison. The day of reckoning came in April 1878 when Mock Cop Comstock posed as a customer buying contraceptive pills for his wife. She had had too many pregnancies, he said, and he feared the next might be her last. Restell sold him some of her medications and he left as a satisfied customer. The next day he returned with the police. Alone in New York since the death of Lohman in 1876, approaching seventy years of age and facing a trial with only one outcome, Restell lay down in a warm bath and cut her throat. After her death, countless letters of gratitude came to light from women she had saved from dismissal, divorce, disgrace and even death.

Which way now?

Thanks to Comstock, the Act for the 'Suppression of Trade in, and Circulation of, Obscene Literature and Articles of Immoral Use' became law in 1873. This made it a federal crime to disseminate 'obscene' objects like contraceptive pills, or even to send leaflets on the subject through the post.

Around the turn of the century, Margaret Sanger realised that she had to rescue the public idea of contraception from the belief that every time a birth was prevented, a child was killed. This grotesque but damaging accusation had been levelled not only at abortionists like Madame Restell, but also at the Dutch doctor Aletta Jacobs, who developed the cervical cap. Sanger showed her flair by inventing the term 'birth control', which shifted the emphasis from blocking the process of contraception to its purpose, making positive the idea of being in control out of the negative suggestion of destroying a new life. But as she foresaw when she and her colleagues launched the *Birth Control Review* in 1917, the way ahead looked bleak. 'The struggle will be bitter,' she wrote.

'It may be long. All the methods known to tyranny will be used to force the people back into the darkness from which they are striving to emerge.'

Sanger already knew how hard it could be. When she opened her first birth control clinic in Brooklyn in 1916, it was raided and shut down three times in its first month of existence, before the police forced her landlord to terminate her lease, and closed her down for good. Sanger was arrested, charged with 'maintaining a public nuisance', tried and offered a suspended sentence on condition that she would never repeat the offence. She refused, and was sent to prison for thirty days. Also jailed was Sanger's first husband, loyally taking a stand for the cause even after they had parted, while her devoted second husband risked the same fate by smuggling illegal cervical caps across the border from Canada.

Here is Margaret Sanger in full cry against the Comstock laws:

> Woman has always been the chief sufferer under this merciless machinery of the statutory law. Humbly she has borne the weight of man-made laws, surrendering to their tyranny even her right over her own body ... Against the State, against the Church, against the silence of the medical profession, against the whole machinery of dead institutions of the past, the woman of today arises ... She is here to assert herself, to take back those rights which were formerly hers and hers alone. If she must break the law to establish her right to voluntary motherhood, then the law shall be broken.

Marie Stopes showed Britain the ropes

The privileged background of Marie Stopes, thousands of miles away in Britain, could hardly have been more different from Sanger's poor and painful origins. The only child of well-to-do and enlightened parents, Stopes flew through a fine education, heaping up first-class scientific degrees and doctorates at an early age, before moving easily into academic life as the first female lecturer at Manchester University in 1904.

And there she might have remained. But at thirty, the virginal bluestocking met a fellow scientist, Reginald Ruggles Gates, and made a whirlwind marriage that lasted for less than three years. The dry legal reason for the annulment – 'unconsummated' – conveys nothing of the misery they both endured, and it prompted her to embark on an entirely new career to spare others the same distress. Encouraged by Margaret Sanger at a chance meeting in London, Stopes published *Married Love* in 1918, and her open-hearted defence of her mission still has the power to move. 'In my own marriage,' she wrote, 'I paid such a terrible price for sex-ignorance that I feel knowledge gained at such a cost should be placed at the service of humanity.'

The outcry was immediate, but so was the success. While leading doctors, churchmen and newspaper editors fell over themselves to denounce it as 'lewd' and 'obscene' (*those words again*), the book was flying off the shelves at the rate of two thousand copies within a fortnight of publication, and selling almost three-quarters of a million copies by 1931. In hindsight, the hysteria and vitriol of the attacks seem extraordinary in the light of Stopes's romantic, indeed lyrical approach to what she chastely calls 'the act':

Assuming ... that the two are in the closest mental and spiritual, as well as sensory harmony: in what position should the act be consummated? Men and women, looking into each other's eyes, kissing tenderly on the mouth, with their arms round each other, meet face to face. And that position is symbolic of the coming together of the two who meet gladly.

It is usual in civilized societies for the man to lie above the woman as she reclines on her back. Indeed a curious idea seems to exist that it is 'immoral' or 'humiliating' for the man if the position is reversed. Yet Ovid recommends it to little women, and . . . there may be an exquisite grace in the event, as though there had entered into it the poetry and beauty of the picture of the sleeping Endymion over whom the floating goddess Diana stooped.

Was it Stopes's artless account of the woman taking an active part in married love that so enraged her critics, or her radical belief that women felt sexual desire just as much as men? Whatever men thought, she knew what she was talking about. Women had already been writing to her in detail with their questions and expressing their distresses, some of which she recorded in *Married Love*: 'one wife [a short woman] told me that she was crushed and nearly suffocated by her husband so that it took her hours to recover after each union, but that "on principle" he refused to attempt any other position than the one he chose to consider normal'.

For women like this and for many others, Stopes set up her first clinic under the banner of 'Constructive Birth Control' in 1921, five years after Margaret Sanger opened in New York. Stopes chose one of London's poorest areas, Holloway, home also to Britain's largest and harshest women's prison at the time. From these early efforts, the worldwide movement for birth control was born. Sanger in particular proved a powerful and tireless ambassador, founding the American Birth Control League in 1921, which grew into the Planned Parenthood Federation of America, with Sanger as its honorary chairman. Two of her greatest gifts were her global vision for women and her ability to draw others into the cause. She organised the first World Population Conference in Geneva in 1927, she was the first president of the International Planned Parenthood Federation in 1953, and throughout her career she worked to establish her campaign for birth control in Asia, especially in India and Japan.

After meeting her in New York in 1920, the pioneering Japanese feminist Katō Shidzue brought Sanger to Japan seven times, although the American's visa was at first flatly refused because ideas of birth control were officially classified as 'dangerous thoughts', and special permission had to be obtained. Like Sanger, Katō was persecuted by the authorities. Her arrest and imprisonment for the same crime of 'dangerous thoughts' in 1937, followed by the advent of the Second World War brought the campaign for women's reproductive rights in Japan to a standstill. In 1948, however, standing as a socialist, Katō was one of the first women elected to the Japanese Diet, and the next year she co-founded the Family Planning Federation of Japan.

My body, my life

Katō's oppression differed from that of Sanger in that there was no element of religion involved. In the West, as dictated by Roman Catholic Christianity, both Church and state worked together to prevent women's access to birth control, or even the knowledge of it. Both held that interfering with the natural process of conception was wrong, and created a panoply of religious and secular punishments to enforce this view. It was not always so. Judaism, Islam, Confucianism, Buddhism – all permitted both contraception and abortion, and no matter what importance was placed on the family, the woman was not prevented from having some control over the size of it. In ancient advice books from Mesopotamia, India, China, Persia and Anglo-Saxon England, preventing conception was routine, and involved neither shame nor blame. If the dung/ monkey brains/mercury didn't work, abortion was simply the next stage, never a crime or a sin. Indeed, older 'civilisations', even the most highly regarded like those of Ancient Greece or Rome, treated infanticide as the logical extension of family limitation, and felt no qualms about exterminating babies, especially girls.

What the Church condemned as a sin, the state could easily re-frame as a crime, especially if it was focused on increasing its population. Both Church and state assumed the unquestioned right to treat the wombs of their females as an exploitable natural resource, and no Christian country was free of that attitude and the legislation to enforce it. As desperate as some women were to avoid getting pregnant, these outside agencies were equally determined that they should.

As Sanger, Stopes and others knew, spreading the use of birth control depended on the support of individual women, many of who were already converts to the cause. The hardest task was winning a general recognition for the right of a woman, most particularly a wife, to an existence of her own apart from her duty and destiny as a mother. The woman who could control her fertility could control her life, but if she achieved that autonomy, what next? Once again, the body was the battleground.

Alas, in one of its more startling upheavals, this century of change dealt a body blow to women's claim to equality by introducing a new and scientific rationale for female inferiority. It was not the first time that science had attempted to categorise and limit women, but this came from a uniquely original and influential source. In his 1859 work *On the Origin of Species*, Charles Darwin unlocked the mystery of evolution, introduced human beings to our ape ancestors and changed the story of the birth of the world. In another discovery that the world found far easier to accept than the descent from apes, he also offered solidly researched and evidence-based 'scientific proof' of the female's innate and inescapable inferiority to the male.

'The less highly evolved female brain . . . '

Highly intelligent and deeply thoughtful though he was, ready to think the unthinkable and to challenge the cherished Judaeo-Christian orthodoxies of his age, Darwin demonstrated one great intellectual black hole in his reading of the world. As he charted the evolution of birds, iguanas and giant tortoises during his lifelong journey unravelling the riddles of millennia, his painful ratiocinations never once led him to consider that the female of the human species could have any of the strength, skill, adaptability or mental capacity for dominance enjoyed by the male.

On the contrary, in *The Descent of Man, and Selection in Relation to Sex* (1871), Darwin stated that the development of a woman was stunted because 'the formation of her skull is said to be intermediate between the child and the man'. As a result women are the intellectual inferiors of men. 'Man is more powerful in body and mind than woman,' Darwin went on, 'and in the savage state he keeps her in a far more abject state of bondage than does the male of any other animal; therefore it is not surprising that he should have gained the power of selection.'

The key word here is *selection*. Selection, and hence evolution, were in the hands of men, leaving women passive and primitive, dominated by instinct and emotions, which constituted their greatest weakness. 'Man' was busy inventing tools and using weapons, thereby increasing the natural power of his already mighty brain. So 'man has ultimately become superior to woman', Darwin wrote: he 'attains a higher eminence, in whatever he takes up, than can woman – whether requiring deep thought, reason, or imagination, or merely the use of the senses and hands'.

Female incapacity: innate or man-ufactured?

Protest swiftly followed. The American abolitionist and former Protestant minister Antoinette Brown Blackwell fearlessly attacked Darwin. Her influential study *The Sexes Throughout Nature* (1875) also took issue with Darwin's enthusiastic disciple, the philosopher Herbert Spencer, previously characterised by his fellow philosopher, the mordant Thomas Carlyle, as 'the wisest fool in Christendom'. Spencer blithely opposed education for women on the grounds that over-taxing the female brain produced 'flat-chested girls' who could never bear 'a well-developed infant'.

But Spencer and his pseudo-scientific claptrap were only a sideshow. What disappointed Blackwell was the failure of Darwin and his followers to go beyond thinking of women as biological specimens and nothing else. Why no account of their essential and irreplaceable social role? Above all, why no attempt even to entertain the idea of women's equality? What hope for the future, Blackwell reflected gloomily, if 'the human race, forever retarding its own advancement ... could not recognize and promote a genuine, broad, and healthful equilibrium of the sexes'.

It's a good question.

What can we say about the less socially evolved Darwin brain?

In private, Darwin was a loving husband and father who valued his girls as highly as his sons. His daughter Henrietta became his 'very dear co-adjutor and fellow-labourer' on his last great work, *The Descent of Man*. As a scholar, Darwin consistently supported the women scientists who wrote to him, but he maintained his views on the superiority of men and its impact on evolution all his life. By what double-think, then, did he square the circle of enlisting his clever daughter to work with him on a book that labels women as dim and backward, a verdict that downgraded the female sex for generations to come? As a final irony, note that Darwin's confirmation of women's biological inferiority was taken as scientific proof, while his theory of human evolution was widely attacked, especially by 'Creationists'.

Creationists, notably in the US and the UK, believed that God had created the world for Man exactly as the Bible described it, day by day. This view commanded a powerful following, insisting that evolution should be taken off the syllabus or introduced as a theory, while creationism would be taught as a matter of fact. Either way, for those promoting Darwinian evolution or Creationist biblical absolutism, the verdict remained the same. Science had proved it and God had ordained it, women were inferior to men, no ifs, no buts.

Old lies never die – they just get born again.

Oh, the ever-rampant, last-prick-standing phallusy of history!

Seconds out for the second round

Contraception was identified by Margaret Sanger as 'the first step' towards freedom. The second was the vote. For women this was the great step two, the queen of rights, the key to all other rights and powers they could achieve. Women first stumbled onto it in the French Revolution, when the March on Versailles allowed them to bring the power-holders to account and to make them pay. That was the power the vote could give to every woman. At the ballot box, all were equal and equally free.

So give women the vote!

How could the Big Boys agree with that? 'Sensible and responsible women do not want to vote!' trumpeted Grover Cleveland, former President of the United States, in 1905. Now what were sensible and responsible women to do? In America, women had been pressing for suffrage since the Women's Rights Convention at Seneca Falls had made international headlines in 1848. In the UK, public action was the chosen tactic of the suffragettes, and one woman in particular came to embody the soul of the cause.

She was a sober-minded forty-year-old spinster when one fine morning in June 1913, she took a train to Epsom Downs for the Derby, one of England's premier race meetings and always attended by the king and queen. She found a place on the rails, waited for the king's horse to approach, then ran on to the course and fell under its hooves. Her injuries were catastrophic and she died four days later. From the purple, green and white flag she was carrying, and another she had wrapped around her body, she was identified as the suffragette Emily Wilding Davison.

'She died for women,' proclaimed Mrs Pankhurst. As the leader of the Women's Social and Political Union, she instantly grasped the publicity value of the first martyr dying for the cause. This slogan of sacrifice decorated the WSPU banners when an estimated six thousand white-clad suffragettes marched with the hearse in Davison's funeral procession, while thousands more turned out to pay their respects as it passed.

All the world loves a virgin martyr, and 'she threw herself under the king's horse' was the authorised version of Emily Wilding Davison's death. It's a great story, and the suffragettes milked it for all it was worth. Sadly, like so many good stories, it wasn't true.

She died for women, right?

The funeral procession of Emily Wilding Davison, 14 June 1913.

Wrong.

Even at the time, sceptics questioned whether Davison meant to kill herself. There was no doubt that she was ready to take risks, face danger and endure pain: in the course of many arrests she had been force-fed forty-nine times, a process far more painful and damaging than is generally understood. That day in 1913 the race was filmed by three separate cameras, and a hundred years after Davison 'threw herself under the king's horse', twenty-first century software allowed investigators to revisit the footage. Once they had digitised, cleaned and combined the three extracts, a different story emerged.

The new film strongly suggested that Davison intended to gain the maximum publicity for the women's cause, but *not to die*. Her plan was to create a spectacular disruption that would be captured on the Pathé Pictorial News cameras recording the race and shown in newsreels worldwide. As the cameras roll, there is no '*running onto the course and throwing herself under the horse's hooves*'. Davison is seen stepping forward calmly, holding a suffragette flag. She raises her hands in front of the galloping colt, then makes a grab for his bridle, trying to tie on her flag so that the slogan 'Votes For Women' would be fluttering before all the cameras at the end of the race. Seconds later, the horse hit her, and they both went down. He survived, and so did his jockey. She did not.

Davison had another flag to use elsewhere on the course and the return half of her ticket taking her back to London was found in her purse after she died. It seems clear that demonstration, not death, was her intention that day.

Not now, girls, not yet

In the north of England, Emmeline Goulden, later to be Mrs Pankhurst, heard her first suffrage speech as a fourteen-year-old in the 1860s. As the decades dragged by, hundreds of women put in thousands of hours under the leadership of the mild-mannered Millicent Fawcett, marching, leafletting and lobbying, without result. Fawcett herself said that the movement for women's suffrage was 'like a glacier; slow moving but unstoppable'. To Pankhurst, the glacial progress was intolerable. Gallant New Zealand, a small country split between two islands, shamed the so-called Great Powers by giving all its women the vote as early as 1893, while Australia followed region by region in 1894, 1899 and 1902, thereby becoming the first country in the world to grant its women full citizenship: not only the right to vote but also to stand for election to Parliament, joining the ranks of the governing body, no longer simply the governed.

Kate Sheppard, the wonderfully wise and level-headed leader of the New Zealand campaign for women's suffrage, attributed their success to simple persistence, because they petitioned and kept on petitioning till the vote was won. Sheppard shared with Mrs Pankhurst a flair for a dramatic gesture: the final and successful petition she introduced to the House of Representatives was 270 metres long, spilling all over the floor of the parliamentary chamber.

Sheppard was much in demand as a speaker when the women of other countries clamoured to learn how the NZ vote was won. New Zealand was a slender colonial sliver on the edge of the British Empire, yet it led the world for women while the major powers dithered, dallied and dug in their heels. Generous in victory, New Zealand sent a delegation to England in 1910 to support the sisterhood there. Already involved in the struggle was Anna Stout, a veteran of the campaign in New Zealand, who had moved to London with her husband the year before. A woman ahead of her time who supported rights for the Maori population and for sex workers, Stout brought her considerable experience to the British struggle, relishing the heightened activity as the movement gathered pace.

Kiwi women had had the vote for a full ten years when Pankhurst's patience finally ran out. In 1903 she founded the Women's Social and Political Union with her three daughters Christabel, Sylvia and Adela, determined to give the 'polite and tame' movement of the suffragists more urgency and bite. Christabel, always the most belligerent of the foursome, argued forcefully for creating public protests provocative enough to get the protesters imprisoned, a tactic that would infallibly draw attention to the cause. The others agreed. 'We threw away all our conventional notions of what was "ladylike" and "good form",' Mrs Pankhurst remembered, 'and we applied to our methods the one test question: Will it help?'

So was born the split between Fawcett's suffragists, committed to acting within the law, and Pankhurst's suffragettes, determined to break it. As a first foray in 1903, Christabel and Annie Kenney, a former Oldham factory hand and keen supporter, disrupted a Liberal Party meeting in Manchester by repeatedly demanding to know if the Liberal Party would give women the vote. As they were roughly bundled out, Christabel spat at a policeman, deliberately committing an imprisonable offence, and to jail they went. Initially unsure about the new strategy and the first militant action of the campaign, Mrs Pankhurst was entranced by its impact. The passage of time only strengthened her conviction that employing force against the power of the state was both necessary and right. 'I would rather be a rebel than a slave,' she later declared. 'Kill me, or give me my freedom.'

Suffrage hopes centred on the Liberal Party, then in opposition, as the more likely to enfranchise women when they came to power than the Conservatives. But Herbert Asquith, one of its leading lights, was a hardcore anti-suffragist motivated wholly by party tribalism, wrongly convinced that women would always by nature vote Conservative, and would keep the Liberals out of office. When he became Prime Minister in 1908, his view did not change. On 18 November 1910, a date later known as Black Friday, three hundred women led by Emmeline Pankhurst marched to the Houses of Parliament, where the police were waiting for them. Woman after woman reported uniformed officers and plain-clothes men handling them in ways designed to hurt and humiliate, raising their skirts above their heads to expose their underwear, mauling their breasts and beating them with batons, while taking no action against the men in the crowd who joined in the assault on the women.

The women activists always had to be prepared for attacks from men. Even a simple speaking engagement or platform meeting put suffragettes at risk. Like the old-time miscreants in the pillory, they were pelted with fish heads, rotten eggs, sticks and brickbats, while some local trouble-makers would release sacks of mice and rats to run between their feet. Today's action women often ask why the Pankhurst SAS went into battle in such outsize hats and veils. The heavy-duty headgear served as vital protection not only from flying bottles and half-bricks but also from the cayenne pepper and chilli powder it amused their tormentors to blow into their eyes. It became safer to commit a violent public offence and to be immediately removed by the police than to carry out a peaceful demonstration and undergo the rough handling that was sure to follow.

Whatever happened, Asquith was unmoved. Worse, the women came to see that he and his deputy, David Lloyd George, were playing politics with them *and enjoying it*. Something with a higher shock value was needed to move the game along. Mrs Pankhurst declared war on the three things she considered most dear to the heart of society and to the hearts of the men who ran it – 'money, property and pleasure'. The WSPU now began to target their attacks in a more systematic way. The intention was plain: *hit them where it hurts*.

Is that a hammer in your handbag . . . ?

Londoners stood aghast as hundreds of well-dressed women appeared without warning in Piccadilly and Bond Street, whipped out whatever weapons they had brought along, and set about smashing plate glass shop fronts. Two hundred and twenty protesters were arrested at that unprecedented display of massed woman power in 1912, and one Emmeline Pankhurst was on the list of culprits.

The popular idea of the suffragette is of a young woman chained to the railings of the Houses of Parliament, or lobbing a brick through a window or two. In reality, attacking official buildings, bombing churches and burning down the country houses of the great and the good became regular operations as the suffragettes extended their repertoire. Another misconception locates the suffrage struggle in London, the seat of power. In 1912, Dublin suffragettes tried to fire-bomb the Theatre Royal when Asquith was watching a matinée there. Glasgow Art Gallery saw a flying suffragette raid that left glass exhibition cases smashed to smithereens, and all the telegraph wires were cut along the main road at Potters Bar. Acts of suffragette violence great and small were recorded all over the country, with banks and post boxes the favourite targets. In February 1913, four Dundee postmen were left with phosphorus burns, 'as a result of diabolical outrage by suffragettes', according to the *Dundee Courier.*

At the height of the militant campaign, around a thousand suffragettes were in prison in Britain, and many went on hunger strike to keep up the pressure on the government. In 1913, an enraged Parliament brought in the so-called Cat and Mouse Act. This law allowed convicted suffragettes to be repeatedly force-fed, a process that required a number of female warders to hold the woman down while a doctor pushed thick tubing into her mouth or nose and down her throat so forcibly that it overwhelmed the natural gag reflex, then down the oesophagus and into the stomach, tearing soft tissues as it went. This rape of the alimentary canal made women so ill that they had to be allowed out of prison to recover, then the law mandated that they were recalled for more of the same. At least one woman who suffered this quasi-torture, Lady Constance Lytton, already in poor health, later had a heart attack and a stroke, and died at the early age of fifty-four.

The authorities did not relent, but neither did the suffragettes. It was a deadlock neatly satirised by the woman who wrote to the *Daily Telegraph* in 1913:

*Sir, Everyone seems to agree upon the necessity of putting a stop
to Suffragist outrages; but no one seems certain how to do so.
There are two, and only two, ways in which this can be done.
Both will be effectual.*

   1. Kill every woman in the United Kingdom.

   2. Give women the vote.

                                    Yours truly, Bertha Brewster.

Nice one, Bertha.

But 'deeds, not words' had been the slogan of the suffragettes
from the first, and the end glorified the means. When the country house of the Chancellor of the Exchequer, Lloyd George,
was fire-bombed, Christabel proudly proclaimed 'We are fighting a revolution!' So it was that one day in March 1914 a small,
respectable-looking woman in her early thirties stepped into the
National Gallery and musing in front of one of the treasures of
the collection from the Spanish Golden Age, *The Toilet of Venus*
by Diego Velázquez, produced a meat cleaver and set about
slashing it, inflicting several deep cuts before she was stopped.

She was sentenced to three years in jail, where she had been
sent on a number of occasions before. Later she expressed what
drove her on: 'I must pay the full price demanded of a suffragette . . . I belonged nowhere; I had no home, and so there was
nobody who would worry over me and over whom I need
worry. From the start it had been this knowledge that made
me feel I must do more than my fair share to make up for the
women who stood back from militancy, because of the sorrow
their actions would have caused some loved one.'

Like many of the suffragettes, Mary Richardson had an almost
religious devotion to Mrs Pankhurst, stating that she chose the
Rokeby Venus for destruction because the image of a beautiful
woman should not survive when the government was torturing
this real-life beautiful woman to death. Others served the cause

with a disrespect reminiscent of the mass mooning by the female convict transports at the Female Factory in Van Diemen's Land in 1838. Here are some of the sixty women arrested on the last militant event of the campaign, a march on Buckingham Palace to petition the king in May 1914. They had all refused to give their names, so had to be arraigned by numbers:

Number 1 was brought in on her knees, Number 3 was dragged in and refused to be tried ... The next woman turned her back on [the court] – another was only prevented by four policemen from climbing over the dock rails ... [then] a bag of flour was thrown by one of the spectators ...

Sir John Dickinson [the magistrate] ordered the court to be cleared and there was a new start. Number 11 threw her boot at the magistrate; Number 14 shouted 'Hip, hip, hurrah!' continuously. The next two women were put in the dock together and as one called Sir John 'a rusty tool of a corrupt government' the other referred to him as 'a wicked old man'. A succession of women made similar comments, and after refusing to be bound over, were discharged.

Whatever they did, Pankhurst's irregulars captured hearts, minds and headlines, especially when a fatuous and compla-cent opposition offered them an open goal. Denying that there was any sexual discrimination and declaring that 'of course' women were admitted to the Walton Heath Golf Club in Surrey, an official joked 'Who do you think makes the teas?' In the same spirit of waggish humour, suffragettes burned the club down.

Meanwhile, the tenacious, low-key and unsung work of Millicent Garrett Fawcett and her suffragists went on. Who won the vote for British women, then, Fawcett or Pankhurst? Many on the Fawcett side were convinced that the actions of the suffragettes only made enemies of the men who would decide the issue, while also angering the general public with the reckless violence of their campaign. Arthur Conan Doyle, the creator of Sherlock Holmes, denounced them as 'female hooligans', while Winston Churchill dismissed the entire movement as liars and terrorists, an insult to womanhood. The level of hatred and contempt expressed by the males of the establishment for the suffragettes was so high, reflected the writer Rebecca West, that 'women ... for the first time knew what many men really thought of them'.

Pankhurst apologists insisted that their high-profile campaign had succeeded in propelling women's suffrage to the top of the national agenda and forced the power-holders into action. Pankhurst's shock troops unquestionably won the publicity battle hands down, but Fawcett had the numbers. In 1913, her National Union of Women's Suffrage Societies had some fifty thousand members, compared with around two thousand in the WSPU. Notably, however, both women refused to be drawn into the kind of female 'cat-fight' so beloved of the gutter press. Fawcett paid an unstinting tribute to the militants in a letter to *The Times* in October 1906: 'I take this opportunity of saying that in my opinion, far from having injured the movement, they have done more during the last twelve months to bring it within the realms of practical politics than we have been able to accomplish in the same number of years.'

But for all this, both wings of the suffrage movement in Britain were still getting 'words, not deeds' from the powers that be. What would it take to give women the vote?

'Give us one reason why we should'

So the opinion formers and power holders always replied. The case against women as voters always came down to their simple incapacity, their undeveloped mental powers that left them in a permanently childlike state. We can only wonder what the '*our-brains-are-bigger-than-yours*' brigade made of Marie Skłodowska Curie. In 1903 she became the first woman to win a Nobel Prize. She was also the first person and only woman to date to win it twice, and she remains the only person to have won twice in two different sciences, physics and chemistry. The only other double-discipline laureate, Linus Pauling, was honoured for his contributions to chemistry and peace.

Yet Curie's life in science garlanded with its highest awards, her international acclaim and her impeccable professionalism did little to protect her when she embarked on a relationship with a fellow physicist four years after her husband Pierre had died. She was forty-three, he was thirty-eight, and married. A ravening press fell on the story and pilloried her as a home-breaker, a whore, a Jew and a Pole.

Home-breaker?

No. Paul Langevin never left his wife and family.

Whore? When she had sex with only two men in her life?

Jew? Sorry, guys, no, not even by marriage.

Pole, yes. She could not escape the charge of being 'a foreigner'.

One conviction out of four is not a great crime sheet, but whoever needed a reason to attack a woman deemed to have broken the rules? Her academic enemies even attempted to block her from receiving her second Nobel Prize in 1911, on the grounds that the King of Sweden should not have to shake the hand of an adulteress. Curie returned home to Paris from the world-class Solvay Conference to find a mob besieging her house, and was forced to flee with her daughters and take shelter with friends. Magnificently, she mounted a successful counter-attack and lived down the metaphorical public stoning of 'the woman taken in adultery', as the Bible has it, garnering greater international recognition and more glittering prizes until her death in 1934.

Marie Curie has achieved an iconic status as the only female scientist that almost everyone in the world has heard of, but there were many other valiant women working with maths and matter. The women staffing the Harvard College Observatory from the 1880s to the mid-twentieth century, initially at just thirty cents an hour, were called 'computers', because their job was simply to count the stars they saw. But in 1908, one of them measured the stars she was counting, analysed their size and brightness, and proved that the universe was not stable, but expanding.

This discovery was such a complete contradiction of the accepted theory that it went nowhere. Only when the American astronomer Edwin Hubble took up the idea did it gain any traction, and became what is now known as Hubble's Law, winning him a nomination for the Nobel Prize before his sudden death in 1953. To his credit, Hubble repeatedly said that the original discoverer, Henrietta Swan Leavitt, should have been a Nobel laureate, and in 1924 she was nominated by the Swedish mathematician Gösta Mittag-Leffler, only for her champion to discover that she was dead and therefore ineligible.

Let's take a moment to appreciate this good man, a lifelong supporter of women. He first displayed his feminist leanings as a twenty-year-old student when he added his mother's maiden name, Mittag, to his father's, and carried both forward into his professional career. He saw first-hand the difficulties of his sister, Anne Charlotte Leffler, torn between her desire to become a writer and her guilt about moving out of her feminine role, despite a talent that was to establish her as a leading playwright and author. As a member of the Nobel Committee in 1903, Mittag-Leffler insisted that the prize in physics had to go to Marie and Pierre Curie, and not to Pierre alone. Another woman, the Russian Sofia Kovalevskaya, owed her entire career to him when he arranged for her to become a full professor of mathematics in Stockholm in 1889, the first woman in the world to hold that role.

So what about the vote?

Curie, Leavitt and others all over the world were proving that when girls were educated, they could achieve. But however well individual women performed, votes for women at large also had to surmount deep barriers of class and race. Even liberal thinkers like John Stuart Mill, one of the strongest supporters of women in the nineteenth century, assumed that suffrage would be limited to women of the educated classes. Other sympathisers, male and female, argued that a woman could be allowed to vote if she were a property owner, but working-class women whatever their background or ability were so far outside the universe of the male, educated, landowning and white establishment that they might have been on another planet.

As a microcosm of women's struggle for equality, female suffrage had to fight for its right to exist from the very start. Some American feminists claimed the right to vote on the grounds of women's moral superiority to men, which made them God's police, the essential custodians of society and of men: they deserved it. Catholic and other religious suffragists argued their case on the basis of their extensive voluntary and charitable work: they had earned it. In Germany, women based their claim to the vote on the fact that only they could bear the future cannon-fodder (*sorry, warriors!*) of the Fatherland, and they should be rewarded.

That a woman should have the vote because she was the human equivalent of any adult man was unthinkable. She had to have womanhood *plus* – *plus* property, *plus* land, *plus* education, *plus* morality, *plus* service in the community, *plus* motherhood. In short, she had to demonstrate an impeccable super-womanhood in every female aspect, when by now the ballot box was open to the lowliest man. Nowhere was the vote for women presented or promoted as a right. A British suffrage poster of 1912 satirised the discrepancy:

- What a Woman may be and yet not have the Vote:
  - Mayor
  - Nurse
  - Mother
  - Teacher
  - Factory Hand

- What a Man may have been and yet not lose the Vote
  - Convict
  - Lunatic
  - Proprietor of White Slaves
  - Unfit for Service
  - Drunkard

'Failure is impossible'

So Susan B. Anthony declared at her last public appearance, a party held to celebrate her eighty-eighth birthday in early 1906. But more than half a century of battles had borne little fruit. Anthony and many others tried repeatedly to force their way into public elections, including the great Grimké sisters, now crankier than ever and splendidly refusing to mellow into serene old age. Finally a Supreme Court judgment of 1874 criminalised the very attempt. The law cases and the protests against them carried on until 1886, when a Women's Suffrage

Amendment reached the floor of the US Senate, only to be defeated two to one.

As the years passed, so did the valiant standard bearers, one by one. Lucy Stone died in 1893, and Elizabeth Cady Stanton succumbed to pneumonia in 1902. Four years later Susan B. Anthony followed her. They were both so closely wedded to the cause that theirs was arguably one of the most productive political partnerships in history. For all their decades of dedication, not one of the famous American triumvirate (*tri-feminate?*) lived to cast their vote.

In Britain too, despite the massive effort they had put in, both the suffragists and suffragettes had to accept a soul-shrivelling lack of success. A decade or so after Pankhurst had formed the WSPU, and almost fifty years since the foundation of the National Society for Women's Suffrage, they had nothing to show for it but the determination to carry on. And even that was about to be stopped in its tracks. Two giant steps forward, the arrival of birth control and the campaign for the vote, had seen women well on their way to gaining personal autonomy and full civic identity. The one step back, the derogatory classification of women as the less evolved sex would simply have to be lived through and lived down.

But like a scorpion, the nineteenth century still had a sting in its tail. While the women in America, the UK and elsewhere had spent the last half century trying to create a new model of a female life, the boys in Europe had been busy with Man Stuff. That meant throwing their countries into nation creation (read: *fuelling aggressive nationalism*), winning military glory (read: *glorifying militarism which fuelled nationalism*), and forging strong alliances (read: *signing grandiose and half-cocked treaties whose consequences none of them had foreseen*).

Is this an exaggeration?

Only to make it more like it was.

It was a toxic brew of ignorance and arrogance spiked with 100 per cent pure testosterone, and it had a low boiling point.

No surprise, then, that one day in 1914 the pot boiled over, and the world blew up.

It was the First World War.

CHAPTER 6

FOOTPRINTS OF BLOOD

It is far easier to make war than to make peace.

GEORGES CLEMENCEAU

Without women, victory will tarry and the victory which tarries means a victory whose footprints are footprints of blood.

DAVID LLOYD GEORGE

Rather, ten times, die in the surf, heralding the way to a new world, than stand idly on the shore.

FLORENCE NIGHTINGALE

As the world fell apart during the First World War, so much else fell away too. For fifty years and more, nothing had been more important to the cause of women than the fight for the vote. That was recognised as the cornerstone of women's rights as early as the Seneca Falls Convention in 1848, because it promised access to all the other rights and freedoms available to men. Decades of campaigning for female suffrage had taken place in Britain and the United States, in Europe, as far afield as Russia and India, and throughout South America. Now it had to be put on hold. Mrs Pankhurst, and later Lucy Stone when the United States joined the war in 1917, agreed to call off the campaign for the vote, and to direct all their members' energy into the war effort.

When men make war, women's lives change profoundly, though they may never see action or hear a gun fired. As the old world broke down, the birth of the new offered Western women and girls unprecedented opportunities to take advantage of the crumbling of the old conventions that had held them back. Now they had chances to redirect their life course, to experiment, to innovate, *to act*.

One who did that and more was Florence Nightingale, already in full rebellion against the stultifying regime of her repressive parents when war in the Balkans provided a unique outlet for her outstanding drive, and her mission to do good. She succeeded so well that she became world-famous, immortalised as 'The Lady with the Lamp', an icon of tender womanhood selflessly caring for men in the Crimean War. In the deep religiosity of the time, this image also carried a strong association with the much-loved Holman Hunt painting of 1853, *The Light of the World*, where Jesus is portrayed as a saintly figure in the shadows, carrying a lantern to lighten the globe.

And here it is, the origin of the story from the pen of the legendary war correspondent William Russell, in *The Times* of 8 February 1855:

She is a 'ministering angel' without any exaggeration in these hospitals, and as her slender form glides quietly along each corridor, every poor fellow's face softens with gratitude at the sight of her. When all the medical officers have retired for the night and silence and darkness have settled down upon those miles of prostrate sick, she may be observed alone, with a little lamp in her hand, making her solitary rounds.

All together now: *aaaaahhhh!*

Heart-warming, or what?

Sadly, like so many good stories, it was too good to be true. The heroine of the Crimea? She was based in Scutari, hundreds of miles away. Gliding round the wards? Her achievement lay in organising the wards and training nurses to run them, and her tough-minded, austere nature would have revolted at the idea of milking the gratitude of sick soldiers by playing the angel of mercy at dead of night.

And 'The Lady with the Lamp'? In reality, Nightingale was known to the troops as 'The Lady with the Hammer' after she broke into a locked store room to release much-needed medical supplies, in defiance of a military commander who had blocked her every move. But as Russell knew, a powerful, belligerent, rebel woman would be far too coarse and unladylike for the readers of *The Times*, so he simply made the story up. The sentimental, saccharine fiction he created was lapped up by the good folks back home, and swallowed round the world. It continues to this day, distorting the memory of Florence Nightingale for all time. Important as her work at Scutari was, and the nursing school she founded at St Thomas' Hospital, London in 1860 that offered the world's first secular training for women who wanted to be nurses, not nuns, these were only stepping stones to a life of change and reform. 'Were there none who were discontented with what they have,' she said, 'the world would never reach anything better.'

Back in London and bed-ridden for most of her life with an illness now thought to be a virulent form of brucellosis, Nightingale continued waging war on ignorance and disease by publishing books and pamphlets on every subject from public health to patient mortality and military hospitals, not forgetting midwifery and prostitution. The woman popularly remembered as a glorified nurse is now also recognised as a pioneer statistician, mobilising figures to back up her facts. In another innovation, she created ground-breaking graphical work in the presentation of information and statistics, re-inventing the pie chart among her other feats.

Nor was Nightingale the only heroine of the Crimea. Also active was the nurse, traveller and trader from Jamaica, Mary Seacole, who like Florence Nightingale became nationally known as a heroine of the Crimea when she published her memoirs in 1857. Here she remembers one of the battlefields where she tended the injured and dying:

> I derived no little satisfaction from being able to treat the wounds of several [enemy] Russians; indeed, they were treated as kindly as any. One of them was badly shot in the lower jaw and was beyond my or any human skill. Incautiously I inserted my finger into his mouth to feel where the ball had lodged, and his teeth closed upon it in the agonies of death so tightly that I had to call to those around to release it, which was not done till it had been bitten so deeply that I shall carry the scar with me to my grave.

A battlefield was no place for the faint-hearted, but women of spirit found ways to make themselves at home there. Two British nurses of the First World War, Elsie Knocker and Mairi Chisholm, met while working as motorcycle despatch riders and, understanding the vital importance of speed, were dismayed to find that their field station in Flanders was so far from the battle lines that only the lightly wounded could hope to survive. Commandeering a bombed-out house so close to the front line that it was little more than a ruin, they set up their own medical post in the cellar and used their own ambulance to bring in the casualties. Operating under constant bombardment and sniper fire from 1914 to 1918, they saved countless lives and limbs until an almost-fatal gas attack left them too badly injured to carry on. Both lived to be laden with honours, and were among the most photographed individuals of the war. Knocker even returned to the fray in the Second World War and served with such distinction that she was mentioned in dispatches.

Elsie and Mairi were only two of the many women serving in the First World War who could not only drive cars and motorcycles, but maintain and service them too. Here we can note in passing the demise of another powerful male myth, the mystic union of man and machine. When women proved that they could get under a bonnet to find a dipstick or change a spark plug, and that they knew the difference between their sumps and their big ends, an important barricade was breached. Indeed, the barriers to female involvement were going down all over Europe.

Leave it to the men?

The myth of epic from the *Iliad* onwards, was that war is men's work: men must fight while women weep, and wait and weep yet more. Very poetic, but completely untrue. Women have always fought. Everywhere we turn in history or geography, the facts explode the age-old dichotomy of male/female, hawk/dove. Women and girls have been active in every war since time began. History abounds with stories of fighting women from the days of the Amazons of Ancient Greece, no longer a myth but now known to be real women warriors from Scythia, modern-day eastern Iraq. When the Romans exterminated the druids on the island of Mona off the coast of Wales in 61 CE, women fought side by side with men. The Roman commander,

Gaius Suetonius Paulinus, ordered his forces to kill all the female druids first, as the wild-haired, black-clad, screaming, cursing, fighting women in the front line defending the males behind, frightened his soldiers more than the men. These women fought to the last dregs of their strength and courage, because they knew they were going to die.

Equally formidable were the fifteen hundred or so women warriors of the Kingdom of Dahomey in west Africa. First recorded in 1600 and still in action in 1900, they were the king's crack troops, highly trained and experienced in combat.

In fatal contrast to the 'black Amazons' of Dahomey, the six hundred women defenders of Piribebuy, the last stand in Paraguay's doomed struggle against Brazil in 1868, had never faced battle before, but they fought to the death after their ammunition ran out and went down still firing volleys of empty bottle and stones, finally hurling handfuls of sand at the troops who killed them all. In the same spirit, the women who were on the barricades of the Paris Commune alongside men in France's republican uprising of 1871 resisted the ferocious bombardment and final onslaught of the government battalions to their last breath. 'They fought like devils, far better than the men,' recorded an anonymous English medical student who was in Paris at the time. 'I had the pain of seeing fifty-two of them shot down, even when they had been surrounded by troops and disarmed.'

The world loves stories like this, of any woman who takes up arms to defend her home, her city, her king or country. History readily polishes these individuals into national heroines like Joan of Arc who can be made into icons or martyrs, especially if they are virgins, and super-specially when (*and it's a when, not an if*) they die. By making the 'supreme sacrifice', they are washed clean of any blood they may have spilled, shining like stars through all the mud, the blood, the guts, the stink and the slime. Like Christ, the prototype of the spotless virgin unless you believe the romantic gufferoo about him and Mary Magdalene, Joan of Arc took wounds but never inflicted them, becoming the perfect warrior saint.

In reality, women in war had to fight and act as men did, and like men chart a safe path through the equally demanding politics of war. Inevitably, then, they repeatedly show not only courage in combat but well-grounded military skill and leadership. Harriet Tubman, the former slave and liberator we met earlier as the conductor of the Underground Railroad, earned the honorary title of 'General' Tubman when she led an armed assault during the American Civil War to rescue more than 750 slaves in the Combahee River Raid of 1863. All over the world, women have shown themselves to be capable of the same skill and courage as men. Lakshmi Bai, the Rani of Jhansi, was renowned for resisting the colonisation of the British in the Indian Uprising of 1857. As troop upon troop of redcoats closed in on her fortress, Lakshmi Bai fought back with seemingly endless reserves of brute courage and raw nerve. In one tight corner, she reportedly leaped from the battlements of her fort with her young son on her back to land on a waiting horse below and make their escape.

At last, her army overwhelmed by sheer force of numbers, she was shot by a lowly redcoat, resisting the might of the British Raj to the last. A flood of elegies commemorated her phenomenal horsemanship, fighting skills and courage in defence of her realm. Twenty years after her death, she drew this tribute from the British army officer Colonel George Malleson: 'Whatever her faults in British eyes may have been, her countrymen will ever remember that she was driven into rebellion due to ill-treatment by the helmsmen of the East India Company, and that she lived and died for her country.'

Hundreds, no, thousands of women like these give the lie to the old lie that women are by nature soft-hearted, fearful and reluctant to fight. In truth the members of the gentler sex can be as hawkish as any man, and can win the loyalty of fighting men if given command. This was the story of the short and myopic trainee teacher Ecaterina Teodoroiu who beat down all official opposition to enlist in the Romanian army as a woman, not in disguise as a man, and became a regular soldier in the First World War. Fighting on the front line, she won three awards for bravery, was promoted to Second Lieutenant, and given command of a platoon in an infantry regiment. With a major offensive looming, her commanding officer urged her to seek safety in the field hospital behind the lines. Refusing to leave her platoon, she led her men into battle, where she was mown down in a hail of machine-gun fire, still shouting as she fell, 'Forward, men! Don't fall back, I'm still with you!'

By contrast with Teodoroiu's conventional background, the Russian soldier Mariya Bochkareva came to war conditioned to conflict by her traumatic early years. Prostituted as a child and only just escaping with her life from two violent husbands, the young Bochkareva won permission from the government in the early days of the Russian Revolution to form an all-woman battalion to fight against Germany on the Eastern Front. 'Our Mother Russia is perishing!' began her appeal for volunteers in May 1917. 'Come with us to save her ... I want women whose hearts are crystal, whose souls are pure.' Fifteen hundred women enlisted that night in the 1st Russian Women's Battalion of Death, and similar units sprang up all over Russia.

Fighting at the front, Bochkareva's shock troops proved a brave and powerful force, only to find that whenever they overran an enemy trench the male soldiers would refuse to go forward and make good the advance, but instead dropped everything to find the alcohol and get blind drunk. Six months later, the Bolshevik Party came to power, disbanded the women's battalions and sentenced Bochkareva to death. She escaped to America in April 1918, but that August she returned to Russia to found another Battalion of Death – to fight for the anti-communist White Russians this time. Instead, she fell into the hand of the Reds, the Bolshevik army, who executed her by firing squad in May 1920. At least she had the final tribute of a soldier's death.

Dancing the skies

The actions of women like Mariya Bochkareva, taken with the massive juggernaut of the First World War bringing huge changes and advances big and small, meant that the Western world gradually developed a greater acceptance of women's skills. One glorious new adventure they embraced from the start was aviation. In keeping with the idea that whatever history delivers there's a woman in there somewhere, consider the delicious image opposite, from the birth of powered flight.

Katharine Wright is now known to be as deeply committed to the business of flight as either of her brothers, and the one who kept the whole show on the road. She ran the business as well as the household, while also taking care of Orville and Wilbur and supporting their work.

With their vast country and open skies, Americans predictably took to flying like ducks to water. The young Katherine Stinson was such a natural that she only needed four hours of instruction before she flew alone. As an aeronautical acrobat, she was the first woman to loop the loop, and later created her own version to make the stunt more sensational – and far more dangerous – by adding an extra 'snap roll' at the top of the loop when the plane was at its slowest and heaviest. The public adored her for it, and she performed the stunt countless times without mishap. Despite all this, Stinson was flatly rejected when she answered the call for pilots to fly for the United States

It's the Wrights! See the famous brothers Orville *(left)* and Wilbur seated, with the third and largely unknown leg of the family triangle, their sister Katharine. Note the touching device to protect her modesty, the piece of string tied round her legs to keep her skirt from blowing up, not a problem the men ever had to face.

after the country joined the First World War in 1917. But her younger sister Marjorie, another fine pilot, was hired to train almost one hundred cadets in San Antonio, Texas, all of whom went on to serve in the military during the conflict.

In Europe, the versatile Hélène Dutrieu, cyclist, stuntwoman, actor and journalist, became Belgium's first qualified woman pilot and was later awarded the Légion d'honneur, although her prize-winning long-distance and high-altitude records never commanded as much press interest as the revelation that she flew without corsets. Like Katherine Stinson, Dutrieu did not fly in the war, finding herself similarly stuck on the ground driving ambulances. Russia, meanwhile, was home to one of the world's first female military pilots known to be active in warfare. The magnificently mad cousin of the last Russian tsar, Nicholas II,

Princess Eugenie Shakhovskaya flew numerous cocaine-fuelled reconnaissance missions in the First World War, and survived the Bolshevik Revolution only to die in a drunken shoot-out at a wild party when she was thirty-one.

They flew by night

Bigger steps were to come when Marina Raskova became the driving force behind the formation of no less than three all-women pilot combat units in the Second World War. Between them, the units flew over thirty-thousand missions for the Soviet Air Force on the Eastern Front despite being given the worst of the planes to fly, old crates of wood and canvas barely held together with glue. As the machines were far too slow to evade counter-attack, the women learned to cut their engines and glide down onto the target. The eerie sound of the wind whistling through the plane's struts and wires as they flew in for the kill, along with a growing fear of their apparently supernatural skills, earned the 588th Night Bomber Regiment the nickname of 'the Night Witches'.

The undisputed star was the fighter pilot Lily Litvak, the 'White Rose of Stalingrad', who had been flying since she was fourteen. In her 168 combat missions against the Germans, Litvak downed twelve enemy planes herself, and had three shared victories. She was held in such awe by the Luftwaffe that, according to reports, it took eight of their fighter pilots to bring her down. This they did in August 1943, a grievous loss to the Russians, who could take comfort only from the knowledge that the war was not going according to the Führer's master plan. By April 1945, the Great Architect of the Thousand Year Reich had bunkered down in Berlin, where one of his last acts was to send for his personal pilot Hanna Reitsch, 'Hitler's Valkyrie'.

Young, naive and almost mystically focused on the magic of flight, Reitsch was ordered to fly into Berlin under heavy Allied bombardment, braving a barrage of bursting shells to bring a senior Luftwaffe officer to Hitler's side. Charged with the deranged dictator's last orders (*'Arrest Heinrich Himmler!'*) the odd couple took off again two days later with the city a sea of flame below, dodged the shelling and finally landed safely at Plön, headquarters of the surviving members of Hitler's high command. In less than two weeks, Hitler was dead, Germany had surrendered, Reitsch's passenger had killed himself and she had been taken into American custody. She lived to build a post-war flying career in Germany and America by taking up gliding, achieving a level of success that culminated in an invitation to the White House in 1961. She never lost her love of flight, advising Prime Minister Nehru on establishing a national gliding school in India, and moving to Ghana in 1962 to do the same. There, despite her indoctrination in Nazi theories of racial purity, she forged a close relationship with Ghana's leader Kwame Nkrumah and stayed for four years. Back in the US, she continued to break records, including her own, right up to her death in 1979.

Hanna Reitsch risked her life more times than she could count for the Fatherland that she was ready to die for. But perhaps the most closely entwined with the future of her country was the first Turkish woman aviator, Sahiba Gökçen. Gökçen was the adopted daughter of the founder of Turkey, Kemal Atatürk, and became a feature of his campaign to bring the country into the modern world and to educate its women, thereby releasing them from the constraints of Islamic traditions like the veil. Sahiba, he decided, was to be his 'creature of the air'. Given the name Gökçen, 'belonging to the sky', she was taught to fly as a living symbol that women were soaring into freedom under Atatürk's regime. In 1936 she trained as Turkey's first female military pilot, flying bomber and fighter planes, and deployed on bombing raids against Kurdish insurgents the following year.

Gökçen loved flying and never seems to have resented being made Atatürk's trophy rebel, even when he ordered her to fly with a loaded pistol, ready to shoot herself if she fell into enemy hands. Her active service on this military operation in 1937 made her the world's first female combat pilot, and she was decorated for her outstanding performance in the air. During her career in the Turkish Air Force, Gökçen flew twenty-two different types of aircraft and logged more than eight thousand flying hours, thirty-two of them under enemy bombardment. In 1996, the US Air Force featured her in a series of posters honouring the Twenty Greatest Aviators in History – the only woman to make the cut. In later years she became the chief trainer at the Turkish Flight School, bringing on younger female pilots to take her place. She is commemorated today in the Sahiba Gökçen airport at Istanbul, a fitting companion to the main airport, Atatürk.

A rose by any other name

Equally committed to her country was the Japanese-American radio broadcaster Iva Ikoku Toguri, known to US troops as 'Tokyo Rose'. The name was invented by Allied soldiers and used for all the female English-speaking radio broadcasters pumping out Japanese propaganda in the Second World War, but Toguri became identified with it, and it stuck. Heaping insults on the forces in the Pacific, she greeted her listeners every morning with the bracing call 'Hello, boneheads!' and kept on broadcasting right up to the Japanese surrender in August 1945. Like Reitsch, Toguri later paid for her patriotism and heavily, when she was sentenced to ten years in prison on a single charge of treason. It later emerged that the witnesses had perjured themselves and that the trial was rigged. The American judge admitted that he had given her the maximum sentence within his powers because his son had served in the Pacific.

We can't all be patriots, noble heroines and national treasures in times of crisis. What of the women who got through by moving entirely for themselves, piggy-backing on the spirit of patriotism and nationalism to do their own thing? Any war gives a certain type of woman her chance, as it does men. Creatures of spirit, enterprise and not too much scruple, while vigorously pretending to keep the home fires burning, could carve out lives that peacetime could never afford. From a rich gallery of frauds and fantasists, posers, winners and losers, queen of them all could well be the French 'pioneer aviatrix' Marthe Richard, who managed to make herself a patriot, a heroine and a national treasure in both world wars.

Richard's entire life reads like an epic of self-reinvention. Registered as a prostitute at sixteen in her home town of Nancy, she left for Paris and married a rich man who owned a plane, then set about claiming records for flights she never made. Spying for the Germans, she later invented a career as an underground agent for the French Resistance, published the bestseller *My Life in the French Secret Service* and was awarded the Légion d'honneur. Becoming a politician in 1945 and protected by a series of powerful lovers, she successfully campaigned for the closure of brothels in Paris (no solidarity with her former fellow-sex workers there, *hélas*). Opponents at the time felt that the city's crying shortage of food, drink and basic utilities like electricity might have been a better focus for her attention, but her status and self-belief carried her through a variety of further adventures until 1982, when she died at the age of ninety-two.

Now what about the vote . . . ?

'In war, there is a place for mad people,' said Field Marshal Bernard Montgomery, the hero of the Battle of El Alamein, in 1942. The madness of war can infect any participant from the commander to the cookhouse cat, overriding all else, no matter how important to others. Was it purely a coincidence, then, that a century of revolution when women's fight for equality had convulsed the globe was followed by another in which two world wars brutally reinforced the domination of the male? That so many countries embraced the chance to glorify male violence and to promote militaristic structures of men in charge after an era in which men's traditional dominance had repeatedly been challenged and overthrown, and in which women had claimed and won rights and freedoms which were never theirs before?

Including the long-sought-for pearl beyond price, the long-fought-for queen of rights, *winning the vote*. With the outbreak of the First World War and its agreed restrictions on campaigning activity in the UK and the US, the cause dwindled into irrelevance against the horrors of the conflict, the slaughter, the blood, the rats, the cries of the dying, and the stink of an entire generation of young men, the flowers of the field, rotting where they fell. Against this background, the formal, legal granting of votes for women slipped out almost unnoticed.

In Britain, the first tranche of women won the vote in 1918, as a reward, so it was said – and is still widely believed – for their good behaviour during the war. They had stopped the suffragette attacks, they had contributed to the war effort, they had worked and served, they had been good girls, *they deserved it*.

This is a fiction.

Once again it negates the reality that votes for women were

and are *a basic human right*. Why should a woman have to earn it when a man did not?

In reality, opinion at this stage had been coming round to female suffrage for some time. In the summer of 1915, the founding president of the Women's National Anti-Suffrage League, the novelist Mrs Humphry Ward, confessed, 'I sometimes wonder in my secret thoughts whether we are not already beaten.' In Parliament, a committee of MPs from all parties who met during October 1916 agreed on extending the vote to certain women, and early in 1917 Lloyd George, now Prime Minister, assured a deputation of suffragists that a draft bill giving women the vote was prepared and ready to pass through Parliament. The Representation of the People Act, which gave over eight million women the vote, was passed on 6 February 1918, *nine months* before the signing of the Armistice brought the war to an end. This led to Parliament passing the Parliament (Qualification of Women) Act on 21 November, which allowed women to become MPs for the first time, and seventeen women, including Christabel Pankhurst, stood as candidates in the general election of 14 December. In light of this timetable, it is ludicrous to suggest that this was any kind of 'reward' for the women of the UK. It was simply a right that could no longer be refused.

Playing catch-up

British suffragists had privately agreed to accept the limitation of the vote to women over the age of thirty, in the correct assessment that once some women were enfranchised, the rest must follow. The vote was finally extended to all women over twenty-one, the same age as men, ten years later. Over in the US, the daughter of Elizabeth Cady Stanton had gingered up the entire suffrage movement by introducing banner parades, street speakers and non-violent picketing, all proving highly effective in waking up a somnolent New World. Harriot Stanton Blatch formed the group which became the Women's Political Union in 1910, and freely acknowledged that her radical and attention-grabbing tactics were all borrowed from the British suffragettes.

Another innovator was the Iowa powerhouse Carrie Chapman Catt. The only female of her graduating class at Iowa Agricultural College, she plunged into the suffrage campaign in her twenties, and twenty years later succeeded Susan B. Anthony at the head of the National American Woman Suffrage Association in 1900. There she devised what she confidently called her 'winning plan' to win round each of the states of America that previously had refused to back votes for women, one by one. The plan worked. In August 1920, less than two years after the end of the First World War, American women were granted the vote.

Catt would have been the first to acknowledge that the victory was not hers alone, but built on the heroic work of the fighting foremothers of the US women's suffrage campaign, now mostly gone. Happily Catt survived to cast her vote in the presidential election of November 1920, which she did in the company of Mary 'Mollie' Garrett Hay, a linchpin of the suffragist organisation in New York. Married twice and widowed twice, Catt spent her time travelling and campaigning with Hay, and after her second husband's death, they lived together for many years.

It was quietly understood within their close circle that the two women had a 'special relationship'. Luckily this did not prevent Catt from being showered with honours and going down in history as one of the builders of the nation. When Catt died in 1947, almost twenty years after Hay, she chose to be buried with neither of her husbands but with Mollie, beneath a headstone engraved HERE LIE TWO, UNITED IN FRIENDSHIP FOR THIRTY-EIGHT YEARS THROUGH CONSTANT SERVICE TO A GREAT CAUSE.

Over the seas and far away

Carrie could rest in peace, knowing that the women who won the vote had changed history, ushering in a new world. And what was this world made new in which women were becoming equal to men? Very different from the one our heroines had confronted at the start of the nineteenth century when the modern fight for women's rights began. While some women (and men too) had been working for women's freedom and autonomy on the domestic front, many men (and women too) had been occupied overseas in the global outreach of empire building. By 1900, Russia had one of the largest empires in the history of the world.

But Britain was already ahead in the great game of smash and grab, seizing princely states of India, as well as Burma, Assam, Ceylon and South Africa by force between 1796 and 1818. Afghanistan, Kashmir, the Punjab, Singapore and Hong Kong were added to the haul by the end of the First Opium War in 1842. Not to be outdone, France, Belgium, Italy, the Netherlands and Portugal, the strongest of the European powers, eyed up the rest of the globe and eagerly snaffled up land wherever they could. Meanwhile America intensified its great drive westward, extending the imperialist impulses of the founders and establishing an internal empire.

Ripping yarns

Imperial ventures have consequently been presented as *The Big Book of Boy's Own Adventures*, tales of duty and derring do, the exploits of men's men with the odd dusky maiden thrown in. The works of Rider Haggard and Rudyard Kipling heave and throb with masculine imperial excitations. Invasion and conquest were seen as bringing enlightenment to 'subject races', with the women in a man's world being seen as the largest subject race of all – for, as Kipling wrote with or without irony, 'a woman is only a woman, but a good cigar is a *smoke*'.

In these adventures, women are notably absent. 'I can safely say that there is not a *petticoat* in the whole history,' harrumphs Rider Haggard in *King Solomon's Mines* (1886). But the imperial adventurers of every nation honoured their women *in absentia* by naming mountains, rivers, towns and territories after them, notably the US state of Virginia, Sir Walter Ralegh's tribute to England's Virgin Queen in 1584. Another British queen became the most commemorated person in history, making the mini-monarch's moniker the most commonplace name in the world as Queen Victoria was immortalised everywhere from streets in city slums to the grandeur of Victoria Falls.

Victoria was created Empress of India in 1876, a position placing her as ruler far above her lowly 'subject races'. But women were everywhere in the empire, and some did not see themselves as subject to anyone, not even the great white queen. Hence the case of *Regina vs Nehanda*, when a fifty-eight-year-old Mashona woman was prosecuted for the murder of Henry Hawkins Pollard, a white Native Commissioner in Matabeleland, now part of modern-day Zimbabwe.

Pollard was widely known as a violent oppressor of the Mashona, one of the dead-eyed brutes who 'smell of tobacco and blood' in Kipling's phrase, while Nehanda was highly revered as the incarnation of the ancestral spirit of her people. She led the resistance to the regime of the British South Africa Company, the creation of Cecil Rhodes, and was convicted of the murder of Pollard on evidence no better than hearsay that she had ordered his death. Hanged shortly afterwards, the tiny Nehanda went to the gallows fighting all the way, shouting, screaming and ululating in defiance, a rebel to the last.

From a Queen Empress to a convicted criminal, the range of women involved in the empire was immense, and one in particular, the British explorer Gertrude Bell, became a highly influential British political adviser. Her government white paper of 1920 on the Middle East, 'Review of the Civil Administration of Mesopotamia', was the first report at that level to be written by a woman, and it mapped out the borders of Iraq.

Bell was no stranger to firsts, as the first woman to win first-class honours in history at Oxford (although as a woman she was not allowed to graduate), which she did in two years instead of the normal three. Rebelling against the normal fate of the educated young woman of her class (*going back home to keep Mother company, taking tea and going to church*) she learned Persian and Pashto, and pushed off to the Middle East. Once there, the rest was history and she helped to make it. She became the first English woman to travel alone in the Syrian desert, the first female officer in British military intelligence, and the first female colonial administrator.

Later dubbed the 'Queen of the Desert', Bell was also remarkable for the rapport she developed with the Arabs of the region, meeting their sheiks and leaders with a greater ease and depth of understanding than any of the army officers or male diplomats. She was the only British official, it was said afterwards, who could be remembered with any respect or affection. At the Cairo Conference in March 1921, convened to restructure the Middle East, she was the only woman in a gathering of the world's leading experts and politicians, including Winston Churchill and T. E. Lawrence 'of Arabia', and she helped to shape the outcome with her support for Arab aspirations for self-government and national identity. She built a dazzling career, and was the prime mover in creating two important commemorations of Arab art and culture in what are now the National Library and the National Museum of Iraq. At her death in 1926, as a former British political officer and adviser on military intelligence, she was buried in Baghdad with full imperial honours, a tribute to her unique combination of duty and daring.

Desert queen or flotsam and jetsam, wherever empire building took place women found their opportunity, and often in the teeth of desperate events. As the newly united country of America spread westward in the nineteenth century, colonising vast swathes of Native American land, Texas had enjoyed nine years as a nation in its own right. This followed its 1836 declaration of independence from the Republic of Mexico, triggering a savage war with the Texans ('*Remember the Alamo!*'), and a rough country it remained. In 1864, nine-year-old Libby Thompson was snatched by a Comanche raiding party and returned home to Texas four years later. What had happened to her in the time her parents spent searching for her and raising the ransom needed to get her back? In plain terms, was she still a virgin? No one knew, but she was treated thereafter as a 'soiled dove', Wild West-speak for a fallen woman, and ostracised by the community, to the shame and anguish of her whole family.

Libby had one champion in town, an older man who wanted to marry her, but her father shot him dead. A year later she ran away from home to join a Dodge City dance hall specialising in diversions of the horizontal variety, where she rose swiftly through the ranks of the good-time girls. By now known as 'Squirrel Tooth Alice', she opened her own establishment, offering a wide range of terpsichorean delights. Her success as a madam allowed her to retire young and live in comfort till the age of ninety-eight.

Decline and fall

From the Assyrian empire of 859–612 BCE to the British, world-powerful from about 1700 to 1950, each one carried the seeds of its own decay. Colonial administrators of the vast expansion into Africa thought little of overthrowing ancient tribal customs that placed women in charge of salt production, for instance, or agriculture. They chose instead to hand over to men questions of land ownership, the right of decision-making and, crucially, the financial subsidies allotted for improvement.

Money, Honey!

Can we blame the men for high-tailing it into town to spend the cash on cigs, tarts, gambling and drink, with no thought for the panning, drying and sorting or ploughing, weeding and seeding, all the work that had to be done in return? 'In Africa,' commented the economists Lisa Leghorn and Katherine Parker in 1981, 'women still do 70 per cent of the agricultural work while almost all the agricultural aid has gone to men.' In many parts of Africa too, the same thinking permitted, no, *encouraged*, the direct rule of men, which meant the breaking of age-old structures of tribal monarchy in which women held power. Female rulers like the supremely crafty queen Njinga Mbandi, who in the seventeenth century ran rings around the Portuguese colonial invaders in what is now Angola, were all but forgotten. The long line of African queens may have begun with the biblical Queen of Sheba. It certainly continued for centuries with the Kandakes of Kush, an ancient kingdom between Egypt and Sudan, one of whom appears in the New Testament. They were followed by the fifteenth-century war chief Amina of Nigeria and others we have already met, in a tradition leading on to Yaa Asantewaa of Ghana, who led an army of five thousand against British colonial forces in 1900. Who now remembers them when the very memory of their existence is reduced to the name of a clapped-out old barge in the 1951 film *The African Queen*?

Now you see it . . .

. . . that good old freedom and equality for women, and now you don't. By the time the next world war broke out in 1939, the position of women darkened before the first shot was fired. The rise of Fascism created a force violently hostile to women's freedom and determined to crush it. The movement springing up in the Italy of the 1920s spread like a virulent pox over to Spain. In both countries it glorified an ideal of the family that closely mirrored the reactionary, hierarchical and tyrannically religious structure of these firmly Catholic states, and defined women in a rigidly repressive way.

The founder and leader of the Fascist movement in Italy, Benito Mussolini, had no doubt about the role of women in the life of the nation and his life in particular. In 1914 he married a successful businesswomen, Ida Daiser, who obligingly funded the start of his political career and became pregnant with his child. The next year, before the baby was born, Mussolini also married his long-term mistress, Rachele, who had borne him a child in 1910. Outraged, Ida mounted a public protest on behalf of herself and her son, and maintained her claim to be Mussolini's wife. When he seized power in 1922, the dictator ordered his secret police to search out and destroy any records of the marriage. He then had the still-protesting Ida kidnapped, beaten and committed to a lunatic asylum, where she died fifteen years later of a 'brain haemorrhage'. The same fate befell her son Benito after his father's rise to power: he was told that his mother was dead, and put up for adoption as an orphan. When he persisted in claiming that Mussolini was his father, he too was forcibly confined in a lunatic asylum, where he was murdered in 1922.

And women's rights? Here is *Il Duce* in 1922, two years after American women won the vote:

> I am not thinking of extending the vote to women. There would be no point. My blood opposes all kinds of feminism when it comes to women participating in state affairs ... I'd be laughed at! In our state [women] must not count.

Nor should women either study or work, in the view of the man whose own education had ended in a qualification as an infant school teaching assistant, and who, after fleeing military conscription in 1902, never held a proper job in his life. When Mussolini became prime minister in 1925, female students had to pay double the fees of males to attend schools and universities. In the Italian economic crisis of the 1930s, the Great Leader also ordered all working women to leave their jobs because they were 'thieves who reach out to steal men's bread, and who are responsible for men's unproductiveness'.

Yet the Great Satan was Nazism, a political movement fed by virility fantasies of the ideal warrior. The hyper-masculine identity of the warrior was founded on a primal flight from the female, a fear of weakness and effeminacy, of a nation gone soft with the loss of its manhood after Germany's defeat in the First World War. For the proto-Nazis after 1918, one of the main tasks in rebuilding the country was the rooting out of all things female in the culture, and they began with the repression of women and girls.

Why on earth were German women so eager to sign up to a party which from the beginning meant to bring them down, down, *down*, and made no secret of it? The first Articles of the Nazi Party Constitution in 1921 and 1922 prohibited women from holding any office or taking any active roles. There was to be no place in the public world for them, only domestic femininity. Women should not work or even wear trousers, according to the Nazi rules of female behaviour, because 'the mission of women is to be beautiful and to bring children into the world,' as Joseph Goebbels later pronounced.

This was not so easy as it sounds. From her school days, a girl had to learn every aspect of housekeeping, cooking, cleaning and sewing, while also studying hygiene, first aid and basic nursing care in order to deal with family accidents and illnesses. As a mother, her task was not only to rear healthy, blond, blue-eyed Aryan children but to educate them in the values of the Fatherland. Oh, and she had to be an ever-lovely, ever-loving wife to her man – again not easy, when the ideal Nazi woman did not wear make-up or high-heeled shoes, curl or colour her hair, or ever diet to try to lose weight, because she was supposed to be perfect without tampering with nature.

With all this to keep her busy, the Nazi government that came to power in 1933 also ensured that the inferiority of the female was to be institutionally entrenched. If Latin was a requirement for university, let's ban girls from taking it, it's too much for their little brains. And why would girls need education anyway? In Nazi thinking that owed a lot to Darwinism, females were a lower level of the human race, no more than a higher kind of animal.

This particularly applied to the foreign women and enemy captives who formed a substantial proportion of the slave labour the Nazis relied on to keep the wheels of war turning when the Second World War began. They were expected to carry out the kind of manual work that normally fell to men, however hard it was, as Heinrich Himmler commented in 1943: 'Whether ten thousand Russian females fall down from exhaustion while digging an anti-tank ditch interests me only in so far as the anti-tank ditch for Germany is finished.' Inevitably, they were also used as sex slaves in military brothels and in those set up in concentration camps, where they were expected to service a different man every twenty minutes.

Despite official policies relegating Aryan women to the home, an overstretched Nazi regime had been compelled to resort to the employment of a sizeable home-grown female workforce by the end of the war. In 1945 the armed forces of the Third Reich had half a million female auxiliary workers, mainly occupied in support roles in hospitals and offices, manning telephone lines or working in civil defence. Despite this effort, it was too little, too late.

As it turned out, the Nazis' rigid refusal to see women as anything other than workhorses and brood mares proved to be one of the key factors in the German defeat of 1945. When its enemies were drawing on all their people to join the fight, regardless of sex or age, Germany paid the ultimate price for banning women from any activity outside *Kinder, Küche, Kirche* (children, kitchen, church). Modern warfare demanded the services of millions of women worldwide, in the factories, in military support services, in their communities and on farms.

For the Allies, female labour was vital to the war effort from the start. In Britain, the Women's Land Army, first established to increase food production in the First World War, was officially re-started in June 1939, before war was declared. Full mobilisation of British women took place in 1941, and in the following years hundreds of thousands of women were called up in Britain, Russia and America as a key part of the political programme to win the Second World War.

The greatest commitment came from the Soviet Union, which conscripted an estimated *eight hundred thousand women*, and deployed them far and wide. Not everyone was impressed. 'Why are you bringing those girls here?' was the enraged cry of one Red Army field commander when he saw the first detachment of Soviet women soldiers clambering down from their trucks. '*Because you can't win the war without us!*' they might have replied. Drafting women like these Ivanas to serve on the front line, in tank battles and in 'hot' combat zones, went against the grain of every traditional military prejudice, but it turned the tide. Nazi Germany's decision to exclude half its population from war work for so long had meant fighting with one hand tied behind its back. Without the women who toiled tirelessly for their countries, the Allied victory would have been far from certain, and certainly far more long drawn-out.

A cool and lonely courage

And as it turned out, women proved to be particularly suited to a form of war work in which the tame and docile Nazi haus-fraus would not have been deployed. The Second World War saw the first widespread use of women as undercover agents since the American Civil War, when the 'Wild Rose of the Confederacy', the highly effective spy Rosie O'Neal Greenhow, delivered intelligence that gave the South victory in 1861 and 1862 against the Union in both Battles of Bull Run. From 1940, a larger number of female spies served in secrecy than has ever been acknowledged, criss-crossing Occupied Europe trading on the reputation of women as the non-combatant sex and exploiting the Nazis' apparent inability to suspect the fresh-faced girl bowling round the countryside on her bicycle or the old lady rearranging the flower pots in her window. Yet the bicycle basket would be carrying vitally important radio parts and the flower pots were a signal to the Resistance as women everywhere proved that they could be capable of the covert work men normally undertook.

Yet spying was still deadly dangerous for the female agents, with beatings, rape, torture and death their likely fate only weeks or days into their active service in the field. Winston

Churchill himself questioned the advisability of sending women into an enemy zone to face risks like these. But Selwyn Jepson, head of recruiting for F Section of the Special Operations Executive, argued that 'women were very much better than men for the work ... Women have a far greater capacity for cool and lonely courage than men. Men usually want a mate with them. Men don't work alone, their lives tend to be always in company with other men.'

And he was right. Women agents became the key to victory, as the intelligence they supplied informed the strategic Allied actions that undermined the military supremacy of the Axis powers. Who can we single out from this roll call of brave women, many of them hardly more than girls? Indeed the wide-eyed Belgian Resistance heroine Andrée de Jongh looked so young and innocent in her white ankle socks that the Gestapo never suspected her of being the creator and mastermind of the largest and most successful escape line in Occupied Europe, one that delivered a total of six hundred downed pilots and Allied soldiers to safety in Spain. Not without cost. She was eventually caught and endured over two years in concentration camps before being freed by the Allies in 1945. Her father was also taken by the Gestapo, and executed.

Equally impressive was the unquenchable American Virginia Hall, who served with distinction as a spy in both the British and US secret services. With no training in sabotage, Hall succeeded in blowing up four bridges, severing a railway line and derailing numerous freight trains, as well as keeping up a steady supply of intelligence as she cycled round France disguised as an old lady, muffled up in an ancient black gabardine and an assortment of unsavoury scarves. Using the 'Comet Line' route de Jongh had established, Hall had to make the final desperate dash for safety when the Germans closed in, escaping over the frozen, wind-lashed mountains, stumbling along tracks hardly fit for goats into neutral northern Spain, with the dogs, the guns and the mountain men of the Wehrmacht hot on her trail.

Hall's daring exploits were all the more remarkable as she had lost a foot in a pre-war shooting accident and used a brass prosthesis, which she affectionately christened 'Cuthbert', to get about. Fleeing for her life, Hall telegraphed ahead to London to announce that she was on her way back, but Cuthbert might slow her down. Back bounced the glorious response IF CUTHBERT IS TIRESOME HAVE HIM ELIMINATED. Like James Bond, Hall had a licence to kill. Unlike 007, she lived and died by the word 'secret' in her wartime service, and her tally of hits, if any, remains unknown.

War the great leveller

For many women, the conflict brought a welcome levelling of the playing field, a rough equality they had never tasted before. Conscription and war work opened a magic door to the public world, broadening horizons they hardly knew existed and helping them to find a new idea of themselves. This was the message behind the iconic and inspirational poster of a woman worker later dubbed 'Rosie the Riveter', the centrepiece of a 1942 recruitment campaign encouraging American women to fill the vacancies in factories and shipyards, thereby replacing the men called up to fight. Baring her forearm and raising a clenched fist, Rosie stares out proudly from under her red and white spotted bandana, encouraging other women with the slogan 'We Can Do It!' in what became one of the most well-known pieces of graphic propaganda of the war.

And whatever their work, for the first time large numbers of women had proper jobs. And jobs meant money, another first, money of their own. Of course they were paid less than men, but what did that matter now they did not have to answer to a man if they wanted to treat themselves to a packet of Lucky Strikes or the ultimate thrill, a tiny bottle of the most famous fragrance of the war, *Soir de Paris* by Bourjois? Day after day, the manufacture of arms, tanks, ships and flying machines, all the vital materiel needed to make war, gobbled up iron and steel, rubber and plastic, along with 'aloominum', as the Americans called it. The women too were simply part of the system, conscripted to work as hard as their counterparts in the First World War, the female arms-makers known as 'munitionettes'.

But by night . . . they could be something, to themselves at least. After the war, many women fondly recalled those evenings when they rouged their lips, boot-blacked their eyelashes, dabbed *Soir de Paris* behind their ears and sallied forth for a night on the town. And whatever the fun, they would still be back at their benches, lathes and conveyer belts the next day. For as the women of two world wars took on 'men's work', one thing became clear: in many if not most instances the female of the species could do the job every bit as well as the male. This was a reversal of pre-war thinking, an unsung revolution destined to become more and more evident both in peace and war.

Early on in the twentieth century, both war and empire seemed to open doors for the women of the world, offering the freedom to travel, the chance to work, the promise of a salary, a sense of significance in their lives. The women who survived had cast off their corsets and cast their first votes, held down real jobs and learned to take charge, to drive, to fly and to fight. With this experience behind them, the list of new-found freedoms promised a female-friendly future of discovery, adventure, independence and growth.

Yet somehow, as peace dawned, freedom and equality were as far away as ever. And throughout what the West blithely called the post-war period after the final defeat of Germany and its allies in 1945, the wars went on. Sudden and violent eruptions of fighting continued to break out in regions that were formerly strategic empire strongholds or contested territories, to no obvious gain. As Eleanor Roosevelt sombrely observed in 1948, 'I can not believe that war is the best solution. No one won the last war, and no one will win the next war.'

Meanwhile, trained ears could already detect the distant rumblings of another kind of war, one not destined to break out into open hostilities again, but serious enough to carry the threat that it might. Dubbed the 'Cold War', it was still hot enough to provide another external factor that would dominate and re-shape women's lives.

Women had helped to win the last two wars.

Now it was time to help win the peace.

3

Some Like It Cold

Oh, if I could but live another century and see the fruition of all the work for women! There is so much yet to be done.

SUSAN B. ANTHONY

CHAPTER 7

IRON CURTAINS AND IDEAL HOMES

The kitchen is your natural setting as a woman and
you should look beautiful, not bedraggled, in it ...
pinafores, organdies ... gay cotton wrap-arounds ...
why look like Cinderella's crotchety stepmother when
you can be a lyrical embodiment of all that home and
hearth means!

ANNE FOGARTY

Are you now or have you ever been a member of the
Communist Party?

US SENATOR JOE MCCARTHY

The battle for the individual rights of women is one
of long standing and none of us should countenance
anything which undermines it.

ELEANOR ROOSEVELT

1945, and at last the peace that had taken so long to win. All over the world, soldiers trailed back to wives and families who had not seen their menfolk for years, and in some cases did not know who they were. A Welsh army wife answered her front door one morning to an unknown soldier, dirty, dishevelled and desperate, who forced his way into the house and raped her on the floor, only yards away from her children playing in the front room. Getting to her feet afterwards, she told him to clear out. 'Don't you know me, woman?' he shouted. '*I'm your husband!*'

There were thousands of stories like this. In the aftermath of war, the problems of peace were as monumental as the gaunt and towering ruins of cathedrals, factories and cities looming across Europe. Some of the greatest minds and souls of the time wrestled with the task of dealing with war criminals and child refugees, the shortages of food, of housing and of almost everything else, all searching for ways to heal the rifts that the war had opened between races and nations.

Home, sweet home

The return of the troops triggered a powerful fantasy of pre-war life, where Father went off to work in the morning, Mother was at home keeping house, and women who worked outside the home were an abnormality. This drive was particularly strong in the US, where towns and cities throughout the country succumbed to a rose-tinted vision of 'the way things used to be', and strained every nerve to get everything 'back to normal'. So when the munitions plants returned to peacetime production, all the riveting Rosies had to be laid off to make way for the men. Losing their income (and with it their independence) meant that women were forced back into a role that owed more to the Victorian than to the Atomic age.

Large swathes of Western women and girls were subjected

to a mind-numbing, soul-eroding re-education programme of excruciating domesticity. The lowliest grunt in the armed forces was to be king in his own home, not only the breadwinner but the centre of the female universe. In the UK, women were taught that to be the perfect wife they had to mould themselves around their husbands' lives, then their children's, and expect nothing for themselves. Education for girls should focus on cookery, dressmaking, nursing, mothercraft, housecraft and horticulture, nothing more. The influential British journalist Marjorie Proops, by-lined as 'the Queen of Fleet Street', inveighed against 'intelligent girls who spend their youth getting themselves highly educated'. That meant they would 'have little time to devote to the art of making themselves delectable for the opposite sex'.

Dedicating themselves to the opposite sex was the work of every married woman, who was sinking, if not drowning, under a tidal wave of advice and advertising promoting a pernicious, even abusive, domesticity. With hindsight, it was all too clearly designed to restore and reinforce the domination of the male that had been eroded by the competence women had displayed in the Second World War.

The pressure to be a devoted little wife who built her life around her husband was inescapable. And to think that this godalmighty guff was aimed at women who had served in two world wars as farmers and factory hands, tank drivers, ship builders and, not least, riveters like Rosie. Now the centrality of the male was presented as absolute. In order to conform to his standards and his decisions, 'his' female has to demean and diminish herself to live the half-life of a woman described by Elizabeth Cady Stanton over a hundred years earlier at the Seneca Falls Convention: '[Man] has endeavored, in every way that he could, to destroy her confidence in her own powers, to lessen her self-respect, and to make her willing to lead a dependent and abject life.'

show her it's a man's world

So the Van Heusen Man wears his tie in bed ... Is there a semiologist in the house?

This post-war image of the Good Wife proved to be remarkably static for decades. 'Hey, little girl, comb your hair, fix your make-up, soon he will open the door,' warbled Jack Jones, winning a Grammy for Best Vocal Performance in 1963. The song itself became a hit covered by stars as big as Frank Sinatra and Ella Fitzgerald. Let's take a moment to feel out the message behind the boppy Bacharach beat.

- Think rings on fingers but DON'T count on them – you're only here on approval.
- DO NOT let him see you in hair rollers when he is going to work, or he'll just have to fuck the first girl he bumps into in the lift to get over it, and of course all the women he meets at work only want to ensnare a man.
- DO remember that there's only one way to keep hubby happy, according to the warnings rolled out by good ol' Uncle Hal David, the wordsmith of the Bacharach melodies: soft lighting, sweet music, and get him sloshed. Then what follows, he'll think is love, *hey, result, girl, good job, job done!*

OK, babe, you with me?
Put out or he'll push off, that's the deal.
Notice the two strands of this mid-century Guide to Good Wifery, the strict list of verbal instructions and the sappy tune both focus on the moment the husband comes home from work and *Lights! Camera! Action!* the wife is ON. If anything speaks of the distance the world has travelled since 1963, it is the ease with which we can now identify these elements that combined to make it one of the most sexist pop tunes ever produced, even in the sexist 1960s.

What am I today?

Home-maker, lover, mother? The conflicts and contortions required to fulfil all these demands are rarely acknowledged, because the Good Wife made it all look seamless, or else she was getting it wrong – *if they can see how hard you're working, you're not working hard enough!* In addition, these are all roles that define women in relation to other people, never to themselves. Nor is it ever acknowledged that much housework and wife-work is unnecessary, designed to keep the little woman constantly on the go. The American feminist Charlotte Perkins Gilman robustly summed it up: 'A house does not need a wife any more than it does a husband.'

Gilman came to this radical belief after struggling to reconcile the contradictory demands imposed on the Good Wife and the consequent loss of self, something she felt led inexorably to the death of the soul. In her harrowing and semi-autobiographical story of a woman's breakdown, *The Yellow Wallpaper* (1892), we see the destruction at work. Compare this with the novel *All Passion Spent* published decades later in 1931, where marriage means a wasted life for the woman who has destroyed herself by trying to live within it. The author, Vita Sackville-West, born in the year that *The Yellow Wallpaper* was published, offers a bleak conclusion in which the heroine is told:

> Your children, your husband, your splendour, were nothing but obstacles that kept you from yourself. They were what you chose to substitute for your real vocation. You were too young, I suppose, to know any better, but when you chose that life you sinned against the light.

The woman protests, 'But you mustn't blame my husband.'

'I don't,' her accuser replies. 'According to his lights, he gave you all you could desire. He merely killed you, that's all. Men do kill women. Most women enjoy being killed; so I am told.'

Whose revolution is it, exactly?

Was that true? And if so, can it explain why so many women accepted, even embraced, regimes that ran counter to every hope they may have had of freedom and independence as a woman, with the right to decide for themselves?

Fascism, Nazism and communism, for all they promised, meant nothing for women but more of the same. The communist/anarchist communities of Spain in the Civil War of 1936–9 struck out for equality when they began, but could not get beyond the age-old assumption of men's right to dictate the rules of the game. Where women were heard, their voices echo hollowly down the decades, like that of the anti-fascist leader Dolores Ibárruri. Known as La Pasionaria, she became famous for heartening the Republican troops at the Battle of Madrid in 1936 with the ringing cry, '*No pasaran!*' ('They shall not pass!')

They did, of course.

One of the century's most famous women politicians, Ibárruri went from the trenches of the Spanish battlefields to exile in Russia and finally to a seat in the Spanish Parliament at the age of eighty-one. In a career of blazing dedication and furious action, she focused on the plight of Spanish women and their children, founding the women's anti-Fascist organisation Mujeres Antifascistas in 1933. A woman ahead of her time and working in one of the most priest-ridden and male-dominated countries of the Western world, Ibárruri challenged the macho culture of Spain by identifying and promoting the needs of women. Ironically enough, among the thousands who fell under her spell was Mr Macho himself, the young American writer and wannabe war reporter Ernest Hemingway. He killed himself in 1961, but his 1940 portrayal of Ibárruri as Maria, the heroine of his Spanish Civil War novel *For Whom the Bell Tolls*, is unlikely to die.

Best little whorehouse in Buenos Aires – or so they said

But women are not always on the side of free speech, democracy, freedom from tyranny and all that good stuff. One who wholeheartedly embraced the tiger of totalitarianism and rode it to the pinnacle of power was the charismatic Eva Duarte Perón. Her ascent was all the more surprising because the strongly conservative establishment of Argentina loathed her from the start for being low-born and illegitimate, labelling (and libelling) her as a *puta de casa de putas* ('a whore from the house of whores').

It did not hold her back.

Around town one night, the young Eva met the man who was soon to be President of Argentina. She was bright, beautiful, busty and brilliantly blond, courtesy of hydrogen peroxide, the brunette's best friend. He was the widowed Colonel Juan Perón, at forty-eight twice Eva's age and a denizen of another world. That night they slept together, and awoke as a couple. To the astonishment of all, the handsome, charming, powerful Perón, who could have chosen any woman in the world, formed a bond with Eva that lasted until her death.

So began a political career that would have been extraordinary for a man, let alone a woman operating in one of the most macho countries of South America at the time. Married to Perón in 1945, Eva created for herself the role of First Lady and used it to promote welfare programmes for the wretchedly poor, known as the *descamisados* – those without shirts, an echo of the *sans-culottes* of the French Revolution. Eva also established a feminist wing of her husband's ruling party, and ensured that the women of Argentina were granted the vote in 1947.

Not everything associated with Eva was sweetness and light. For a sympathiser with the poor, she had an unfortunate fondness for a luxurious turn-out, and saw no contradiction between other women's straitened way of life and her Dior ball gowns, fine furs and immaculate *coiffure*. Her lowly origins fostered the belief that she was milking the donations to her charitable foundation to heap up cash in overseas bank accounts, a rumour supported by a tour of Europe she made in 1947, delegated by Perón to repair and renew relations with European countries after the end of the war. On that tour, it was later insinuated, Eva received jewels and gold as bribes from former Nazis to smooth their way to safe haven in Argentina. Perón ruled as a strong man in a country familiar with military dictatorships, and to their opponents he and Eva were not friends to the poor but rather demagogues and dictators. The control Eva had at her height over both the President and the people made her arguably the most powerful woman in the world, with a remit few female politicians have held before or since. As a nobody from nowhere and missing the magic factor of being male, how did she do it?

By a magic of her own, as it turned out. An outstanding speaker, Eva Perón had the animal magnetism to connect emotionally and intimately with vast crowds in a way that bordered on the uncanny, convincing every person there that she was talking only to them. Argentina's powerful establishment, the landowners, the military, the Church and the rich, all despised and detested her as a bastard, an *arriviste* and jumped-up hustler who had made a poodle of their President, forcing him to jump through unnatural hoops such as granting women the right to vote. But her hold on the poor and the powerless that they contemptuously dismissed as 'blackheads' was unassailable, not least because she made no secret of the fact that she had been one of them herself. She outlined her agenda for equality and social justice in no uncertain terms:

> It is not philanthropy, nor is it charity … It is not even social welfare; to me, it is strict justice … I do nothing but return to the poor what the rest of us owe them, because we had taken it away from them unjustly.

Revolutionary talk, or what? Eva always had the power to make the privileged shake in their hand-made shoes.

To her death, Eva never lost that power. But like the luckless Diana, Princess of Wales, Eva was forced to accept that the power she derived from the adoration of the people meant nothing without a power base of her own. So when Juan Perón ran for re-election in 1951, she seized the chance to stand as his vice-president. At her final rally in Buenos Aires she drew a crowd of an estimated *two million* supporters, the largest turn-out ever known for a female politician. Packed together under the blistering sun, the people stood for hours weeping, begging and chanting 'Now, Evita, NOW!'. Within sight of political legitimacy, however, Eva was brutally reminded that her loyal constituency counted for nothing in the world of realpolitik. Behind the scenes Argentina's military leaders were preparing a coup, and all the forces of the establishment were massing against her with one imperative: 'Stop this woman, NOW!'

And as it happened, the vice-presidency was already receding from her grasp. Inexplicably fainting and bleeding from January 1950, Eva consulted the most highly esteemed and highly paid doctors from the US, and they all lied. That was the way of it in those old days. The liar-in-chief was her husband, who never allowed Eva to know that she was dying of uterine cancer at the age of thirty-three. But for Eva? Nobody's fool, living with endless pain, blood flooding from her vagina and her weight dwindling to seventy-nine pounds, what was she to think? Still, her man was running for office and the show must go on. Even when she was too weak to stand, Perón continued to use her in his re-election campaign: check out the photographs showing Perón crouched behind Eva with his hands around her waist, holding her up as she woos the crowds on his behalf.

Eva campaigning for Juan Perón in October 1951. Note his hands around her waist, holding her up.

This was not to be Eva's last experience of presidential power. As the cancer progressed and Eva reportedly became unpredictable and aggressive, Peron authorised a pre-frontal lobotomy, a drastic and now disgraced surgical procedure widely used from 1930s to the 1960s that involved cutting through the important connections in the brain. This reduced the patient's spontaneity, initiative and control, leaving them dulled and dependent. Was this the act of a tender, loving husband trying to spare his wife's awareness of her situation in her final months? Or did Eva threaten to become a liability to the President? As it was, she remained an asset to the end. At Perón's triumphal victory parade in June 1952, she dazzled in a long and luxurious fur coat that concealed the padded metal frame holding her upright. A few weeks later, she was dead.

Something in the zeitgeist

Blessed with better health than Eva and a longer life, Eleanor Roosevelt changed the future direction of the world when she led the United Nations General Assembly to adopt the Universal Declaration of Human Rights in 1948. Before the twentieth century, most of the world had not moved far from the view of Aristotle that the human race was divided into separate groups, some of whom had more value than others. It took centuries for this concept of a fixed hierarchy of worth to make way for the radical and shocking idea that all human lives are of equal value and should enjoy equal rights. Furthermore, as Eleanor always insisted, this principle had to be accepted without exception or reservation.

How did Eleanor Roosevelt come to this depth of understanding? Orphaned by the age of ten and handed over to the indifferent care of relatives, she was saved by the charismatic French educator Marie Souvestre. A free-thinker, a feminist and a lesbian, Souvestre turned the awkward fifteen-year-old into a fluent French speaker and opened her mind, as she did with another of her celebrated pupils, the American lesbian, modernist and maverick Natalie Barney.

From France, Eleanor was ordered home by her grandmother to make her debut in society, sheer torture for a painfully shy, six foot tall, big-boned and buck-toothed teenager. Her luck turned when a chance meeting with a distant cousin, Franklin Delano Roosevelt, led to a flurry of love letters and marriage at twenty, after which she bore six children in ten years while her husband focused on the political career that brought him to the White House in 1933. Eleanor, still ill at ease in public, at first recoiled from a life in the spotlight as America's First Lady. But, bowing to the inevitable, she made the role her own.

What does a First Lady do?

First Ladies before Eleanor had been ornamental rather than useful, but she created for herself something to *do*, not just something to *be*. Her activities were all female-centred, from the League of Women Voters and the Women's Trade Union League to the National Consumer League, overseeing the products women used in the home. As First Lady, she rewrote the protocol, transforming the role from that of a non-speaking consort, fashion plate and political nonentity into that of a vibrant communicator and opinion leader on matters great and small.

From the first her approach was logical and professional. Ideas had to be supported by facts, aims prioritised, and work organised for results to flow through. And work Eleanor did, as she had done since her husband lost the use of his legs at the age of thirty-nine after an attack of polio in 1921. Franklin's paralysis was airbrushed from any record at the time, for fear that the public knowledge of his disability would spell death at the polls. From then on, Eleanor had to handle the cover-up while acting as his legs, his eyes and his ears, often standing in for him at events where his inability to walk or to move at all unaided could not be concealed.

But Eleanor had her own agenda too. During her twelve years in the White House, she displayed both the rigour of her early intellectual training and an appetite amounting to a gift for the nuts and bolts of politics, the dry-as-dust workings of the government machine. Day by day, she read the *Congressional Record*, studied committee reports, reviewed the drafts of future legislation, spoke at public meetings and met with Congressmen and Senators to take the prevailing temperature on Capitol Hill. Night after night, she made her own digests and analyses of what she gathered, assessed the progress of projects in hand and devised strategies and tactics for the next stage.

Hard and relentless work with progress measured in centimetres at best, but Eleanor loved it, and she was good at it. Before Franklin became President, she had already made her mark as a teacher, as a writer who contributed numerous articles to the newspapers on social and political affairs, and as an activist and organiser who succeeded in translating her words into deeds. She became the first and only First Lady of the US who

- actively promoted civil rights, counting African Americans as colleagues and friends at a time when the all-American conscience had barely registered the oppression of blacks, and lynchings were common
- took the same attitude to workers' rights, supporting trade unions and legislation to curb the power of the mighty industrialists
- travelled the length and breadth of the country, seeking out neglected rural communities and anywhere the local poor were to be found, to direct national funding to forgotten settlements
- stood in for the President and represented her country abroad, most memorably heartening America's beleaguered ally Britain with a morale-boosting visit in the dark days of 1942, when the Nazis were the military masters of Europe
- summoned different interest groups to the White House, and chaired national and international conferences to get difficult topics onto the agenda
- held regular press conferences and aimed to make government and the White House as open and transparent as possible
- published books – over fifty of them – on topics from democracy to etiquette and the future of India
- made more than three hundred radio broadcasts during her time in the White House including a regular weekly slot,

and wrote a daily newspaper column, 'My Day', which was syndicated to ninety newspapers across the US.

This full and fulfilling life came to an abrupt end in the spring of 1945, when Franklin had a massive stroke and died. Like Eva Perón, Eleanor had parlayed her place at the side of the President into a position of power, but like Eva again, she had no power base of her own. At the end of her forty-year marriage and with the loss of the man who had been her political partner all her adult life, her future gaped before her like an open grave.

Single again and deep in middle age, what was she to do? America knew.

Forget the widow's cap and shawl, lady, came the message from Franklin's successor, Harry S. Truman, when in December 1945 he nominated Eleanor Roosevelt as a delegate to the newly formed United Nations. It was a brilliant appointment. Eleanor's analytical but open mind sweeping the landscape like a search light, her subtle sense of all the players in the game whether or not they were present at the table, her forensic ability to detect the rocks and hard places in the negotiation ahead, and her skill in piloting all comers through the whirlpool of their clashing needs to bring their ships to the shore: these were all attributes too valuable for her country to waste.

Far harder work was handling the rugged opposition and settled enmity of the Soviet bloc in one of the bitterest phases of the Cold War. Throw in the sheer bloody-mindedness of Saudi Arabia and South Africa, both regimes founded on gross inequality and a fixed belief in hierarchies of worth, and it is little short of astonishing that Eleanor succeeded in driving through the creation of a Universal Declaration of Human Rights. Nor did she assume, as many had done before, that 'human rights' only meant the rights of man. As she had said earlier in her career, 'the battle for the individual rights of women is one of long standing and none of us should countenance anything which undermines it'.

The Declaration was formally adopted by the UN General Assembly on 10 December 1948. It remains a landmark in the dialogue between nations and individuals, despite the subsequent behaviour of signatories like Saudi Arabia and Russia. Eleanor herself considered it to be her finest achievement. Less well known was her success in overcoming a lifetime of indifference, malice, bullying, betrayal and hate.

It began with Eleanor's mother, Anna Hall Roosevelt, who nicknamed her 'very plain' and 'old-fashioned' child 'Granny'. Meeting her cousin Franklin, also a Roosevelt, brought the eighteen-year-old Eleanor into the orbit of his pathologically domineering mother, Sara Delano Roosevelt, a woman for whom every day was Mother's Day, *or else*. Widowed for many years, Sara was so possessive of her only son that when the young couple got married she bought the house next door, and knocked through the party wall so that she could come and go as she pleased. In public Sara also constantly criticised Eleanor's hair, clothes and lack of style. Franklin himself was not above joining in the fun at his wife's expense, on one occasion leading a dinner table demand for 'Eleanor Roosevelt jokes' with the hilarious question mocking her protruding front teeth: 'Who's the only woman in America who can eat corn through a fence?'

Secrets and lies

Still, Franklin loved Eleanor enough to defy his mother and marry her, he fostered her political ability before she recognised it in herself, and he knew how much she had contributed to his career. But this coexisted with a series of infidelities, most notably an affair with Eleanor's secretary, Lucy Mercer, at the same time as he was reportedly conducting another with his own.

When Eleanor came across a tell-tale bundle of love letters from Lucy in September 1918, her mother-in-law furiously forbade a divorce and she agreed to carry on. Franklin told his mistress that Eleanor had refused to divorce him and told Eleanor that the affair was over, then he too carried on as before.

Politically, Roosevelt was widely respected for the New Deal, his programme of recovery from the worst economic collapse the industrialised world had ever seen – the catastrophic New York Stock Market crash of 1929. But in his personal life, it was the Old Deal all the way. When he died suddenly in 1945, the Roosevelts' daughter Anna, involved by her father in her childhood as the lovers' go-between, had to tell her mother that the relationship with Lucy had continued even after she had married another man, and Franklin had died in her arms. How did Eleanor deal with this? Only by an extraordinary greatness of soul that seems to have been the hallmark of her character. Going through Franklin's effects afterwards, she came across the watercolour of a portrait of him that Lucy had arranged, and sent it to her to show that she bore no ill will. Lucy was overwhelmed by this selfless generosity.

Communism, tovarich?

Eleanor also turned to the age-old panacea for grief, her work. Busy at the UN developing a protocol for equality and human rights, and dealing with opposition from the political right as well as from the left, she met none more hostile to these ideals than the communists. Like all the new twentieth-century ideologies, communism never confronted or even acknowledged the contradiction at its heart that whatever the rhetoric surrounding its dogma of equality, the revolution of 1917 brought no change to the primeval structures of inequality and to women's imposed inferiority.

Communism versus capitalism: capitalism too could not contemplate or even conceive of making its women more equal than they were. This did not stop political leaders from playing the domestic card when it suited them. At the opening of the American National Exhibition in Moscow in 1959, the Russian president Nikita Khrushchev and the US Vice-President Richard Nixon met in a mock-up of an all-American kitchen and engaged in what was called without irony the 'Kitchen Debate', when in all likelihood neither man could have so much as boiled an egg.

The two men scrapped vigorously over the way they treated the female half of the population. In the blue corner, Nixon maintained that America valued its women in the home where they kept the family together and where they were rewarded with the finest, fanciest fridges, food blenders, washing machines and all the domestic appliances that US engineers could create. In the red corner, Khrushchev dismissed the very idea of confining women to a life of domesticity and house-bound consumerism. 'Your capitalistic attitude toward women does not occur under communism,' he reproved Nixon loftily. Writing in the comments book, Russian visitors to the exhibition agreed that the 'miracle kitchen' set up by General Electric was unnecessary. 'We don't need it,' one declared, 'because we are striving to free our women from kitchen work entirely.' Far from liberating women from domestic labour, the new model kitchen represented a new form of enslavement: house arrest, if you will.

A classic example of political posturing, Khrushchev's assertion went unchallenged at the time. But under communism a woman's much-vaunted freedom to work outside the home came at the cost first faced by British women in the Industrial Revolution. Toiling like men in factories, mills and fields, every woman came home for the second, far more punishing, domestic shift, and a shortened life as a result.

Reds under the bed

In post-war America, despite the wartime alliance with Russia, the relationship had begun to sour before the ink on Germany's surrender had time to dry. One of the great psychopaths of history, Stalin spent more money, manpower and time during the war spying upon his allies than he did on his enemies. So when the guns fell silent in 1945, he upped the ante to treat allies and former enemies alike. Soviet intelligence forces set up undercover networks throughout the major nations of the world, from Britain to Finland and Germany and France, and from Japan to the United States.

Once this was understood, the full implications of the Cold War became clear. In this atmosphere of generalised anxiety and even paranoia, one man grossly exploited the public's fear that hundreds of communists had infiltrated the government and had to be rooted out. To anyone who could count, Senator Joseph McCarthy was a wrong 'un from the start. Launching his crusade at the Republican Women's Club of West Virginia in 1950, he claimed to have in his pocket a list of two hundred and five communists, a figure that changed to fifty-seven, then eighty-one, and soared into the hundreds and thousands as his power and popularity rose.

In the way that women often have of seeing through male fantasy and braggadocio, the first person to question McCarthy's campaign was a fellow Republican, Margaret Chase Smith. She was a widely respected Senator from Maine, who found it contrary to fundamental American values and devoid of 'political integrity or intellectual honesty'. But McCarthy's assertions chimed too well with the nation's fears, and the first line of the famous interrogation, or rather intimidation, 'Are you now or have you ever been a member of the Communist Party?' became as familiar to Americans as 'Twinkle, twinkle, little star'.

If the US had only listened to Margaret Chase Smith, decades of shame and suffering would have been spared. Investigative reporters later exposed a thorough and thuggish persecution of anyone who showed up on McCarthy's radar, politicians and civil servants, actors, writers and producers, a good many of whom were blacklisted and ruined for life. The poet and writer Dorothy Parker had contributed as a screenwriter to films like *A Star is Born* and *The Little Foxes*, and had been nominated for several Academy Awards. But her last screenplay was Otto Preminger's *The Fan* in 1949. After she appeared on a list of 'communist sympathisers' in 1950, she never worked in Hollywood again.

It happened across the board. Lillian Hellman, despite her many successes on stage and screen, was reportedly so nervous when answering a summons to appear before McCarthy's House Un-American Activities Committee that she reached for a flamboyant gesture to make herself feel better, and tipped the taxi driver who took her there a hundred dollars. She had previously told the Committee, 'I cannot and will not cut my conscience to fit this year's fashions,' offering to admit anything about herself, but refusing to name anyone else. Her offer was refused, and she too was washed up in Hollywood at the height of her career.

But the America that had allowed McCarthy to conduct his witch hunt was the same America that finally called this fraudster, fantasist and fear-monger to account. The great American conscience kicked in, and just as one woman, the senator Margaret Chase Smith, was the first to call him out, so another triggered the process that brought him down. Targeting major international and hugely powerful invisible enemies of America was one thing. But when his mysterious commie-detecting machine lit on an insignificant, respectable and hard-working woman, it proved to be too much for the country to take.

And Annie Lee Moss was indeed all of the above, a lowly communications clerk working for the Army Signals Corps at the Pentagon who came to McCarthy's attention when he sought to prove that the military was 'riddled with communists'. The standard McCarthy method of accusation without evidence was laid bare when the headline-grabbing claim that Moss was a danger to national security because she dealt with 'the encoding and decoding of confidential and top-secret messages' was flatly contradicted by the information that everything at her grade was encrypted, and she had no access to anything of any importance.

Moss's lack of sophistication was obvious when she appeared before the House Permanent Sub-committee on Investigations on 11 March 1954. Questioned about Karl Marx, she asked, 'Who's that?' Her grilling by McCarthy's chief counsel, Roy

Annie Lee Moss under interrogation by the McCarthy Committee.

Cohn, aroused deep concern, provoking the journalist Ed Murrow to produce a TV report he called 'a little picture about a little woman'.

Murrow's focus on the treatment of Moss and its clear abuse of American processes and values resonated through the country. According to Drew Pearson, another respected journalist in McCarthy's home state, 'Wisconsin folks saw her as a nice old colored lady who wasn't harming anyone and they didn't like their senator picking on her.' A 'Joe Must Go!' campaign swept through the land, the Senate passed a vote of censure and McCarthy's political career was over.

And little old harmless Annie?

In fact she *was* a card-carrying communist (and only forty-nine at the time of her testimony) although the evidence for this, including her Communist Party card, did not emerge until after her death in 1996. It was also clear from the outset that she had not worked as a spy, nor had any contact with Soviet agents in America. But other women had traded on the kind of non-threatening ordinariness that Moss embodied, and exploited the general assumption that women were just part of the furniture. Let's meet Melita Norwood, the insignificant Englishwoman the Russians prized as one of the most valuable spies in their entire network, and who served the cause longer than any other of their overseas agents.

Norwood drudged at the British Non-Ferrous Metals Research Association as a secretary so drab that even when the British got wind of her they thought she was no more than a tiny cog in the machine. In truth, Norwood *was* the machine. Not one of the men working with her noticed the small woman flitting quietly between the filing cabinets in her beige cardigan and white blouse, or clocked the fact that as secretary to the project director of the British Atomic Works Project, all his files passed across her desk. During a working life of forty years, she handed over a stream of secrets to Moscow, most notably the blueprint for the atom bomb, which enabled the Russians to build their own bomb within the year.

Norwood was never paid for any of this. A convinced communist, she later said that she had acted to defend the 'new system' that cared for its people so well, although she never visited Russia or saw communism in action. In 1992 the senior KGB officer in the Soviet Foreign Intelligence Directorate, Vasili Mitrokhin, defected to Britain and revealed exactly what Norwood had done to make her such a huge asset to Soviet intelligence. But no one believed him. Norwood was never arrested, prosecuted or even questioned, and lived on into a peaceful, beige retirement in the peaceful, beige suburb of Bexleyheath.

The American communist Ethel Rosenberg met a different fate. Implicated with her husband Julius in spying for Russia at the height of the Cold War, she was accused of selling her country's atom bomb secrets to the Russians, the very offence from which Melita Norwood would skip away scot free. Unlike Norwood, who methodically betrayed her country's secrets for decades, the extent of Ethel's 'spying' lay in acting as a typist and assistant to her husband Julius. When she refused to give evidence against him, she was prosecuted and sentenced to death, in the belief that she would then crack and incriminate him, to save her own life for the sake of their two young children. She did not. Ethel Rosenberg was the only woman and one of the only two people (the other being Julius) executed for un-American activities in the whole of the Cold War.

A world free for all!

... was the rallying cry at the end of the Second World War. *Free, did they say?*

Not for women, and not yet.

Both East and West were taken up for much of the century with wars great and small, each one followed by an uneasy, queasy peace until war, hot or cold, broke out again like the plague.

That was the story of Vietnam. The post-1945 struggle of the Vietnamese against their imperial master, France, morphed into a full-blown war in 1955, when Uncle Sam came calling with his pockets full of gold. American 'aid' to South Vietnam lasted until 1975, and created the longest and worst conflict in US history, tying up their military, their economy and their politics for twenty years. It cost over $168 billion, fifty-eight thousand American lives, and an estimated two million lives of Vietnamese − thirty-five times as many as those lost by their invaders. In addition, it became one of the most widely condemned wars of all time, with protest marches and demonstrations around the globe.

And where were the women in all this?

They were right there in the thick of it, over eleven thousand of them.

Some ten thousand American servicewomen were stationed in-country during the conflict, wearing the uniforms of the US Army, Air Force, Navy and Marine Corps. Also serving were more than one thousand non-military female personnel, almost all of them volunteers, who worked as librarians, clerks, air traffic controllers, communications specialists and intelligence officers. Other women were there as missionaries and officers of various charities, often with overlapping roles such as missionary doctors and nurses. In a guerrilla war like this, there was no safety behind the lines and whatever their role, many were drawn into the combat. Sixty-seven women lost their lives in Vietnam, mainly civilians. Of the eight military women who perished, only two died from natural causes (pneumonia and a stroke), while six were shot down in helicopters or fatally wounded under attack. All their names are listed on the monument to the fallen known as 'The Wall', part of the Vietnam Veterans Memorial in Washington DC.

Of the other fifty-nine, thirty-seven volunteers were killed during the disastrous Operation Babylift of 1975, when a plane evacuating South Vietnamese orphans crashed shortly after take-off. Other volunteers, mainly from religious or missionary organisations, died in bomb incidents, jeep accidents or random actions of the Viet Cong. Dr Eleanor Vietti, an American missionary working at a leper colony, was taken by guerrillas in May 1962, presumably to tend their wounded, and never seen again. Rumours of a doctor treating the Viet Cong, of a white woman in a remote village pleading for a copy of the Bible, continued to surface until the 1970s. But by 1991, Vietti was listed as 'presumed dead' on the official Prisoner of War/Missing in Action roll. She is the only American female casualty of the Vietnam War who remains unaccounted for, and the only woman left behind.

In contrast, the families of the US nurses Beatrice Kosin and Evelyn Anderson might well have chosen not to know what happened to them. Working at a missionary hospital in Laos that treated all comers, the two women were taken prisoner in a Viet Cong attack of October 1972. Hidden in a hut, Anderson and Kosin were secured back to back, wired by their wrists to the central roof pole. A search and rescue operation was already in the air when the command came from the US embassy to abort the mission. Peace negotiations were 'pending', and it would not do to embarrass the North Vietnamese. To both sides, the women were disposable. Ready to move on, their captors set fire to the hut and burned them alive.

The story of the women in this war has been long buried. Those who survived to come home then had to face the general revulsion displayed towards all the veterans of this peculiarly bitter engagement. Claire Brisebois Starnes, who had served as a staff sergeant in the US Army Signal Corps and in the Military Office of Information, was not the only returner who reported being heckled and spat on at the airport as soon as they got off the plane. Trying to join a group therapy session for veterans, Starnes also found herself being rejected by the men she had fought alongside in Vietnam, who now shouted at her and drove her away. Frequently attacked and abused as 'baby-killers' themselves, the men apparently took out their anger and shame on the women, unable to believe that they could have understood or shared the horror and the misery of it all.

The women soon learned to conceal or deny that they had played any part in the conflict, said Starnes. This rule of silence continued until 1999 when she and others formed the Vietnam Women Veterans group. But at the time they most needed understanding and support, the public had yet to accept the declaration that appears on the Women's Memorial at the Arlington National Cemetery:

> Let the generations know that women in uniform also guaranteed their freedom.

'Revolution is an act of love'

So said Jane Fonda: 'We are the children of revolution, born to be rebels. It runs in our blood.' Taking a stand against the Vietnam War and in favour of the Viet Cong made her the best-known woman of the entire conflict, and for a time the most hated female in America. A natural rebel, she had already been involved in the counter-culture of the 1960s, active in both civil rights protests and in the early days of the women's movement, before turning her attention to Vietnam. As the fighting intensified, public dissatisfaction grew. 'Our government was lying to us and men were dying because of it, and I felt I had to do anything that I could to expose the lies and help end the war,' Fonda would later explain. She began by raising funds for the Vietnam Veterans Against the War campaign in the early 1970s, then in 1972 she travelled to Hanoi to see for herself.

So began an episode that proved hard, if not impossible, to shrug off. Meeting with the communist North Vietnamese, Fonda was seen as fraternising with the enemy. In the eyes of the American public, her broadcasts on Hanoi Radio reporting the damage the US had inflicted put her on a par with Second World War enemy broadcasters like Tokyo Rose. A photograph of Fonda sitting on a Viet Cong anti-aircraft gun earned her the nickname 'Hanoi Jane' and the undying hatred of millions. At aged eighty-one she remains an activist, now for the climate change group Extinction Rebellion.

The Vietnam War was one that no one could win. But some tried. The woman known as 'Madame Nhu' became the First Lady of South Vietnam in 1955 because the President, Ngô Đình Diêm, her brother-in-law, was unmarried. High-born, petite and doe-eyed, Madame Nhu had the face of an angel, the instincts of Ivan the Terrible and a sense of entitlement twice as big as the Ritz. By the time of the Vietnam War, the sheer force of her personality had made her so powerful that President Diêm himself was afraid of her. To the horror of all, she famously ordered him in public to 'Shut up!', and when one angry general threatened to overthrow Diêm and then take her for himself, she screamed at him that he hadn't got the balls for either, and she'd claw his throat out first.

Small wonder then that she was called the 'Dragon Lady' throughout the region, after a well-known cartoon character of the time. Claiming credit as a moderniser, she proudly championed women's rights and in 1962 formed the Women's

Solidarity Movement, an all-female elite paramilitary organisation twenty-five thousand strong, of which membership was not voluntary. At the same time, the nation's First Feminist was busy ramming through parliament various laws banning contraception, abortion, adultery and divorce, in line with her new-found Catholic beliefs. Her religious conversion only strengthened her animosity towards her cradle faith, Buddhism, and she openly displayed her vicious aversion to the monks who burned themselves alive in protest against the government she now controlled. 'I would clap my hands at seeing another monk barbecue show!' she crowed, and offered to bring along the mustard.

US officials, from the newest State Department gopher to Lyndon Johnson himself, were forced to deal with her as the President's representative, and found themselves constantly infuriated by her inflammatory rhetoric and unsettled by her violence. But baffled, bamboozled, wrong-footed and simply ignored by her, they entirely failed to get her under any kind of control. Her attitude to the US was like that of a gold-digger to a doting, enfeebled sugar daddy: rapacious and contemptuous in equal measure. At her insistence Uncle Sam coughed up a magnificent twenty thousand dollars in 1962 to pay for a statue of the legendary Tru'ng sisters, Vietnamese heroines who, when the finished work was revealed, both proved to have a close resemblance to Madame Nhu herself. American observers could also see their tax dollars at work on other vanity projects, when funds intended for government spending on the army, for instance, were diverted to pay for the First Lady's all-female paramilitary posers, her model army of high-born women all serving her with the sole purpose of advancing their husbands' careers.

'Power is wonderful,' she gloated. 'Total power is totally wonderful.' Forget the money: nothing could ever be enough for Madame Nhu until the US had pounded North Vietnam into extinction, wiping it from the face of the earth. Under pressure from the Dragon Lady, and indeed from his own generals and industrialists who were doing well out of the war, President Johnson threw over half a million troops into the death trap of the Mekong Delta in support of the South. At her behest, it was said, the President ordered punitive air strikes to pulverise the undefended North, attacks that had no military justification and succeeded only in strengthening the resolve of this small and underdeveloped country to fight back.

Johnson's aides whispered behind their hands that the President was afraid of her – as was everyone else. The then Defense Secretary, Robert McNamara, noted that he 'saw Madame Nhu as bright, forceful, and beautiful, but also diabolical and scheming – a true sorceress'. But he too was defeated by the volcanic power of her uniquely demanding personality. He later wrote that America 'could and should have withdrawn from South Vietnam' in late 1963, and admitted that his judgement had simply failed.

Confucius rules, OK?

Madame Nhu was that unusual thing, an out-and-out female monster who survived the consequences of her machinations to die in her own bed – on the French Riviera, no less. In contrast, the lesser women in Vietnam, as she would have rated them, had no power and no rights. They were born into the social structure that had evolved from the writings of the great sage Confucius, who mansplained in all his teachings that women owed total obedience to every man in their lives, from the local lord to their youngest son. The French invaders (*sorry, colonists delivering the benefits of civilisation*) saw no reason to challenge such a serviceable arrangement, and vigorously exercised their imperial *droit de seigneur* when and where they pleased.

Little wonder then that the women of North Vietnam had every reason to fight the French and to hate the Americans, who had created the war in order to protect the world from the evils of communism and had only succeeded in blowing their country apart. And in the tracks of the Tru'ng sisters, the warrior queens who had defeated the Chinese army in 40 CE, along they came to join the struggle in droves. Understandably, the American soldiers never considered that these women, no more than tiny childlike creatures to them, could pose any kind of threat, let alone become guerrilla fighters as effective as any man. Despite their size, the women also served as porters, carrying massive loads for miles along the Ho Chi Minh Trail to keep the North Vietnam forces supplied. Like the eight hundred thousand Russian women who served in the Second World War, the women of Vietnam made a significant difference to the war on the ground, and played an incalculable part in America's eventual withdrawal.

'For you, Big Boy, the war is over.'

The Vietnam War ended in 1975, but the repercussions were immense. Vietnam was increasingly seen as a dirty, low-down, dishonest business in which President Johnson and advisers like Robert McNamara had recklessly squandered the goodwill the country had built up in previous wars, as evidenced by the difference between the reception the Vietnam vets received and the heroes' welcome accorded to the soldiers of the Second World War. The rage expressed in the worldwide anti-war protests emerged throughout popular culture in films like *The Deer Hunter* (1978), and fostered a generation of disaffected and often dangerously angry youth.

The twentieth century delivered two world wars and a thousand lesser conflicts, along with assorted mini-revolutions, rebellions and revolts. Militarism, communism, fascism, totalitarianism had strutted their stuff, and after all this, were women any better off than before? That well-known cultural commissar of Hollywood and a veteran of nine marriages, Zsa Zsa Gabor, summed it up: 'I've been married to a communist and a fascist, and neither of them would take out the trash.'

What would it take to change that?

CHAPTER 8

IS THIS ALL?

We really believed that we were building a new world.

DOROTHY HEIGHT

It is *new* for women to be making history – not just
a few queens, empresses or exceptional geniuses, but
hundreds, thousands, millions of women now entering
history, knowing we have made history – by changing
our own lives.

BETTY FRIEDAN

Vimochana.

SANSKRIT: 'LIBERATION'

All the world was racked with uncertainty in the unsettled post-war years. The lost millions of Europe were not alone in their experience of displacement and fear. A similar experience met black GIs, who came back to a colour bar so strong that most of them could not get a job. What should have been a joyous return was poisoned by the realisation that the US government could throw thousands of troops and millions of dollars into fighting for freedom in Europe, but had no interest in freedom for black Americans back home.

This proved a powerful impetus for the birth of the civil rights movement in the 1960s. Yet the male vocabulary of the fight for black freedom perpetuated the notion that it was men who needed freedom. In a legendary speech at the Democratic Party Convention of 1948, Senator Hubert Humphrey urged his party to fight racial segregation and to walk 'into the bright sunshine of human rights'. 'We place our faith in the brotherhood of man under the fatherhood of God,' he declaimed. America offered 'the last best hope on earth . . . of a land when all men are free and equal and each man uses his freedom equally and well'. Did the well-meaning senator think that the women of the Land of the Free were also free and equal?

Uncivil rights

Rosa Parks is remembered as the person sitting quietly in the 'coloured' section of a bus in Alabama in 1955 who refused to give up her seat when four white passengers came on board. The segregation operated in Southern buses had long been a running sore for blacks, forced to pay their fare at the front then walk back to use the 'coloureds' entrance at the rear (if the driver had not already had a little 'fun' by driving away without them).

Parks was not the first to confront these customs head on. The writer, editor, feminist, suffragist and civil rights activist Ida B. Wells had refused to give up a 'white' seat on a train as early as 1884, and was forcibly removed by the driver and two conductors.

Wells sued, only to find that her first lawyer (black) was being bribed by the train company to ensure that the case failed. Hiring another (white) she won her case, and five hundred dollars in damages. When the train company appealed, the Tennessee Supreme Court ruled that Wells was not the victim deserving damages but the damage itself. She was ordered to pay the court costs, or go to prison. Wells's response to the judgment came *de profundis*: 'O God, is there no redress, no peace, no justice in this land for us?'

But who did she mean by *us*?

Here is Martin Luther King:

> We know through painful experience that freedom is never voluntarily given by the oppressor; it must be demanded by the oppressed.

But the oppressed spoken for, lived and died for, were men. When Rosa Parks started working at her local branch of the National Association for the Advancement of Colored People in 1943, her boss, the Alabama civil rights leader Edgar Nixon, told her that 'Women don't need to be nowhere but in the kitchen.' To the question 'What about me?' he replied, 'I need a secretary, and you're a good one.' She was in that role for the next fourteen years.

Over the years, Ida B. Wells and many other women came to see that the 'us' they thought they were fighting for constituted only the male half of the population. Intent on the cause of civil rights, they fully understood oppression as outlined by William Du Bois: individuals deprived of rights, condemned to perpetual inferiority and given only the smallest chance of advancement, if that. And like the white women abolitionists who came to see that they were fighting to give rights to slaves that they would never have themselves, so it became clear to the black women involved in the civil rights movement that these very terms of oppression applied to them not only as people of colour, but as females too.

Just as American women's struggle for the vote sprang from their involvement in the fight against slavery, many women – and men too – came to the 1960s struggle for women's liberation through their work in civil rights. But the subordination of women and the corresponding centralisation of men was so *embedded* that they were invisible even to those who concerned themselves deeply and sincerely with the injustices of the world. In 1962 a group of ardent young American thinkers formed Students for a Democratic Society. In a searing manifesto they attacked the atom bomb, capitalism, the military–industrial complex, the US government for supporting right-wing governments overseas, and the leaders of the USSR for suppressing left-wing protest at home – no turn unstoned. But even they fell in with the idea that 'man' was universal:

> We regard men as infinitely precious and possessed of unfulfilled capacities for reason, freedom and love ... human brotherhood must be willed, however, as a condition of future survival and as the most appropriate form of social relations. Personal links between man and man are needed, especially to go beyond the partial and fragmentary bonds of function that bind men only as worker to worker, employer to employee, teacher to student, American to Russian.

Well, whadda y'know, it's that MAN again. It took the women's liberation movement to tell the world that 'mankind' really did mean man – and it didn't include woman.

Women and children last . . .

Of all the battles of the post-war world, none was harder than the fight for women to establish lives of their own. The use of 'man' for human being, 'mankind' for the human race and 'men' to include all women was so commonplace that it was never questioned, and remains enshrined in legislation and documentation throughout the English-speaking world. Un-thinking the power of man, identifying and dismantling the props that have shored up human mental processes for millennia, was a hard and painful process for women and men alike.

And so long drawn-out. The first call to arms in the twentieth century came from Simone de Beauvoir, who published *The Second Sex* in 1949. Already famous for her own writing as well as for her relationship with her fellow philosopher Jean-Paul Sartre, de Beauvoir drew on history, biology, culture, myth and literature to expose how women were treated as inferior to men from birth, and trained to be secondary in every aspect of life. Man was the standard and the norm and woman was the 'other', everything that man was not. It was immediately recognised as a major work both of philosophy and feminism, selling twenty-two thousand copies in its first week and getting banned by the Vatican. Making its way to the English-speaking world via a 1953 translation, it influenced many emerging feminists, including Betty Friedan and Kate Millett.

No one who knew de Beauvoir was surprised by her success. Academically precocious, she graduated from the Sorbonne as one of only a handful of women, and became the youngest person to pass the highly competitive postgraduate philosophy examination of the École Normale Supérieure at the age of twenty-one. Originally marked for first prize, she was downgraded in favour of Sartre because he was a student at the École (an all-male college she could not have joined), and because the examiners considered that he needed a leg-up on his second attempt, having failed the first time. De Beauvoir, knowing none of this, accepted the verdict without reservation. 'I was intelligent, certainly,' she said later, 'but Sartre was a genius.'

Sartre went on to become one of France's most revered writers and philosophers, but de Beauvoir too built a worldwide reputation with the success of *The Second Sex*. In the 1970s she involved herself in the women's liberation movement in France, drawing up the (in)famous *Manifesto of the 343* in April 1971. 'The 343' were women who, like her, had had abortions, then illegal in Catholic France. The famous among them, such as Catherine Deneuve, Sonia Rykiel and Françoise Sagan, were courting public hate and vitriolic censure, and they were all at risk of criminal prosecution and imprisonment.

To offer the women some legal protection, the feminist lawyer Gisèle Halimi, herself one of the 343, founded the group Choisir ('To Choose'). Not one of the 343 was prosecuted and 331 doctors later published a manifesto stating that they had all carried out abortions. In January 1975 abortion became legal in France. After two thousand years, Feminism with a capital F was coming to life again.

The gender agenda

'Women's liberation', as it was known, was the product of half a century of growing disillusion in the aftermath of winning the vote. The heroic, costly and divisive struggles of the early twentieth century had led to women supposedly being able to vote as men did, get an education and enter the professions as men did, work outside the house as men did – and yet they found that they were still denied key civic and legal rights. Every married woman in the West was defined by her partnership with a man, and much of society still operated on the age-old rule of English common law that 'man and wife is one flesh' and that was the man's. The world had changed, history had changed, women had changed, and men? Men ... were still thinking about it and often trying not to think about it, especially as it touched their own lives.

'Let woman out of the home, let man into it, should be the aim of education,' advised the American activist and Nobel Prize-winning writer Pearl S. Buck. 'The home needs man, and the world outside needs woman.' *Let women also create the home* was the motto of the women architects who broke through in the twentieth century. Irish-born Eileen Gray had trained to design and build houses, not merely to decorate homes. In 1919 she was commissioned to redesign the Rue de Lota flat of the Paris fashionista and society hostess Madame Mathieu Lévy. Gray stripped the walls and floor of colour to create a clean, simple background, then filled the space with lacquered tables, white leather furniture and animal skins. The final effect was a perfect blend of Modernism's austere mantra 'less is more' with the rich luxury befitting her patron's tastes and expectations, a signature look she was to perfect in the years to come.

Gray also counted the fashion leader Elsa Schiaparelli among her wealthy and famous clients in the South of France, where she had made her home. Additionally, she created iconic pieces of furniture regarded as works of art in themselves. She gave them names as if they were alive, and her breath-taking *Fauteuil aux Dragons* (Dragons' Armchair), made between 1917 and 1919, became a particular treasure in the collection of Yves Saint Laurent. It later sold for a record £19.4 million in 2009, achieving the highest price then paid at auction for a piece of twentieth-century design.

But Gray's masterpiece was undoubtedly the pale concrete house she designed and built in 1929 on a cliff overlooking the Mediterranean, as a romantic hideaway for her and her secret lover, the French-Romanian architect and critic Jean Badovici. An unexpected and intriguing blend of steps, balconies, solid shapes and space, the building known as E-1027 was immediately recognised as a *tour de force* for Gray's inspired response to the difficult location, and for her transformation of the blank interiors beloved by the male Modernists into something welcoming, warm and kind. The much-admired buildings designed by Le Corbusier had proved hard to live in, bleak white blocky cubes in which tables and chairs and signs of human comfort struggled to find a place.

But in the world of Modernism, Le Corbusier was king. Fast-forward to 1938, when the love affair was over, Gray had left the house and Badovici invited Le Corbusier for a visit. Was it professional jealousy? Unlike Gray, Le Corbusier had never completed an architectural course or gained any qualification in his life. Or was it rage that a woman had created a Modernist work that was seen as a rebuke to his own? Whatever the reason and with or without Badovici's permission (accounts vary), Le Corbusier picked up a paintbrush and set about covering the plain-washed and peaceful walls of Gray's beloved home with crude and lurid murals, an act of deliberate vandalism that Badovici did nothing to prevent. In the words of the British art critic Rowan Moore, 'As an act of naked phallocracy, Corbusier's actions are hard to top.'

How long, O Lord, how long?

Alas, Le Corbusier was not the last nor the worst of the great phallocrats. When those heroic gender warriors, the Cambridge scientists James Watson and Francis Crick, used the crucial work of Rosalind Franklin in the discovery of DNA in 1953, she got the el-bow and they got the Nob-el. Franklin had died in 1958 and so would not have been eligible for the prize, but there is no doubt that her critical role in this iconic discovery went unacknowledged for many years

A similar fate befell the British astrophysicist Jocelyn Bell Burnell, when her superior and his deputy were both recognised for their work on the discovery of pulsars in 1974. Bell Burnell, then a research student, was central to this breakthrough, because she was the first to notice and record the strange and inexplicable signals, but she resolutely resisted expressing any resentment. 'Arguably, my student status and perhaps my gender were my downfall with respect to the Nobel Prize,' she said. 'At that time, science was still perceived as being carried out by distinguished men leading teams of unrecognised minions who did their bidding and did not themselves contribute anything other than as instructed!'

Be that as it may, sometimes she who laughs last, laughs all the way to her place in history. Bell Burnell was subsequently recognised for her discovery and loaded with honours worldwide, including a damehood from the British establishment and the Herschel Medal, a pleasing link to Caroline, her sister star-reader from an earlier epoch. In 2018, she was chosen by a panel of leading scientists to receive the $3 million Breakthrough Prize in Fundamental Physics for her landmark work on pulsars and a lifetime of inspiring leadership in the scientific community, the crowning achievement of a truly stellar career. 'I've done very well out of not getting a Nobel Prize,' she quipped, and immediately donated the entire sum to the Institute of Physics for the UK and Ireland, to establish research opportunities for people from groups underrepresented in physics.

But what hope for the average woman when exceptional talents like Gray, Franklin and Bell Burnell faced resistance like this? Self-doubt and anxiety among women at home grew and spread like mould, all the more inexplicable because it was so hard to pin down. Millions of them sensed it, but at the forefront of those who felt it and smelt it, got to grips with it and gave it to the world was Betty Friedan. A standing ovation, then, for one of the mothers of the modern women's movement, a driving force in one of the greatest rebellions of the twentieth century and beyond.

Betty Friedan, the Mother of the Women's Liberation Movement and first among equals in the work to change the world.

Magnificently cantankerous in her later years when I knew her, Friedan was a rebel from early on, never at ease in her staid community of Peoria, Illinois. As a girl denied the chance to write for the school newspaper, she started her own. A keen student, she left college with an armful of awards, a fellowship to study for a PhD and a bright future ahead. But her then boyfriend persuaded her to give it all up, and she settled for a life dictated by the domestic, not the intellectual, nor the professional, nor anything else that a brilliant male graduate would have taken for granted. Marriage followed, and three children.

At a college reunion fourteen years later, she was struck by how many of the women there had made the same choice. They had thrown all their intelligence, all their dedication, all their capacity for hard work, into becoming the Good Wife and Perfect Mother. They were living up to the all-American image of womanly fulfilment and doing their level best to make it work. But deep in their souls, as Friedan discovered, there was a question that would not go away:

> The problem lay buried, unspoken, for many years in the minds of American women. It was a strange stirring, a sense of dissatisfaction, a yearning that women suffered in the middle of the twentieth century in the United States. Each suburban wife struggled with it alone. As she made the beds, shopped for groceries, matched slip-cover material, ate peanut butter sandwiches with her children, chauffeured Cub Scouts and Brownies, lay beside her husband at night – she was afraid to ask even of herself the silent question – 'Is this all?'

Is this all?

Painstakingly interviewing woman after woman, Friedan pieced together the evidence for what she called 'the feminine mystique' in her break-out book of that title which appeared in 1963. Women who had for years been happy to fill in 'Occupation: Housewife' on official forms, now described feeling 'empty, somehow', and 'incomplete', 'as if I don't exist'. Friedan understood. She saw that for every one of these women her status, her very existence depended on being some man's wife. Any hope of independence, of autonomy or personal authority, all had to be sacrificed on the altar of the extreme ideal of womanhood called 'femininity'. As she dug deeper, the pressure on a woman to live up to it was, in Friedan's eyes, inherently destructive of her life, her soul, her self.

Friedan was not alone in suggesting that this deep and unacknowledged suffering of women's strangled selfhood lay behind other 'female' diseases like depression, sexual frigidity, mental breakdown and even suicide. Charlotte Perkins Gilman had drawn that same conclusion almost a century before. Unlike Gilman, however, Friedan did not lay the blame on men. 'Man is not the enemy here,' Friedan insisted, 'but the fellow victim. The real enemy is women's denigration of themselves, fostered by the feminine mystique.' But the unquestioned and unquestionable power vested in men, and the resentment and rage it generated in women and girls, was being ignored, denied, dismissed and suppressed as it had been throughout history.

This time, it did not go away. Friedan named it 'the problem that has no name', and spelled it out for the women who could not say it for themselves: 'I want something more than my husband and my children and my home.' Armed with the strength of this conviction, Friedan announced *enough of the ideal-home-making, to hell with the table-scaping, let women out of the kitchen and into the world!*

The result was 'hundreds, thousands, millions of women entering history', as Friedan said, making history by changing themselves and changing the world. At a US conference on Equal Opportunity in June 1966, twenty-seven women, frustrated by the lack of action to end sex discrimination in employment, came together with Friedan in her hotel room and founded the National Organization for Women (NOW). The names of the founders read like a roll-call of the often unsung mothers of modern feminism, among them Mary Eastwood, Kathryn F. Clarenbach, Alice S. Rossi and Pauli Murray. Friedan was elected as the first president with the mission 'to take action to bring women into full participation in the mainstream of American society now, exercising all privileges and responsibilities thereof in truly equal partnership with men'.

Five years later came the creation of the National Women's Political Caucus, a non-partisan organisation aiming to increase the number of women in political life at every level from the mayor of Ozone, Idaho, to the heights of Capitol Hill. Again, its founders and members among the 320 attending the first meeting, included heavy-hitters like these: Dorothy Height, president of the National Council of Negro Women; Jill Ruckelshaus, US Civil Rights Commissioner; Elly Peterson, former vice-chair of the Republican National Committee; LaDonna Harris, Native American rights leader; and Congresswoman Eleanor Holmes Norton, former chair of the Equal Employment Opportunity Commission. Other prominent figures were:

Bella Abzug, 'Battling Bella', lawyer, Congresswoman and activist. 'Our struggle today is not to have a female Einstein get appointed as an assistant professor,' she said later. 'It is for a woman *schlemiel* to get as quickly promoted as a male *schlemiel*.'

Shirley Chisholm, educator, politician and writer, who in 1972 became the first black woman to run for the Democratic Party's presidential nomination. 'When I ran for the Congress, when I ran for president,' she declared, 'I met more discrimination as a woman than for being black. Men are men.'

Mildred 'Millie' McWilliams Jeffrey, the life-long union organiser and first senior female in the United Automobile Workers labour union. In politics she worked closely with both John F. and Bobby Kennedy, and championed civil rights and the women's movement.

Virginia Allan, Republican businesswoman and former chair of Richard Nixon's 1969 Task Force on Women's

Rights and Responsibilities. 'I just knew that there was discrimination,' she said of women in government, 'and I really felt very keenly about doing something that would correct the situation so that discrimination could be wiped out.'

And there were many, many more. But the glory of that day in July 1971 went to the aptly named Gloria Steinem, whose keynote Address to the Women of America at the National Women's Political Caucus was, well, *Steinemite*! Here she is in full flow:

This is no simple reform. It really is a revolution. Sex and race, because they are easy, visible differences, have been the primary ways of organizing human beings into superior and inferior groups, and into the cheap labour on which this system still depends. We are talking about a society in which there will be no roles other than those chosen, or those earned. We are really talking about humanism.

Steinem's childhood had been fractured by her parents' divorce and her mother's mental instability, and Steinem, ten years old when her father left home, saw Ruth Steinem's efforts to obtain either work or help being constantly, painfully thwarted by what her daughter came to identify as a rooted prejudice against women in society. After college, she found her way to feminism when the editor of *Esquire* commissioned her to investigate contraception in 1962, and she was struck again by the way women were restricted in comparison with men. Her article showed that in the land of the free, women were not free to get married and have a career like any ordinary man, but instead were only permitted one of the two. There was clearly something in the zeitgeist, as Steinem's article emerged at the same time as Betty Friedan was working on the self-same theme in *The Feminine Mystique*.

From that beginning Steinem took on the life of a feminist activist, speaking, marching, protesting and campaigning, overcoming a natural diffidence to make her voice heard. It is likely, though, that she will be remembered as much for her writing as for her activism, and for two pieces in particular. 'A Bunny's Tale', published in 1963, was Steinem's account of going undercover to work at the New York branch of the Playboy Club, and her deadpan reporting tellingly exposed the degradation and exploitation of the women who worked as 'Bunnies', while being constantly told what an 'exciting' and 'glamorous' job they had. Here is Gloria being shoe-horned into her bunny outfit by the wardrobe mistress, ready to go to work:

> It was so tight that the zipper caught my skin as she fastened the back. The bottom was cut up so high that it left my hip bones exposed, as well as a good five inches of untanned *derrière*. The boning in the waist would have made Scarlett O'Hara blanch, and the entire construction tended to push all available flesh up to the bosom. I was sure it would be perilous to bend over.
>
> 'Not too bad,' said the wardrobe mistress, and began to stuff an entire plastic dry cleaning bag into the top of my costume. A blue satin band with matching Bunny ears attached was fitted around my head like an enlarged bicycle clip, and a grapefruit-sized hemisphere of white fluff was attached to hooks at the costume's rear-most point. 'Okay, baby,' she said, 'put on your high heels and go show Sheralee ...'

Equally celebrated was a satirical article triggered, so Steinem said, by 'an old Irish woman taxi driver in Boston', who told her 'if men could get pregnant, abortion would be a sacrament'.

Yes indeed, she mused.
And if men could menstruate . . .

Men would brag about how long and how much.

Young boys would talk about it as the envied beginning of manhood. Gifts, religious ceremonies, family dinners, and stag parties would mark the day . . .

Sanitary supplies would be federally funded and free. Of course, some men would still pay for the prestige of such commercial brands as Paul Newman Tampons, Muhammad Ali's Rope-a-Dope Pads, John Wayne Maxi Pads, and Joe Namath Jock Shields – 'For Those Light Bachelor Days' . . .

Generals, right-wing politicians, and religious fundamentalists would cite menstruation ('*men*-struation') as proof that only men could serve God and country in combat ('You have to give blood to take blood'), occupy high political office ('Can women be properly fierce without a monthly cycle governed by the planet Mars?'), be priests, ministers, God Himself ('He gave this blood for our sins'), or rabbis ('Without a monthly purge of impurities, women are unclean').

In short, we would discover, as we might already guess, that logic is in the eye of the logician.

The truth is that if men could menstruate, the power justifications would go on and on.

If we let them.

The enemy within

'We are really talking about humanism,' Steinem had told the National Women's Political Caucus in 1971. Humanism, humanity, the human race – of course women wanted to be part of that. But the age-old struggle of women to possess their own minds, their bodies, their role in life and their place in the world is unlike any other power struggle in history. Greeks against Persians, Christians against Moors, Sunnis against Shias, Catholics against Protestants, communism against capitalism: none comes close. When the two opposing sides of any conflict drew up to give battle, they had rarely, if ever, spent time together, let alone fallen in love. One had not shared a bed with the other and got up to make his breakfast, take care of his children, clean his house, wash his dirty laundry and then make ready to welcome him home that night with a kiss and a hot meal. And however equal the relationship may have seemed to be in the home, it was based on an unexamined acceptance of the superior importance and centrality of the man in the world outside. This inequality was demonstrated in all the everyday structures of work, finance, the law and society, which reflected back to women incessant reminders of their lowlier position.

Feminism had a slogan for it: the personal is political. This was scorchingly illustrated in *The Female Eunuch*, Germaine Greer's 1970 hand-grenade of a book. She juggled this with a parallel life building a profile in television, journalism and film, and threw herself into the budding counter-culture of Britain, writing for the controversial magazine *Oz*. More controversially, she co-founded *Suck*, the self-proclaimed 'First European Sexpaper' that ran from 1969 to 1974 offering a platform for 'a new pornography' that would 'demystify male and female bodies' at a stroke.

For Greer in those torrid, florid early hippy years, sexual liberation was as important as women's liberation: indeed they were one and the same and could/should not be separated. Defining herself as a 'liberation feminist', she attacked the idea of women achieving equality, declaring at the All About Women festival as late as 2015 that 'it wouldn't change anything'. Men were not free, she argued, so why would women want to join their club? She had made the point more fully in the introduction to *The Whole Woman*, her 1999 sequel to *The Female Eunuch*:

> In 1970 the movement was called 'women's liberation' or, contemptuously, 'women's lib'. When the name 'libbers' was dropped for 'feminists', we were all relieved. What none of us noticed was that the idea of liberation was fading out with the word. We were settling for equality. Liberation struggles are not about assimilation but about asserting difference, endowing that difference with dignity and prestige, and insisting on it as a condition of self-definition and self-determination. The aim of women's liberation is to do as much for female people as has been done for colonized nations. Women's liberation did not see the female's potential in terms of the male's actual; the visionary feminists of the late sixties and early seventies could never find freedom by agreeing to live the lives of unfree men. Seekers after equality clamoured to be admitted to smoke-filled male haunts. Liberationists sought the world over for clues as to what women's lives could be if they were free to define their own values, order their own priorities and decide their own fate.

The Female Eunuch had not argued for equality, but in fact weighed in strongly against it. The book, an overnight bestseller, established Greer as Britain's answer to Betty Friedan in the front rank of international feminists. Years of intense education had larded Greer with degrees and qualifications, but had done nothing to tame her larrikin spirit, her hair-raising pugnacity and her coruscating anger against all the dinosaurs and drongos holding women down, a firestorm of fury that many of us remember with a deep affection and considerable awe. Greer was our Mrs Pankhurst in those glory days, and more.

The British journalist and writer Helen Lewis summed it up:

Germaine Greer is feminism's arsonist ... Her value to feminism is as a destructive force, tearing down stereotypes and smashing taboos. She is living testament to the idea that women don't have to do what has always been expected of them: be good girls, get married, have kids, be nice and shut up. As a public intellectual, she had self-confidence you could bounce rocks off. She was never ashamed of being clever. She demanded to be heard.

And she was.

The ascent of woman

As Greer abundantly demonstrated in her later work on women artists and poets, one of the strengths of feminism and one of the key factors in its success was that its central idea could be applied to any other school of thought or academic discipline, and used to turn it upside down and inside out. Take sociology, history, biology, say, and ask the key question, *is this all?* Or was there another way of looking at the material that would offer a different conclusion from the standard view? In particular, if the aim of women's liberation was to bring women into the mainstream of society and to claim equality with men, how were they being represented in existing accounts of the world?

In the 1960s the writer Elaine Morgan came across a little-known scientific thesis that the human race began not on the African savannah but on the margins of the sea. After years of research, she published *The Descent of Woman* in 1972, a book that radically rewrote the story of 'early man'. Instead of Man the Hunter, Man the Toolmaker, Man as *Homo sapiens* doing all the evolving for all the rest of the human race, Morgan proposed a new model of the dawn of time, a woman-centred story of human evolution taking place in warm seas, with mothers on hand and ample food all around.

Morgan had an outstanding academic mind, winning a scholarship to Oxford from a desperately poor mining background in Wales, and returning to university to do graduate research on what became known as 'the aquatic ape hypothesis'. Nevertheless Morgan's book drew a number of furious onslaughts from male scientists outraged both by her lack of scientific background and by her sex. Indeed her own publisher described her as 'a fifty-two-year-old Welsh housewife', implying that she had just rustled up the book in between scouring her front doorstep, baking welshcakes and singing 'Cwm Rhondda' at chapel.

This was only one of the countless attacks on anything that smacked of 'women's lib'. Particular fury was reserved for any concrete proposals for change. What did we want? The women's movement of the 1970s had four simple goals:

- equal pay
- equal education and job opportunities
- free contraception and abortion on demand
- free twenty-four-hour nurseries

Any one of these would have changed the life of any woman who obtained it.

Not one of them has been achieved anywhere in the world.

But the work went on.

Betty Friedan's deceptively simple and deliciously subversive question *is this all?* found a determined response. In 1974, Judy Chicago, the founder of the first feminist art programme in the United States, encountered the academic Gerda Lerner, the founder of the first academic programme of women's history. Lerner's work convinced Chicago that women would only succeed when they could band together, draw strength from one another and claim their place in the public world. Inspired, she brought together some of the most powerful female figures in world history for an imaginary dinner party, and created a massive installation honouring their names. Her great work, built in a triangle to echo the eternal feminine symbol of Venus, the vulva and the vagina, featured 1038 women's names in all, with thirty-nine singled out for a place at the table. The guests ranged from Kali to Georgia O'Keeffe, and this radical feminist piece travelled the world in all its glory between 1974 and 1979, and is now a permanent installation in the Brooklyn Museum.

Just because she's a woman . . .

. . . doesn't mean she's a sister. This part of the story does not have a happy ending. As the successes of the 1960s swelled into the 70s and 80s, it seemed that the pendulum of history had swung women's way at last. The time was right to go for the Big One, a new amendment to the mighty Constitution of the United States, the founding document of American democracy and the cornerstone of its ideals of freedom and equality.

Any amendment is a deeply serious thing, consciously adopted to shape the future of the country for the better, like the historic 13th that abolished slavery, and the 19th that granted women the vote. Surely there could be an Equal Rights Amendment to enshrine in law the right of every woman to be treated on equal terms with every man?

Why not? said the leaders of the women's movement and their millions of supporters, as the ERA sailed through Congress in 1972 and was sent out to each of the individual state legislatures for ratification by 1979.

Why on God's earth? said a deeply Catholic, deeply conservative housewife and mother of six from St Louis, Missouri. And

Phyllis Stewart Schlafly hijacked the ERA train and drove it into the buffers, just like that!

No one had expected such a crushing reversal. The idea of an amendment had been current since 1923, when the head of the National Women's Party, Alice Paul, proposed to Congress that 'men and women shall have equal rights'. Paul had won her spurs as a doughty campaigner for women's rights in Britain, where she and another suffragette once disguised themselves as cleaners to gain entry to London's Guildhall, and ambushed the Prime Minister when he rose to speak by smashing a stained glass window and shouting 'Votes for Women!' Despite suffering hard labour and forced feeding in prison, which damaged her health for the rest of her life, Paul stuck with the equal rights proposal for the next fifty years, and it was her wording of the amendment that was finally agreed by Congress.

The ERA had been approved by both the Republican and Democratic parties, both houses of Congress, and two successive Presidents, Gerald Ford and Jimmy Carter. It also enjoyed such wide support in the country that thirty states had ratified it as early as 1973, only eight short of the number required to pass the amendment into law. This appears to be the point at which Mrs Schlafly felt a little tickle from the hand of God and knew that he wanted her to stop it. 'Feminism is doomed to failure,' she trumpeted, 'because it is based on an attempt to repeal and restructure human nature.' Schlafly also knew human nature well enough to play upon its fears and weaknesses, and she began with the women. From the dustbin of history she plucked out all the arguments previously used against women in the struggle for the vote.

If women gained legal equality with men, she pronounced, they would all:

- lose the right to be supported by their husbands
- become bad wives by neglecting their 'household duties'

- be bad mothers and endanger their children
- be tempted to work in the unsafe world outside the home
- be forced to enrol in the military and be sent into combat
- lose their privacy in public places, being forced to accept mixed lavatories and worse
- see all sorts of sinfulness like abortions and gay marriages taking over their towns, and eviltude everywhere.

Through all this political dirty dancing, Schlafly loved to play the regular-housewife-and-mother card, despite having two academic degrees and a legal education culminating in a JD, just as Margaret Thatcher soft-pedalled her Oxford degree and qualification as a barrister, happily posing for the cameras with a shopping basket and rattling on about the price of milk. And like Thatcher again, Schlafly saw no contradiction in opposing equal rights for other women, condemning them to full-time home-making while she enjoyed a career as a lawyer, writer, activist and speaker, and finally as the CEO of her own right-wing pressure group, Eagle Forum, which she founded in 1972.

Schlafly also gained support from an ad hoc alliance of women-haters, antediluvianists and antifeminists like traditional, evangelical and fundamentalist church groups, as well as business and industry, who unsurprisingly acted as one to block any amendment that could mean women getting equal pay. The results of her crusade were startling. By 1982 the campaign for equality had fallen short of the numbers it required to succeed. Schlafly's triumph was total. The ERA had failed.

The defeat of the Equal Rights Amendment was a body blow to the women's movement. As a result, some of the leaders felt a loss of authority to speak on behalf of other women, while many members lost confidence in its future direction and not least in its power to bring change. *Hey ho and on we go*, muttered the tougher survivors of the 1982 *dégringolade*. Feminism had arrived, whether Mrs Schlafly liked it or not, and it was on its way to real and enduring change.

In the UK, the Equal Pay Act passed in 1970 came into effect in 1975.

Change indeed.

And not only in the West.

The same, only different

As Western women were gearing up to renew the struggle, women of India and China were fighting for the same rights, with the same conviction, but on very different grounds. Like the women of the West, they identified their targets on the basis of their own experience, which was often more complex and nuanced than that of the uniformly privileged middle class, well-educated and white feminists, as the early 'women's libbers' were perceived to be. This was of course a caricature, but it fed the belief that the Western movement was limited to the one idea that the women of the world were oppressed simply as women, and all they wanted was to get themselves into the all-male elite echelons of business and finance, and get their hands on their share of the rewards.

In countries like China and India, this broad-brush explanation took no account of the interlocking distinctions that were applied to women on the grounds of their caste, class, religion, ethnicity or politics, all potentially as powerful in defining an individual as their gender. There was, however, one gender-specific practice that they and some other countries shared: a long tradition of killing baby girls.

In 2016, a UN report estimated that between India and China alone, somewhere in the region of *two hundred million* female babies had now to be counted, in the powerful phrase of the Nobel Prize-winning economist and philosopher Amartya Sen, as '*missing women*'. This genocidal tradition was facilitated and extended the 1970s onwards by the use of amniocentesis and ultrasound as tools designed to save lives were used to enable sex-selective abortion, and the mass destruction of female foetuses.

For the Chinese, only a son could act for his parent in life and perform the correct rituals after death, making them essential to the smooth running of the social, financial, legal and religious systems. Girls had no such value. On the contrary, they would burden their family with the need to provide a dowry, and so were routinely suffocated or drowned at birth. This age-old practice was suspended from 1934 to 1976 by Mao Zedong as part of his policy to raise the birth rate. But in 1979 China introduced the one-child policy to tackle the crisis of over-population, and if Chinese couples had to choose, they had to have a boy.

As a result, China faced the future with a population imbalance of thirty million more men than women when the twenty-first century began. But the Chinese government introduced more woman-friendly legislation, on marriage and divorce in 2001, on sexual harassment in 2005, and domestic violence in 2015. In addition, equality for women on the same terms as men had been enshrined in the constitution of the Chinese Communist Party from the beginning, and women were encouraged to leave home and work to build the new nation, with the result that the country reportedly developed the largest female workforce in the world.

There were some signs of women's growing confidence. In 2012, a machine operator in the southern Chinese region of Guangdong, Luo Hong Mein, badly injured her arm and after a fierce struggle to win paltry compensation, set up the Sunflower Women Workers' Association to help other women in similar situations. The next year a young woman using the pseudonym of Cao Ju won the first gender discrimination lawsuit to be launched in China, after she applied for the post of executive assistant at a private tutorial academy in Beijing and was rejected on the grounds that the school was only appointing males. Offering no defence, the school apologised and the court awarded her the sum of thirty thousand yuan, about four thousand US dollars, in damages.

These and other events had been underpinned by the academic work of scholars like Li Xiaojiang, who published *Xiawa de Tansuo* ('In Search of Eve') in 1983. Two years later she set up the Henan Women's Study Center, followed it with a nation-wide non-government conference, and launched what is believed to be the first academic course on women and gender in China. She followed this up with directing the first publication of the major series of academic studies on women while also establishing the ground-breaking Women's Research Centre at Zhengzhou University in 1987, and holding a national women's academic conference in 1990.

To some, Li Xiaojiang is a problematic figure, frequently disagreeing with the leaders of the state-sponsored All-China Women's Federation. It could be argued, however, that debate and dissent are the mark of any mature organisation as the work on women continued to spread, and twenty-first century China boasts an increasing number of feminist scholars and centres for research into women and gender. Wang Zheng, a research scientist at the Institute of Research into Women and Gender at the University of Michigan, explored the history of women in China to establish what she called a 'Chinese feminist genealogy', to recover some of the lost stories of the pioneers. Wang's approach included promoting creative action, encouraging the creation of feminist drama which she described as 'the Chinese version of *The Vagina Monologues*', and in 2014 she founded and co-directed the UM-Fudan Joint Institute for Gender Studies, a collaboration between the University of Michigan and Fudan University, Shanghai.

But despite the central importance given to gender equality at the founding of the People's Republic of China in 1949, Chinese feminists discovered as their Russian sisters did, that communism did not concern itself with women's freedom, assuming that it was simply part of the class war, and that in any event, it had to take second place. Meanwhile, the rigid state control meant no freedom of speech nor of the press, and no authority outside the Party to whom women could complain.

In response, China's modern feminists began building an online community of workers, students and young professionals to share their concerns about discrimination against women, domestic violence and sexual harassment. In 2009, the activist Lü Pin founded Feminist Voices, declaring 'the feminist movement is about women's everyday concerns and building a community, rather than just having one or two famous individuals who can enlighten everybody else'. The network was hampered by various interventions from the state authorities, and in 2018 it was permanently shut down – on 8 March, International Women's Day, no less.

Making things change

In India, women journalists were more free than those in China to speak out, and the report of Sumita Thapar for *The Hindu* of 19 March 2007, 'Save the Girl Child', was one of a number from the 1970s onwards drawing attention to the growth of foetal sex determination and sex-selective abortions throughout the subcontinent. In the same year, Meena Sharma, a TV reporter from Rajasthan, took four pregnant women round different states across India, and found that over two-thirds of the 140 doctors she contacted were willing to give the women an abortion if the baby was a girl, some as late as twenty-eight weeks. The lawyer and activist Varsha Deshpande pointed out that the law banning the abuse of prenatal diagnostic techniques was highly effective and easy to use. 'We have done seventeen sting operations across Maharashtra and got action taken against more than twenty-five doctors,' she commented.

Individual women have also found that the law in India can support them in their fight for their rights. In 1991, the High Court of Kerala banned females between the ages of ten and fifty from entering the Sabarimala temple complex housing one of India's most sacred shrines, as menstruating women would be an offence to the celibate god. Following legal challenges, a judgment of the Supreme Court in September 2018 decreed that any discrimination against women on the grounds of their gender was a violation of the Constitution, and the ban was struck down. Violent protests followed, but a number of undaunted women subsequently exercised their newfound right.

One world, one word

The Vimochana Forum for Women's Rights, founded in 1979 to save battered women in Bangalore, confronted dowry harassment and bride-burning, but in the words of one of the co-founders, Dr Corinne Kumar, they soon found that the 'liberation' promised in their name was 'as important and essential to men as to women. It is transformatory for all.' This was brilliantly illustrated by the involvement of men in the Bangalore women's 'reclaim the night' march of 21 January 2017, #IWillGoOut. One of the male marchers, clad in shorts and T-shirt, carried a placard proclaiming 'I AM HALF NAKED AND SURROUNDED BY MEMBERS OF THE OPPOSITE SEX ... BUT I FEEL PROTECTED, NOT INTIMIDATED. I WANT THE SAME FOR THEM!'

That is all modern women want for themselves.

Vimochana.

Liberation.

And what great changes would happen when women were free?

CHAPTER 9

ROOM AT THE TOP

The cock may crow, but it's the hen that lays the eggs.

MARGARET THATCHER

No more phallic imperialism! Women have moved forward from demanding equal opportunity and now demand equal power.

ANDREA DWORKIN

Once, power was considered a masculine attribute. In fact power has no sex.

KATHARINE GRAHAM

'There will not be a woman prime minister in my lifetime,' declared Britain's leading female politician in 1970. 'The male population is too prejudiced.' Nine years later she became the country's first woman premier. A confirmed antifeminist, Margaret Thatcher repeatedly denied that she owed anything to the women's movement, but there she was, right at the top of the tree. Women were breaking through politically, managerially, commercially, socially, at every level in the Western world.

Australia had elected its first female Senator as early as 1943, the social reformer Dorothy Tangney, whose twenty-five years in post established her as the longest-serving Australian woman parliamentarian in the twentieth century. The years after the Second World War also saw the appointment of another impressive pioneer, Australia's first female Cabinet minister, Enid Lyons. Married at seventeen, Lyons took her husband's Catholic faith and bore twelve children. Widowed at forty-two, she went on to serve the government in a wide range of elected offices while looking after a family of eleven – one son had died of meningitis at ten months. Political and maternal, she was a powerhouse in her native land. Lyons was the first woman to be awarded not one but two damehoods, of the Order of Australia and the Order of the British Empire, and thoroughly deserved them both.

Women and power

How did these women find their way to the top? Margaret Thatcher rebelled against the headmistress who had refused to let her apply to Oxford, organised private tuition to learn Latin (an unavoidable requirement), and won a place to read chemistry. Once there, she joined the Oxford University Conservative Association, became its president, and went on to become the first female leader of the Conservative Party, a series of no mean feats. Thatcher herself always said that her proudest achievement was not becoming the first woman anything, but the first scientist to be a British prime minister.

But in the 1970s, Thatcher was already late on the scene. Her famous prophecy that there would never be a woman prime minister in her lifetime meant only in the UK, because Sirimavo

Bandaranaike had served as prime minister of Ceylon (as Sri Lanka then was) from 1960 to 1965, and was re-elected in 1970. Bandaranaike came to power in, if not quite at, the wake of her prime minister husband, S. W. D. R. Bandaranaike, offering herself as his successor after his assassination in 1959 with the artless remark, 'Mr Bandaranaike would not have been a happy husband if I had not thrown myself into politics.' She served as prime minister three times between 1960 and 2000, and is described everywhere as the world's first female head of state.

She was not.

The world's first elected female government leader had come to power twenty years earlier in April 1940, when Khertek Anchimaa was voted chair of the Little Khural [Parliament] of the state of Tannu Tuva. Once a remote Siberian backwater of the Qing Empire, Tuva became a Russian Protectorate in 1914. Russian officials arriving to survey their newly acquired territory found that none of the bewildered locals could answer the question, 'Do you know where Moscow is?' All except one. 'No,' the young Khertek stoutly replied. 'But if you send me there, I will.'

Khertek's education in Moscow at the Communist University of the Toilers in the East (*I am not being satirical*) gave her the first step up the ladder. Returning to Tuva in 1935, she worked her way up to become head of the local Communist Party. Following Moscow's famous Great Purge of 1936–8, tiny Tuva was quick to play catch-up, enthusiastically rooting out 'counter revolutionaries', 'opportunists of the right' and 'Japanese spies'. And as in Moscow again, the Party found them all guilty and condemned them all to death.

Then came the Second World War. By now head of state, Khertek threw the entire future of her little republic behind Russia in 1940. In the same year she embarked on a home-based defensive manoeuvre of her own, marrying the general

Khertek Anchimaa, date not known. Observe the look Mrs Thatcher was later to perfect, the strong reassuring masculine suit paired with the little frilly feminine pie-crust collar and the lady-bow at the neck.

secretary of Tuva's Communist Party, one Salchak Toka, who, like her, had deftly seen off his political rivals in the purges.

Another forgotten woman leader, Sükhbaataryn Yanjmaa of Mongolia, attended the same Toilers' University as Anchimaa. Also the survivor of a wretchedly poor background, she too found in the Communist Party a future, a family and a home. She met her husband as a young revolutionary and after his death in 1923 she intensified her efforts, representing the Mongolian People's Revolutionary Party at the Third International Conference of Communist Women the following year, where she met the revolutionary leaders Nadezhda Krupskaya and Clara Zetkin. In 1925 she involved herself in setting up Mongolia's first trade union, and doggedly worked her way up through the ranks until she was elected president of Mongolia's Great State Khurai [Supreme Parliament] in 1953. In that role, Yanjmaa became only the second woman in history, after Khertek Anchimaa, to be elected as a non-hereditary head of state and like Khertek again, she lived to a ripe old age.

Pathways to power

Such unaided success was rare. When statecraft, business and industry were the exclusive preserve of the male, access to man-power only came by working through men, in a number of ways:

Husband-power

All through history, women too numerous to count have risen to high office purely through the men they married, often pro-testing all the while that they were only doing it for their men. This form of preferment, called 'widow's succession', is well known in every country, and it put Keiko Nagaoka of Japan into her husband's seat in the national Diet when he commit-ted suicide in 2005. Meanwhile, America has lost count of the number of widows and wives who have taken over their hus-bands' (often still warm) seats in Congress: hubby-power at its most naked and unashamed.

Father-power

Indira Gandhi was also promoted to fill in for the absent male, in this case the son her prime minister father never had. Pandit Jawaharlal Nehru dealt with the ultimate tragedy of the patri-arch by grooming the only child, albeit a female, who could follow him into politics from an early age.

Papa-power also worked well for the first woman president of Indonesia, Megawati Sukarnoputri, the daughter of the coun-try's first premier. Even where there are brothers, the father's choice will often alight on an able girl if she outshines the male mediocrities in the family, as happened with Benazir Bhutto, the first woman to become prime minister of Pakistan.

Clan-power

Otherwise known as the dynamics of dynasty. Traditionally females have been more useful to powerful political families as pawns rather than as performers. Under Henry VIII, the Howard family contrived to marry two of their girls to the King to gain power and influence, although that backfired when both Anne Boleyn and Catherine Howard signally failed to give satisfaction, and were beheaded. In the modern world, America has the Roosevelts, the Bushes and the Kennedys, of course, and we can add the Clintons and the Trumps.

Being the offspring of the man in power has historically proved to be an advantage rather than the reverse, and the advent of the First Daughter in the presidency of Donald Trump was no exception. Her promotion into government, along with her husband, acting in a nebulous advisory capacity as soon as her father was elected in 2016, was seen as a portent. Will Ivanka Trump become the first female president of the United States? We can only wait and see.

Whore's-power

Prepare for a fanfare of strumpets as we retrace the steps of those women who have trodden this well-worn and time-dishonoured pathway to power. Whether or not they ever worked in the sex trade, they were all vulnerable to the slur that they had slept their way to the top. This sticky label was particularly easy to slap on women who had previously been actors or performers, like Eva Perón.

But any woman became a target if she stepped out of line. As an American with two living husbands and at the time only one divorce, plus a lively past and a reputation for giving the best sex since Cleopatra's handshake rocked the Nile, the last lover of King Edward VIII slipped readily into the slot of the whore on the make, digging for power and gold. But Wallis Simpson was not the primary culprit in this crisis. Desperate to abdicate, Edward cast her as the sole and total excuse to share the blame for an action that he knew would be universally reviled, and to support that romantic fiction he had to marry her. As the Duke and Duchess of Windsor, they were to spend the next forty-five years trapped in an exquisitely empty marriage, like flies watching the slow-rising amber and powerless to escape.

For another woman, however, the strategic deployment of her sexual skills led to a seat at the top table of one of the largest and most dangerous countries in the world. When Mao Zedong founded the People's Republic of China in 1949, at his side was the film star Jiang Qinq and there she stayed for the next thirty years. Only twenty-four when they met in 1938 and half Mao's age, she had little difficulty in prising him away from his middle-aged wife and five children. Just as important, she was already a hard-line communist of iron-clad conviction and implacable rigour.

As Mao embarked on the twenty-seven-year reign that caused the deaths of tens of millions of people, Jiang Qing, now Madame Mao, spearheaded his public programmes, destroyed his enemies and pursued many dark initiatives of her own. From 1961, when Mao placed all the might of his dictatorship under her control, Jiang could and did do anything she wanted. As the supreme architect of the Cultural Revolution, she had a private army of thousands of Red Guards at her command and was recognised as the most powerful woman in the world. The scope this gave her was immense, her range apparently limitless, and her rage for destruction terrifying. After Mao complained about the 'feudal and bourgeois' tendencies of traditional Chinese opera, she took the opportunity to destroy this intricate and hallowed form, in its place producing crude creations churning out simple communist and revolutionary themes. Her other 'reforms' focused on literature and art, ensuring the virtual extinction of creative work in China in favour of promoting political propaganda along lines she rigidly controlled.

These were her public works. Jiang devoted the same manic fervour to her private vendettas, avenging herself on anyone who had injured her in any way, however long ago. These attacks ranged from those who had disparaged her talent in her now-distant acting days to her main rival for power, the prime minister Zhou Enlai. She had his son killed and his daughter tortured to death, then ordered the ashes to be scattered so that Zhou could never lay his child to rest as tradition required.

As China's head of government and Mao's presumed successor, Zhou Enlai did at least pose a political threat to Jiang's supremacy. Others she seems to have destroyed just for fun, such as the wife of her second husband, a man she had dumped years before on her ascent to power. Another victim was the third wife of Mao, a woman he had abandoned as soon as he met Jiang. In addition, there is no reliable record of the numbers tortured and killed in the decade when she whipped on the Red Guards to run riot all over China, carrying the Cultural Revolution wherever they saw fit. Millions died at Jiang's behest, while Mao looked on, saw Jiang consolidating his power, and found it good.

Jiang was safe as long as Mao was alive. But any reliance on power borrowed from a man comes at a cost.

From her first entry into politics, Indira Gandhi was widely mocked as a *goongi gudiya* (Hindi for 'wooden doll, bimbo'). Even when she was elected as India's first woman prime minister in 1966, she was still dismissed as 'Daddy's girl', and the puppet of party bosses exploiting her name and her connection with the man who was not only her father but the Father of Modern India. Gandhi outgrew the belittlement, rebelled against Nehru's influence, and carved out her own policies. Her finest tribute came when the president of her party pronounced 'India is Indira and Indira is India'.

Indira Gandhi made much of her role as the mother of the country, and to the many millions in the world's largest democracy, she was Mother India.

And then they killed her.

Bang bang, they shot them down

In any era, power goes hand in hand with the risk of death. Gandhi died in a hail of gunfire in 1984, shot by Sikh dissidents, her own bodyguards no less. Thatcher was politically assassinated in an open attack by her own party, all the prime minister's men lining up to stab her in the front. For both of them, the end was swift. For Jiang Qing, her power evaporated in 1976 with Mao's last breath. Less than four weeks later, she was arrested and tried as a counter-revolutionary, a rich irony considering how wholeheartedly she had thrown herself into the revolution, as she was at pains to point out. At her trial, she furiously protested her innocence. '*I was Mao's dog!*' she screamed. 'What he said to bite, I bit.' She was sentenced to death. Later reprieved, she was given life imprisonment and hanged herself in 1991.

Jiang Qing's career closely paralleled that of Eva Perón, both of them able and ambitious politicians whose power was derived entirely from the man they married, and who had to watch it vanish like fairy gold for want of a power base of their own. But Eva's successor became the first female president in the whole of the Americas. Isabel Perón's road to power came via her husband Juan, Eva's widower, who placed her on the ticket as his vice-president when he ran for the presidency in 1973. Perón's poor health meant that 'Isabelita' was in effect acting as president from the time of his election, and his death in 1974 only confirmed her place at the top. But while headlines around the globe celebrated her as the only female president of any country in the world, one question remained unanswered when she was ousted in 1976 by a military coup: how far was she responsible for the violent political suppression, ingenious tortures and mass killing that took place under her regime? When thousands of 'leftist' dissidents like lawyers, students, trade unionists, writers and artists were exterminated or simply 'disappeared', what did she know? The question remains. Charged with human rights abuses after her fall, La Presidente lay low in exile in Spain and the statute of limitations saved her from facing trial.

She who must be obeyed

As this shows, women in power does not necessarily mean good women in power. Imelda Marcos grabbed it with both hands during her busy career as the First Lady of the Philippines and rewarded herself accordingly, although First Ladies do not usually deem themselves worth the ten billion dollars that she and her husband Ferdinand Marcos are widely believed to have lifted from the national coffers between 1965 and 1986, a figure that puts her in the first rank of the Great International Kleptocracy. But who could judge the luscious Imelda until they had walked a mile in one of her 2784 pairs of shoes? 'I did not have three thousand pairs of shoes, I had one thousand and sixty!' she squealed, denying the figure recorded by US Marines, shoe by shoe, after the couple fled the People Power Revolution in 1986. 'People say I'm extravagant because I want to be surrounded by beauty,' she protested. 'But tell me, who wants to be surrounded by garbage?' Not Imelda. Her position was always clear: 'Win or lose, we go shopping after the election!'

But Imelda was a rank amateur in comparison with those who used their access to money and power to far darker ends. Look no further than some of the women leaders of failing states all over the world, like Joice Mujuru, the second vice-president of Zimbabwe and Robert Mugabe's former deputy. Joining the Liberation War as a teenager in 1966 and calling herself Teurai Ropa ('Spill Blood') she made her name as a violent terrorist, married a fellow-fighter Solomon Mujuru and won a reputation as a brave soldier, even in late pregnancy.

Once in power, Robert Mugabe made Joice the youngest minister in his independence Cabinet of 1980, and continued to promote her through the ranks. In 2001 her husband directed the violent seizure of a multi-million-dollar farm called Alamein, and the couple moved in to live there, ignoring a judgment made a year later by the Supreme Court of Zimbabwe declaring their land-grab illegal. Mugabe subsequently made Joice Mujuru his deputy, and she was his presumed successor for ten years from 2004. That decade saw the persecution and killing of white farmers, a riot of plunder and corruption, and the accelerating destruction of the country under the fatally incompetent and deranged Mugabe.

Monsters make monsters, and Joice Mujuru was one of Mugabe's. When the European Union first sanctioned Zimbabweans for financial violations and human rights abuses in 2002, Joice was on the list. Joice might have been the public face of the power couple, but few doubted that husband Solomon was a full partner in all his wife's dealings. His own business interests ranged from mining and agriculture to tourism and construction, and that meant no shortage of suspects in August 2011 when he died in a sudden and violent fire at Alamein Farm suspected of being an arson attack.

Yet the police investigation yielded no useful information and no arrests were made. In the toxic political landscape of

Zimbabwe, Joice kept going until the end of 2014, when she was unexpectedly accused of conspiring against Mugabe, sacked from her powerful position as vice-president, and driven out of ZANU-PF. She promptly formed her own political party, and contested the 2018 presidential election held after Mugabe was deposed. Her poor performance in the polls may have suggested that her public career was over, but it would be foolish to believe that one so accomplished in the black arts of power and politics as the former 'Spill Blood' could easily be written off.

Equally sad or bad or both was the course of the 'Great Mam', Winnie Mandela, once the ardent young lover, devoted wife and revolutionary partner of Nelson Mandela and for the twenty-seven years of his imprisonment his only channel to the outside world. 'They think because they have put my husband on an island that he will be forgotten,' she announced after Mandela was sent to Robben Island in 1964, where he remained for the next eighteen years. 'They are wrong. The harder they try to silence him, the louder I will become!' She then lived through her own quarter of a century of official persecution, banishment, imprisonment, beating and torture without him and alone. Did that lead to her creation in 1985 of the Mandela United Football Club?

The Club, however, never played much soccer. Winnie used it as her own private hit squad to carry out random arrests, punishment beatings, abduction, torture and murder. From a kangaroo court at the back of her house, she dealt out summary justice, and the death of Stompie Moeketsi, a fourteen-year-old boy suspected of being a police spy, was only one of many grievous assaults she was believed to have authorised. Bank fraud and larceny, both on a massive scale, also featured on the crime sheet as time went by.

But Winnie's link with Mandela and her own iconic status as the 'Mother of the Nation' made her virtually untouchable.

Tried and convicted for her part in the murder of Moeketsi in 1991 and again for a bank fraud in 2001, she was sentenced to jail on both occasions, but the sentences were overturned on appeal. Over the years, both the criminal courts and South Africa's Truth and Reconciliation Commission were given ample evidence of Winnie's involvement in many crimes and the proof of her guilt. But as a part of the foundation myth of the 'rainbow nation' of the new South Africa and a major player in the life of Mandela, she quite simply and literally got away with murder.

Crime not compulsory

Happily, among the women who got their hands on the levers of state, Winnie Mandela, Joice Mujuru and Imelda Marcos proved the exception, not the rule. In the second half of the twentieth century, almost two hundred women scaled the heights of political power to become prime minister or head of state or both. Who to single out for special mention, from Turkey to Costa Rica, from Nicaragua to Bangladesh, when every one of them had proved herself? Here are a few who illustrate the range and conviction rebel women brought to the top table, as soon as they broke through the door and got into the corridors of power:

> **Eugenia Charles** became the first prime minister of Dominica in 1980 and was in office for fifteen years, making her the world's longest continually serving female prime minister to date. Also Dominica's first female lawyer, she entered politics to fight a government bid to stifle opposition nicknamed the 'shut your mouth' bill. Known as the 'Iron Lady of the Caribbean' for her integrity and strength of character, she also opposed another bill to enforce a repressively formal dress code in parliament by turning up for work in a swimsuit.

Mary Robinson, a human rights lawyer, became the first female president of Ireland in 1990 and the first feminist, the first activist and the first liberal to hold power in that torn and tortured isle. 'I was elected by the women of Ireland,' she said, 'who instead of rocking the cradle, rocked the system.' Her success as a liberalising force in Ireland led to her appointment to the United Nations High Commission for Human Rights in 1997, a post she held until 2002.

Jenny Shipley, the first woman prime minister of New Zealand in 1997, was the first to attend Auckland's Hero Parade, giving establishment backing to recognising LGBT+ rights. Shipley was nicknamed the 'Perfumed Steamroller' for her ability to bulldoze her projects through. 'This ain't a damn beauty contest,' was one of her firm beliefs. 'If you come into politics to be popular, then you've picked the wrong sport.' Shipley lost power in 1999 to another woman politician, Helen Clark – another first in New Zealand history. Clark was in office until 2008, and nine years later New Zealand's Jacinda Ardern became the country's third female premier.

Ellen Johnson Sirleaf became the first elected female head of state in Africa when she was installed as president of Liberia in 2006. Her previous political career involved exile, repeated imprisonment and a narrow escape from a firing squad. As president, Sirleaf made education for elementary school children both compulsory and free. She signed into law a Freedom of Information Act to check corruption, and successfully negotiated for Liberia the highest debt relief of any African country. In 2011 she was awarded the Nobel Peace Prize, and was rated by *The Economist* as 'arguably the best president the country has ever had'. Sirleaf shared the Nobel Prize with

Leymah Gbowee, who led what became the Women of Liberia Mass Action for Peace, a movement credited with helping to end the Second Liberian Civil War in 2003. The third laureate of this all-female group was Tawakkol Karman, a journalist, freedom fighter and women's rights activist, who became the first Yemeni and the first Arab woman to receive it. 'Women should stop feeling they are part of the problem, and become part of the solution,' Karman said.

And the list goes on. In 1996 the American businesswoman and activist Laura Liswood co-founded the Council of Women World Leaders with Vigdís Finnbogadóttir of Iceland, who made history as the world's first democratically elected female president in 1980. Finnbogadóttir served as the Council's first chair after making history again as a president who had made such a success of her tenure that she was repeatedly re-elected to serve a record-breaking sixteen years. As she explained, she was guided always by her personal mantra, 'Never let the women down':

Because I was the first woman to be elected president, I had to live up to those expectations to prove that a woman could do it. I had this gusto, this feeling that I couldn't fail – it was my duty not to fail on behalf of the women of the world.

Despite all this, Finnbogadóttir did not allow her career to consume her life. One of the first single women in Iceland to adopt a child, she took office as the divorced mother of a nine-year-old daughter. But then, where you have women, you have children. As prime minister of Pakistan, Benazir Bhutto was the first head of government to give birth while in power, having a daughter during her first term of office and a son in her second. She was followed in 2018 by Jacinda Ardern, and by Ruth Davidson, the former leader of the Conservative Party in Scotland, who married her female partner and gave birth to a boy while in office.

Around the world, women were quietly disproving negative myths about women in power. In 2017, Ana Brnabić was not only the first woman, but the first openly gay person to be elected as prime minister of Serbia. Her sexual orientation proved to be of less interest to voters than her reforms of the country's antiquated infrastructure. A messianic moderniser, she pushed through an IT programme to renew government documents like driving licences online rather than queuing up to do it in person, which saved Serbians an estimated *six million* hours a year.

And power is –

Among other things, the power to make change. When the Texas Republican Kay Bailey Hutchison was elected to the US Senate in 1993, she found that her efforts to get mammograms for women covered by state medical insurance were blocked by the male party bosses. She then discovered that while refusing to fund a test which saved women's lives, insurers would pay for penile implants to pump up men's flagging erections – breast cancer blown off as unnecessary, but a bonanza for every weary willy in the Lone Star State. With this revelation, suddenly it was *open sesame*! The state coffers coughed up the cash for women after all.

The power to make change in politics only lasts until the next election, but the ownership and control of money can be pure power in itself. As the owner of the Washington Post Company, a multi-billion-dollar media empire that also included the magazine *Newsweek* and six TV stations, Katharine Graham had it, and used it too. The first female publisher of a major American newspaper, the first female head of a Fortune 500 company and one of the most influential women in the US, she led the *Post* through a major national crisis when her reporters uncovered the Watergate scandal that blasted Richard Nixon, the President himself, out of the White House.

Graham was not at all prepared for this, and lacked the confidence that she could handle it. Like Eleanor Roosevelt, she had been undermined by her mother and then by her husband, Philip Graham, who enjoyed making her the target of family jokes. Brilliant and bipolar, he planned to leave her to marry his mistress, and to take over the ownership of the *Post*, which he had been running for his father-in-law.

Graham later recalled that she understood the situation, but felt powerless to change it: 'The end result of all this was that many of us, by middle age, arrived at the state we were trying most to avoid: we bored our husbands, who had done their fair share in helping reduce us to this condition, and they wandered off to younger, greener pastures.' Then Philip shot himself in 1963, and she found herself in control of the company. Once at the helm, the downtrodden and insecure Graham discovered her inner rebel, as soon as she had something serious to rebel against.

And few things could have been more serious than defying the power of the law, the state and the President. The *Washington Post* had had a previous run-in with the political establishment in 1971, when it went to court for permission to publish the Pentagon Papers, secret reports by the Department of Defense on the conduct of the Vietnam War that revealed gross lying and deception at the highest level of government. Katharine Graham's partner in resisting the government's attempts to bury that story was her editor Benjamin C. Bradlee, whose talent she had noticed when he was the Washington bureau chief for *Newsweek*, and brought him over to the *Post* to run the show. But their finest hour came the following year when two of the paper's reporters,

Bob Woodward and Carl Bernstein, picked up an account of an attempted break-in at the Democratic National Committee headquarters in a Washington office complex called Watergate.

This started a two-year investigation during which the dogged work of Woodward and Bernstein uncovered an intricate web of wrongdoing that led to the heart of the Republican administration and to the president himself. It was the biggest political scandal in the history of the United States, involving break-ins, burglary, wire-tapping, fraud, spying, money-laundering, political corruption and the obstruction of justice. Rumour and hysteria swept the capital as the extent of the 'black operations'· came to light. Throughout all this, Graham was the still centre of a rising storm as pressure mounted to cover up the criminality and to silence the press.

As she remembered it, 'the only way I can describe the extent of my anxiety is to say that I felt as if I were pregnant with a rock'. Nixon's chief enforcer, the Attorney General John Mitchell, issued a lewd personal threat: 'Katie Graham's gonna get her tit caught in a big fat wringer if that's published.' This was only one of the attacks intended to break Graham's nerve and to shut the investigation down. They failed. Sixty-nine men were brought to trial, with forty-eight convictions followed by jail sentences and fines. Although he clung on in the teeth of mounting public and political fury, President Nixon was finally forced to resign.

The legacy of Watergate was a raft of reforms, beginning with a Freedom of Information Act in 1974 and taking in swingeing reorganisation of the US election processes. These were the events that gave Graham her status as the most powerful woman in publishing. As chairman and principal owner of the Washington Post Company, she controlled the fifth-largest publishing empire in the nation so successfully that in the period from 1975 to 1985, profits grew at more than 20 per cent a year.

Honoured with the S. Roger Horchow Award for Greatest
Public Service by a Private Citizen, she recognised the work
of Woodward, Bernstein and Ben Bradlee, and later insisted,
'Whatever power I exert is collegial.'

Let's talk money

Old or new, money is power, and few have ever made as much
in one lifetime as the phenomenal Muriel 'Mickie' Siebert.
Visiting the New York Stock Exchange as a teenager from
Ohio, Siebert felt what she called 'the buzz of thousands of
deals' and knew at once what she wanted to do. She had a gift
for figures that verged on the supernatural, saying 'I could look
at a page of numbers, and they would light up like a Broadway
marquee.' She used it to establish a brokerage business in 1967
that made her the first female self-made paper billionaire after
her company went public in 1996. Known throughout the US
and beyond as the 'First Woman of Finance', Siebert was the
first non-male to own a seat on the New York Stock Exchange
and to head up one of its member firms.

If that makes Mickie's barrier-busting career sound an easy
ride, it was anything but. Arriving in New York with nothing
but 'five hundred dollars, a used old Studebaker, and a dream'
to buy a seat on the Stock Exchange, Siebert found that she
had to pay thirty thousand dollars more than the Exchange
charged the men. Needing a backer, she was rejected by nine
male colleagues before the tenth agreed. Blonde, blue-eyed
and glamorous, she developed a standard response to the anti-
Semitism she met in the Stock Exchange, sending a bouquet of
flowers to the offender with the following verse:

Roses are red,
Violets are blue-ish.

You may not know it
But I am Jewish.

That humour, that style, stayed with her all her life.

As did her lifelong faith in women and her commitment to the cause. When I met her through the International Women's Forum in the 1990s, she described the group as her 'soul food', and she readily encouraged women to grasp new opportunities

Muriel 'Mickie' Siebert doing what she loved best – watching the numbers 'light up like a Broadway marquee'.

when the chance arose. With the power to make things happen, she endowed a foundation to promote financial literacy as a life skill no one should be without. Above all, she brooked no obstacles. Many a woman, including me, would find herself earnestly explaining to Mickie all the reasons why something could not be done, only to spark a piercing glint in her eye. She would raise her eyebrows and utter one word in her raspy, measured, unforgettable voice. '*So?*'

Let's code

Mickie Siebert's ascendancy provided a powerful example of how well a woman could do in finance, given half a chance. As president and CEO of Yahoo! Marissa Mayer made history in 2013 as the only person to feature in all three of *Fortune* magazine's annual lists in the same issue: at number 10 in Businessperson of the Year, number eight in Most Powerful Women, and as one of the Top 40 Under 40. What was the secret of Mayer's success? As a pre-medical student concerned by the high cost of her course at Stanford University, she decided that computer science might be better value for money, a decision that led to her becoming the first woman engineer at Google in 1999. 'I'm a geek,' she later said blithely. 'I like to code.' Finding her world had another bonus too: 'If you can find something that you're really passionate about, whether you're a man or a woman becomes a lot less important. Passion is a gender-neutralizing force.'

This may have been Mayer's story, but in the arena of commercial IT, the opposite proved true. From its brand-new beginnings in the twentieth century, the technology sector displayed one of the worst old-style gender imbalances of any profession in the developed world. How did that come about? It stemmed from the foundation myth of Silicon Valley, with its *faux-naïf* narrative of simple start-ups: just a couple of kids playing around with computers in a garage, except that they both happened to be male.

From its infancy, the tech sector consciously sought to shape a new reality with its dress-down, open-office-or-no-office restructuring of work, and its dismantling of traditional conventions considered to have held back innovation (read: *ambitious young men*). With its idea of itself as having shaken off the dead hand of the past and focusing on horizon-scanning and blue-sky thinking, it set about hiring other tech-minded young men. Like recruited like, and very few of the first companies established a human resources department, since none of the boys ever thought they needed one.

Another key factor was the reputation the San Francisco Bay Area soon acquired as a magic money machine, when the Santa Clara Valley replaced Wall Street as a national and international site of wealth and power. Melinda Gates, ex-Microsoft and an advocate for women in tech, argued that the domination of men at every level in IT gave them a licence to misbehave. 'I don't think there's a woman who has worked in tech who hasn't experienced some form of bias or sexual harassment along the way,' she said in an interview in 2017: 'the asymmetry of power is ripe for abuse.' A weak representation of women in any group inevitably weighted the culture in favour of male attitudes and male norms. From male humour to matters of finance, the prevailing tone, already exclusive of women, easily became hostile and even ugly when the wrong stars were aligned.

So what's new? you may say. Did it matter, as long as some women could get through? Two reasons made the world of IT a special case. One is that under its wing, a peculiarly harsh attitude to women evolved that all too easily plumbed extraordinary depths of hatred and femicidal rage. In 2013, Zoë Quinn, an independent game developer, attracted online rape and death threats for releasing *Depression Quest*, a game that marked a departure from the standard fare of alpha-male heroes doing alpha-male things.

The attack on Quinn intensified with increasingly obscene and sadistic activity on social media until it grew into a massive online mob. The thugs then targeted another female developer, Brianna Wu, and the media critic Anita Sarkeesian. Sarkeesian's only offence was to have made a series of YouTube videos showing that the roles played by female characters in video games were typically limited to sex objects, or damsels in distress.

With 'Gamergate', as it was called, the outside world had its first clear and irrefutable introduction to the seething misogyny at work in the tech universe. The rage against the three women only increased during 2014, and the anonymous 'cyber warriors' published the women's personal details and home addresses in what Sarkeesian called 'an organized, concerted effort to destroy' their lives. Online messages repeatedly urged 'Gamergaters' to kill the women in any number of hideous ways, so that all three had to leave their homes on a number of occasions and go into hiding for months at a time.

This particular act of gender terrorism died away as the hunting pack moved on. The FBI had been involved, but the agents made no arrests and soon closed the case. Were they deflected or defeated by the cyber-thugs' unique combination of stone age brutality and space age control, or were the attacks simply not rated as important enough for in-depth investigation? Either way, no country, state or nation should consent to the exclusion of women and girls en masse from the world of IT. This takes us to the second reason why it deserved special attention.

The technology industry of the early twenty-first century was of prime importance to every man, woman and child from its very beginning, because it was forming and deforming their daily lives in the here and now, making it up as it went along.

At the same time it was building the highway to the future, similarly without the knowledge or consent of the great mass of its consumers. Like the financial sphere, it drew in the brightest graduates from all over the globe, and promised them not only rich rewards but a chance to change the world. That meant the industry's ideas and ideals, even its way of doing things, would impact the way people lived for generations to come, and who should ever, no matter what the circumstances, consent to the exclusion of the female half of the population from that?

Let's do business

In contrast to tech, older trades and businesses proved readier to open their doors to women and to new ideas. In her day, Rosalía Mera, co-founder with her then husband Armancio Ortega of the Zara clothing and homewares chain, was named as the world's most successful self-made female entrepreneur by *Forbes* magazine in 2013, with an estimated personal fortune of $6.1 billion. Her secret? She more or less invented fast fashion. But the biggie must surely be the triumph of Mary Barra, who became the first woman to run any major global car manufacturer when she was appointed as the CEO and chair of America's General Motors Company in 2014. Barra's appointment was hailed as 'a landmark moment' in manufacturing, 'one of the most macho areas of the car industry'.

But Barra had slogged her way up through GM in departments ranging from human resources to car design and marketing, while also gaining an engineering degree and an MBA from Stanford. Soon after she became CEO, a scandal involving defective ignition switches and around 124 deaths linked to the fault forced the recall of over two and a half million cars. In contrast to the traditional corporate keep-quiet-and-cover-up response, Barra fired those found responsible and told GM workers,

'I want to put this painful experience permanently in our collective memories.' She then brought in new policies to encourage employees to flag up any problems in advance.

Barra's decision to throw the weight of GM behind all-electric and self-driving cars was a radical shift of emphasis that many found hard to accept. But when she was featured on the cover of *Time* magazine's '100 Most Influential People in the World' in 2014, and rated number one in *Fortune*'s list of America's Most Powerful Business Women for the third year running in 2017, Barra could afford to smile and wave from the driving seat, and keep on motoring.

What women did

All over the world, women were fulfilling their potential and changing the face of public life. Let's meet some of them:

   In 2002 South African **Gail Kelly** became the first female CEO of a major Australian bank. **Hamdiyah Mahmood Faraj Al-Jaff** became the chairman of the board, president and CEO of the Trade Bank of Iraq after joining it in 2011. **Ana Patricia Botín-Sanz de Sautuola O'Shea** was appointed executive chairman of Spain's Santander Group in 2014.

   In politics, the election of women to the role of state governor in the US was dominated for half a century by the tradition of keep-it-in-the-family. As we have seen, wives and widows were usually well to the fore. This dated from the election of **Nellie Tayloe Ross**, the first woman governor of Wyoming in 1924, when her husband died after less than a year in office. Elected in the same year, **'Ma' (Miriam Amanda) Ferguson** guilelessly made it plain that she would be the mouthpiece of her crooked husband (impeached, convicted and banned from public office in 1917) when she told voters that Texas would get 'two governors for the price of one'. **Ella Grasso** then made history as the first woman to be elected a state governor without being the wife or widow of a man who held the office before when she won Connecticut in 1974.

Salima Ghezali became the first female newspaper editor in the Arab world when she took over Algeria's liberal *La Nation* in 1993. Between January 1995 and December 1996, the paper was banned nine times on the grounds of 'endangering state security' by the military authorities then running the country following an anti-Islamist coup. In 1997 Ghezali announced that *La Nation* refused to cover the murky events called 'security incidents', because government restrictions made objective reporting impossible. The anger this roused in the regime drove her into years of hiding her two young daughters with her female relatives and slipping round town sleeping in different beds every night to dodge the death threats that came every day. Continuing as a powerful activist for women, Ghezali was awarded the Sakharov Prize and the Olaf Palme Prize in 1997.

British banker **Alison Streeter**, the 'Queen of the English Channel', swam it forty-three times, a record outstripping any other swimmer to date. She also made a non-stop triple crossing in 1990, a feat unequalled for twenty-five years. **Chloe McCardel** of Australia set the world record for the longest unassisted ocean swim in 2014, when she completed over seventy-seven miles in the Bahamas. America's **Diana Nyad** began breaking endurance records in her twenties and continued into her sixties, when in 2013 she swam from Havana, Cuba to Key West in Florida, 110 miles in fifty-three hours. In 2019 American **Sarah Thomas** completed a four-way non-stop Channel crossing, swimming 134 miles instead of a planned eighty-four when currents, winds and tides forced her off course.

When **Sue Sally Hale** was a girl in California, polo clubs were not open to women, even though she was so good that one sports commentator later recorded that 'she could ride a horse like a Comanche and hit the ball like a Mack truck'. Courtesy of her stuntman stepfather, who taught her his riding tricks and arranged her transformation into a moustachioed youth with the help of a studio make-up artist, Hale played polo as a young man for fifteen years. Then some of her team mates, who knew the secret of her masquerade, threatened to embarrass the authorities by revealing how copiously they had been duped, and forced the US Polo Association to admit her as a member in 1972.

Along with sport, business, politics and finance, rebel women made their way into the church, the military and the highest echelons of art and music. *A woman bishop? Come talk to the General. Oh, she's busy with that orchestra director, what's her name?* Fill in the blanks. Throughout the modern period, the increasing visibility of women at the top helped to normalise those in everyday roles, 'lady doctors' for instance, bank managers and justices, as well as firefighters, engineers and chefs. At every level, women were coming through, a development that also welcomed men into traditionally all-female jobs like au pairs, nursery school assistants, carers and midwives.

These were the winners. What of the others, the unnoticed working women of the daytime world and the unseen, unsung armies of the night, the millions of female office cleaners, hospital workers, laundry maids and sandwich-makers?

From the very start of the women's movement, activists knew that the answers would only be found when enough women made their way into enough structures of power to change that outside world, where male centrality was deemed as natural and normal as sunlight and fresh air. What kind of world had they entered as girls that would have blessed or blighted their chances of developing their potential, their personal power? What images and information were they given to shape their idea of womanhood?

4

The Longest March

How are men and women to think about their maleness and femaleness in this twentieth century, in which so many of our old ideas must be made new?

MARGARET MEAD

CHAPTER 10

MASS HYSTERIA

The mass media molds everyone into more passive roles, into roles of more frantic consuming, into human beings with fragmented views of society. But what it does to everyone it does to women even more.

ALICE EMBREE

The movie industry is full of crazy people who think that they are God.

ANTHONY HOPKINS

My Prince Charming is a Princess.

T-SHIRT SLOGAN

'JACK THE RIPPER CLAIMS 5TH VICTIM WOMAN BRUTALLY HACKED TO DEATH.'

The story of a mangled, sexually assaulted female body has rarely failed to arouse public interest, and reports like this had been the lifeblood of newspapers since the sixteenth century. But the widespread rise in literacy, the growth of city living and the march of technology from the nineteenth century onwards made it possible to flood the streets with accounts of the latest scandal or gruesome murder far faster, and in far greater numbers, than ever before. The ensuing sales and profits vividly demonstrated and arguably encouraged the human hunger for salacious information, and pointed the way ahead. In the twentieth century, then, it became possible to reach a vast number of people and to give them all the same message at the same time, with a corresponding increase in both cash and control. Later known as 'mass communication' or the 'mass media', it re-shaped the world of the twentieth century and beyond.

The massification of media took old forms such as print and developed new products: paperback books, glossy magazines, pull-out and pop-up supplements and many more publications. Meanwhile, the existing technologies of telegraphy and radio expanded to give a hungry world television, film, pop music, advertising, video games, mobile phones, computer software and the internet. Each medium prospered by seeking out and consolidating its own following, delivering the news of events but also creating a new kind of complicity with a new kind of consumer. Working on a level of the human psyche hitherto unrecognised, the mass media created and fed the fantasies, fads and crazes of men and women with an unprecedented speed, intensity and depth.

And with time, the new-fangled toys normalised their presence and took over the mainstream of public opinion with a confidence and enthusiasm not seen since the days of the Roman Empire, when 'bread and circuses' kept the people docile, and distracted them from their woes. Karl Marx saw religion as 'the opiate of the masses', performing the same function, but he could not foresee – *who could?* – the ways in which the immediate and insistent nature of mass communication offered an alternative to religion. Above all, the ever-multiplying media outlets took readily to the task of acting as the moral guardians of society, and in particular in setting out suitable images and rules for womanhood.

This mission was embraced with an especial vigour by the popular press. One woman who attracted the attention of American journalists was the illiterate Irish cook Mary Mallon, identified as the source of a 1906 typhoid outbreak in New York. Only two or three deaths were ever linked to Mallon, a blameless, symptomless carrier of the disease. But labelled 'Typhoid Mary', she was branded THE MOST DANGEROUS WOMAN IN AMERICA in screaming headlines all over the country. Arrested and detained without charge, she was kept in isolation for twenty-six years before she died, still a prisoner.

Mallon was an illustration of one of the rapidly emerging unwritten rules of media production: that the public must be given someone to love and someone to hate. The mass media traditionally insist that they only reflect society, they do not shape it, a refuge from the truth no longer available now that their subtle, complex and far-reaching effects are better understood. But it is hard to eradicate the time-honoured tropes, especially those defining and describing the female.

Mallon was among the first in a long line of candidates for the most hated woman of her time.

And the most loved?

The fairy-tale bride

This is, of course, the old folk tale of Cinderella, the girl who finds her Prince Charming and becomes the Princess Bride, destined to live with him happily ever after. One happy-ever-after in 1956 kept the media in ecstasies for months, when a real-life film star married a real-life prince in a real-life palace, in what was christened the Wedding of the Century. For Grace

Kelly, the marriage offered the starring role of a lifetime. For the impoverished Prince Rainier III in his tiny decrepit principality, it bestowed a cascade of glamour and stardust, putting Monaco on the map for American visitors and super-wealthy future residents.

Equally welcome must have been the pot of gold that appears in all the best fairy tales, the two million dollars Rainier charged Kelly's father for marrying his lovely daughter, archaically described as her 'dowry' when the details came to light. But Kelly's life as a princess, shorn of her film career and restricted to her royal role, was far from fairy tale, and it ended with a cliff-top car accident in which she was killed. By some extraordinary prophetic irony, the person sent to represent the British royal family at Kelly's funeral was another ill-starred Princess Bride, the hapless girl awaiting her own fatal car crash, Diana, Princess of Wales.

Diana

The mass media have always had the power to make or break. In the case of Lady Diana Spencer, they did both. First she was cast as the Virgin Bride, the perfect answer to Prince Charles's long search for the perfect future queen. When they married in 1981, over 750 million people watched the wedding on television, and soon Diana was the Ideal Wife and Mother (*an heir and a spare, job done!*). As the marriage began to fail, Diana became the Wronged Wife and then the Brave Single Mum Trying to Give Her Boys a Normal Upbringing, amid a flurry of photos on log flumes at theme parks. Finally she emerged as a Famous Fighter for the Cause of Women, standing up to the royal family when she hired top London lawyers to handle her divorce and to win a fair settlement from her ex-fairy-tale prince.

From her first emergence as a touching teenager, 'shy Di'

won the hearts of hardened media professionals and the general public alike. So there was little or no coverage of the lovers that Diana was thought to have taken both before and after her divorce, ranging from a car salesman to her police bodyguard and her riding instructor. The media also protected the Princess in 1993 when hundreds of silent calls were made to the home of her married lover, the art dealer Oliver Hoare, and again when she was fruitlessly pursuing the man she told her closest friends was the love of her life, the Pakistani heart surgeon Hasnat Khan. Spurned by him, she took up with the Egyptian playboy Dodi Fayed in July 1997, and only a few weeks later she was dead.

In truth, 'DIANA DEAD', as the headlines splashed the news, proved to be as serviceable to the media as she had been when alive, still generating headlines, full-page spreads and TV documentaries more than twenty years later, and her mystique only grew with the orgy of public grief and hysteria that ran round the globe. 'She wasn't seen as posh, she was one of the people', opined *Time* magazine. Not posh, as a direct descendant of Charles II? And 'one of the people'? 'The People's Princess' was a cheesy invention of the then prime minister, Tony Blair, part of a self-aggrandising fiction in which he cast himself as the man in charge after Diana's death, directing the Queen's response because he had to show the poor old thing what to do.

As the clouds gathered over her marriage, Diana took the decision to turn to the media to win public sympathy, and to show that she was not to blame. Photographed with Aids patients, disabled children and the elderly, she emerged as the nation's darling in a series of powerful and touching images that often seemed to carry the wistful subtext, so *why doesn't my husband love me when everyone else does?*

As her popularity spread, all the world wanted a piece of her, and the more she fed that hunger, the more it grew. The very media that had lovingly tracked her development from a gawky girl to fashion leader and 'Queen of Hearts', the same outlets that had loyally suppressed reports of her less royal activities, expected their pound of flesh, not to mention blood, demanding access to her at all times: in his eulogy at her funeral, Diana's brother, the Earl Spencer, declared that Diana was not the *hunter*, as her name implied, but the *hunted*. So it was that when she left the Ritz Hotel in Paris at midnight on 31 August 1997 after dinner with Dodi, she was trailed by a posse of paparazzi to her death.

The world now knows that Diana used the media to fight her corner, tipping off the newspapers for photo opportunities and giving Andrew Morton the intimate and incendiary material for his 1992 tell-all biography, *Diana: Her True Story*. Diana has never received her due recognition as one of the most successful creators of her own public image, and one of the most astute mass media manipulators of the modern age.

There's a fairy at the bottom of the garden

Naturally, women were not only the subject of the media but involved in making media too. The world's first film-maker was a woman, French-born Alice Guy-Blaché who wrote and directed over a thousand films. Her first short movie of 1896, *La Fée aux choux* (The Fairy Among the Cabbages), a satirical take on an old European folk tale that boys are born underneath cabbages and girls under roses, is now recognised as the world's first narrative film. For ten years afterwards, Guy-Blaché was the only woman making films in France and America, where she owned and ran her own studio. She shared with her contemporary Georges Méliès a delight in visual effects, but the gentle humour and sense of absurdity are all her own.

Check out the film industry in almost any country, and

women were there from the start. Fatma Begum made history in the India of 1922 when she broke not only the social taboo against women appearing in public but also the long-standing stage convention that only men could play female parts. After starring in *Veer Abhimayu* (The Hero Abhimayu), a tragic Hindu warrior myth, she formed her own production company, Fatma Films, in 1926 and made her debut as a writer, director, producer and actor with *Bulbule-Paristan*. As a director, Begum loved special effects and happily pioneered fantasy cinema and science fiction. Her three daughters all became superstars of the silent movies, and the eldest, Zubeida, starred in the 1931 smash hit *Alam Ara* ('The Ornament of the World'). This love story between a prince and a gypsy girl made history as India's first talkie with songs, a clear forerunner of the Bollywood to come.

In the US, the shrewd Canadian-American Mary Pickford also saw the potential of the movie business early on. As a teenager she had no hesitation about giving up a much more prestigious stage career for silent films as soon as director D. W. Griffith offered her ten dollars a day, exactly double what she could make treading the boards. From her debut in black-and-white silents like *The Little Teacher* and *The Awakening*, two of the fifty-one films she made in 1909, she won the heart of film-goers with her sweet smile and cluster of golden curls.

These girlish attributes earned her the nickname 'Blondilocks', and ensured that she was cast as a juvenile long into adulthood. But her public didn't care. After a venture into more mature roles fell flat, she devised and wrote for herself the silent comedy-drama *Little Annie Rooney*, featuring a spunky young orphan getting through life with her dog. Pickford played the twelve-year-old heroine at the age of thirty-three, and generated one of the top money-spinners of 1925.

But the rebel in Pickford looked beyond her dazzling earnings as an actor into the heart of the movie machine, where the real money was made. Within three years of joining the industry, she successfully leveraged her popularity at the box office to gain ever-increasing control not only of subject, script, casting and crew, plus direction and production, but significantly of the film's afterlife: its distribution, circulation and by extension its profits. As early as 1919, she moved into production and distribution, first founding the Pickford-Fairbanks Studio with her secret lover and later husband Douglas Fairbanks, then joining forces with Fairbanks and two other giants of the trade, D. W. Griffith and Charlie Chaplin, to create United Artists. In a career of lifelong success as one of the most powerful women in this cut-throat industry, her only miscalculation was to underestimate the arrival of sound, comparing it to slapping lipstick on the Venus de Milo. Retiring from performance, she continued to be a major Hollywood mover and shaker, and received a Lifetime Academy Award in recognition of her services to the film industry in 1976, almost half a century after her first Oscar for Best Actress in 1929.

Who loves ya, baby?

As Pickford discovered, Hollywood loved to see women on screen looking beautiful and young, and some were very young. Shirley Temple was singing and tap-tapping away for money from the age of three, as were Frances Ethel Gumm from Grand Rapids, Minnesota, better known as Judy Garland, and Peggy 'Merry Dancing' Ryan, who started in her parent's vaudeville act when she was two. Of the three girls, Ryan was the only one to miss the standard starlet horrors of domineering studios with their formulaic demands, body shaming and liberal supplies of uppers and downers. She failed to conform to what became a favourite media narrative, 'A Star is Torn', which is why few people have ever heard of her.

Temple later recalled her driven, obsessive mother curling her hair every night in fifty-six precisely situated ringlets to ensure continuity for the next day's filming. It was a punishing routine with a workload that bordered on the abusive, and it warped her life. Addressing a US conference of the International Women's Forum in the 1990s, she spoke of her life as a child star, and behind the supremely professional dignity and calm I could hear, like every other woman in the assembly, the deep thrum of the resentment she still harboured at this treatment. It had taken decades, she said, before she had come to see how she had been exploited. Whatever the studio bosses paid her, it was a drop in the ocean compared with how much they had made.

Temple's image and her unique selling point were her sweet innocence and her dimpled smile, shown to perfection in her breakthrough movie of 1934, *Bright Eyes*, the first time she sang 'On the Good Ship Lollipop', which became her signature tune. In *Curly Top* a year later, she had another hit movie and another world-famous song, 'Animal Crackers in My Soup'. She was Hollywood's number one box-office draw from 1935 to 1938, with the studio raking in millions from her films and their spin-offs: half a million copies of the sheet music of 'On the Good Ship Lollipop' flew off the shelves in the first three months after the release of *Bright Eyes*. There were also mountains of Shirley dolls and other Shirley-themed merchandise – cash cows all, and she saw none of it.

While Mary Pickford at thirty-three had cast herself as a feisty ragamuffin almost a third of her age, Shirley Temple was required to play roles that were way beyond her years, displaying an unfailing capacity for command and control as her child character sorted everything out. Another questionable aspect of Shirley Temple's career lay in the fact that she also had to show off her all-singing, all-dancing physical prowess in skimpy clothes and short skirts. The moral ambiguity of promoting a performer as young as she was with a deliberately sexualised adult agenda, was noted by Graham Greene in a 1937 review of *Wee Willie Winkie*:

> Already two years ago she was a fancy little piece ... Now in *Wee Willie Winkie* she is a complete totsy ... Her admirers – middle-aged men and clergymen – respond to her dubious coquetry, to the sight of her well-shaped and desirable little body, packed with enormous vitality, only because the safety curtain of story and dialogue drops between their intelligence and their desire.

> Twentieth Century Fox sued Greene for libel, and won. And that was the end of that.

Is that a gun in your pocket . . .?

But those promoting Temple as an innocent and wholesome example of American womanhood in training were only part of the story. Like most of the American West, Hollywood was a magnet for those born to be wild, and the early film industry was a natural home for those inclined to break rules. While Temple's films came out under babyish titles like *Our Little Girl* and *Dimples*, the writer, actor, director and producer Mae West had already stormed Broadway in 1926 with an indisputably adult play she called *Sex*. Her early years as a hoofer and songbird in the rough and tumble of vaudeville had made her tough, and she loved a good dust-up. A high-profile run-in with the outraged New York authorities killed the show, but the publicity it generated set her up for life. Two years later her play *Diamond Lil*, with West herself starring as the satisfyingly salacious and fast-talking, free-booting heroine, proved such a hit that she revived it successfully for the rest of her career.

And so to Hollywood. Continuing to run her own show,

West became the number one cheerleader for women in film from the 1930s onwards. Launching her stellar movie career at the late age of thirty-nine, she had the maturity and experience denied to Tinseltown beginners, when, in her own words, 'a dame that knows the ropes isn't likely to get tied up'. As a writer, West created an effortless flow of lines like this, and as a performer, she knew how to deliver them. Her humour had universality and authority, so that when she said 'To err is human, but it feels divine' or 'You only live once, but if you do it right once is enough,' all the world knew what she meant.

Her rebel wit created the character for which she is remembered, that of the independent woman who both earns and controls her own money, knowing exactly how many beans make five. She satisfies her every desire, from fox furs to fancy men, but shuns marriage like the plague because a husband would only cramp her style. With lines like 'When I'm good, I'm very very good, but when I'm bad, I'm better,' she mocked the cherished ideal of the good wife and mother, and merrily promoted herself as a turbo-charged sex goddess whose victims queued up for the promise of ecstasy, even at the risk of the agony of expiring in the throes of such utter bliss. Nothing was sacred. Men? 'Ten men at the door?' she quipped. 'Send one of them home, I'm tired.' Motherhood? 'That guy's no good. His mother should have thrown him away and kept the stork.' Virginity? 'I used to be Snow White, but I drifted.'

The cutting one-liner was only one of West's techniques for making sport with sex. She also had an unparalleled gift for what the Ancient Romans called innuendo and the French *double entendre*, a process so foreign to good, clean all-American minds that they have no word for it. What would respectable bridge parties of the 1930s, for instance, have made of her declaration that 'Good sex is like good bridge. If you don't have a good partner, you'd better have a good hand'?

West clearly enjoyed rebelling against convention, and her fearless flouting of good-womanly behaviour brought her into constant conflict with the moral zealots who created the notorious American Motion Picture Production Code. This rigid set of rules for film-makers, uniquely powerful from 1930 to 1968, was a list of *Dos* and *Don'ts* (mainly *Don'ts*) drawn up by two Catholic guardians of public purity, a layman, Martin Quigley, and Father Daniel Lord, a Jesuit priest. The Catholic authorship was kept secret, although insiders keenly relished the irony of a Jewish industry imposing Catholic morality on Protestant America. 'America's favourite hussy', as Mae was called, was impervious to disapproval: 'Those who are easily shocked should be shocked more often.' They were, of course. The wonder is that she got away with it for so long.

Fasten your seatbelts . . .

Unlike Pickford or West, Bette Davis wanted to portray women who could be good or bad or both, complex characters who could be as driven and conflicted as she was herself. Her chance came when the former silent movie idol George Arliss, by now a major star of the talkies, was looking for a girl to play his fiancée in a 1932 production of *The Man Who Played God*. The heroine is caught between her duty to her future husband and her desire for another man, and Arliss had a sense that Davis could bring a greater depth to the character than most of the more one-dimensional *ingénues*. He was right. After one look at the rough cut, Warner Bros signed her up to a contract for five years that eventually lasted for eighteen.

An actor of exceptional power and unique personality, Davis was a measure of the industry's ability to attract women with enough star quality to light the Milky Way. But she was an oddly shaped piece on the chessboard, and the Warner bosses never understood how to play her. Hungry for meaty roles that would showcase her range, Davis welcomed parts that other female stars rejected, and delivered a scorching performance as the cruel, ignorant Mildred who tries to destroy the life of the man who loves her in *Of Human Bondage* (1934).

She was, however, at the mercy of a studio system that rigidly controlled what she was allowed to play, and became convinced that the men in suits were ruining her career by forcing her to appear in feeble films that gave her no chance to shine. Her bid for freedom came in 1936, when she broke her contract and sued Warner Bros in an attempt to be released from it. She lost the case, but her rebellion paid off when a rattled studio placated her with better scripts, higher fees and the increased control she had fought for, and she stayed with Warner for another fourteen years. In that time she earned the nickname of 'The Fourth Warner Brother' for a string of critical and commercial successes, including the classic weepie of 1942, *Now, Voyager,* for which she won an Oscar nomination.

But times changed. The first women in Hollywood lost power as soon as chauvinists like Samuel Goldwyn and Louis B. Mayer, not forgetting the Great British export Alfred Hitchcock, arrived and froze them out. The new boys needed them, they used them, but they kept them in their place as servants to their ideas. Hitchcock's wife, Alma Reville, was an established screenwriter, editor and director's assistant when they met. After that, his career simply swallowed hers whole, and her later work was all behind the scenes, often without any on-screen credit, writing and preparing her husband's scripts and scenarios.

Equally patriarchal was the focus on showing women what they should be doing with their lives instead of getting a job and making their own way in the world. In the 'golden years' of mid-twentieth century Hollywood, the great dream factory made film after film feeding women the fiction that their future lay in finding the right man, and getting him to marry her. These fairy tales were dressed up with songs and dances, sparkling jewellery, glamorous gowns and handsome men. The movie-makers seemed driven by the belief that all a girl wanted was a ring by spring. Post-war Hollywood turned out a series of films in this vein, and even when there was a sparky heroine like Doris Day in the international hit *Calamity Jane* in 1953 and Jane Powell in *Seven Brides for Seven Brothers* a year later, it still cheerily insisted on showing female viewers how to nab that man and with him enjoy a life of domestic fulfilment.

In truth, Hollywood was always a battleground between those who saw its role as the moral guardian and shaper of women and society, and those who recognised it as one of America's greatest gifts to the free world along with jazz and pantyhose. How did film turn in the twentieth century from an art form of wit, humour and invention to a *drip-drip-drip* message to women that women were for men, and should be happy and grateful? This message was so close to the main thrust of all religions that Hollywood gently and invisibly evolved into the Church of America, using its empire – a cinema in every town – to spread the good news.

SHE – and others like her

Film's obsession with the need of every young woman to find a man was echoed and replicated in most of the women's magazines spawned in the mass media age. For women, the advent of modern magazines like *SHE* (first published 1955) put a shiny new edge on an old blade, which began in London as far back as 1693 with the *Ladies' Mercury*. Later iterations of a publication designed solely for women cropped up in Egypt, India, Thailand and the United States. Even the Nazis started one of their own, the *NS-Frauen-Warte*, the Paper of the

National Socialist Women's League, packed from 1934 to 1945 with good-housewife-and-Aryan-mother stuff. In the new mass media age, the topics became more varied, the pictures better, the colour and style more exciting, but the titles said it all. *Good Housekeeping* sailed over from America to build a British readership in the hundreds of thousands, but there was still room for *Woman*, *Woman's Own* and *Woman and Home*. The story read the same all over the world, with *Family Circle* in the US and *Homemakers* in Canada, while Australia's *Better Homes and Gardens* introduced a competitive spark to keep readers on their toes.

You'd better be better . . .

These publications are aimed at women who focus on their womanhood and their home as their main priority, and while they offer their readers pleasure and relaxation, they also play constantly on any insecurities they may have. 'New year, new you!' they trill, 'new' being one of the handful of words shown by research to be the most effective in sales and marketing. Or 'new wallpaper/new look for a tired bedroom/new ideas for a small hallway/new loo!' In other words, *consult your own sense of inadequacy or competitiveness and get busy making new, new, new!*

Marry, or . . . ?

But where you have women, you have rebels, and a famous early fighter, Helen Gurley Brown, raised the flag in 1962 with her first book, *Sex and the Single Girl*. When the mantra of the time was 'You can marry him, or you can say no', Brown created the dazzlingly successful *Cosmopolitan* magazine by laying down the guidelines for a woman who wanted to do neither. Almost single-handedly she de-coupled sex from marriage, derailing the social and religious fixation that they go together like a horse and carriage.

Another innovation was her dismissal of the long-instilled commandment that in sex the only pleasure that counted was the man's, and the good wifey-woman lay back and thought of England – or of America, or of hats and shoes. While Brown blithely taught her readers how to make a man happy by publishing her own personal blow-by-blow account of giving oral sex, she always remembered that the sexual pleasure of the *Cosmo* girl was her number one priority, and she never forgot to remind women to look out for themselves.

A rebel, then? Certainly she anticipated the taboo-breaking of the hippy revolution and helped to consign the worship of virginity to the trash can in the US, and in at least some of the one hundred-plus other countries where the magazine was sold. And certainly she developed if not created the concept and the protocol of a woman's sexual needs and rights long before most of the world's females realised they had either. Although softly spoken and reserved when I knew her in the 1990s, she fearlessly put sex on every agenda, demystifying it and dispelling any embarrassment or shame. She was not disturbed when *National Lampoon* parodied her editor's letter column 'Step into my Parlor' as 'Step into my Panties', or when *Private Eye* spoofed a *Cosmo* cover with a strapline rejoicing 'PAINT YOUR TOE-NAILS GOLD AND WIN 5 ORGASMS FOR CHRISTMAS!' She knew what she was doing when she made the magazine into the biggest-selling women's magazine in the world, and she had faith in all of it.

To her critics, however, both she and the magazine had one central flaw: the core belief in the centrality of men in the life of every *Cosmo* girl. True, by the time I came on board as a writer the emphasis had shifted from 'How to marry an airline pilot/barrister/top executive' to 'How to *become*' all of the above, and HGB herself always stressed financial literacy as an essential element of a woman's life. But it fell to the next generation to devise a magazine for women offering an alternative to a life built around men. *Ms* magazine was launched in 1972 as a direct challenge to all existing women's magazines where women were in charge as editors, but never in control. At *Ms*, editorial power, ownership and control resided with co-founders Gloria Steinem and Dorothy Pitman Hughes, along with a strong team of women writers and activists such as Letty Cottin Pogrebin, a founder member with Steinem of the National Women's Political Caucus the year before.

The mission of *Ms* was to present work on subjects about women and by women that were not being covered in mainstream magazines. The team made history in its first year when it published the names of women prepared to admit that they had had an illegal abortion, an echo of the 'Manifesto of the 343' published in France the year before. In 1976 *Ms* became the first national magazine to promote awareness of violence against women by printing a ground-breaking cover showing a bruised and battered female face. These were the 'women-and-home' stories that were not being told, and not everyone wanted to hear. When *Spare Rib* began in the UK the same year as the launch of *Ms*, founded with the same mission to promote women's liberation, WH Smith refused to handle such incendiary material. Run by a collective, *Spare Rib* won a reputation for investigative journalism by running an early probe into the wage gap, and by highlighting other don't-ask-don't-tell stories such as sex trafficking and date rape.

A new Dawn

And things changed again, all through the media world. In Hollywood, the prospects for women improved as the tidal wave of the women's movement washed through the 1970s. A 1973 survey by the Women's Committee of the Writers'

Guild of America showed that virtually all films and television shows were produced, written and directed by men, the crews were men and the companies behind them were run by men. Most of the shows had no women writers at all – a particular irony when a female character was central to the story, as in the Oscar-nominated *Nicholas and Alexandra* and *Mary, Queen of Scots*. In the ensuing discussions about finding women to fill the gaps, the newly promoted Columbia executive Renée Valente, later the first female president of the Producers' Guild of America, asked one male colleague what he did not like about women in the business. 'Women in the business,' he replied.

But the women were not inclined to go away. Bursting through the celluloid ceiling, Sherry Lansing was the first woman to head a Hollywood film studio when she became president of production at 20th Century Fox in 1980. By 1992, she was running Paramount Pictures, overseeing a steady stream of its most critically successful and profitable movies since the 1930s, including *Titanic* (1997), one of the highest-grossing films of all time. Lansing's courteous management style led to her being called the 'Queen of Cool', and even Hollywood cynics had to agree that she was a welcome variation on the old-school media moguls like the producer David O. Selznick, who regularly boasted, 'I don't get ulcers, I give 'em.'

The next woman to run a major studio was the very different Dawn Steel, whose colourful background as the hardball heroine of various . . . shall we say complex? . . . commercial ventures (including ripping off the Gucci logo to sell a line of toilet rolls) was in no way considered an obstacle to her advancement in the cloacal world of Hollywood. As production chief at Paramount in 1985, Steel was responsible for such hits as *Flashdance*, *Beverly Hills Cop* and *Top Gun*. Moving to Columbia Pictures as president in 1987, she hit pay dirt again with another international success, *When Harry Met Sally*. This film made history with Meg Ryan's famous faked female orgasm.

So they were free, were they, these rebel women, winning power and control in a major modern medium? Not always. Sherry Lansing survived twelve years at Paramount before she stepped down, and was immediately offered a string of other top-level posts. Dawn Steel's reign at Columbia lasted only two. She was fired after a string of flops in 1989, having failed to turn the company around from a series of unsuccessful ventures left behind by the previous CEO, David Puttnam. The blow fell when she was in labour with her first child (*timing, huh?*), and unsurprisingly, her career never recovered. From the first, the rising Dawn had encountered a general resistance to her authority as a woman and specific hostility to her as a person. It did not help that while Sherry Lansing was mocked for her emollient style, Steel's was described as 'Take no prisoners!', and she was both famed and feared for her strong, often shouty, leadership.

But in her time at Columbia she made a point of bringing on other women, as Nora Ephron, the screenwriter of *When Harry Met Sally*, recalled at Steel's death in 1997:

> Dawn certainly wasn't the first woman to become powerful in Hollywood, but she was the first woman to understand that part of her responsibility was to make sure that eventually there were lots of other powerful women. She hired women as executives, women as producers and directors, women as marketing people. The situation we have today, with a huge number of women in powerful positions, is largely because of Dawn Steel.

How did this all work through? Is it a coincidence that the breakthrough years of the women's movement also saw the onslaught of films trumpeting the danger of the female sex?

Exaggeration?
How about these?

- *Rosemary's Baby* (1968)
- *The Exorcist* (1973)
- *Carrie* (1976)
- *Looking for Mr Goodbar* (1977)

In a Technicolor jumble of fears ancient and modern, these films portrayed women as dangerous, disgusting and fraught with horror and sin. And remember *Fatal Attraction* (1987), when a deranged woman threatens a perfect American marriage and the unfaithful husband comes out free and clear while she meets a watery end like an old-time witch plunged into the village pond? The wicked Bunny Boiler even displays supernatural powers when she rises from the dead after our hero has drowned her in the bath, and to cleanse his house and save his family she has to be killed all over again. Glenn Close's character Alex, the unhinged New York book editor, is an all-out attack on the figure of the single, successful, happily employed and high-earning female professional, with the clear message that a life like hers would drive any woman mad, and when they go mad, *all they want is a man.* Some saw this as a portrayal of a woman driven into mental breakdown by a man, representing all men. To others, she was just a horny, crazy bitch who got what she deserved.

Like sexism, racism was another unacknowledged and unmentionable elephant in the studio from the dawn of movie-making, one that made the lives of women of colour doubly difficult in the world of the Great White Male. Even in the twenty-first century, female actors of colour still had to pass the 'paper bag test', said Viola Davis, the star of the 2011 film *The Help.* Dating from the days of slavery, this form of racial discrimination rated an individual's acceptability on the basis of their skin tone: the lighter, the better.

Above all for women, Davis added: 'If you are darker than a [brown] paper bag, then you are not sexy, you are not a woman, you shouldn't be in the realm of anything that men should desire.' If you are older, too, she might have said: she was fifty at the time. Nevertheless, Davis was the first black woman actor to be nominated for three Academy Awards and the first to achieve the US Triple Crown of Acting. That meant one of just twenty-four performers at time of writing to win a Tony, an Emmy and an Oscar, interestingly enough, nine men and fifteen women – *rebel women still moving forward!*

Getting conversations started

There's another test for the representation of women in fiction, films and on television, the Bechdel–Wallace test. This is named for the American cartoonist Alison Bechdel, who came up with three rules in her 1985 comic strip *Dykes to Watch Out For*. The scene/story has to have:

1. at least two women in it
2. who talk to each other
3. about something besides a man.

Bechdel at first intended it as just a lesbian joke, but struck home with so many that it has become a virtually infallible way or measuring equality on the page and on the screen.

Mad about the girl

Film always saw itself as the main player on the media field. But from the 1950s, television caught up and overtook it. Given a place of honour at the heart of every home, the TV became the household oracle that interpreted the outside world to those by definition on the inside, and thereby exerted a considerable influence over the public response. Over time, this unthreatening domestic medium succeeded in reshaping, if not reversing, old attitudes of the popular press, including the deep-rooted prejudice against women loving women.

Yet Sapphists, named for Sappho of Lesbos, were not always seen as different from other women, or dangerous. Sappho's own interest in women posed no problem for her enthusiastically homosexual male contemporaries in Ancient Greece, nor for the other writers of her day, who recognised her as one of their greatest poets. Later ages took a different view, as did the fathers of the early Christian Church. Today only around 650 lines of her poetry survive of the ten thousand or so she wrote, after the Pope ordered her poems to be burned in Rome and Constantinople in 1073, and other Christian leaders followed suit.

For centuries, women's sexuality was controlled by the compulsory heterosexuality of marriage. Nonetheless, 'romantic friendships' were often quietly tolerated, like the discreet 'Boston marriages' of late-nineteenth-century America. Most of these women spent their lives hiding in plain sight, working on the silent, self-censoring principle of *don't ask, don't tell*. But the progress of medical knowledge in the nineteenth century, and the spread of psychology in the twentieth, led to an earnest desire to discover, diagnose and classify various conditions that had not been identified as pathologies before. And what better candidate for being pathologised as 'unnatural' than a woman who spurned the entire species of man in favour of another woman?

The German psychiatrist Richard von Krafft-Ebing led the charge with the discovery that lesbianism was a neurological disease. Since the entire purpose of sex was procreation, any-thing that did not lead to that outcome was not only a vice, but a perversion of nature. 'In almost all such cases,' he wrote, 'the individual subject to the perverse instinct displays a neuropathic predisposition in several directions ... this anomaly of psycho-sexual feeling may be called, clinically, a functional sign of degeneration.' Krafft-Ebing's attitude towards women's love in his *Psychopathia Sexualis* (1886) is clear from his use of terms like this. It was degenerate, diseased, unnatural, abnormal, flying in the face of nature.

Defining gay women as suffering from a mental and physical illness may seem both insulting to them and damaging to any hope of social acceptance. But against the background of the age-old belief that anything but the straightest of straight sex was both a sin and a crime, Krafft-Ebing was remarkable for his ability to move beyond condemning lesbians for acting out their 'unnatural vice'. Lesbianism, he argued, originated in biologi-cal damage to the infant in the womb that produced a 'sexual inversion' of the brain, and this marked an important advance in removing blame from lesbians for the way they were. They were not deliberately choosing to flout civilised standards, but simply living out the dictates of their nature. They were, in Krafft-Ebing's explanation, 'inverts', individuals whose natural and innate attraction to the opposite sex had been turned inside out, through no fault of their own.

His British disciple Henry Havelock Ellis agreed that lesbi-anism was a form of insanity, but did not agree that it could be permanent: many women who thought they loved other women got over it as soon as they had experience of marriage and 'a practical life'. But others were 'true inverts', he said, a 'Third Sex' who rejected 'normal' female life and chose to live as men, free to pursue their 'masculine' desires.

*

No woman embraced this concept more eagerly than the writer Marguerite Radclyffe Hall, who had studied *Psychopathia Sexualis* in detail and resolved to bring the theoretical concept of the invert vividly to life in her work. Born the only daughter of a rich man longing for a son then inheriting his wealth as an adult and with it his sense of entitlement, she eagerly dumped the flowery identity of Marguerite in favour of 'John', the love-name bestowed on her by her first lesbian partner, and a good-looking young man she made, too.

Radclyffe Hall earned her place in history for daring to write and publish the first mainstream novel in English with a lesbian heroine and a lesbian plot. A devout Catholic, she struggled all her life to square her profound belief in God with her attraction to women and with the comfort she drew from her circle of lesbian friends and lovers, a conflict she longed to resolve.

By 1926, the outlook seemed favourable. Her most recent novel, *Adam's Breed*, enjoyed commercial and literary success, winning major awards including the French Prix Femina. Riding high in Europe and the UK, she was also warmly encouraged by Havelock Ellis. 'I have read *The Well of Loneliness* with great interest,' he wrote in a letter commenting on an early draft that later became the introduction to the first edition of the novel, 'because – apart from its fine qualities as a novel by a writer of accomplished art – it possesses a notable psychological and sociological significance. So far as I know, it is the first English novel which presents, in a completely faithful and uncompromising form, one particular aspect of sexual life as it exists among us today.' Accordingly, Radclyffe Hall decided in 1928 that the time was right to publish her novel.

Alas, she was wrong, disastrously wrong. Convicted of obscenity after an excoriating trial, Radclyffe Hall was ruined, financially and socially, and left England with her partner Una

'John' in the Paris days of the brilliant circle around the American lesbian Natalie Barney, painted by Charles Buchel, 1918.

Troubridge to live in France. But *The Well of Loneliness* survived to give hope to generations. And the climax, where the heroine on the verge of suicide cries out to God on behalf of all 'inverts', still stands as a powerful plea:

'Acknowledge us, oh God, before the whole world. Give us also the right to our existence!'

Way out west

Radclyffe Hall paid heavily for breaking the social code and the harsh law of her time. The flamboyant Spanish-Cuban poet, playwright and novelist Mercedes de Acosta found a more accommodating scene in the early Hollywood of the 1920s, reportedly boasting 'I can get any woman off any man!' Known as the Spanish Lothario, she made good her claim by having open affairs with Isadora Duncan, Marlene Dietrich, Greta Garbo and the Russian silent-film star Alla Nazimova among many others. Her friend and possibly one-time lover Alice B. Toklas, partner of Gertrude Stein, summed it up: 'Say what you will about Mercedes, she's had the most important women of the twentieth century.'

Predatory, ruthless and reckless, de Acosta was a rare bird even by the standards of the jungle that was Hollywood, red in tooth and claw. Most women attracted to women knew that they had to keep quiet. When Eleanor Roosevelt fell in love with a woman, the reporter Lorena 'Hick' Hickok, breaking cover was not an option. For the wife of any politician, it would be unthinkable. For the wife of the president, impossible.

Many of Eleanor's admirers have always denied that this 'close friendship' was a lesbian affair, despite the evidence: 'I want to put my arms around you, I ache to hold you close' is one of Eleanor's many tender tributes to Hick. But for all the love between them, Hick did not attend Eleanor's funeral, fearing that media coverage would confirm the gossip that had been hovering around them for years. She also burned an unknown number of letters they exchanged before she died. Through acts and attitudes like these, lesbian love often passed unnoticed or unacknowledged, shielded as it was from scrutiny by the safety of marriage, money, status and high birth, or else by the innocence, ignorance or denial of both men and women that it had always been a part of human life, and still was.

Nowhere was this monocular view of women's sexual activity more deeply held than in the mass media. The American Babe Didrikson became one of the world's first celebrity athletes, when everything she touched turned to gold. At the 1932 Olympics she won two gold medals, for high jump and javelin, and she displayed equal prowess at hurdling, basketball, baseball and softball, as well as diving, roller skating and bowling. She was so awesome in action that the hardened sports writer Grantland Rice could hardly contain himself. 'She is beyond all belief until you see her perform,' he raved. 'Then you finally understand that you are looking at the most flawless section of muscle harmony, of complete mental and physical coordination, the world of sport has ever seen.' Coming late to golf at the age of twenty-four, Babe hit another winning streak that led to her being rated as one the greatest golfers of all time.

Babe was America's wonder woman, and she knew it. But she also knew that the Great American Public of 1950 would not approve if they knew that she was in love with a fellow golfer nineteen years her junior, Betty Dodd, and that Dodd adored her too. Like so many women before and since, they remained underground, and Babe's husband went along with it.

Just good friends

It's the old paradox, the familiar patchwork of reality, that for centuries the US has been the most open, progressive and modern society on the planet. Yet at the same time it was the most puritanical, evangelical peddler of sickening if not suffocating stereotypes of female subordination, stressing the 'normalcy' of heterosexuality and the divine rightness of male control. Whatever the brilliant, bold and beautiful Babe had done for America, she could have no faith that her country would extend a scintilla of understanding to her.

Yet slowly and below the surface, the old attitudes were shifting. The freedom to learn, to earn, to work and live outside the family benefited many women, but arguably lesbians most of all. With these freedoms came the chance to meet other women, and to begin building a community that would in time refuse to be dismissed. *Qui se rassemble, s'assemble*, say the French: those who are like another, find the way to get together. At Gateways, the legendary London club that ran from the 1930s to 1985, former member, the academic Dr Jane Traies, remembered clearly the comfort and strength the women drew from being together:

> I was a typical femme [in the 1960s], a little girl in a short skirt. Most people were terrified in those days and didn't dare be out as lesbians, but at the Gates we were safe, we could be ourselves. You were seen as abnormal everywhere else.

Being safe, being together, these were the embryonic stirrings of the sisterly solidarity that would help women who did not fit the mould find a way to break out of it. The tough-talking American writer, activist and chronicler of lesbian life, Rita Mae Brown, summed it up in *Rubyfruit Jungle*, her truth-telling novel of 1973:

> I didn't even want a husband or any man for that matter. I wanted to go my own way. That's all I think I ever wanted, to go my own way and maybe find some love here and there.

Love, but not the now and forever kind with chains around
your vagina and a short circuit in your brain.

And among the mass media, television was a prime mover
in the process of changing attitudes. Two long-running series,
one in Britain and the second in the US, are commemorated
for broadcasting the first openly lesbian scenes and storylines in
mainstream popular entertainment. Britain is widely believed
to have led the way in 1994, when an episode of the soap opera
Brookside featured a passionate kiss between two women. In
fact, twenty years earlier the BBC had broadcast a TV drama,
Girl, the story of two women army officers that showed the pair
kissing, but it was handled so gingerly that it created little stir.
Similarly, *Brookside* caused some comment for broadcasting a
lesbian scene before the watershed, but there was not much fuss.

The British reaction contrasts strongly with the frenzy that
gripped the US at the end of April 1997, when viewers tuned
in to see the central character of the series *Ellen* come out as
gay. The star of the series that ran for five years between 1994
and 1998, Ellen DeGeneres, came out at the same time in an
interview with Oprah Winfrey. The 'Puppy Episode', so called
after the codename that kept it secret in production, has been
hailed as 'the most hyped, anticipated, and possibly influential
gay moment on television' and as paving the way for other
programmes to deal with LGBT+ issues as a regular fact of life.

And Ellen DeGeneres deserves all the credit for putting her
personal life on the line and bringing it into the show to reach
the wider world. The series using her name and tracking the life
of a single woman began to run out of reasons why the character
dated men but nothing ever came of it, and the feeling grew
between the actor and her production team that it was time for
her to come out. When she did, with the simple words 'I'm gay',
the show was watched by forty-two million people and though

there was some critical backlash and the show was not renewed beyond the next season, it was generally well received.

DeGeneres herself considered that the show achieved its aim, and has stood the test of time. 'I think it helped a lot of people,' she said in 2008, 'and still to this day I hear about parents and children being able to have an honest conversation through watching that show. That's ultimately what television can be: it can get conversations started.' Later she told the audience on her talk show, *The Ellen DeGeneres Show*, what a relief the whole process had been: 'It was the hardest thing that I ever had to do in my life. I would not change one moment of it because it led me to be exactly where I am today – standing in front of all of you, which is a joy. And the fact that all of you and everyone at home is watching me and willing to accept me into your homes every day, when no one thought that would ever happen again – it means the world to me.'

Under the net

Just as television supplanted film, so the internet took the world by surprise in outstripping TV and all other media as the primary medium of mass communication in the late twentieth century. More than a century after Ada, Countess of Lovelace had recognised that computers could do far more than just add up, the US Navy officer 'Amazing' Grace Hopper taught them how to speak. Her work led to the birth of COBOL in 1959, a computer language still in use today. With the same leap of imagination, the British engineer Tim Berners-Lee created a new medium in 1989 and called it the World Wide Web. His mother, the computer scientist Mary Lee Berners-Lee, had opened the door for him and she was among the many women involved in the computer revolution as it created a new universe of unmapped galaxies.

Reaching out

As the internet opened up new channels of communication all over the world, it helped to break down the isolation central to the subordination of women, especially in tyrannical regimes. In 2009 eleven-year-old Malala Yousafzai began a blog for BBC Urdu that reached America, Europe and beyond. Rebelling against the repression that she and her fellow-pupils suffered under the Taliban in her part of Pakistan led to her being shot in the head on her way home from school. Her renewed determination to promote the cause of education for girls saw her honoured as the youngest-ever winner of the Nobel Peace Prize in 2014 .

Another rebel made famous by the internet was the young Saudi woman seen in an online video wandering through a deserted town in a miniskirt and crop top. Cue outrage in 'The Kingdom' where the law forces women to wear the full-length black abaya in public, plus a headscarf or full-face veil, on pain of punishment. Cue too the joy of the international press when they could run headlines like WOMAN ARRESTED FOR WEARING A SKIRT!

More fun was to follow. What was the charge, public indecency? There was no public. What was the offence, insulting Islam? No reference to religion had been made. What had she done? Revealed to the world the state secret that Saudi women had legs, waists, arms and hair? Or was it that she was seen out on her own, challenging Saudi Arabia's 'male guardianship' system that decrees females must always remain under the control of men and so, like little children, they can never be allowed out on their own? Lacking any reason to detain her, the authorities quietly released this dangerous offender without charge.

Fairy tales, secrets, oppression and lies, the mass media offered all these to the women of the modern world, and more. But there was no denying its part in women's growing power, confidence and significance as the century wore on. Ambivalent as its mixed messages could be, pop music picked up the spirit of the time in heralding women's new-found control of their own lives.

First in the field was Helen Reddy's 1971 hit, 'I Am Woman'. Destined to become an unofficial feminist anthem, it caught the spirit of the times with the defiant promise, 'No one's ever gonna keep me down again.' In 1977 Bette Midler sang 'You're Moving Out Today', celebrating a woman's ownership of her own home and her right to decide who lived there, and *who didn't*.

The equally powerful 'Sisters Are Doin' It for Themselves' released by Eurythmics in 1985, similarly hailed 'the conscious liberation of the female state', and it didn't stop there. Women were going forward with every ounce of the grit, guts and gumption implied by Reddy's pledge, because the game was moving on.

CHAPTER 11

OUR BODIES, OUR SELVES

The body is the socket of the soul.

OLD ENGLISH PROVERB

The basic freedom of the world is woman's freedom.

MARGARET SANGER

Another world is not only possible, she is on her way.
On a quiet day, I can hear her breathing.

ARUNDHATI ROY

In the still-unfolding scroll of women's achievements in the modern era, winning control of their bodies is a major and ongoing task, because it forms or deforms the whole of their lives. One of the triumphs of the last two hundred years has been the progress made towards freeing women from being seen as prisoners of their biology and also subject to men's views of how women should look and behave.

What women achieved was all the more remarkable when we remember how limiting these expectations could be.

Throughout the age of revolutions and despite the vagaries of fashion, most women still confined and restricted their bodies with a series of physical restraints that had gone unchanged for centuries, stiff bodices and heavy full-length skirts underpinned by various kinds of corseting. The majority of these were rigid body forms made of layers of dense fabric stuck together with glue and reinforced with 'stays' (a word that became short-hand for the whole garment) of whalebone or iron, and fitted with laces at the back designed to produce the tiniest waist by being drawn together as tightly as the wearer could tolerate. Uncomfortable, often painful and always restricting a woman's ability to move about or breathe freely, they constituted a daily reminder of women's secondary status to men, who could walk or run wherever they wanted to go.

Mothers of invention

Casting off the corset in the 1920s was one of the greatest free-doms Western women ever won. But free of the corset, what next for rebel girls? Hurrah for the bra, an icon of the new female spirit at large. The classic nineteenth-century corset had pro-duced the fashionable and supposedly desirable 'pouter pigeon' silhouette, a massive swollen mono-bosom admiringly named *le balcon* (the balcony) by Belle Époque French men-about-town. Aiming for the more elegant outline of two pillows rather than one bolster, in 1910 the American debutante Mary Jacob – later better known as Caresse Crosby – devised the first bra from a pair of silk handkerchiefs and a length of pink ribbon with the help of her maid, and wore it to a society event that night.

The story of what became a mainstay, if you'll pardon the pun, of most female wardrobes included others besides Mary Jacob, but in 1914 she became the first to patent it, and the first to begin trading, establishing the Fashion Form Brassiere

Company in Boston in 1920. Four years later, her husband pressured her to sell the patent. Caresse got fifteen hundred dollars, and the buyer made millions of dollars for decades afterwards.

And that was only one version of a piece of bodywear that took on as many different shapes as the women who bought them. The bold young women who bobbed their hair in the 1920s wanted tight breast bands to produce the fashionable boyish look, a type of brassière that corsetières of the twenty-first century still call 'The Minimiser'. This one also suited the demands of wartime service or factory work, but peacetime and leisure after the Second World War created variations on 'The Maximiser': the push-up, the padded, the underwired, the strapless, and possibly the acme of structural engineering, the circle–stitch style guaranteed to produce two perfectly pointed and symmetrical cones, as seen on Marilyn Monroe and others in the 1950s.

If that was a high point in bra history, a low occurred at the birth of the women's liberation movement in the 1960s, when bra-burning came to symbolise women casting off male oppression. Unfortunately for the myth of ball-busting, man-hating Amazons, not one woman ever burnt her bra. It was all made up by the press. Sadly, some hacks still trot out this pitiful fiction, unfettered by accuracy or truth.

The bottom half of the female body also went through a sequence of re-imaginings, from the suspender (US garter) belt, to what were euphemistically called girdles. These were all pretty grim, as I remember them in the UK, tight elasticated tubes we called 'roll-ons' worn between waist and thigh, hot and sticky in summer, clammy and cold in winter, a torment always. Finally, in the 1960s, women were granted the supreme liberation of tights, or pantyhose. What a relief from all the fiddle-faddle of suspenders and stocking tops, much as some men adored them. These inventions followed the decade when tampons came to supplement 'sanitary pads' (*why were women ever insanitary?*), which had themselves proved a welcome liberation from the chore of boiling out the monthly menstrual rags.

But the next step was the greatest.

One small step for a man – one great step for womankind?

Of all the famous female firsts in the twentieth century, a life-changing event was the arrival in 1958 of the oral contraceptive almost immediately known simply as 'the pill'. And what a gift that was! The condom was tricky because it was outside women's control (*would he buy one? Would he bother to use it? Could he get it on right?*). The cervical diaphragm or Dutch cap was a big improvement because it was in a woman's hands, but it required a liberal application of cold and slimy spermicidal jelly and a passion-killing attempt at positioning it that could be quite demoralising when you couldn't tell your cervix from the parson's nose, and handsome Joe Bedworthy was knocking at the door.

Knowing all this, the great Margaret Sanger, the Mother of Birth Control, was determined to see a contraceptive that a woman could take as easily as she popped an aspirin for a head-ache. From her own research, she became convinced that the route must lie through understanding the hormones regulating ovulation. If the release of a woman's egg could be prevented, there would be no need for barrier methods, because there would be nothing for the sperm to fertilise. At a dinner party one night in 1950, Sanger met the scientist Gregory Pincus, whose work lay in that field. Abraham Stone, the host who brought them together that evening, was not only the director of the Margaret Sanger Research Bureau, but also the medical director and vice-president of the Planned Parent Federation of America, which soon put up the funds to begin the work.

But the money ran out, and no university or pharmaceutical company would take up the project. All were reluctant to be seen rocking the boat by promoting contraception in a country where birth control was against the law in thirty states. In addition, very few believed that Sanger's 'magic pill' was even possible. One who did was the scientist and feminist Katharine McCormick, who luckily had already developed a keen interest in hormonal research. One of the first women graduates of Massachusetts Institute of Technology, McCormick had also been a suffragist and luckily again, she was well placed to advance the project because she had a great deal of money, which she placed at Sanger's disposal to complete the work.

It was thanks to McCormick's time, dedication and above all her generosity with her inheritance that within four years of her involvement in 1953, a miracle was born. Pincus and his team came up with a pill that was small and easily swallowed, required no preparation before sex, lasted around the clock and was also affordable, reliable and entirely within the woman's control.

But how to get the pill from the lab to the women? Many people still believed that contraception was a form of abortion and hence a mortal sin, because every act preventing an egg from being fertilised meant a life snuffed out. But the marketing men of the day were up to the challenge. In deference to the damnation-believers, to the many honest doubters and to the doctors who had to control the distribution, the pill was originally licensed by the American Food and Drug Administration and marketed as a medication to regulate menstrual disorders. Now who could possibly object to that?

It seemed a crucial breakthrough for Catholics when Pope Pius XII ruled that the use of the pill to treat gynaecological problems was not contrary to Catholic morals. For one of the Pincus team, the Catholic Dr John Rock, it meant more than most. The Church had already approved the so-called rhythm method of avoiding conception in the early 1930s, and Rock had vigorously promoted this idea to Catholic couples, seeing no contradiction between contraception and his passionate faith.

The rhythm method was known as 'natural conception', based on the theology that God was happy with everything in nature because he had created it, so he could have no quarrel with its high failure rate. But as soon as science invented a new, radical and above all *reliable* barrier to pregnancy, the old battle to control women's bodies began anew. The primary objection was the 'artificial' nature of the ingredients in the pill. Rock fought hard to convince opponents that oestrogen and progesterone, the key elements of the pill, were also natural, because they already occurred in women's bodies.

He failed. In 1968 Pope Paul VI put out a hard-line decree, 'On the Regulation of Birth', restoring the blanket ban on every 'artificial means of contraception'. For Catholic women, it was back to rhythm method, the torturous monthly game of Vatican roulette. But *how dare they tell us what to do?* was a question even good Catholic women were beginning to ask. Others were too. Despite the Pope's proscription of contraception, once the pill was available millions of women took up the chance to rebel against their previously inescapable biologically determined fate. These women had been given a freedom and control that their foremothers would have done anything to possess.

A quick question:

In view of all they did for women, for men, for families and for Mother Earth, did Gregory Pincus or anyone involved in making the pill and bringing it to market ever win the Nobel Prize?

What do you think?

Roe v. Wade

Until the radical legal and social changes of the mid-twentieth century, women lived in an unacknowledged system of public wardship, whereby the state reserved the right to use their bodies as baby machines, to increase the population and to produce cannon fodder for future wars. In Japan, the government banned the pill until as late as 1999, bowing to pressure from an unholy alliance of condom manufacturers and the lucrative abortion industry, deliberately denying women access to the contraceptive that had the highest reliability rate and the greatest ease of use and control for forty years after it was invented.

In the United States, the attempt to assert control over women's bodies peaked in a court case that became known across the world as *Roe v. Wade* 1973. This judgment of the Supreme Court affirmed the constitutional right of every American woman to safe and legal abortion, in the teeth of opposition from all sides, religious, fundamentalist, traditionalist and misogynist. Britain permitted abortion by an Act of Parliament in 1967, that despite heated debate and strongly felt opposition was passed by a majority on a free vote.

The US federal system of government meant that America had no one single law that could be challenged and overturned. The case had to be fought on the grounds that the anti-abortion laws infringed a woman's right to terminate a pregnancy and for that, a pregnant woman was required. In 1969 that woman was a twenty-one-year-old Texan mother of two, Norma McCorvey, who was given the pseudonym 'Jane Roe'.

Troubled as McCorvey was by a highly destabilising past, one thing she knew for sure was that she did not want this baby. At the time, the Dallas attorneys Linda Coffee and Sarah Weddington were looking for a candidate to enable them to mount a challenge to the archaic anti-abortion law, and they took McCorvey on. The lawsuit had first to be brought in a federal court against the local district attorney, who represented the state of Texas. This was Henry Wade. They won the case, and won again when the judgment was referred to the Supreme

Court for the final arbitration, and it made history. It was noted too that an action that changed the future for American women was brought by a woman and fought by women, for women, without the intervention of men.

'If you're going to San Francisco . . .'

. . . be sure to wear some flowers in your hair', carolled the silvery tenor Scott McKenzie in the hit song that became the unofficial anthem of the Summer of Love. However powerful it became as a symbol of the new America, *Roe v. Wade* was only one sign of the breakdown of former standards and the massive social upheaval that contraception sparked in the 'Swinging Sixties'. With this small but powerful pill, women could now switch off their fertility and enjoy their bodies any which way they chose. The female half of the hundred thousand or so flower children who flocked to San Francisco in 1967 and to Woodstock in '69 constituted the first generation of women who could separate copulation from conception, and focus entirely on sensation and satisfaction as men had always been able to do.

Few captured the rebel spirit of this chaotic, exhilarating and unforgettable time better than Erica Jong, the internationally acclaimed prophet, poet and high priestess of women's sexual liberation. Her astonishing first novel, *Fear of Flying* (1973), projected to sell three thousand copies, went on to sell more than twenty-seven million and still counting, not least for her compelling fantasy of the 'zipless fuck' – sex with a handsome stranger, hot and happy, without commitment, without even words. 'The zipless fuck is the purest thing there is,' Jong wrote. 'And it is rarer than the unicorn. And I have never had one.'

This unique blend of power and pathos, the story of Isadora Wing's abundant sensuality and rampant sexuality set against her mixed fortunes in dealing with men, hit a nerve in the female

The spirit of the age. You'll have noticed the joint.

reading public. It was one that most women didn't know they had – and not all of them wanted to find out. To some, she was the Mother of Too Much Information (did she really need to tell us that her husband had '*the cleanest balls I had ever tasted*'?). To others, she held up a beacon like the angel at the gate of the New Jerusalem, lighting the way to an unknown land where women could take sex as men did, without shame or complications.

In the women's movement Jong was attacked by some for the novel's focus on men as the most important thing in any woman's life. But that was the truth of many women's lives. Their daily reality consisted of focusing on their men, their children, their home and family, doing most of the domestic drudgery even when they were working full-time outside the home. And while they were doing that, they could happily dream of the zipless fuck.

If they wanted to.

Not every woman hankered to be a flower child, ready to

turn on, tune in and drop out, as recommended by the LSD evangelist and lost soul, Dr Timothy Leary. Still less did they see themselves wandering the world like Jong's heroine, having sex with any and every man or woman she met. But Jong made many women feel that they deserved a more exciting life, one that delivered at least some of the fun, freedom and sexual variety that comes so naturally to her heroine. And despite mishaps, Isadora owns, controls and uses her body for her own pleasure, a situation bound to arouse curiosity, if not hope of emulation.

My body, my choice

Every woman has the right to possess her own body, and to decide what to do with it. Pornography flourishes in the denial of that right, and grows out of the social consensus that if men want it, they must have it. One heroic attempt to challenge this principle came in 1983 from two activists in the US women's movement, the lawyer Catharine MacKinnon and the radical feminist and writer Andrea Dworkin. At a series of hearings held by the City Council of Minneapolis on how to deal with the rising number of businesses selling pornographic materials, they argued that it constituted a violation of women's civil rights. By promoting, as they defined it, 'the sexual, explicit subordination of women', and thereby increasing sexual violence against them, it amounted to discrimination and as such should be banned. At the public hearings, women workers in pornographic films gave evidence, notably Linda Boreman Marchiano, aka 'Linda Lovelace', the 'star' of *Deep Throat* (1972), arguably the best-known pornographic movie of all time.

The Minnesota hearings were judicious and fair, and the proposal was immediately passed by the almost exclusively male council. It was just as immediately vetoed by the mayor of Minneapolis, and vetoed again when it came back to him a year later. That same year in Indianapolis, the same ordinance was signed by the mayor.

Enter the massed muscle of the defenders of the 1st Amendment of the US Constitution, hustling to the Supreme Court to uphold the right to free speech. The gallant 'free speechers' won the day and the new Indianapolis law banning pornography was overturned by the Supreme Court as 'unconstitutional'. At a stroke, pornography had been deemed constitutional, even in its most extreme forms. What would the Founding Fathers of the Constitution have made of that?

And it spread. With the connivance of the rest of the mass media, pornography made its way into the mainstream of Western culture. Its themes and images, its ever-increasing use of female nudity and its stress on violence and women under threat, all came to permeate fashion, photography, advertising, crime novels, rap music, film, TV and social media. Meanwhile Hugh Hefner and Paul Raymond, the self-styled 'King of Soho' in Britain, kept up the flow of only-just-legal magazines like *Playboy*, *Men Only* and *Knave*.

Both men were loyally supported by their daughters, who gave their lives to the business, as their fathers had. Christie Hefner worked for the Playboy empire for more than thirty years, serving as its president, chairman and CEO, before stepping down in 2008. Debbie Raymond likewise proved her worth to her father as editor-in-chief of his magazines, and also worked with him on his highly successful property ventures. She too was moving towards taking control of the business when she died at the age of thirty-six in 1992, after an evening of cocaine, heroin and vodka.

However successful women like these may appear, in pornography male dominance is the name of the game. What to make, then, of a woman writer who romanticised the relationship between a naïve young woman and a rich, dominant, older and sadomasochistic male? E. L. James, in her 2011 novel *Fifty Shades of Grey* spawned a publishing sensation like no other. What began as a blog became the fastest-selling paperback of all time in the UK, and the novel and its sequels had sold a combined total of more than 125 million copies worldwide by 2018. Some saw it as the creation of a new genre, 'mummy porn', making pornography respectable for women by giving them what men had always had. To others, it argued the failure of the fight against porn, and served as a painful reminder of the persistence of male domination and women's willingness to go along with it.

The war on women – and the fightback

Historically a wife belonged to her husband, and the law stated that by marrying him, she had given her consent to sex whenever he wanted it, for the rest of her life. Legislation in the UK and US against marital rape was not passed until the late 1980s and early 1990s, largely due to the revaluation of women's role and status in society arising from the women's liberation movement. But even today, the legal and judicial process tends to treat rape within marriage differently from other rapes, a clear indication that the belief of a husband's ownership of his wife's body lingers on, and his right to possess it at will.

As does the concept that any rape, especially outside the home, must be the woman's fault.

These ancient, powerful and pervasive beliefs were subjected to a searing re-assessment by Susan Brownmiller in her landmark study *Against Our Will: Men, Women, and Rape* (1975). She showed us what the threat of violence and rape was doing to our sense of ourselves. Brownmiller first demonstrated that rape was more about power than sex, and then that society expected women to protect themselves; that it was the responsibility of the 'victim' to make sure she didn't get raped by being in the wrong place, wearing the wrong clothes and so on. It was a wake-up call to women. The narrative was a dramatic pivot in consciousness, shifting the story from women-blaming. But rape – however we understand it – goes on and even today a pitiful number of reports of rape end with convictions. So far from women attracting rape, she showed, men chose to use it, not to get sex, but as an instrument of power.

Brownmiller's work was a radical challenge to centuries of traditional thinking about rape. However, almost half a century after its publication, it has yet to change the general idea of rape in the modern world, where pitifully few rapes are ever reported. Women know that they still run the risk of being blamed and shamed, and they also know that the legal system has yet to address its own systemic failure to bring rapists to justice, when the few reported crimes result in even fewer cases of conviction and punishment.

The deliberate use of rape as a weapon of triumph and terror is nowhere clearer than in time of war. The figures speak for themselves: in the twentieth century, *millions* of women were raped by soldiers during the Second World War. The first step towards recognising the need to protect women from sexual violence during armed conflict came at the Geneva Conference of 1949, where it represented an important advance on the traditional view that 'rape and pillage' were simply part of the collateral damage of any war. Nevertheless, it took many more years before what had always been seen as a private and individual crime was recognised as a public statement.

This milestone came in 2008 when the United Nations passed a resolution that 'crimes of sexual violence committed during conflict, particularly those committed systematically as a weapon or tactic of war to terrorise, humiliate and wipe out or forcibly relocate whole communities, prolongs, deepens and promotes conflict'. These acts were now officially designated as war crimes and as crimes against humanity, and treating women in war with respect and dignity was given a place of prime importance 'at the heart of the peace and reconstruction processes'. This constitutes a full acknowledgement that the infliction of mass collective rape is the most heinous form of violence against women. As with the deeper structural changes of attitudes towards women and men in modern society have taken time to work through, so progress in accepting this particular revolution in thought may be slow, but it will not be reversed.

And many of the women themselves have found their strength to speak out and add their weight to the struggle.

Nadia Murad, a nineteen-year-old Yazidi, was abducted from her village in Iraq in 2014 after an ISIL war band killed her mother, executed her six brothers, and slaughtered all the rest of the villagers except the women they could use as sex slaves, and sell on. She was beaten, burned with cigarettes and repeatedly raped before she managed to escape. From a refugee camp, Murad gave an interview in February 2015 to a Western newspaper, *La Libre Belgique*.

Not without cost. As Murad later said, 'Deciding to be honest was one of the hardest decisions I have ever made, and also the most important.' In December 2015 she addressed a United Nations assembly on human trafficking, and was appointed a UN Goodwill Ambassador on behalf of all who had suffered as she did. In that role she has campaigned widely for the safety of women and children, and founded Nadia's Initiative, a non-profit organisation working against genocide, mass atrocities and human trafficking. In 2018 Murad was awarded the Nobel Peace Prize along with the Congolese surgeon Dr Denis Mukwege, as the citation stated, 'for their efforts to end the use of sexual violence as a weapon of war and armed conflict'. Her co-laureate had dedicated his life and career to repairing the gynaecological injuries inflicted on women raped in conflict and both were honoured for giving women fresh hope for the future by offering them a way out of the traumas of the past.

Living with Mr Punch

Whatever the dangers on the streets, many women feel safer there than in their home. In 2016 the UK Office of National Statistics (ONS) recorded a man attacking a woman every seventy-five seconds of every day of the year. Figures also showed that women did not make a complaint until they had suffered an average of fifty such assaults. By 2018, an estimated 1.3 million women had experienced violence in the home, and legal and social service records showed a rise of 23 per cent on the previous year. According to the ONS, 'this in part reflects an increased willingness of victims to come forward'.

But change is painfully slow. Many women have children, and no jobs or money they could call their own. Middle-class women with money, status and jobs often struggled in vain to convince others that their respectable husbands – the doctor, the lawyer, the professor – could subject them to the beatings commonly attributed to the lowest class of men. Typically too, the woman had been bullied for so long that she had lost any sense of herself, and any instinct for self-preservation.

And if she wanted to leave, where could she go? That question was answered by the change-maker Erin Pizzey, who in 1971 established the world's first refuge for women trying to escape a violent partner. Without planning permission, because the local authorities had never considered the need for such a thing, Pizzey and her helpers opened the shelter anyway. The house was already home to established colonies of rats and cockroaches, and the Dickensian accommodation consisted of bedding on the floor. Nevertheless, 150 women and children 'squeezed like sardines' into the eight bedrooms as soon as

Chiswick Women's Aid opened its doors, all saying 'over and over and over again that it was far better being in the refuge in that state than being beaten at home'. A born rebel and a formidable fighter, Pizzey battled council bosses, the laws, the bye-laws and every authority whose primary impulse was to shut the whole thing down. Against the odds, it survived.

And *women helping women* – the message spread. In 1974, the Women's Aid Federation of England was established to draw together over forty independent women's centres into a national network that blossomed into more than 180 groups servicing over three hundred life-saving havens for women in distress. Meanwhile, Chiswick Women's Aid grew into Refuge, and went on to provide a UK network of specialist services, including emergency accommodation for women in crisis, legal advice and outreach into the community. With Women's Aid, it also set up the National Domestic Violence Helpline.

Erin Pizzey holding the hand of a child in the Chiswick Women's Refuge, ready to deal with bemused local officials and violent men. Note the cramped and overcrowded space, and the lack of furniture.

The concept and initiative expanded worldwide. Shelters sprang up in more than forty-five other countries, all beginning with empty begging bowls but armed with unquenchable determination and rebel grit. They won help, support and funding from governments, non-profit organisations, charitable foundations and private donors, grants that ensured their survival and growth. In Australia, the strong-minded Anne Summers had been in training for women-centred action since her Aunt Janet taught her as a child, 'Never iron a man's shirts.' From Sydney, she telephoned Pizzey in London to ask her how to set up a women's refuge. 'Just do it!' came Pizzey's reply.

And Summers did. With co-founder Bessie Guthrie and a committed group of other Sydney activists, Summers broke into a pair of abandoned houses in the path of a proposed freeway in 1970, and established Australia's first Women's Refuge Night Shelter. Called 'Elsie', because that was the name of the house, the refuge relied for its security in the early days on one of the women standing guard at the door, armed with a cricket bat. In this role one of the watchwomen mistook a government minister for a marauding husband and chased him away. Unexpectedly, the minister proved ready to offer financial support, impressed by how well the shelter was defended.

The courage and conviction of the founders won support from all sides, as locals donated everything from food and water to washing machines. Later on a proposed freeway was re-routed, and the refuge was granted a lease and government funding to carry on. Summers subsequently helped carry the cause of women into Australian public life when she served as a political adviser to two prime ministers in the Officer of the Status of Women in Canberra.

Within a decade, Erin Pizzey's revelation of the crying need for women's refuges had been confirmed by the Colorado psychologist Lenore E. Walker in her breakthrough book *The*

Battered Woman (1979). Walker argued that violence in the home was not a random series of one-off incidents, but a recurring and self-perpetuating cycle. There was a structure of abuse that worked to destroy a woman's self-confidence and with it her free will, keeping her mentally chained to her partner and powerless to escape. This occurred when normal domestic tensions led to an explosion of violence, followed by remorse, forgiveness, reconciliation, and a honeymoon period before the everyday pressures of life kicked in to start the process all over again. Only the woman leaving the man and getting out of the home could break the vicious cycle.

As long as she had somewhere to go.

This simple but crucial factor had to be rediscovered again and again as the refuge movement gained ground. The first centre in America dedicated to providing a safe haven for women in flight from a brutal partner grew out of a domestic violence hotline set up in 1987 in St Paul, Minnesota, by the group Women's Advocates, to provide information and support. But the first call-handlers soon realised that the women usually needed a place of safety far more urgently than they needed advice, and so that shelter was born.

A place to call my own

Modern refuges have changed dramatically from the run-down, overcrowded and insanitary house in London where it all began. A state-of-the-art facility in San Antonio, Texas, La Paloma De La Paz, the Battered Women's and Children's Centre opened in 2002 as a shelter complex on a wide green campus housing up to 220 people, with individual units for each family. Once safe inside the house of 'the Dove of Peace', the women and children have the services of a school, a medical and dental clinic, and full support to make a clean break from the home. This can mean offering legal advice, job training and the services of psychologists and psychiatrists, as well as providing clothing and shoes to attend job interviews. Another highly valued innovation is the cosmetic help and/or surgery for women whose partners had disfigured them in the ways familiar to the workers in the field.

However valuable their efforts, all refuges typically face an ongoing struggle for money. Anything that can raise awareness and bring in donations is worth its weight in gold. In Britain, the work of Refuge (and its coffers) received a wholly unexpected boost when *The Archers* radio soap opera included a storyline about Helen Titchener, a daughter of the founding family, who had not only been the victim of her husband Rob's physical abuse, but also of his coercive control. He slowly set about breaking her down by criticising her actions, her clothes and her friends under the guise of a concerned and protective love. In a grippingly accurate narrative running from 2013 to 2016, Rob was shown to manipulate Helen so subtly and successfully that she feared she was losing her mind.

During the show's transmission, the UK government passed a new law in December 2015 making 'controlling or coercive behaviour in intimate or familial relationships' a criminal offence. The first prosecution and conviction for this offence took place in February 2018, resulting in a jail sentence, and 235 convictions were recorded by the July of that year, offering the Helens of the future the hope of some redress. The great British public also responded in droves when listener Paul Trueman set up an online fundraising page for real-life women in Helen's situation, with the hope of raising a thousand pounds for charity. The money poured in, often in painfully small amounts ('£10 for our daughter'), and the appeal finally produced more than £170,000 for Refuge. CEO Sandra Horley expressed the charity's gratitude for the 'incredibly powerful – and sadly all too accurate' portrayal of the process of inflicting prolonged abuse. 'Talking about domestic violence is still taboo,' she said, 'and the storyline has given Refuge a brilliant opportunity to raise awareness, reaching women who might be experiencing the same kind of abuse.'

Breaking the silence

The Helen and Rob storyline received widespread publicity, and so succeeded in getting the subject talked about in work-places, pub and gatherings throughout the land. This was vital progress in shifting the burden of blame from the victim to the perpetrator. Jasvinder Sanghera, a British Sikh, wrote about rebelling against a forced marriage in her bestselling memoir, *Shame* (2007). She was the source of it in her family when she ran away to marry another man, while her three older sisters had submitted to their father's choice. One of them, Robina, only found her way out of her unbearable marriage by burning herself to death, and in her memory Sanghera set up a helpline in Leeds to support victims of forced marriage and so-called 'honour-based' abuse. Four thousand women contacted Karma Nirvana in the year after it opened in 2008.

'When a woman tells the truth, she is creating the possibility for more truth around her,' said the American poet and an early hero of the women's movement Adrienne Rich. Sanghera and her team freed a good number of women from the grave of eternal silence. Their work was part of a groundswell of opinion beginning to question cultural practices that overrode a woman's right to determine what happened to her body, and consequently her life. Among those who campaigned against forced marriage were the actor and writer Meera Syal, the Yorkshire MP Ann Cryer and the Asian women's group Southall Black Sisters, resulting in the ground-breaking UK prohibition of forced marriages introduced in 2014. Only a year later a thirty-four-year-old Cardiff businessman became the first person in Britain to be jailed for forcing a woman into marriage. The young woman, a devout Muslim, found the strength to identify her abuser and to testify against him, and he was sentenced to sixteen years in prison.

As Karma Nirvana declared from its foundation, just because arranged marriages and family control were part of a long tradition, that did not make them either lawful or right. Tradition does not mean that the living are dead, said G. K. Chesterton. 'It means that the dead are living.' It is the *only* area of society where ancient customs and beliefs have been allowed to trump the 1948 UN Declaration of Human Rights in the ongoing abuse of women and their bodies.

Another time-honoured tradition that has proved strongly resistant to change has been the practice of surgically reducing and rearranging the genital organs of girls and women. An estimated two hundred million of them from countries in Asia, the Middle East and Africa have been victims of female genital mutilation (FGM), also known as 'cutting'. A girl can be cut from birth up to young adulthood, but her time will generally come between the ages of five and nine, to make sure that she is 'clean' for a husband before she gets her first period.

What is 'clean'?

The clitoris is the only organ in the human body, male or female, that exists purely for sexual pleasure, so its amputation radically compromises the possibility of a full and fulfilled adult female life. In what is regarded as the 'mildest' form of FGM, all or most of the clitoris, its hood and the sheath below are cut out. The next stage involves slicing off the inner lips of the vulva, the *labia minora*. The most radical form, carried out in an estimated 20 per cent of cases, involves scraping away the flesh inside the outer lips, the *labia majora*, then stitching together the remaining skin to close off the vaginal opening, leaving a hole of no more than two centimetres in diameter for the passage of urine and menstrual blood. The traditional practitioner worked with a sharpened stone, a shell, a piece of glass or an iron blade, and used long thorns to sew up the wound. The instruments improved with the advent of modern medicine, but the result was the same. During the process, the child was held down by female relatives and typically remained conscious.

Although practised in Muslim countries, FGM pre-dates Islam, and is not mentioned in the Qur'an. Christians are also known to practise FGM with no support from the Bible. In Kenya girls were routinely cut before it was made illegal in 2011, with some success. Local initiatives were strongly supported by the United Nations, where the Secretary-General announced 6 February 2019 the International Day of Zero Tolerance for FGM, and pledged to work towards its eradication by 2030. Whatever the country or religion, the belief of centuries was that girls had to be kept chaste and that FGM preserved them in a state of virginal innocence and ignorance until marriage. Towards the end of the twentieth century, however, survivors of the traditional ritual began to question the reason for their childhood suffering, and the absence of libido as grown women.

Prominent among the protesters was Somalia-born Waris Dirie, already a rebel at thirteen when she fled an arranged marriage to a man more than four times her age. Dirie went on to establish an international career as a fashion model, but could never forget what had happened to her about the age of five. 'When they tried to convince me that God wants this,' she recalled, 'I said: "Did my God hate me so much?" I remember telling my mother, "If He hates me, then I don't want Him."' After what she termed 'female circumcision', Dirie lay there, bargaining with God: 'Make me stay alive. You owe me this now.'

As an adult, she identified the tradition as 'pure violence against girls, and it destroys the rest of their lives. And for what? For who?' Like others who broke their silence, Dirie felt compelled to make public what would otherwise have remained purely private, and gave a starkly outspoken interview to *Marie Claire* magazine in February 1997. The next year she brought out her autobiography *Desert Flower*, and gave up modelling to campaign full time. 'I just knew that I had to tell the world that there was torture, an undercover war against women,' she later said. 'What really made me take a stand was that nobody was doing anything.' Group action was essential if the practice was to be eradicated: 'This is not one person's war – all of us have to do something.'

Let the girls walk free

By the end of the twentieth century, Europe had stopped pretending that this war on women was a problem that occurred elsewhere. The End FGM European Campaign led by Amnesty International brought in the first action plan to combat the practice, and saw it adopted by the European Parliament in 2013. A treaty of the Council of Europe in force from 2014 was the first formal and legal recognition that FGM took place in Europe. Western countries and their politicians, who had long invoked the need to respect the 'different cultural traditions' of their ethnic minorities as a justification for turning a blind eye to what went on, were now under notice that their evasions would no longer be accepted.

Dirie was a highly effective advocate against cutting, and the example she set continued to empower other women to reveal their own experiences. Little was known of the Dawoodi Bohra sect of Shia Muslims until the Pakistani writer Mariya Karimjee went public in 2015 with a graphic account of her own FGM at the age of seven. She never forgot the pain she had felt as a child, and it returned with a vengeance the first time she tried to have sex, as a student in the US. Fortunately Karimjee had access to American consultants in FGM and, following treatment and counselling, she discovered that she was capable of enjoying sex.

All over the world, step by tiny step, FGM slowly became no longer traditional, inevitable and acceptable, but unjustifiable, intolerable, and criminal. When the two men appeared in court who were responsible for the death of thirteen-year-old Soheir al-Batea in 2014 as a result of FGM, both the father who had arranged the operation and the doctor who had carried it out were acquitted. But Egypt's Appeal Court reversed the decision and sentenced the father to three months in jail (suspended), while the doctor, convicted of manslaughter and of performing an illegal operation, was jailed for two years and three months and his clinic was closed down for a year.

Only one case and with arguably over-light penalties, but it was a crucial breakthrough, sending a signal not only to parents but to the mutilators too, that FGM was medically unjustified and therefore against the law of the land. Other countries followed suit. In 2015 a court in Australia sentenced two Dawoodi Bohra Muslims and a retired midwife to prison for crimes related to FGM. Two years later came the first prosecution under US federal law. A Detroit doctor, Jumana Nagarwala, was indicted for mutilating a number of girls, along with seven others allegedly involved in the offence. Regrettably, these charges had to be dropped on a legal technicality. The twenty-year-old law making FGM illegal throughout the country in fact contravened the right to determine its own laws granted to each state under the US Constitution, so the case could not proceed. This apparent failure, however, helped rather than hindered the attempts to outlaw the practice, because the thirty-three states who had no laws against it were compelled to respond to the massive publicity generated by the case, and to get started on framing their own.

No turning back

It is hard to exaggerate the importance of advances that have been made all over the world in overthrowing customs and traditions that in many cases date back thousands of years. From the first acknowledgement in the West that the female body did not need the physical support of 'stays' to the global action against practices that have been recognised as unnecessary, cruel and destructive, change and progress are evident worldwide. Women are not yet out of danger. Attacks on their bodies, both physical and symbolic, continue in the form of pornography, sexual violence and rape. Equally serious are the repeated assaults on the hard-won laws in the West that asserted every woman's right to have the sole say in what happens to her body, particularly in relation to her reproductive rights. As Margaret Atwood so clearly summed it up: 'Young women of reproductive age are always in the minority in any society', and yet they have decisions 'made about them, and about their entire future and fate and body and health'. Inspired by her novel *The Handmaid's Tale* (1985), we have watched as women all over the world, dressed in red robes and white bonnets, have protested against the renewed attacks on their rights, which we now know must be constantly defended and cannot be taken for granted, even in the modern world.

And women will no longer be silenced, as long as they are free to speak. They know that the control of their bodies, previously ceded to parents, husbands, doctors and priests without their consent, is now no longer the rule of law, in the West at least. In the words of Britain's premier judge, the President of the Supreme Court Lady Hale, 'Abortion is a hideous moral problem, but it's the woman's problem.'

Our bodies, then, our lives and our selves. And our right to choose our own futures, and to determine the way ahead, whatever that brings.

CHAPTER 12

THE LAST REVOLUTION

My fellow citizens, is it not time we women had a revolution too?

OLYMPE DE GOUGES

The True Republic: Men, their rights and nothing more. Women, their rights and nothing less.

Revolution, THE FEMINIST NEWSPAPER

I neither think I'm God nor Mary not anyone special, but merely a full grown WOMAN. Yes! Rock on ... Ride on ... REVOLUTION!

SINEAD, MOTHER BERNADETTE MARIA O'CONNOR

'It really is a revolution,' said Gloria Steinem in July 1971 when she delivered her Address to the Women of America, stressing the scope and significance of the change women sought at the founding of the National Women's Political Caucus of America. The radical reversal of women's historical second-class status that Steinem envisaged is still ongoing. Like most deep-laid conflicts, it has never been one steady advance but a series of defeats and retreats, with the survivors rallying and regrouping to fight again another day.

The recognition of women not as Simone de Beauvoir's 'second sex' but as people of primary importance to the world has been – and still is – a long time coming. But in many countries and across many nations, rebel women have won three major victories and gained these game-changing rights:

- To control their bodies.
- To develop their minds.
- To achieve an existence separate from men by winning civil rights and the vote.

We can do it!

With these three revolutionary changes around the world, women could change society, and they did. In the twenty-first century, the world boasts women engineers, mountaineers, rocket scientists, chess grandmasters, priests, bus drivers and military leaders, women in art, music, business, sport, science and the law, all proving that females could be as capable as males even in the fields previously considered well beyond their natural powers. Many of them also combined these activities with motherhood. As Patricia Schroeder, member of the US House of Representatives and mother of two, put it, 'I have a brain and a uterus and I use both.'

Another revolution came with the growing realisation that women were central to the survival and success of the human race, not merely a support system for the activities of men. Women's concerns became international concerns as countries accepted that the health and education of women and girls were fundamental to the well-being of their nation. Education was acknowledged as the key to limiting the numbers of children a woman would have, and one that profoundly affected both her health and that of her children too. Their level of attainment in life also related directly to the mother's educational level, not to the father's.

> If you educate a man, you educate an individual.
> If you educate a woman, you educate a family.

Education, yes, but health first. The health of the woman is the health of the earth, and the ability to control childbirth is the world's only way out of poverty, particularly in developing nations. This was the thrust of the first International Conference on Population and Development held by the United Nations in 1994. There the Norwegian prime minister Gro Harlem Brundtland denounced religions that took women's lives by forbidding birth control. 'Morality becomes hypocrisy,' she declared, 'if it means mothers suffering or dying in connection with unwanted pregnancies and illegal abortions of unwanted children.'

The head of the Iranian delegation, Mohammad Ali Taskhiri, took this as an attack on the religion that 'is our whole life', responsible for 'the progress of humanity', and stated that it would lead to 'unbearable social problems'. He demanded that Brundtland withdraw her comments. She did not. She also received unexpected support from Benazir Bhutto, who had defied severe pressure from conservative Islamists not to attend. In what was hailed as a powerful endorsement of Brundtland's statement, Bhutto spoke out strongly in favour of women's rights. 'Development policies must give women the means to make economically independent decisions free of male prejudice,' she stated to rising applause. 'Empowerment of women is a means to reach population stabilisation.'

She who wears the crown

That conference was in the mid-1990s. Since then:

Two of the world's oldest monarchies, Denmark and England, both dating back to the eighth or ninth centuries, have voluntarily accepted the female right to rule as equal to the male. In the UK, the law of male succession to the crown was abolished in 2011, following Denmark, Sweden, Norway and Belgium, who all allow first-born females to accede to the throne. The third and oldest, Japan, with a pedigree of around 2700 years, has been edging towards it since the early 2000s due to an unfortunate shortage of males.

In politics the world over, women have risen to run political parties and to become world leaders from the Netherlands to Nicaragua. In the US of 1969, there were only ten women in the House of Representatives and one in the Senate, compared with eighty-four and twenty-three respectively in 2018. In Britain, the rebel queens Catherine Mayer and Sandi Toksvig founded the Women's Equality Party on International Women's Day 2015. The following year, when Theresa May ran for election as the leader of the Conservative Party, her nearest rival was another female politician, Andrea Leadsom, who became the Leader of the House of Commons and the first Conservative woman to have been appointed to this role. America may not yet have a female president, but Theresa May was the UK's second woman prime minister.

In Iceland, Jóhanna Sigurðardóttir made history as the world's first openly gay prime minister in 2009. The following year, her government banned strip clubs and any other means of making money from the nudity of employees, female *or* male, another first among Western democracies. Sigurðardóttir declared that 'the Nordic countries are leading the way on women's equality, recognizing women as equal citizens rather than commodities for sale'. And to Finland goes the honour of appointing the world's youngest serving state minister with Sanna Marin, who will lead an all-female cabinet.

In the course of their professional lives, all these women showed their ability to move onto the world stage. The twentieth century also gave birth to a movement driven by women and girls to save the world itself. 'Where have all the flowers gone?' sang Marlene Dietrich at a concert in 1962. The question was raised the same year by the American biologist Rachel Carson when she learned that hundreds of new industrial chemicals designed to control weeds, insects, rats and mice, were in fact killing almost everything else around them. Haunted by the fear of a world without bird song and where the chemicals in the soil would long outlive those who created them, Carson took aim at the post-war petrochemical industry in the US, whose massive profits were made without any apparent concern for the consequences. 'How could intelligent beings,' she wondered, 'seek to control a few unwanted species by a method that contaminated the entire environment and brought the threat of disease and death even to their own kind?'

Recognised as one of the most important scientific works of all time, Carson's *Silent Spring* also established her as the Mother of the Conservation Movement to protect the environment and to save the Earth. This took on a greater relevance over time as the issues she highlighted continued to be ignored. In 1977 the Kenyan activist Wangari Maathai founded the Green

Belt movement to combat the ongoing deforestation of Africa. More than forty million trees were planted in over two thousand designated public green spaces throughout the continent. Maathai also repeatedly rebelled against the Kenyan regime, at great personal cost, including persecution and imprisonment. But she twice succeeded in preventing a massive privatisation by the president of public forest land, and in 2004 became the first African woman and the first environmentalist to receive the Nobel Peace Prize.

In August 2018, a fifteen-year-old Swedish schoolgirl, Greta Thunberg, brought new life to the cause when she began a weekly demonstration outside the parliament in Stockholm, cutting school to call for immediate action on climate change. 'I am doing this,' she said, 'because you adults are shitting on my future.' Her simple message 'School Strike for the Climate' caught on, and at the end of December that year, more than twenty thousand students had held Friday school strikes in at least 270 cities. By 15 March 2019, her fervour had ignited the young worldwide, and an estimated total of a million and a half school pupils in over a hundred countries struck too. As the protests continued, Thunberg was showered with prizes and awards, invited to attend a UN summit on climate change, nominated for the Nobel Peace Prize and became the youngest-ever *Time* magazine Person of the Year.

A different reception greeted the protesters of the Extinction Rebellion movement, who were heavily criticised when they brought central London to a standstill in April 2019. Citing Emmeline Pankhurst and Mohandas Gandhi as her models for direct action, the British scientist Dr Gail Bradbrook, co-founder of Extinction Rebellion, justified her determination to use shock tactics to wake up the world she saw as sleepwalking to its doom. 'The way I see it,' she said, 'we are fighting to keep all our children safe and ensure they have a future.'

Despite strong censure from government officials and the police, the group held further demonstrations in other British cities, carrying their message across the country as new supporters continued to rally to the cause.

And success breeds the confidence to act outside the box. In 2019 the Brazilian forward 'Magic' Marta Vieira da Silva became the all-time FIFA World Cup top goal-scorer, breaking the previous records held by men as well as by women. In this once-in-a-lifetime, top-of-the-world position, da Silva did not hesitate to use her power to kick the demand for women's rights into the political arena where it belongs. Promising to 'push for more equality and women's empowerment', she told BBC Sport's Tom Garry, 'this is a struggle for equality across the board'. 'Magic' Marta was striking out for women in football everywhere. At the FIFA Women's World Cup in 2019, the total prize money was $30 million – but there had been a $400 million prize purse at the Men's World Cup the previous year. In March 2019, all twenty-eight of the US Women's National Team squad lodged an equal pay action against the US Soccer Federation. The case was scheduled to go to trial in May 2020.

Da Silva harks back to another shining sports star, the world No. 1 tennis player who defined and dominated the game in the 1970s, Billie Jean King. Challenged by Bobby Riggs, the fifty-five-year-old former world No. 1 and 1939 Wimbledon champion, on a mission to prove the superiority of the male in what was billed as the Battle of the Sexes, King took him on in an exhibition match in September 1973, and won. That same year and thanks to King's campaigning, the US Open offered equal prize money for men and women for the first time. It would be another thirty-four years before Wimbledon did the same.

Sharp elbows and flying feet: Magic Marta takes the ball past Kim Hyeri of Japan in the 2015 FIFA Women's World Cup.

Lead us, heavenly Mother, lead us

We saw earlier that about 2300 years BCE, the chief priest of Sumeria, now Iraq, was Enheduanna, the Moon-Minister to the Most High. She composed 'The Exaltation of Innana' to honour the Goddess, showing that the world's first known deity, its first priest and its first poet were all female.

The 'Most High' was, of course, the Great Mother Goddess, the divinity worshipped throughout most of the ancient world. Then came the rise of the Father Gods driving out and destroying any traces of the time when God was a woman, followed by thousands of years of resistance to women in the ministry of each and every faith. The older the structure, the stronger the resistance to women, and few things were more feral than the fight of men in frocks to keep out vicars in knickers. Over time, however, rebel women succeeded in reclaiming their former roles as full participants in religion. Unsurprisingly, non-conformists were readier to include women in their ministry than the established Anglican churches, and female Methodist lay preachers were active in Britain from the 1760s onwards. One of them, Elizabeth Evans – the aunt of Mary Ann, better known as George Eliot – served as the model for the preacher Dinah Morris in Eliot's 1859 novel *Adam Bede*.

The older organisations took longer to accept that women could be equal to men in religion. The first woman to be ordained as a rabbi? Check out the inspirational rebel Regina Jonas, officially certified in Berlin in 1935. Yet Jonas was not the first woman to act as a rabbi. Scholars of Jewish history recognise the seventeenth-century Jewish Kurdish scholar and writer Asenath Barzani, who was also the earliest recorded female leader in Kurdish history.

Almost forty years after Jonas, in 1972, twenty-five-year-old American Sally Priesand became the second female rabbi to be ordained, and the first in the US. Priesand knew at the age of sixteen that the customary female life was not for her. She believed that she could be a female rabbi and in defiance of tradition she made it come true. Priesand steered clear of calling herself a feminist, but insisted 'I do think the feminist movement is important because it is time for us to overcome psychological and emotional objections. We must fulfil our potential as creative individuals.' In 1986, at Monmouth Reform Temple in New Jersey, Priesand made history again when she and cantor Ellen Sussman became the first all-women team of rabbi and cantor to conduct a service.

And the rebels kept coming. Jackie Tabick, born in Dublin,

also notched up a number of firsts when she became the first female rabbi in the UK in 1975, the first to marry another rabbi and the first woman rabbi to have a child. Six years later, Australia's first female rabbi, the American-born Karen Soria, was also the first to serve with the US Marines, then became the first female rabbi in the Canadian Armed Forces.

Regina Jonas pictured after her ordination.

In Christianity, the first female Anglican priest, Florence Li Tim-Oi, was ordained in Occupied China in 1944, the year Rabbi Jonas would die in Auschwitz, where she ministered to her first and only resident flock. The call for female priests in Britain led to the foundation of the Anglican Group for the Ordination of Women to the Historic Ministry of the Church in 1930, a pressure group with high-profile supporters such as Dame Sybil Thorndike, and with the Bishop of Lichfield and the Dean of Canterbury as its founding vice-presidents.

It took another forty years, but in 1971 Joyce Mary Bennet was the first Englishwoman to be ordained a priest in the Anglican communion, taking holy orders in Hong Kong. The recognition of women in the ministry picked up speed in the following decades. On 12 March 1994, thirty-two women were ordained in the Church of England, in alphabetical order, which gave Angela Berners-Wilson the honour of becoming the first female priest in the Anglican communion of the UK. Women bishops were already known in Canada, the USA, New Zealand and Australia when Libby Lane was created the first in Britain on 26 January 2015.

Judaism and Christianity triumphed over tradition to grant women the right to lead a religious ceremony. What of Islam? Why not female imams? Supporters argued that nothing in the Qur'an or in the life of Muhammad precluded it, and many were listening. Between 1995 and 2018, Muslim women began taking action and leading prayers in the USA, Canada, the UK, Denmark, Germany and India. A rebel twice over was the South African Shamima Shaikh, an activist previously involved in protesting apartheid who pioneered a revolution in her Johannesburg community in 1995 by leading women into mosques at Ramadan to pray side by side with men. The response was strong. 'It was very intimidating at first,' Shaikh admitted, 'but our perseverance saw us through. The protests fizzled out as the nights went by.'

Shaikh's campaigning continued until her early death from breast cancer in 1998. Ten years later, an American professor of religion and philosophy, Amina Wadud, became the first woman in the modern era to lead the Friday prayers of Muslims, and in a mixed group of about a hundred men and women. On that historic day in New York, 18 March 2005, Wadud was supported by a number of progressive female activists and another woman, Suheyla El-Attar, also gave the call to prayer. Banned from using a mosque, Wadud held the gathering in a meeting room of an Episcopal cathedral, where some of the worshippers joked that there were more media present than Muslims. One of the organisers, the academic Asra Quratulain Nomani, confirmed the significance of what had taken place:

> We are standing up for our rights as women in Islam. We will no longer accept the back door or the shadows. At the end of the day, we'll be leaders in the Muslim world. We are ushering Islam into the twenty-first century, reclaiming the voice that the Prophet gave us 1400 years ago.

While Wadud continued leading prayers as far afield as Denmark, Jamida Beevi led the first Friday worship to be held by a woman in India, again before a mixed congregation, at a village in Kerala in January 2018. Like every one of the women who have made their way into the ministry of Judaism, Christianity, Islam or any of their offshoots, Beevi was subjected to protests, violent opposition and death threats. She took it in her stride. 'I believe in the Qur'an and the Qur'an teaches equality between the sexes,' she said. 'All this discrimination against women is man-made, imposed by the male clergy, and I want to change it.'

When did you last see your father?

'History, if you read it right, is the record of the attempts to tame Father,' said the US writer Max Lerner. 'The greatest triumph of what we call civilisation was the domestication of the human male.' It is a measure of the success of the women's movement that it encouraged women all over the world to question the unchecked dominance of the male, and to reject the sense of entitlement that it conveyed.

But ...

Never underestimate the power of the patriarchy to reconstruct itself. In the political sphere, the early twenty-first century saw the re-emergence of the 'strong leader' in Russia, America, Turkey, Austria and Brazil. When Hillary Clinton stood for election as president of the USA, her opponent was a reality TV star with no experience in politics, a public speaker blind to any boundaries of honesty, decency or impulse control, and a man who boasted on the campaign trail about the size of his penis and his penchant for grabbing women by the 'pussy'. Clinton won the third highest number of votes ever cast in a US election, after President Obama in his victories of 2008 and 2012, and as expected, she beat Donald Trump by *almost three million* votes at the final count.

But in the arcane electoral system of the US devised by the Founding Fathers, Trump notched up the states that counted, and became president. Only later did it emerge that America's new 'strong man' had got there by dint of illegal interference by his Russian counterpart, Vladimir Putin. US political and intelligence agencies confirmed that the Russian dictator had authorised a massive internet attack on Clinton, to undermine her campaign and ensure a Trump victory.

And at home the 'strong leader' could always display his strength by encouraging other men to display theirs, especially against women. A 2010 report from the UN gave an estimated figure of fourteen thousand Russian women killed every year by husbands or male relations. In 2017, Vladimir Putin passed a law that reduced the penalty for beating a wife from two years in jail to two weeks or a fine, as long as the attack broke no bones and it was inflicted only once a year. The state press informed its female readers that they should be proud of their blood and bruises, because aggressive men fathered male children, so the women would be lucky and have boys.

My body, not yours

The strong man of the new millennium was also ready to reassert his control of women's bodies. For women in the West, the major struggles like winning the vote, gaining entry to higher education and the right to divorce, once won, were done. Not so women's right to regulate their own bodies. Both the UK Abortion Act 1967 and the epoch-making *Roe v. Wade* 1973 in the US endured repeated attacks over the years. By 2018, President Trump's appointment of the cradle Catholic and deeply conservative Judge Brett Kavanaugh gave the US Supreme Court a weighting thought likely to assist any future challenge to abortion law. In 2019, a number of states from Alabama to Ohio passed anti-abortion laws designed to elicit a new Supreme Court ruling, in the confident expectation that *Roe v. Wade* would be overturned.

Yet in the Catholic stronghold of the Emerald Isle, the tide was running the other way. 'This is Ireland, it's the law,' said the consultant who refused the thirty-one-year-old Indian dentist Savita Halappanavar life-saving surgery in 2012, when she suffered an incomplete miscarriage only four months into a long-planned pregnancy. Halappanavar and her husband were neither Irish nor Catholic and the foetus had no chance of survival, but because a foetal heartbeat could still be detected the doctors would not act. Halappanavar died of sepsis.

Her death provoked a worldwide response. A 2018 referendum on overturning the Republic's abortion ban galvanised women and men too, to return to Ireland in their thousands to vote 'Yes!', many brandishing placards promising NEVER AGAIN! When flights from London to Dublin were sold out, those going 'home to vote', as the campaign slogan had it, drove for hours to catch ferries that took hours to arrive, and willingly drove for hours more on the Irish side. One woman crowdfunded her air fare to get back from her job in Abu Dhabi, while a young man delighted his 'mam' with a surprise return to vote for her, for his sisters and for all Irish women. One voter tweeted that she was voting for the women of Northern Ireland, who at the time remained subject to strict anti-abortion laws. Among the posters and placards, one of the starkest read 'DO IT FOR SAVITA HALAPPANAVAR'.

And they did. The result was a landslide, when the Republic of Ireland voted overwhelmingly to repeal the 8th amendment – removing the constitutional ban on abortion – by over 66.4 per cent to 33.6 per cent. The taoiseach, Leo Varadkar, a 'yes'-voter himself, hailed the 'culmination of a quiet revolution' as 'an extraordinary victory for women's rights, marking the country's transformation from a bastion of religious conservatism to one of Europe's most tolerant democracies'. This result triggered a similar revolution in Northern Ireland, where abortion was decriminalised by a popular vote in 2019.

Calling it out

Where there was wrong, many women found the knowledge, the confidence and the power to speak out against it. A pandemic of abuse emerged all over the world: by men in industry, in entertainment, in politics, in the church, everywhere. It was not easy. Every woman who came forward spoke of long-hidden pain, often redoubled when the initial shock and sense of powerlessness gave way to the realisation that she had no hope of redress. If she told what had happened, she would be disbelieved, and possibly branded as a troublemaker and sacked. Women also kept quiet for fear of being blamed by a parent, a husband, even an adult son. Women rarely confided in each other, paralysed by the same fear and shame.

What made men think that they were entitled to behave like this? Only centuries of unchallenged licence that women, one by one, were beginning to bring to an end. The first denunciations came slowly. Entertainers including Bill Cosby had been fending off rumours and accusations of sexual misconduct for years before they were finally exposed. But eventually Cosby, adjudged a violent predator in 2018, was tried, convicted, fined and sentenced to three to ten years in jail.

Even in the twenty-first century, when many assumed that the fight for women's equality was over and done, resisting the demands of a powerful man was often hard, and for some women impossible. For Rose McGowan it began as a regular Hollywood invitation to meet a producer, the mega-mogul Harvey Weinstein. It ended in a violent sex attack. When she tried to speak out about it afterwards, he allegedly had her blacklisted to ruin her career. When she complained, her agent dropped her. When she tried to sue, a lawyer told her, 'You'll never win.' With nothing left to lose, she went public with her story in 2016. On 5 October 2017, two investigative reporters from the *New York Times*, Jodi Kantor and Megan Twohey, revealed the numerous sexual harassment allegations that women had made against Weinstein, dating back to the 1990s.

Ronan Farrow then followed with an article for the *New Yorker*, and the dam burst. A flood of accusations revealed Weinstein to be a serial sex offender who had been attacking and raping women for years, then silencing them with punitive legal agreements backed up with hush money. Reviled, ostracised and sacked from Miramax, the film company that he founded, Weinstein was hounded out of town. Revulsion at his behaviour and also at the impunity he had engineered, provoked a tornado of disgust throughout the industry and the world beyond. The #MeToo movement ran around the globe, leaping from country to country like a forest fire. And one by one they fell, men previously thought too important to question, let alone to bring down. The trickle of revelations became a torrent as thousands

of women told of thousands of sexual assaults typically hidden
for decades and now out there for all to see.

Stormy weather

#MeToo generated a sister movement, Time's Up, launched
in the *New York Times* on 1 January 2018 to raise the money
needed to allow lower-income women to take legal action
against their abusers. It was also intended to support those with
little or no access to media like the female farm workers of
America, as well as men who were being oppressed, people of
colour and the LGBT+ community. One woman showed the
way by taking on the first president of the USA to be elected
despite having admitted to a history of sexually assaulting
women. Among the tumults of his tempestuous first term, special mention must be made of the American porn actor, writer
and director Stormy Daniels.

Daniels was paid $130,000 by Trump's attorney in October
2016, one month before the election, cash she claimed was to
buy her silence about sexual encounters that the presidential
hopeful needed to go away.

She memorably rebelled against a legal gag imposed by
Trump's lawyer, and made history when she defied the law,
the president and large swathes of public opinion to spill the
beans about the affair in her memoir *Full Disclosure*, published in
2018. Stormy had no regrets. 'The deck has always been stacked
against me,' she wrote. 'I own my story and the choices I made.'

That, of course, was the power that the women's movement
wanted every woman to possess. #MeToo reversed the tide of
history because women – and men who had never spoken out
before – raised their voices and clamoured to be heard. The
worldwide coverage by the mass media helped to validate the first
truth-tellers, supported the second wave, and created a safe space

where those who came forward could know that they were not alone. Between them, then, #MeToo and the mass media had a radical and powerful impact during 2017–18. It was a textbook demonstration of the strength of solidarity and group action, when women in their millions revolted against the abusers' age-old rule of *omertà*, and could tell their own truth. It was epic, it was global, it was world-shaking, and it felt like the revolution at last.

Let's hear it for the f-word

In December 2017, Merriam-Webster crowned 'feminism' its Word of the Year based on the massive surge in searches for the word in the online dictionary, up by 70 per cent on 2016. There was a corresponding surge in action too. The Women's March of 21 January 2017 was originally planned for Washington DC, but it spread throughout the world. With half a million protesters in DC alone, the numbers were far greater than those of the supporters that had appeared at Trump's inauguration the day before, and taken with the estimated four to five million attending the 408 marches taking place in the rest of the country, it was the largest single-day protest in American history. A further 673 marches were also organised in eighty-four other countries, from Mexico to Antarctica, with an estimated number of participants exceeding five million.

Come the revolution . . .

In the last two hundred years, revolutions have taken place in America, France, Austria, Hungary, Italy, Germany, Poland and Greece. In every one of these, rebel women raised their revolutionary claim for human rights, for freedom and equality on the same terms as men, and over two centuries later the claim is unresolved. In every revolution women have faced a double revolution, once against the known oppressor and then against the unknown, unrecognised oppressor, the power of patriarchy in their family, in their school, in their church, the man in their marriage, in their bed and in their head. That is why *all revolutions, all democratic movements, all demands for equality have stopped short of sexual equality.*

But anyone with an eye on history will recognise the eternal power of the pendulum effect. The rise of women to take part in a world that in early civilisations had worshipped them as goddesses and later did not even guarantee them the right to life, has been phenomenal. Most bias is unconscious and simply absorbed, not chosen, and the massive changes that have taken place in attitude have been inspirational.

One thing remains – a very big thing.

The women's revolution is the greatest piece of unfinished business in the history of the world.

It must be a revolution, because we are calling for a full turn of the wheel, not just the slow erosion of women's supposed inferiority which has already taken hundreds of years. As the nineteenth-century suffragists found, rational argument about female subjection, appealing to ideas of justice to right this huge and ancient wrong, did not give women the vote or bring equality. A revolution for women is therefore necessary and overdue. Women have tried everything else, including patience. Two thousand years of waiting for things to change have shown that the revolution will come when women grasp the reality that the change they seek is within their grasp, and *it is already under way.* I believe it will be guided by the power of reason, propelled by moral and emotional force, and inspired by the shining justice of the cause.

Not by women alone

'If the world can be saved,' said Vigdís Finnbogadóttir, 'it will be by women – with the help and friendship of men.' All we need is a few good men. In fact, there have been many of them in the long history of the world. 'The women are coming up, blessed be God, and a few of the men are coming up with them,' Sojourner Truth told the Ohio Women's Rights Convention in 1851. That great and tireless campaigner identified the last piece in the puzzle that women sorely need in this long drawn-out campaign: the active engagement not only of the precious few, but of all good men. Without them, who knows where women would still be? With them, women achieved the major successes of the modern age. Contraception, education, suffrage, mental and physical freedom, the good guys have been on the women's march for justice every step of the way, and there have been thousands, if not millions of them over time.

Will they now join with women to form an army of non-violent revolutionaries?

To bring equality for women, what must men do?

The award-winning Carrie Gracie, who resigned as the BBC's China Editor because of unequal pay, has this clear advice for men:

- If you believe in equal pay for women, do something to show it.
- Equal pay is a snakes-and-ladders board. A male comparator can help a woman move from square nine to square ninety by saying her work is equal.

Equal pay is only one part of life where women have lagged behind. Men can also bring change in other areas if they care enough about women and girls:

- Stand up for women and girls, support them and speak out, even when other men do not see anything wrong.

- Question the indignities and injustices they know women suffer.
- Consider their own actions at home and in the world.
- Bear in mind that women have always been unequal, and equality is the goal.

We began with revolution, and that is where we end. Remember the call to arms of Olympe de Gouges? 'Women, wake up ... recognise your rights! ... Whatever the barriers set up against you, it is in your power to overcome them; you only have to want it!' In 2019, women outnumbered men in the US, the UK, the whole of Europe, Russia, Australia and New Zealand and elsewhere, and most of them are still discovering their strength. Following these statistics through into the twenty-first century, *the future will be female.*

The lamplighters are already showing the way ahead. Every decade of the last two hundred years has produced women who changed the past and lit the way to a brighter future, one where equality is real, natural and normal, and not just a wishful dream.

And life will be easier and happier for us all. The American anarchist Emma Goldman summed up the love and laughter to come:

> If I can't dance, it's not my revolution.
> If I can't dance, I don't want your revolution.
> A revolution without dancing is not a revolution
>   worth having.
> If there won't be dancing at the revolution, I'm not coming.
> Our rebel women have blazed the path and shown the
>   way ahead.
> Will you be coming?
> On we go, then.
> *See you there!*

THE WOMEN'S MANIFESTO FOR EQUALITY

A Blueprint For Revolution

Give women human rights, not 'women's rights'

There are no sub-sections, no exceptions, no qualifications to human rights. Equality for women means what it means for men: life, liberty, freedom from fear, freedom from violence, the right to control their bodies and to determine their own lives, to learn, to earn, and above all, the right to define their own future.

Establish women's equality before the law

Recognise women's legal existence on the same terms as men's: as competent to bear witness, to inherit, to own and control. One law, one marriage, for both participants: consign polygamy to the past and make women equal in marriage and divorce. Men, equality and nothing more. Women, equality and nothing less.

Protect the female body

Develop the political will to defend every woman's right to make her own decisions about her body. Educate girls to know their bodies and their reproductive rights, and ensure ready access to menstrual products and contraception. Strengthen and enforce the laws against all forms of gender-based violence, from sex-selective abortion and femicide to FGM, forced marriage and coercive control.

Free the female mind

Educate women and girls for the female future. Give them literacy and a full education. Two-thirds of the world's illiterate adults are female, when women's access to education is recognised as the key to population control and to the education that their children will achieve. Help parents to value the human capital of a girl's mind on a level with that of a boy's

And free the male

Dismantle the belief in the inevitability of male aggression in favour of training for non-violence. Educate boys out of using violence and girls out of accepting it. Amplify and extend the definitions of masculinity to give more room for all. Bring up boys and educate men to see equality with women and girls as the norm.

Find and define yourself

Your rebel woman.

NOTES

PART 1: TURNING THE WHEEL

xiii *As I sat watching*: Shaw, *Man and Superman*.

1: Rights – for Women?

1 *Bliss it was in that dawn*: William Wordsworth, 'The French Revolution as It Appeared to Enthusiasts at Its Commencement', in *Poems* (1815).

1 *So you think revolutions*: De Chamfort delivered this stinging rebuke in 1789 to his fellow writer Jean-François Marmontel, who questioned him about the senseless slaughter of the French Revolution. See Marmontel's memoirs in volume 2 of his *Works* (1818). As a rousing slogan it has been misattributed to Lord Byron and Edward Bulwer Lytton.

1 *The position of women*: This was Carmichael's response to a document of 1964, 'Position Paper: Women in the Movement', written and circulated anonymously by female workers in the civil rights movement to challenge the behaviour of the men.

2 *Yesterday, at seven o'clock*: A report in *Le Moniteur Universel*, the main French newspaper during the French Revolution. Quoted in Mousset, *Women's Rights and the French Revolution*.

7 *'Women were in the forward ranks . . . '*: Mignet, *History of the French Revolution*. See also Rudé, *The Crowd in the French Revolution*, who marvels that '*même des femmes à chapeau*' – even women who wore hats rather than the rough head-cloths of the fishwives – joined them on the march.

8 *famously foul-mouthed fishwives*: For the fishwives' command of the march and their impressive repertoire of obscenities, see Hibbert, *The French Revolution*.

9 *newly formed Fraternal Society*: The club Etta Palm d'Aelders joined in 1790 was the Fraternal Society of Patriots of Both Sexes, Defenders of the

Constitution – Société Fraternelle des Patriotes de l'un et l'autre sexe, Défenseurs de la Constitution – to give it its full title.

10 *'Political power grows out of the barrel of a gun'*: Mao Zedong issued this dark diktat on 6 November 1938 in a speech addressing the sixth Plenary Session of the Central Committee of the Chinese Communist Party.

13 *whose husband*: The husband of Sophie was the Marquis de Condorcet, also known as Nicolas de Condorcet, who published *De l'admission des femmes au droit de cité* (On the Admission of Women to the Rights of Citizenship) in 1790.

20 *'Impudent women . . . '* : See Levy and Applewhite, 'Women and Militant Citizenship in Revolutionary Paris'.

20 *'Let us be terrible'*: Speech to the National Convention, March 1793. Danton was responding to savage outbreaks of public violence by arguing that only a more extreme and government-imposed rule of terror could stop the people from breaking the law to deliver their own terrible form of rough justice. The Extraordinary Criminal Tribunal of the Revolution was established that month.

22 *'I am a woman . . . '*: Quoted in Mousset, *Women's Rights and the French Revolution*.

22 *A newspaper report of the verdict*: Quoted in ibid.

22 *'unmuzzled tigers'*: Letter to Citizen Degouges, 2 November 1793, in Ian Donnachie and Carmen Lavin (eds), *From Enlightenment to Romanticism: Anthology 1* (Manchester: Manchester University Press, 2003).

23 *'That hyena in petticoats'*: Letter to Hannah More, 26 January 1795. Like many men, Walpole cherished tender feelings for Marie Antoinette, and attacked Wollstonecraft for her derogatory portrayal of the ill-fated queen in her 1794 essay *An Historical and Moral Review of the Origin and Progress of the French Revolution; and the Effect it has produced in Europe*.

30 *Liberty leading the people*: France's prime minister Manuel Valls declared in 2016 that Marianne's bare breasts embodied the spirit of the Republic, showing that she did not have to cover her body because she was free. Amid the howls of protest from historians (*'moronic!'*) and feminists (*'crétin!'*), it emerged that M. Valls did not know of any other versions of Marianne, and that the 'Liberty' of Delacroix is the only one to show her bursting out of her décolletage for the sake of la Patrie. See 'Marianne, le voile et les droits des femmes: les propos de Valls agacent une historienne', Le Monde, 30 August 2016, https://www.lemonde.fr/big-browser/article/2016/08/30/marianne-le-voile-et-les-droits-des-femmes-les-propos-de-manuel-valls-agacent-une-historienne_4989910_4832693.html.

2: New Worlds and Old Ways

32 *The conduct of the women*: For the official report on the conduct of the women, see Daniels and Murnane, *Uphill all the Way*.

32 *Nature intended women to be our slaves*: See the record for the year 1817 in Trager, *The Women's Chronology*, and Gaspard Gourgaud (trans. Elizabeth Wormeley Latimer), *Talks of Napoleon at St Helena with General Baron Gourgaud, together with the journal kept by Gourgard on their journey from Waterloo to St Helena*, translated by Elizabeth Wormeley Latimer (Chicago: A. C. McClurg & Co., 1904).

32 *The process of industrialisation*: Thompson, *The Making of the English Working Class*.

33 *in an essay of 1855*: George Eliot, 'Margaret Fuller and Mary Wollstonecraft', *Leader*, VI (13 October 1855).

33 *Emma Rauschenbusch-Clough*: For the globe-trotting Miss Emma Rauschenbusch-Clough, see the American Baptist History Society website, particularly 'Emma Rauschenbusch-Clough and the Rights of Women', 8 August 2016, https://abhsarchives.org/emma-rauschenbusch-clough-rights-women/. Her doctorate from Berne was a remarkable indication of the power of Wollstonecraft's *Vindication* to reach unexpected audiences.

34 *One young woman of the Eora nation*: Patyegarang owes her place in history to another scholarly Australian woman, the archivist Phyllis Mander-Jones, who in 1972 discovered the three surviving notebooks of William Dawes in the basement of the School of Oriental and African Studies library at the University of London University, untouched for 136 years. The notebooks are now available online at www.williamdawes.org.

36 *an encounter in 1790*: See Tench, *A Complete Account of the Settlement at Port Jackson*. See also Karskens, 'Barangaroo and the Eora Fisherwomen'.

37 *The 1931 story of three young girls*: Follow the Rabbit-Proof Fence, an account of the children's journey, was written over sixty years later by Molly's daughter Doris Pilkington Garimara, to celebrate a wild leap of daring and a display of human endurance exceptional even in Australia's remarkable history.

38 *'feed the female famine', 'of breeding age'*: Phrases and ideas like these were current since the Ancient Greeks established the first colonies in about 1000 BCE. The need for women and 'young girls to make wives' resurfaced during the English colonisation of North America with Francis Bacon's instructions to the Royal Council for Virginia in 1609.

39 *borrowed her mistress's fine kid gloves*: This story, passed down by the young woman's descendants, was related to me on the Gold Coast by an Australian women who took great pride in her convict ancestry.

39 *'No, no – surely not! . . . '*: Quoted in Hughes, *The Fatal Shore*. Ralph Clark served in the Royal Marines, and like most of those in charge of the convicts, found it easier dealing with the men than the women.

42 *'amazonian* banditti'*: Quoted in Hughes, *The Fatal Shore*.

42 *high jinks*: The 'lively' behaviour of the female convicts in Van Diemen's Land was reported in 1837 in one of the earliest newspapers on the island, *The True Colonist: The Van Diemen's Land Political Despatch, and Agricultural and Commercial Advertiser*. 'Many women [of the respectable settlers],' it noted, 'prefer this class ... There is more fun there than in the others; and

we have been informed, that some of the most sprightly of the ladies divert their companions by acting plays!' See also the wonderfully rich and detailed official documents online via www.nla.gov.au/research-guides/convicts/female-convicts.

42 *the three hundred women*: Quoted in Cassie Crofts, 'The 300 convicts who mooned the Governor', *National Geographic*, 15 January 2016, https://www.nationalgeographic.com.au/history/the-300-convicts-who-mooned-the-governor.aspx.

43 *'in sex, acquirements . . . '*: Letter to Sara Coleridge, November 1802. For a full account of the extraordinary married life of Sara, see Lefebure, *The Bondage of Love*.

44 *Enheduanna of Sumeria* : See Meador and Maier, *Princess, Priestess, Poet* and Friedrich, *The Meaning of Aphrodite*. For a fuller study of the long historical period when the Supreme Deity was female, try *The Great Goddess* by Jean Markdale.

45 *male played a vital role in creating life*: The discovery of biological paternity and its consequences are discussed in Kramer, *The Origins of Fatherhood*.

46 *the phallus took centre stage*: See Keuls, *The Reign of the Phallus*.

46–7 *I have learned that many*: Theano, *On Piety*, *c*. sixth century BCE. Translated by Vicki Lynn Harper, in Mary Ellen Waithe (ed.), *A History of Women Philosophes Volume 1 600 BC–500 AD* (Dordrecht, Boston and Lancaster: Martinus Nijhoff, 1987). Theano also wrote philosophical essays on women, on vice and on virtue, as well as letters, memoirs and works on Pythagoras, all so highly admired that later commentators agreed that they must have been written by a man.

48 *'Man will never be free . . . '*: This statement seems to have been adapted from two lines of his short poem 'Les Eleutheromanes' ('The People Mad for Freedom') in which he imagines that the hands of a free man (*'ni serviteur, ni maître'*, neither servant nor master) will weave together the entrails of a priest for the want of a rope to strangle the kings (*'ourdiraient les entrailles d'un prêtre / Au defaut d'un cordon pour étrangler les rois*). Published in Diderot's *Oeuvres Complètes* (1818–19).

48 *core text*: The encyclopaedia of Denis Diderot and others, to give it its full and final title, was the *Encyclopédie, ou dictionnaire raisonné des sciences, des arts et des métiers, par une société de gens de lettres, mis en ordre par M. Diderot de l'Académie des Sciences et Belles-Lettres de Prusse, et quant à la partie mathématique, par M. d'Alembert de l'Académie royale des Sciences de Paris, de celle de Prusse et de la Société royale de Londres.* (Encyclopedia: or a Systematic Dictionary of the Sciences, Arts, and Crafts, by a Company of Persons of Letters, edited by M. Diderot of the Academy of Sciences and *Belles-Lettres* of Prussia: as to the Mathematical Portion, arranged by M. d'Alembert of the Royal Academy of Sciences of Paris, to the Academy of Sciences in Prussia and to the Royal Society of London), published in France between 1751 (text) and 1772 (illustrations).

52 *'Never forget that all men . . . '*: Quoted in Raven and Weir, *Women in History*.

56 *'Children are taken down . . . '*: *Children's Employment Commission 1842: Report by Robert Hugh Franks, Esq, on the Employment of Children and Young Persons in the Collieries and the Ironworks of South Wales* (1842).

57 *Spinning Jenny*: The Spinning Jenny was not named after the inventor's wife or daughter, as the sentimental fiction has it. Those who spun for a living were almost invariably single women, and a 'Jenny' was the name for anything female, like a donkey.

57 *'spinster'*: Originally, a spinster could be female or male, and simply meant one who spun for a living. That often implied an unmarried woman, and over time the word picked up the derogatory connotations it carried into the nineteenth century and beyond: see Jeffreys, *The Spinster and Her Enemies*.

58 *The common hours of business*: Francis Edward Paget, *The Pageant: or, Pleasure and its Price* (1843)

58 *lives as women*: For an American perspective, see Abbott, *Women in Industry*.

59 *[I] carry water down the mine*: *Children's Employment Commission: Report by Robert Hugh Franks, Esq*.

59 **Mary Price** *outdoor girl*: Ibid.

60 *When well I draw the drams*: Ibid.

61 *A girl named Mary Richards*: John Brown, *A Memoir of Robert Blincoe* (1832).

62 *did not need a living wage*: See Joyce Burnette, 'An investigation of the female–male wage gap during the Industrial Revolution in Britain', *Economic History Review*, 50:2 (May 1997).

62 *'droop and sicken . . . '*: Factories Regulation Bill, *Hansard*, vol. 11, 16 March 1832.

3: All Change

64 *We Abolition Women*: Quoted in Lerner, *The Grimké Sister from South Carolina*.

64 *Tess was no insignificant creature*: Hardy, *Tess of the d'Urbervilles*.

66 *'God gave me a soul . . . '*: Harriet Jacobs had been taught to read and write by one of her female owners, and her memoir, *Incidents In the Life of a Slave Girl*, appeared in 1861.

66 *Sally Hemings*: Little is known of Sally Hemings, but Jefferson's trust in her can be inferred from his charging her with bringing his child from America to Europe. Another glimpse of her as 'an industrious and orderly creature in her behaviour' was given by one of Jefferson's fellow slave owners in the *Fredericktown Herald*, reprinted in the *Richmond Recorder* of 8 December 1802, when the story of their relationship became known.

66 *'mighty near white . . . '*: Isaac Jefferson recalled Sally and other members of her family in his memoirs of around 1847, recorded by a local clergyman, the Reverend Charles Campbell.

67 *Rape and the threat of it*: Annette Gordon-Reed, 'Did Sally Hemings and Thomas Jefferson Love Each Other?', *American Heritage*, 58:5 (fall 2008).

68 *Madison, informed a journalist*: Madison Hemings told his story to S. F. Wetmore, the editor of an Ohio weekly newspaper, the Pike County Republican, where it was first published in 1873.

68 *'solemn pledge'*: One of the strongest arguments for Jefferson's long-disputed paternity of Sally Hemings's children is that, apart from two ancient retainers, they were the only four of his hundreds of slaves he ever freed.

68 *'one-drop rule'*: This notion that one drop of 'black blood' could permeate and contaminate all the blood found in a 'white' human body is memorably dramatised in the 1951 movie *Showboat*, where the mixed-race singer Julie's white lover cuts their skin to mix his blood with hers.

68 *found ways to rebel*: Paton, 'Enslaved Women and Slavery before and after 1807'.

69 *cutting sugar cane*: At six feet tall and extremely tough, canes were exceptionally dangerous work for men, let alone for perinatal women. But sugar was 'white gold', so profitable that nothing was allowed to stand in the way of production.

69 *unable to breastfeed*: Breastfeeding was known to reduced fertility, so enslaved women usually continued as long as they could. The owners, keen to get the mothers back to work, constantly sought to reduce it and inflicted harsh punishments on the women who disobeyed. See Paton, 'Enslaved Women and Slavery before and after 1807'.

69 *'I was the conductor . . . '*: From Harriet Tubman's address to the Rochester Women's Rights Convention, 1848.

70 *'Poem on the African Slave Trade'*: See Teakle, 'The Works of Mary Birkett Card'.

71 *That man over there*: In 1851, at the Women's Rights Convention in Akron, Ohio, Sojourner Truth delivered a speech so powerful that different versions of it exist. This was published in 1863, and became the most popular.

72 *a letter from their church*: 'Pastoral Letter: The General Association of Congregational Ministers of Massachusetts to Churches under their Care: July 1837', in Sklar, *Women's Rights Emerges within the Antislavery Movement*. Sarah Grimké responded with the swingeing *Letters on the Equality of the Sexes and the Condition of Woman*.

73 *Sarah's counterblast*: Letter to Amos Phelps, 3 August 1837, in Ceplair (ed.), *The Public Years of Sarah and Angelina Grimké*.

73 *What man or woman of common sense*: Letter to C. E. Beecher, 20 July 1837, in Angelina Grimké, *Letters to Catherine E. Beecher in Reply to 'An Essay on Slavery and Abolitionism'* (1838).

74 *'Women ought to feel . . . '*: Angelina Grimké, *An Appeal to the Women of the Nominally Free States* (1837).

74 *'I am persuaded . . . '*: Sarah Grimké, *Letters on the Equality of the Sexes and the Condition of Women*.

74 *Men and women were CREATED EQUAL*: Letter to the General Association

of Congregational Ministers of Massachusetts, 17 July 1837. Sarah's claim is perhaps better known in its shortened version, 'We ask no favours for our sex. All we ask is that men will take their feet from off our necks.'

76 *'The history of mankind . . . '*: Declaration of Sentiments from the Seneca Falls Conference, 1848. Available at https://usa.usembassy.de/etexts/democrac/17. htm.

78 *'at the close of the first session,'*: Letter to Susan B. Anthony, 'From Our Special Collections: Abigail Bush', River Campus Libraries, University of Rochester, https://rbscp.lib.rochester.edu/4627.

79 *'Susan stirred the puddings . . . '*: Quoted in Griffith, *In Her Own Right*.

79 *'I forged the thunderbolts . . . '*: Ibid.

80 *'the first person by whom . . . '*: Quoted in Blackwell, *Lucy Stone*.

80 *'I was a woman . . . '*: *Report of the International Council of Women,* Washington DC, National Woman Suffrage Association, 1888.

83 *'stated that she paid her taxes . . . '*: House of Commons debate, 3 August 1832, *Hansard*, vol. 25 c1068.

84 *Millicent Garrett*: Millicent Garrett worked for many years under her maiden name before she married Henry Fawcett in 1897.

84 *'It is quite clear . . . '*: Strachey, *The Cause*.

86 *The Queen is most anxious*: *Letter* to Sir Theodore Martin, 29 May 1870.

89 *foot-binding*: Better known as foot-breaking, this form of female abuse survived a number of attempts to ban it, and was inflicted on young girls from the tenth century into the twentieth. The Bata Shoe Museum in Toronto has a collection of 'little lotus shoes' that are on average 8 to 10 centimetres long.

90 *'three-inch golden lilies', 'viewed as a sexual organ . . . '*: Ryan, *Chinese Women and the Global Village*.

92 *first words ever transmitted*: The original paper tape of the first telegraph, with Morse's handwritten tribute to Annie, is preserved in the Samuel F. B. Morse Papers at the Library of Congress in Washington DC.

93 *the most joyful of all spectacles*: Macfarlane, *'Democracy'*.

PART 2: ONE WAY PENDULUM

95 *A farce in a new dimension*: Simpson, *One Way Pendulum*.

4: Women Who Dared

97 *Disobedience, in the eyes of anyone*: Oscar Wilde made this defence of free-thinking in 'The Soul of man under Socialism', *Fortnightly Review* (1891).

97 *Well-behaved women seldom make history*: Often attributed to others from Eleanor Roosevelt to Marilyn Monroe, this was written by US academic

Laurel Thatcher Ulrich in a 1976 article for *American Quarterly*. It later appeared on T-shirts, mugs, badges and bumper stickers, and Ulrich published a book using the title in 2007.

97 *A ship in port is safe*: Grace Hopper popularised this expression by using it in a number of her speeches, substituting 'port' for the original 'harbour'. Its first appearance in print dates from a collection of everyday sayings, *Salt from My Attic*, by John Shedd (Portland, ME: Mosher Press, 1928).

98 *Martha Jane Cannary*: Most of the information about Calamity Jane's life comes from the account she dictated in 1896 – see *The Autobiography of Calamity Jane by Calamity Jane, The story of Marthy Cannary Burke*, in her own words, http://gutenberg.net.au/ebooks/w00014.html.

99 *'I would like to see every woman . . . '*: Quoted in Kasper, *Annie Oakley*.

103 *'scribblings', 'unladylike', 'might vex'*: As stated in Dooley, *Frances Burney*.

104 *accounts of male brutality*: Charlotte Brontë's obsession with dark and unfathomable men began with her unrequited love for Constantin Héger, the headmaster of the girls' school in Brussels where she studied in 1842. It forms the basis of her two most autobiographical novels, *Villette* (1853) and *The Professor* (originally *The Master*), published in 1857.

104 *'a strange brute'*: Elizabeth Rigby's attack on *Jane Eyre* appears as one half of a 15,000-word article. '*Vanity Fair* – and *Jane Eyre*' in the *Quarterly Review*, December 1848, coupled with a review of William Thackeray's *Vanity Fair*.

105 *'discoveries, observations, and laborious calculations'*: Citation accompanying Gold Medal for Science, 1846.

107 *Mary Fairfax Somerville*: See Alic, *Hypatia's Heritage*.

107 *'the strain of abstract thought . . . '*: Somerville, *Personal Recollections*.

109 *'except . . . in regard to sex'*: Stiles's assessment of Foote is recorded in Arnstein, *The Admission of Women to Yale College*.

112 *'like lava, so long held back . . . '*: The 'Manifesto of the Vésuviennes' was published in Paris in July 1848. The slogan was created by a male revolutionary, Daniel Borme, and displayed on placards throughout the city, as described by David Allen Harvey in 'Forgotten Feminist: Claude Vignon (1828–1888), revolutionary and femme de lettres', *Women's History Review*, 13:4 (2004). See also Laura S. Struminger, 'The Vésuviennes: Images of women warriors in 1848 and their significance for French history', *History of European Ideas*, 8:4–5 (1987).

113 *wearing culottes in public*: For centuries under the rule of the Catholic Church, women wearing men's clothes was a capital crime, and it was the offence for which Joan of Arc was condemned to burn at the stake, not for heresy, as is commonly believed.

113 *'bloomers'*: The 'Bloomer outfit' consisted of a short dress or tunic worn over a pair of voluminous pants cuffed at the ankles like harem trousers. The aim was freedom and comfort, but many women found it hard to give up their familiar if uncomfortable stays.

114 *'This child is really something . . . '*: Quoted in David Conway, *Jewry in Music:*

Entry to the Profession from the Enlightenment to Richard Wagner (Cambridge: Cambridge University Press, 2011).

114 *'Music will perhaps become . . . '*: Fanny's reproof from her father is quoted in Hensel, *The Mendelssohn Family*. Her brother's discouragement appears in the same source.

114 *publishing Fanny's work as his own*: Musicologists are still investigating how many of the compositions attributed to Felix were in fact written by Fanny. One of the major works attributed to her brother, the *Easter Sonata* (1828), was not established as Fanny's until 2010. The piece was given its first performance under her name on 8 March 2017 – International Women's Day – performed by London's Royal College of Music, and broadcast live on BBC Radio 3.

118 *feminist proposals and actions*: Lady Florence Dixie's five-point plan for women achieved two outright victories after her death. Since 2011, any first child of the British or a number of other European monarchies will inherit the throne. Women all over the world now play football and take part in many other sports, including boxing. For the other three, progress is ongoing.

118–19 *'the girls should enter into . . . '*: Quoted in Richard William Cox, Dave Russell and Wray Vamplew, *Encyclopedia of British Football* (London: Routledge, 2002).

123 *women's use of strike action*: Berenice Carroll, '"Shut Down the Mills!": Women, the Modern Strike, and Revolution', The Public i, March 2012, http://publici.ucimc.org/2012/03/shut-down-the-mills-women-the-modern-strike-and-revolution/.

5: Pearls Beyond Price

126 *Woman must have her freedom*: Margaret Sanger, 'A Parents' Problem or a Woman's?', *Birth Control Review* (March 1919).

126 *No one disputes that the bull*: Darwin, *The Descent of Man*.

126 *We woman suffragists*: Emmeline Pankhurst, speech at the Albert Hall, October 1912.

127 *most life-threatening process*: Risks included potential miscarriage and loss of blood; toxaemia; failed or misplaced placenta; arrest of labour; puerperal sepsis; kidney failure; deep vein thrombosis; running fistula; prolapse of the bladder, uterus and/or vagina; and chronic unresolved depression, among many others.

127 *'No woman can call herself free . . . '*: Margaret Sanger, 'Morality and Birth Control', *Birth Control Review* (February–March 1918).

127–8 *'Regardless of what man's attitude . . . '*: Margaret Sanger, *Woman and the New Race (1920)*. See also Latson, 'Why Birth Control Pioneer Margaret Sanger Kept Getting Arrested'. For the full story, try *The Autobiography of Margaret Sanger* (1938) and Esther Katz (ed.) and Cathy Moran Hajo and Peter C. Engelman (asst eds), *The Selected Papers of Margaret Sanger* (4 vols, 2003–16).

130 *The legendary Giacomo Casanova*: Casanova himself wrote the best account of his exploits, *Histoire de ma vie jusqu'à l'an 1797*, 'The History of my Life until the year 1797'. See also Childs, *Casanova: A New Perspective and Kelly, Casanova: Actor, Lover, Priest, Spy*.

131 *prison with hard labour*: This involved punishments later accepted as forms of torture, including moving heavy rocks from one place to another, then back again. The sentence thought to have hastened the death of one of the last men condemned to it, Oscar Wilde.

131 *Madame Restell*: See Karen Abbott, 'Madame Restell: The Abortionist of Fifth Avenue', SmithsonianMag.com, 27 November 2012, https://www.smithsonianmag.com/history/madame-restell-the-abortionist-of-fifth-avenue-145109198/#301xS7tYyL8gRSii.99. See also Browder, *The Wickedest Woman in New York*.

133 *inducing a miscarriage was not illegal*: Abortion was outlawed by the state of New York in 1845.

135 *cervical cap*: Stopping sperm from entering the uterus was long understood to prevent conception, and scientific experiments by German and Dutch physicians began in the early nineteenth century. The decisive breakthrough came in 1844, when Charles Goodyear patented the vulcanisation of rubber in the US.

135 *'The struggle will be bitter'*: Margaret Sanger's attack on the Comstock legislation, 'Shall We Break This Law?' appeared in the first issue of the *Birth Control Review*, in February 1917. The journal, published by Margaret Sanger, Frederick A. Blossom and Elizabeth Stuyvesant, was 'Dedicated to the Principle of Intelligent and Voluntary Motherhood'.

136 *Woman has always been*: Ibid.

136 *Marie Stopes*: Like Margaret Sanger, Stopes was a prolific author, and a brilliant polymath. Her *interests ranged from fossils, flora and fauna to Japanese theatre, male psychology and venereal disease. She also wrote assorted poems, and some of her plays reached London's West End.*

137–8 *Assuming … that the two*: Stopes, *Married Love*.

141 *'The less highly evolved . . . '*: See the *Darwin and Gender research and education project carried out by Cambridge and Harvard Universities from 2009 to 2013*: https://www.darwinproject.ac.uk/about/research-initiatives/darwin-and-gender-project.

142 *Antoinette Brown Blackwell*: Another great standard-bearer in the struggle, an activist of iron resolve in a long life which included marriage and seven children. At the age of ninety-five, Blackwell was the only woman who had been present at the 1850 Women's Rights Convention in Worcester, Massachusetts, who lived to see the passage of the 19th Amendment, which gave women the right to vote, in 1920.

142 *'very dear co-adjutor and fellow-labourer'*: Charles Darwin, letter to Henrietta Darwin, 28 March 1871. In H. E. Litchfield (ed.), *Emma Darwin, Wife of Charles Darwin: A Century of Family Letters* (vol. 2, 1904).

144 *She died for women, right?*: The new work on the death of Emily Wilding Davison was presented in *Secrets of a Suffragette*, Channel 4, 26 May 2013.

146 *Not now, girls, not yet*: For Mrs Pankhurst, see Purvis, *Emmeline Pankhurst*.

147 *'We threw away all our conventional notions . . . '*: Emmeline Pankhurst, *My Own Story* (1914).

148 *'I would rather be a rebel than a slave'*: Quoted in Purvis, *Emmeline Pankhurst*.

150 *four Dundee postmen*: Fern Riddell, 'Suffragettes, violence and militancy', Votes for Women, bl.uk, 6 February 2018, https://www.bl.uk/votes-for-women/articles/suffragettes-violence-and-militancy.

151 *'I must pay the full price . . . '*: Mary R. Richardson, *Laugh a Defiance* (London: Weidenfeld & Nicolson, 1953). See also Raeburn, *The Militant Suffragettes*.

152 *Number 1 was brought in*: Quoted in Raeburn, *The Militant Suffragettes*.

154 *Marie Skłodowska Curie*: Born in Poland as Maria Skłodowska, the great scientist always used her maiden name with her married name, and was never known as 'Marie Curie'. Although she became a naturalised French citizen, she remained a proud Pole, bringing up her two daughters to speak Polish and naming the first chemical element that she discovered 'polonium' in honour of her native country.

154 *won twice in two different sciences*: John Bardeen won twice for physics, in 1956 and 1972, and Frederick Sanger twice for chemistry, in 1958 and 1980. To date, Maria Skłodowska Curie is the only person to have been awarded the prize for achievement in two different sciences.

155 *'computers'*: The story of the women star-gazers at the Harvard College Observatory is told by Dava Sobel in *The Glass Universe*.

6: Footprints of Blood

160 *It is far easier to make war*: Quoted in Margaret MacMillan, *Peacemakers: The Paris Peace Conference of 1919 and Its Attempt to End War* (London: John Murray, 2001).

160 *Without women, victory will tarry*: Lloyd George was addressing a rally organised by Mrs Pankhurst in 1916 on the theme of 'Women's Right to Serve'.

160 *Rather, ten times, die in the surf*: Florence Nightingale, 'Cassandra: An Essay' (1860).

161 *'The Lady With the Lamp'*: Charles Howard Russell, *The Times*, 8 February 1855.

162 *'The Lady With the Hammer'*: *Votes for Women*, 9 April 1912.

162 *'Were there none . . . '*: Nightingale, 'Cassandra'.

163 *I derived no little satisfaction*: Mary Seacole told this and many other stories in her autobiography, *Wonderful Adventures of Mrs Seacole in Many Lands*.

163 *Elsie Knocker and Mairi Chisholm*: For the full story of 'the heroines of Pervyse', see Atkinson, *Elsie and Mairi Go to War*.

164 *Amazons*: For an account of the battle-scarred female bones buried with

their armour, see the multi-award winning *The Amazons: Lives and Legends of Warrior Women across the Ancient World* by Adrienne Mayor.

164 *druids on the island of Mona*: A graphic account of the 'frenzied women' druids and their massacre was written by the Roman historian Tacitus, the son-in-law of one of the generals who served in the campaign against the Celts. See *Annals* XIV, xxix and xxx.

165 *warriors of the Kingdom of Dahomey*: For the all-female corps of West Africa, see Alpern, *Amazons of Black Sparta*.

165 *Paris Commune*: The astute and humane Clemenceau did his best for the fighting women of the Communards, even though his authority as mayor of Paris was one of the targets of their attack. Gregor Dallas unravels the politics of the situation in *At the Heart of a Tiger*.

165 *'They fought like devils . . . '*: Quoted in Alistair Horne, *The Fall of Paris: The Siege and the Commune 1870–71* (London: Pan, 2012).

166 *Lakshmi Bai*: A brief portrait cannot do justice to this charismatic leader, fearless fighter and superb athlete; see Edwardes, *Red Year*. Colonel Malleson recorded his tribute to Lakshmi Bai in volume III of his *History of the Indian Mutiny*.

167 *Ecaterina Teodoroiu*: Teodoroiu was not the only female to fight openly as a woman in an army of men. Flora Sandes, a vicar's daughter from Yorkshire, began the First World War as a nurse and ended it as a soldier, commanding a battalion of Serbian infantry.

167 *traumatic early years*: Bochkareva's memoir, *Yashka: My Life as Peasant, Exile and Soldier*, dictated by Mariya Bochkareva to Isaac Don Levine and first published in 1919, gives some idea of her terrible start in life.

168 *Dancing the skies*: See 'Women Combat Pilots of WW1', Hargrave: The Pioneers. Aviation and Aeromodelling – Interdependent Evolutions and Histories, www.ctie.monash.edu.au/hargrave/women_combat_pilots_ww1. html. See also Cole, *Women Pilots of World War II*.

170 *'Hitler's Valkyrie'*: Hanna Reitsch's list of flying and gliding records forms an impressive memorial to the woman who called her 1951 autobiography *Fliegen, mein Leben* ('Flying, my Life'). Her Nazi belief in racial purity changed when she was invited to establish gliding schools in India and Ghana, but she continued to wear the Iron Cross (First Class) presented to her by Hitler into her old age.

175 *Women's National Anti-Suffrage League*: The organisation was formally founded in July 1908, and at its height gathered 337,018 signatures on a petition against women being given the vote.

175 *'I sometimes wonder in my secret thoughts . . . '*: Letter to Lord Cromer, July 1915. Quoted in Purvis, *Emmeline Pankhurst*.

178 *'a woman is only a woman . . . '*: Rudyard Kipling, 'The Betrothed', in *Departmental Ditties* (1886). My italics.

178 *'smell of tobacco and blood'*: Rudyard Kipling, *The Light that Failed* (1891).

180 *Libby Thompson*: Laurence E. Gesell tells her story in *Saddle the Wild Wind*.

181 *Decline and fall*: For the acquisition and collapse of empires, see Kriwaczek.

181 *'In Africa'*: Leghorn and Parker, 'Shouldering the High Cost of Development'.

182 *married a successful businesswoman*: Mussolini married twice, the second time without divorcing his first wife. In *The Dark Side of Camelot*, the Pulitzer Prize-winning journalist Seymour Hersh investigated a similar story of John F. Kennedy's first marriage to Palm Beach socialite Durie Malcolm, and found that the church records for the date in question had been disappeared.

183 *I am not thinking of extending the vote*: Mussolini made these statements about women to Maurice de Valeffe, a reporter for the French publication *Journal*, 12 November 1922.

183 *'thieves who reach out . . . '*: Ibid.

183 *primal flight from the female*: The fear of women and the glorification of hypermasculinity as the bedrock of Nazism is analysed in detail by Klaus Theweleit in *Male Fantasies*.

184 *'the mission of women . . . '*: Quoted in George L. Mosse, *Nazi Culture: Intellectual, Cultural, and Social Life in the Third Reich* (Madison: University of Wisconsin Press, 1966).

184 *'Whether ten thousand Russian females . . . '*: Himmler's response is noted in Shirer, *The Rise and Fall of the Third Reich*.

185 *greatest commitment came from the Soviet Union*: For Soviet women's war service, see Alexievich, *The Unwomanly Face of War*.

186 *women as undercover agents*: Hundreds of women acted as undercover agents in the Second World War, but most of their stories have been lost. Their numbers included Susan Travers, British socialite and nurse, and the only female member of the French Foreign Legion; the Indian princess Noor Inayat Khan, code named 'Madeleine' as an agent in the Special Operations Executive; and Marie-Claude Vaillant-Couturier, a French Resistance fighter in Auschwitz and Ravensbrück. As a start, see McIntosh, *Sisterhood of Spies*.

187 *'women were very much better . . . '*: Selwyn Jepson, Imperial War Museum interview, 1986. Available at https://www.iwm.org.uk/collections/item/object/80009120.

188 *the iconic and inspirational poster*: 'Rosie the Riveter' was not based on a wartime volunteer, but Rose Will Monroe, a widow already working full time as a riveter in 1942 to support herself and her two young daughters after her husband was killed in a car accident.

190 *'I can not believe that war . . . '*: Letter to Harry S Truman, 22 March 1948.

PART 3: SOME LIKE IT COLD

191 *Oh, if I could but live*: Quoted in Sherr, *Failure is Impossible*.

7: Iron Curtains and Ideal Homes

193 *The kitchen is your natural setting*: Fogarty, *Wife Dressing*.

193 *The battle for the individual rights*: Eleanor Roosevelt, 'My Day', 7 August 1941. Available at https://www2.gwu.edu/~erpapers/myday/displaydoc. cfm?_y=1941&_f=md055958.

194 'I'm your husband!': Doreen Williams told me this story herself in Tiger Bay, Cardiff, where she lived when I met her not long before she died in 1989. 'And I was not the only one,' she added. 'But we never said anything.'

195 *re-education programme*: See Spencer, *Gender, Work and Education in Britain in the 1950s*.

195 *'intelligent girls who spend . . . '*: These comments appear in Nicholson, *Perfect Wives in Ideal Homes*.

195 *'[Man] has endeavored . . . '*: Elizabeth Cady Stanton, Seneca Falls Declaration (1848). Available at https://usa.usembassy.de/etexts/democrac/17.htm

196 *'Hey, little girl . . . '*: 'Wives and Lovers' by Burt Bacharach and Hal David (1963). Lyrics © Sony/ATV Music Publishing LLC.

197 *one of the most sexist pop tunes*: See 'The 6 Sexiest Songs of the '60s – #1', https://www.flushfido.com/lists/6-sexiest-songs-of-the-60s/6-sexiest-songs-of-the-60s-1.

200 *Eva Duarte Perón*: Eva Perón was the subject of numerous books and the 1978 hit musical *Evita*, and interest in her continued to flourish after her death. Try *Evita, First Lady* by John Barnes.

201 *It is not philanthropy, nor is it charity*: Eva Perón (trans. Ethel Cherry), *My Mission in Life* (New York: Vantage 1953).

203 *pre-frontal lobotomy*: In 2011, Dr Daniel Nijensohn of Yale University Medical School, obtained X-rays of Eva's skeleton and discovered the tell-tale holes in her skull. See D. E. Nijensohn, 'Prefrontal lobotomy on Evita was done for behaviour/personality modification, not just for pain control', *Neurosurgical Focus*, 39:1 (July 2015).

204 *Eleanor Roosevelt*: A woman of the stature of Roosevelt inevitably generated many biographies and analyses, plus some adventures into fictionalising her full and varied life. One of the best ways to get to know her is to read her own writing, beginning with *The Autobiography of Eleanor Roosevelt*.

210 *'Your capitalistic attitude . . . '*: See 'The Kitchen Debate – transcript', 24 July 1959, https://www.cia.gov/library/readingroom/docs/1959-07-24.pdf.

212 *'I cannot and will not . . . '*: Letter to the House Committee on Un-American Activities, 19 May 1952.

213 *'the encoding and decoding . . . '*: Thomas C. Reeves, *The Life and Times of Joe McCarthy: A Biography* (Lanham: Madison Books, 1982).

214 *'a little picture about a little woman'*: Introduction to *See It Now: Annie Lee Moss Before the McCarthy Committee* television documentary, first broadcast 16 March 1954.

214 *'Wisconsin folks saw her . . . '*: Drew Pearson, 'Washington Merry-Go-Round', *Madera Tribune*, 28 April 1954.

214 *Melita Norwood*: David Burke told her story in *The Spy Who Came in From the Co-Op*.

215 *Ethel Rosenberg*: The trial and execution of Ethel and Julius Rosenberg proved so controversial that debate still rages about the justice of their prosecution and conviction, and new evidence continues to come to light concerning the level of Ethel's involvement in Julius's undoubted guilt.

217 *Dr Eleanor Vietti*: See Maggie O'Kane, 'The Only Woman Left Behind', BBC Radio 4, 24 September 1998.

218 *'Revolution is an act of love'*: Quoted in Brittany Knupper, 'A tribute to Jane Fonda and her 50 years of activism', *The Mary Sue*, 26 October 2019, https://www.themarysue.com/a-tribute-to-jane-fonda-activism/.

219 *'Our government was lying . . . '*: Quoted in Rebecca Leung, 'Jane Fonda: Wish I Hadn't', CBSNews.com, 31 March 2005, https://www.cbsnews.com/news/jane-fonda-wish-i-hadnt-31-03-2005/2/.

219 *Madame Nhu*: In *Finding the Dragon Lady*, Monique Brinson Demery argues that the fear of Madame Nhu dominated and even dictated US policy in Vietnam.

220 *'I would clap my hands . . . '*: Quoted in John Clark Pratt (ed.), *Vietnam Voices: Perspectives on the War Years, 1941–1975* (Athens: University of Georgia Press, 1984)

220 *'Power is wonderful'*: Quoted in Steve Phillips, *The Cold War: Conflict in Europe and Asia* (Oxford: Heinemann, 2001).

221 *'saw Madame Nhu as bright . . . '*: McNamara and VanDeMark, *In Retrospect*.

221 *'could and should have withdrawn . . . '*: Ibid.

8: Is This All?

224 *We really believed*: Dorothy Height, *Open Wide the Freedom Gates: A Memoir* (New York: PublicAffairs, 2003).

224 *It is new for women to be making history*: 'Introduction', Friedan, *'It Changed My Life'*.

225 *not the first to confront these customs*: In *Ida B. Wells*, Fradin and Bloom argue that Wells was not only a campaigner against lynchings, but a driving force behind the birth of the civil rights campaign.

226 *'O God, is there no justice . . . '*: Quoted in Wells, *Crusade for Justice*.

226 *We know through painful experience*: Martin Luther King, 'Letter from Birmingham Jail', 16 April 1963. See '"Wait" means "Never"', in MacArthur (ed.), *The Penguin Book of Twentieth-Century Protest*.

226 *'Women don't need to be nowhere . . . '*: See Olson, *Freedom's Daughters*.

227 *We regard men as infinitely precious*: This is taken from the Port Huron Founding Manifesto of the Students for a Democratic Society in 1962; the

group remained active until 1969. For the view of one of the 'sandwich-making chicks' in the group, Joan Baez, see Garman, *Race of Singers*.

229 *'I was intelligent, certainly,'*: Deirdre Blair, 'How Love Came to Simone de Beauvoir', *New York Times*, 8 April 1990.

230 *'Let woman out of the home . . . '*: Pearl S. Buck, *Of Men and Women: How to Be for Each Other* (New York: John Day, 1941).

230 *Gray's masterpiece*: The house that Gray built for her secret love contained their names in code. She called it *E-1027*, E for Eileen, then 10, 2 and 7, representing the tenth letter in the alphabet (J for Jean), the second (B for Badovici), and the seventh (G for Gray).

231 *accounts vary*: The Spanish architectural historian Beatriz Colomina suggests that Le Corbusier intended his wall paintings as a gift to Gray': see 'Battle lines: E.1027', *Journal of Architecture*, 14:4 (1999).

231 *'As an act of naked phallocracy . . . '*: Rowan Moore, 'Eileen Gray's E1027 – review', *Observer*, 30 June 2013. See also the work of the much garlanded and *(be)*knighted British sculptor Sir Antony Gormley, famous for using his naked body as his source of inspiration and installing life-sized nudie-selfie-statues all over the world. According to his defenders, this 'sounds like an extreme form of narcissism', but 'we are embodied creatures – that is how we experience the world – and he is working from that premise': Aidan Dunne, 'Antony Gormley: "Sculpture is the greatest agent of change of all art forms"', *Irish Times*, 6 January 2016.

232 *'Arguably, my student status . . . '*: S. Jocelyn Bell Burnell, 'So Few Pulsars, So Few Females', *Science*, 304:5670 (23 April 2004).

232 *'I've done very well out of not getting . . . '*: Quoted in Ian Sample, 'British astrophysicist overlooked by Nobels wins $3m award for pulsar work', *Guardian*, 6 September 2018.

234 *The problem lay buried*: Friedan, *The Feminine Mystique*.

235 *'Man is not the enemy here . . . '*: 'Woman: The Fourth Dimension', in Friedan, *'It Changed My Life'*.

235 *'I want something more . . . '*: Friedan, *The Feminine Mystique*.

235 *'hundreds, thousands, millions of women . . . '*: 'Introduction', Friedan, *'It Changed My Life'*.

235–6 *'to take action to bring women . . . '*: Statement of Purpose, 1966, National Organization of Women. Available at https://now.org/about/history/statement-of-purpose/.

236 *'Our struggle today is not . . . '*: Quoted in 'Media Matters: So Now The Press Tells Candidates When to Quit?', via Gloriafeldt. com, 30 April 2008, https://gloriafeldt.com/2008/04/30/media-matters-so-now-the-press-tells-candidates-when-to-quit/.

236 *'When I ran for the Congress . . . '*: Quoted in Kwesi Foli, 'Shirley Chisholm's "Unbought and Unbossed" presidential campaign poster', *The Undefeated*, 25 January 2017, https://theundefeated.com/features/shirley-chisholm-unbought-and-unbossed-presidential-campaign-poster-cover-stories/.

237 *'I just knew there was discrimination*: Virginia Allan interview transcript, A Few Good Women Oral History Collection, Penn State University Libraries, https://libraries.psu.edu/about/collections/few-good-women/ virginia-allen-interview-transcript.

237 Steinemite!: Steinem records that this word was invented by her salesman father, Leo Steinem. Even after he fled the family, leaving ten-year-old Gloria in sole charge of her deranged and distressed mother, he would send cheques clipped to a letterhead with no address or contact details, and simply the phrase 'IT'S STEINEMITE!' emblazoned at the top in bright red capitals.

237 *This is no simple reform*: Gloria Steinem, 'Address to the Women of America', 10 July 1971.

238 *It was so tight that the zipper caught*: Gloria Steinem, 'A Bunny's Tale', *Show* (May 1963).

239 *Men would brag about how long*: Gloria Steinem, 'If Men Could Menstruate', first published in *Ms* magazine, October 1978; reprinted in Steinem's memoir *Outrageous Acts and Everyday Rebellions*.

239 *'We are really talking about humanism'*: Steinem, 'Address to the Women of America'.

240 *This inequality . . . the law*: See Kennedy, *Eve Was Framed*.

240 *the personal is political*: The first recorded use of this phrase was by the American feminist Carol Hanisch in her 1969 article of the same name, published in 'Notes from the Second Year: Women's Liberation' the following year. Hanisch argues that the problems of women are usually attributed to their individual personal character or behaviour, while in reality they are created by their political situation, specifically their place in the power structures of society, oppressed by lifelong inequality.

241 *In 1970 the movement*: Greer, *The Whole Woman*.

241–2 *Germaine Greer is feminism's arsonist*: Helen Lewis, in 'What Germaine Greer and The Female Eunuch mean to me', *Observer*, 26 January 2014.

245 *'Feminism is doomed to failure'*: In Phyllis Schlafly, *Feminist Fantasies* (Dallas: Spence, 2003).

246 *career as a lawyer, writer, activist and speaker*: Phyllis Schlafly began writing in 1964 with *A Choice Not an Echo*, a self-published book urging conservatives to reclaim the Republican Party from its liberal wing, which sold more than three million copies. Her last book, *The Conservative Case for Trump*, was published the day after she died in 2016 at the age of ninety-two.

247 *'missing women'*: Amartya Sen, 'More than 100 million women are missing', *New York Review of Books*, 37:20 (20 December 1990).

249 *'Chinese feminist genealogy'*: 'Faculty spotlight: feminist scholarship in China', Institute for Research on Women & Gender, University of Michigan, https://irwg.umich.edu/news/faculty-spotlight-feminist-scholarship-china.

249 *'the Chinese version of* The Vagina Monologues': Ibid.

250 *'the feminist movement is about women's everyday . . . '*: Leta Hong Fincher, 'Chinese women's movement grows despite intense crackdown', *Taipei Times*, 10 March 2019.

250 *'We have done seventeen sting operations . . . '*: Sumita Thapar, 'Save the girl child', *The Hindu*, 19 March 2007. Available at https://www.countercurrents.org/gen-thapar190307.htm.

251 *'as important and essential . . . '*: 'Vision', Vimochana Forum for Women's Rights, https://www.vimochana.co.in/vision/.

9: Room at the Top

252 *The cock may crow*: Margaret Thatcher loved this centuries-old English proverb and often quoted it, because it embodied her fixed belief that men were the clamorous show-offs of the world, while the real work was always done by women.

252 *No more phallic imperialism!*: Quoted in Miles, *Women and Power*.

252 *Once, power was considered*: Katharine Graham, 'How to Get Power the Old-fashioned Way', *Cosmopolitan* (1985). Graham gives a full account of her time at the helm of the *Washington Post* in her Pulitzer Prize-winning *Personal History*.

252 *'There will not be a woman prime minister . . . '*: 'Key Cabinet post for Mrs Thatcher', *Finchley Press*, 26 June 1970.

254 *'Mr Bandaranaike would not . . . '*: Recorded in Uglow (ed.), *The Macmillan Dictionary of Women's Biography*.

259 *'feudal and bourgeois'*: See *Mao Tse-tung on Art and Literature* (Beijing: Foreign Languages Press, 1960).

260 *'India is Indira and Indira is India'*: This tribute from the Indian National Congress, Dev Kant Barooh, is recorded in Ramchandra Guha, *India after Gandhi: The History of the World's Largest Democracy* (New York: HarperCollins, 2007).

260 *'I was Mao's dog!'*: Jiang Qing's statement at her trial was widely publicised. See Rachel Dragan, 'The 25 Most Powerful Women of the Past Century: Leading Ladies', *Time*, 18 November 2010.

261 *Charged with human rights abuses*: See: Rory Carroll, 'Isabel Perón arrested over accusations of human rights abuses', *Guardian*, 13 January 2007; 'Spain: Extradition of Isabel Perón to Argentina Is Rejected by Court', *New York Times*, 29 April 2008.

261 *'I did not have three thousand . . . '*: Quoted in Therese Reyes, 'What Ever Happened to Imelda Marcos' 3,000 Pairs of Shoes?', *Vice*, 14 November 2019, https://www.vice.com/en_asia/article/59n8ab/what-ever-happened-imelda-marcos-3000-pairs-shoes-philippines.

261 *her 2784 pairs of shoes*: How many shoes did Imelda Marcos have? The figure of 2784 was supplied by the Research Library of the US Embassy in London, and was derived from the work of the US Marines charged with counting them.

263 *'They think because they have ....'*: Quoted in K. Riva Levinson, 'Winnie Mandela's complicated legacy – and how to honor it', *The Hill*, 17 April 2018, https://thehill.com/opinion/international/383587-winnie-mandelas-complicated-legacy-and-how-to-honor-it.

265 *'I was elected by the women . . . '*: Mary Robinson, inaugural address as president of Ireland, 1990.

265 *'This ain't a damn beauty contest . . . '*: See 'Jenny Shipley: Biography', New Zealand History, https://nzhistory.govt.nz/people/jenny-shipley.

265 *'arguably the best president . . . '*: 'Liberia's feisty president: another round for Africa's Iron Lady', *The Economist*, 20 May 2010.

266 *'Women should stop feeling that . . . '*: 'Renowned activist and press freedom advocate Tawakul Karman to the *Yemen Times*: "A day will come when all human rights violators pay for what they did to Yemen', *Yemen Times*, 17 June 2010.

266 *Because I was the first woman to be elected*: Anna Andersen, 'Madam President: Vigdís Finnbogadóttir on fashion and the times', *Reykjavík Grapevine*, 24 March 2014, https://grapevine.is/mag/feature/2014/03/24/madam-president/.

267 *Kay Bailey Hutchison*: Mark Potok, 'Texas Hutchison a battler and survivor', *USA Today* 11 June 11 1993.

268 *'The end result of all this . . . '*: Graham, *Personal History*.

269 *'the only way I can describe . . . '*: Ibid.

269 *'Katie Graham's gonna get . . . '*: Quoted in ibid.

270 *'Whatever power I exert . . . '*: Alex S. Jones, 'Katharine Graham at 70; one woman, two lives, many memories', *New York Times*, 1 July 1987.

270 *'the buzz of thousands of deals'*: Muriel Siebert with Aimee Lee Ball, *Changing the Rules: Adventures of a Wall Street Maverick* (New York: Free Press, 2002).

270 *'I could look at a page . . . '*: Ibid

270 *'five hundred dollars . . . '*: 'Muriel "Mickey" Sibert: The First Woman of Finance', The Calla Lily Dialogues, 9 February 2016, http://www.thecallalilydialogues.com/the-dialogues/2016/2/8/muriel-mickey-siebert-the-first-woman-of-finance.

270–1 *Roses are red*: Quoted in Susan Vaughn, 'Wall Street trailblazer listens to her gut instincts', *LA Times*, 10 December 2000.

272 *'I'm a geek'*: Felicia Taylor, 'Google's Marissa Mayer: Passion is a gender-neutralizing force', CNN, 5 April 2012, https://edition.cnn.com/2012/04/05/tech/google-marissa-mayer/index.html?iref=allsearch.

272 *'I like to code'*: Jacob Weisberg, 'Yahoo's Marissa Mayer: Hail to the Chief', *Vogue*, 16 August 2013.

272 *'If you can find something . . . '*: Taylor, 'Google's Marissa Mayer'.

273 *'I don't think there's a woman . . . '*: Sheelah Kolhatkar, 'The tech industry's gender-discrimination problem', *New Yorker*, 13 November 2017.

274 *'an organized, concerted effort . . . '*: Ibid.

275 *'a landmark moment'*: Katty Kay, 'Mary Barra as GM boss is a landmark

moment', BBC News, 10 December 2013, https://www.bbc.co.uk/news/blogs-echochambers-25326214.

275 *'one of the most macho . . . '*: Ibid.

276 *'I want to put this painful experience . . . '*: Geoff Colvin, 'Mary Barra's (unexpected) opportunity', *Fortune*, 18 September 2014.

277 *Salima Ghezali*: See Nicola Graydon, 'A Life in the Day: Salima Ghezhali', *Sunday Times*, 3 January 1999.

277 *In 1997 Ghezali announced*: See 'Freedom of the Press', Algeria: Human Rights Watch, 1997, https://www.hrw.org/reports/1997/algeria/Algeria-09.htm.

278 *'she could ride a horse . . . '*: Quoted in Elaine Woo, 'Sue Sally Hale, 65; first woman of polo played 20 years in disguise', *LA Times*, 1 May 2003.

PART 4: THE LONGEST MARCH

281 *How are men and women*: Mead, *Male and Female*.

10: Mass Hysteria

283 *The mass media molds everyone*: Alice Embree, 'Media Images I: Madison Avenue/Brainwashing – The Facts', in Robin Morgan (ed.), *Sisterhood is Powerful: An Anthology of Writings from the Women's Liberation Movement* (New York: Vintage, 1970).

283 *The movie industry*: Jeanne Wolf, 'Anthony Hopkins: Hollywood is "full of crazy people"', *Parade*, 11 February 2010, https://parade.com/27954/jeannewolf/0211-anthony-hopkins-wolfman/.

283 *'JACK THE RIPPER . . . '*: *London Daily Post*, 9 November 1888.

287 *the art dealer Oliver Hoare*: See Clayton and Craig, *Diana*. Oliver Hoare asked Scotland Yard to drop their investigation. But in August 1994 the story was leaked to the *News of the World* and was printed in detail.

287 *'She wasn't seen as posh . . . '*: Catherine Mayer, 'How Diana transformed Britain', Time, 16 August 2007, http://content.time.com/time/subscriber/article/0,33009,1653460-3,00.html.

289 *writer, director, producer and actor*: Fatma Begum, *actor*, not *actress*. The twenty-first century is still weeding out poet*ess*, sculptr*ess*, temptr*ess*, and many more. Margaret Drabble confessed that she squirmed at using the word 'authoress', but as a stammerer, she had to avoid saying 'woman writer' at all costs.

292 *Already two years ago*: '*Wee Willie Winkie*', *Night and Day*, 28 October 1937.

292 *sued Greene for libel*: For Graham Greene's clash with Twentieth Century Fox, see Edwards, *Shirley Temple*.

292 *Is that a gun in your pocket . . . ?*: For this, and West's other quips, see Joseph Weintraub (ed.), *The Wit and Wisdom of Mae West* (New York: Berkley, 1977).

295 *she lost the case*: Only seven years later another rebel, Olivia de Havilland, took on Warner Bros and won. Her victory gave rise to the so-called De Havilland Law, which is still in use in the state of California.

301 *Dawn certainly wasn't the first*: Quoted in Bernard Weinraub, 'Dawn Steel, studio chief and producer, dies at 51', *New York Times*, 22 December 1997.

303 *'If you are darker . . .'*: Joseph Kapsch, 'Viola Davis defies Hollywood stereotypes as she keeps it real', TheWrap.com, 22 June 2015. See also Kate Spicer, 'I never wanted to be sexy – I wanted to act', *Sunday Times*, 18 October 2015.

305 *'practical life', 'true inverts', 'Third Sex'*: Ellis, *Studies in the Psychology of Sex*.

306 *Convicted of obscenity*: For an analysis of the obscenity trial, see 'The Mythic Moral Panic: Radclyffe Hall and the New Genealogy', the first chapter in Laura Doan's *Fashioning Sapphism: The Origins of a Modern English Lesbian Culture* (New York: Columbia University Press, 2001).

308 *'I want to put my arms . . .'*: Letter, 7 March 1933, in Roger Streitmatter (ed.), *Empty Without You: The Intimate Letters of Eleanor Roosevelt and Lorena Hickok* (New York: Simon & Schuster, 1999).

309 *'She is beyond all belief . . .'*: Quoted in Larry Schwartz, 'Didrikson was a woman ahead of her time', ESPN.com, https://www.espn.com/sportscentury/features/00014147.html.

310 *I was a typical femme*: Julie Bindel, 'Lesbian nightclub the Gateways is celebrated in new show', *Guardian*, 24 June 2013. See also Gardiner, *From the Closet to the Screen*.

311 *'the most hyped, anticipated . . .'*: Rhonda Gibson, 'From Zero to 24–7: Images of Sexual Minorities on Television', in Laura Castañeda and Shannon Campbell (eds), *News and Sexuality: Media Portraits of Diversity* (Thousand Oaks: Sage, 2006).

312 *'I think it helped a lot of people'*: Debra Kaufman, 'Sitcom was true to star's style', *TV Week*, 27 January 2008.

312 *'It was the hardest thing that I ever had to do . . .'*: Quoted in Karen Mizoguchi, 'Ellen DeGeneres gets emotional about iconic coming-out episode', People.com, 27 April 2017, https://people.com/celebrity/ellen-degeneres-emotional-coming-out-episode/.

313 *Malala Yousafzai*: See Yousafzai and Lamb, *I Am Malala*.

313 *released this dangerous offender*: See 'Saudi woman arrested for wearing a skirt is released without charge', *Guardian*, 20 July 2017.

314 *'No one's ever gonna . . .'*: 'I am Woman' by Helen Reddy and Ray Burton. Lyrics © Universal Music Publishing Group, BMG Rights Management.

314 *'the conscious liberation . . .'*: 'Sisters Are Doin' It for Themselves' by Annie Lennox and Dave Stewart. Lyrics © Universal Music Publishing International MGB Ltd, Universal Music MGB Songs.

11: Our Bodies, Our Selves

315 *The body is the socket*: 'Socket' in pre-electrical English meant a hollow made
  to contain something – in this case, the soul. This proverb also appears as
  'the body is a socket for the soul', and is thought to be a bracing Christian
  revision of the starker Greek apothegm 'soma sema', 'a body [is] a tomb'.
315 *The basic freedom of the world*: Margaret Sanger, *Woman and the New Race*
  (New York: Brentanos, 1922).
315 *Another world is not only possible*: Arundhati Roy, *The Ordinary Person's Guide
  to Empire* (London: Flamingo, 2004).
316 *free of the corset*: See Lewis, *Casting Off the Corsets*.
317 *pantyhose*: This was first produced by the American Allen Gant, Sr at his
  textile works after he saw his pregnant wife sewing her stockings to her
  knickers to avoid the discomfort of wearing stockings and a suspender belt.
318 *Dutch cap*: Mary McCarthy in *The Group* and Margaret Drabble in *Jerusalem
  the Golden* give excruciatingly funny and sad accounts of their heroines' close
  encounters with the diaphragm.
319 *vigorously promoted this idea*: John Rock wrote *The Rhythm of Sterility and
  Fertility in Women* (1932) to promote the rhythm method.
320 *a hard-line decree*: The Papal Encyclical *Humanae Vitae* ('On the subject
  of Human Life') was subtitled *On the Regulation of Birth*. Available at
  http://www.vatican.va/content/paul-vi/en/encyclicals/documents/hf_p-
  vi_enc_25071968_humanae-vitae.html.
322 *'If you're going to San Francisco ...'*: 'San Francisco (Be Sure to Wear Flowers
  in Your Hair)' by John Phillips (1967). Lyrics © Universal Music Publishing
  Group.
324 *Timothy Leary*: For his conflicted upbringing, his faith in psychedelics and his
  role as a leader of the 1960s counter-culture, see Lee and Shlain, *Acid Dreams*.
324 *Catharine MacKinnon, Andrea Dworkin*: Dworkin wrote *Pornography and
  Sexual Violence: Evidence of the Links* in 1983. The official record of the legal
  action is listed as 'Public Hearings on Ordinances to Add Pornography as
  Discrimination Against Women', Minneapolis City Council, Government
  Operations Committee, 12 and 13 December 1983. See Dworkin,
  Pornography.
325–6 *Fifty Shades of Grey*: In the summer of 2012, the *Fifty Shades* series sold
  over ten million copies. Since 2015 the series has been expanded with a
  parallel set of novels 'as told by Christian'.
326 *The war on women*: *The War on Women: And the Brave Ones who Fight Back* is
  the title of the last work of the journalist Sue Lloyd-Roberts, CBE.
327 *'crimes of sexual violence ...'*: Journalist Heather Harvey on UN Resolution
  1820, in 'A triumph for women at the UN', *Guardian*, 25 June 2008.
328 *'at the heart ...'*: Ibid.
328 *'Deciding to be honest ...'*: Nadia Murad, 'I was an Isis sex slave. I tell my
  story because it is the best weapon I have', *Guardian*, 6 October 2018.

329 *many women feel safer*: Police reports from England and Wales are collated by the Office of National Statistics. Supporting research is taken from the anti-domestic abuse charity SafeLives. See Richard Kerbaj, 'Domestic violence incident recorded every 75 seconds' *Sunday Times*, 6 March 2016.

329 *'this in part reflects . . . '*: 'Domestic abuse in England and Wales overview: November 2019', Office of National Statistics release (25 November 2019), https://www.ons.gov.uk/peoplepopulationandcommunity/crimeandjustice/ bulletins/domesticabuseinenglandandwalesoverview/november2019.

329 *'squeezed like sardines'*: Ellie Violet Bramley, '"I could have ended up dead": why women's refuges face a fatal new threat', *Guardian*, 11 June 2018.

330 *'over and over . . . '*: Ibid.

331 *'Just do it!'*: Mandy Sayer, '40 years of Elsie', *Sydney Morning Herald*, 12 April 2014.

331 *Lenore E. Walker*: Walker's work on battered women led to a series of successful appeals by women in the UK against their conviction for killing violent men. The defence of a female 'slow-burn' response to prolonged abuse was established in contrast to the standard legal 'trigger' definition of provocation, which favoured men who killed women.

333 *'controlling or coercive behaviour . . . '*: Clause 76, Serious Crime Act 2015, http://www.legislation.gov.uk/ukpga/2015/9/contents/enacted.

333–4 *'incredibly powerful – and sadly all too accurate'*: Quoted in Liam Kay, 'Archers fundraising page raises £100,000 for Refuge', ThirdSector, 6 April 2016, https://www.thirdsector.co.uk/ archers-fundraising-page-raises-100000-refuge/fundraising/article/1390230.

334 *'When a woman tells the truth . . . '*: Adrienne Rich, 'Women and Honor: Some Notes on Lying', in *Arts of the Possible: Essays and Conversations* (New York: W. W. Norton, 2001).

334 *question cultural practices*: Tracy McVeigh, 'Ending the silence on "honour killing"', *Observer*, 25 October 2009.

336 *'When they tried to convince me . . . '*: Emine Saner, 'Waris Dirie: "Female genital mutilation is pure violence against girls"', *Guardian*, 14 October 2013.

337 *'I just knew . . . '*: Ibid.

338 *Mariya Karimjee went public*: 'Damage', The Big Roundtable, 14 January 2015, https://medium.com/thebigroundtable/damage-7e7b16c9814e.

339 *'Young women of reproductive age . . . '*: Quoted in 'Margaret Atwood says thieves targeted Handmaid's Tale sequel', BBC News, 9 September 2019, https://www.bbc.co.uk/news/entertainment-arts-49635236.

340 *'Abortion is a hideous moral problem . . . '*: Lady Hale, conversation with the author.

12: The Last Revolution

341 *My fellow citizens*: Quoted in Camille Naish, *Death Comes to the Maiden: Sex and Execution 1431–1933* (Abingdon: Routledge, 2013).

341 *The True Republic*: Masthead motto of *Revolution*.

341 *I neither think I'm God nor Mary*: 'Diary of a post-modern priestess', *Irish Independent*, 9 May 1999.

342 *'I have a brain and a uterus . . . '*: In 'Patricia Schroeder', *Current Biography* (New York: H. W. Wilson, 1978).

343 *If you educate a man*: This statement is attributed to the Ghanaian scholar and educationalist Dr James Emman Kwegyir Aggrey, who adapted it from a traditional African saying in order to persuade parents to send their daughters to missionary schools as well as their boys.

343 *'Morality become hypocrisy', 'our whole life'*: Quoted in Nicholas Schoon, 'UN Population Conference: Brundtland "attack on faith" riles Iran", *Independent*, 9 September 1994. Against all expectations, the Cairo conference achieved a remarkable consensus that women's reproductive rights and individual freedom lay at the heart of global development, and agreed a twenty-year plan that was reviewed and renewed by the United Nations in 2014.

343 *'Development policies must give women . . . '*: Quoted in Robert Fisk, 'Rights of women top population agenda', *Independent*, 6 September 1994.

345 *'the Nordic countries are leading the way . . . '*: Quoted in Tracy Clark-Flory, 'Iceland's stripping ban', Salon, 26 March 2010, https://www.salon.com/2010/03/26/iceland_bans_stripping_strip_clubs/.

345 *'Where have all the flowers gone?'*: By Pete Seeger. Lyrics © The Bicycle Music Company. Marlene Dietrich performed the song in English, French and German. Singing in Israel in 1962, she broke the post-Second World War taboo on using German in public, a major breakthrough for all the German-speaking Jews who had made their home there after the war.

345 *'How could intelligent beings'*: Carson, *Silent Spring*.

346 *'I am doing this'*: Quoted in David Crouch, 'The Swedish 15-year-old who's cutting class to fight the climate crisis', *Guardian*, 1 September 2018.

346 *'The way I see it'*: Janet Hughes, 'Gloucestershire mum "Godmother" to group bringing London to a standstill', GloucestershireLive.co.uk, 8 October 2019, *https://www.gloucestershirelive.co.uk/news/gloucester-news/london-protest-extinction-rebellion-bridge-2710501*.

347 *'push for more equality . . . '*: Tom Garry, 'Women's World Cup: Brazil forward Marta breaks men's and women's tournament goal record', BBC Sport, 19 June 2019, https://www.bbc.co.uk/sport/football/48685664. Da Silva was talent-spotted at fourteen and went on to win the FIFA Female World Player of the Year every year from 2006 to 2010, plus the Golden Ball and Golden Boot at the 2007 Women's World Cup. She is now recognised as one of the outstanding footballers of all time.

349 *inspirational rebel Regina Jonas*: In 1939, Jonas took the additional name 'Sara', an appellation forced by the Nazis on all female Jews who did not bear 'typically' Jewish names. See 'Law on Alteration of Family and Personal Names', United States Holocaust Memorial Museum,

https://www.ushmm.org/learn/timeline-of-events/1933-1938/
law-on-alteration-of-family-and-personal-names.

349 *'I do think the feminist movement is important . . . '*: George Vecsey, 'Her
ambition is to become a rabbi – and a housewife', *New York Times*, 13 April
1971.

351 *'It was very intimidating at first'*: Ferial Haffejee, 'Women claim the mosques',
Africa South & East, 1994. Available at https://shams.za.org/index.php/
about-shamima/women-claim-the-mosques.

352 *We are standing up for our rights*: 'Woman leads Islamic prayer service',
Washington Times, 18 March 2005.

352 *'I believe in the Qur'an . . . '*: Amrit Dhillon, 'Muslim woman receives death
threats after leading prayers in Kerala', *Guardian*, 30 January 2018. See also
Akash Vashishtha, 'India: Muslim clerics lash out at woman for leading
gender-mixed prayers', BenarNews.org, 30 January 2018, https://www.
benarnews.org/english/news/bengali/woman-prayers-01302018151143.html.

352 *'History, if you read it right . . . '*: In Allen, *Picking on Men*.

353 *women would be lucky*: 'Russian newspaper column domestic violence
victims should be "proud of their bruises"', news.com.au, 11 February
2017, https://www.news.com.au/world/europe/russian-newspaper-
column-domestic-violence-victims-should-be-proud-of-their-bruises/
news-story/46683554688d13c1fb75fb4e8cd6d13b.

354 *A 2018 referendum*: The Irish referendum was a highly emotional and
deeply felt event. See Tanveer Mann, 'Emotional outpouring from Irish
women voting yes to #Repealthe8th', *Metro*, 25 May 2018, https://metro.
co.uk/2018/05/25/emotional-outpouring-irish-women-voting-yes-
repealthe8th-7577343/?ito=cbshare.

355 *'culmination of a quiet revolution'*: Speech at Dublin Castle, 26
May 2018. See 'Result is culmination of quiet revolution,
says Varadkar', RTÉ, 26 May 2018, https://www.rte.ie/news/
eighth-amendment/2018/0526/966132-reaction/.

355 *in the church*: Lisa Miller, 'What would Mary do? How women can save the
Catholic Church from its sins', *Newsweek*, 12 April 2010.

356 *'You'll never win'*: Ashely Louszko, Meagan Redman and Alexa
Valiente, 'Rose McGowan describes alleged rape by Harvey
Weinstein, her thoughts on the Hollywood "system"', ABC News,
30 January 2018, https://abcnews.go.com/Entertainment/rose-
mcgowan-describes-alleged-rape-harvey-weinstein-thoughts/
story?id=52684109.

356 *On 5 October 2017*: Jodi Kantor and Megan Twohey, 'Harvey Weinstein
paid off sexual harassment accusers for decades', *New York Times*, 5 October
2017.

356 *Ronan Farrow then followed*: 'From aggressive overtures to sexual assault:
Harvey Weinstein's accusers tell their stories', *New Yorker*, 10 October 2017.

356 *The #MeToo movement*: The New York community organiser Tarana

Burke created the slogan in 2006 to empower women of colour who had been sexually abused. See Sandra E. Garcia, 'The woman who created #MeToo long before hashtags', *New York Times*, 20 October 2017. On 15 October 2017, the actor Alyssa Milano urged women via Twitter to spread the use of the phrase to give the wider world a clearer 'sense of the magnitude of the problem', https://twitter.com/Alyssa_Milano/status/919665538393083904.

357 *Time's Up, launched*: Cara Buckley, 'Powerful Hollywood women unveil anti-harassment action plan', *New York Times*, 1 January 2018.

357 *'The deck has always been stacked . . . '*: Stormy Daniels with Kevin Carr O'Leary, *Full Disclosure* (London: Macmillan, 2018).

358 *Merriam-Webster crowned*: Phoebe Luckhurst, 'Feminism is the word, for this year and more', *Evening Standard*, 14 December 2017.

359 *'If the world can be saved'*: Anna Andersen, 'Madam President: Vigdís Finnbogadóttir on fashion and the times', *Reykjavík Grapevine*, 24 March 2014, https://grapevine.is/mag/feature/2014/03/24/madam-president/.

360 *clear advice for men*: See Gracie, *Equal*.

361 *'Women, wake up . . . '*: Olympe de Gouges, 'The Rights of Woman and the Female Citizen'. Available at https://www.olympedegouges.eu/rights_of_women.php.

361 *If I can't dance*: These are all variants of a statement Goldman made after a young boy told her at a party that her dancing 'did not behoove' a woman in the Anarchist movement. As she recorded in her memoir *Living My Life*, she loved dancing, so she gave the lad a flea in his ear, and partied on.

LIST OF BOOKS CONSULTED AND SUGGESTIONS FOR FURTHER READING

Abbott, Edith, *Women in Industry: A Study in American Economic History* (New York: D. Appleton & Company, 1910)

Adichie, Chimamanda Ngozi, *We Should All Be Feminists* (London: Fourth Estate, 2014)

Alcott, Louisa May, *Little Women* (2 vols, 1868 and 1869)

Aldred, Gloria with Deborah Caulfield Rybak, *Fight Back and Win: My Thirty-Year Fight Against Injustice – and How You Can Win Your Own Battles* (New York: ReganBooks, 2006)

Alexievich, Svetlana (trans. Richard Peaver and Larissa Volokhonsky), *The Unwomanly Face of War* (London: Penguin, 2017)

Alic, Margaret, *Hypatia's Heritage: A History of Women in Science from Antiquity to the Late Nineteenth Century* (London: Women's Press, 1986)

Allen, Judy, *Picking on Men: The First Honest Collection of Quotations about Men* (New York: Fawcett, 1986)

Allen, Vivien, *Lady Trader: A Biography of Mrs Sarah Heckford* (London: Collins, 1979)

Alpern, Stanley B., *Amazons of Black Sparta: The Women Warriors of Dahomey* (London: Hurst, 1998)

Alsanea, Rajaa (trans. Rajaa Alsanea and Marilyn Booth), *Girls of Riyadh* (London: Fig Tree, 2007)

Anon, *The Epic of Gilgamesh* (c. 2100 BCE)

Armstrong, Karen, *The Gospel According to Woman: Christianity's Creation of the Sex War in the West* (London: Elm Tree, 1986)

Arnold, David and Peter Robb (eds), *Institutions and Ideologies: A SOAS South Asia Reader* (Richmond: RoutledgeCurzon, 1993)

Arnstein, Mary, *The Admission of Women to Yale College* (New Haven: Yale University Press, 1974)

Atkinson, Diane, *Elsie and Mairi Go to War: Two Extraordinary Women on the Western Front* (London: Preface, 2009)

Austen, Jane, *Sense and Sensibility* (1811)

Balabanoff, Angelica, *My Life as a Rebel* (London: Hamish Hamilton, 1938)

Baptist, Edward E., *The Half has Never Been Told: Slavery and the Making of American Capitalism* (New York: Basic Books, 2014)

Bardwick, Judith M., *Women in Transition: How Feminism, Sexual Liberation, and the Search for Self-Fulfilment have Altered our Lives* (Brighton: Harvester, 1980)

Barker, Mary Anne, *Station Life in New Zealand* (1870)

———, *A Year's Housekeeping in South Africa* (1880)

———, *Colonial Memories* (1904)

Barto, Susan Campbell, *Terrible Typhoid Mary: A True Story of the Deadliest Cook in America* (New York: Houghton Mifflin Harcourt, 2015)

Bates, Katharine Lee, 'America, The Beautiful' (1893; first published in the Fourth of July edition of the church periodical *The Congregationalist*, 1895)

Barnes, John, *Evita, First Lady: A Biography of Eva Perón* (New York: Grove Press, 1978)

Bart, Pauline P. and Patricia H. O'Brien, *Stopping Rape: Successful Survival Strategies* (New York: Pergamon, 1985)

Beard, Mary, *Women and Power: A Manifesto* (London: Profile, 2017)

Beard, Mary Ritter, *Women as Force in History: A Study in Traditions and Realities* (New York: Macmillan, 1946)

Bell, Diane, 'Desert politics: choices in the "marriage market"', in Mona Etienne and Eleanor Leacock (eds), *Women and Colonization: Anthropological Perspectives* (New York: Praeger, 1980)

Bell, Gertrude, *The Desert and the Sown: Travels in Palestine and Syria* (London: William Heinemann, 1907)

Bergman, Jerry, 'Darwin's Teaching of Women's Inferiority', Institute for Creation Research, 1 March 1994, https://www.icr.org/article/darwins-teaching-womens-inferiority/

Bernstein, Carl and Bob Woodward, *All the President's Men* (New York: Simon & Schuster, 1974)

———, *The Final Days* (New York: Simon & Schuster, 1976)

Blackwell, Alice Stone, *Lucy Stone: Pioneer of Women's Rights* (Boston: Little, Brown, 1930)

Blackwell, Antoinette Brown, *The Sexes Throughout Nature* (1875)

Bleier, Ruth, *Science and Gender: A Critique of Biology and its Theories on Women* (Oxford: Pergamon Press, 1984)

Brontë, Anne, *The Tenant of Wildfell Hall* (1848)

Brontë, Charlotte, *Jane Eyre: An Autobiography* (1847)

———, *Shirley* (1849)

———, *Villette* (1853)

———, *The Professor* (1857)

Brontë, Emily, *Wuthering Heights* (1847)

Brooks, Geraldine, *Nine Parts of Desire: The Hidden World of Islamic Women* (London: Hamish Hamilton, 1995)

Browder, Clifford, *The Wickedest Woman in New York: Madame Restell, the Abortionist* (Hamden: Archon, 1988)

———, '88. The House of Death, the Mystic Rose, and Avenoodles', No Place for Normal: New York (cbrowder.blogspot.com), 22 September 2013

Brown, Charles Brockden, *Alcuin: A Dialogue on the Rights of Women* (1798)

Brown, Helen Gurley, *Sex and the Single Girl* (New York: Bernard Geis Associates, 1962)

Brown, Rita Mae, *Rubyfruit Jungle* (Plainhead: Daughters, Inc., 1973)

Brownmiller, Susan, *Against Our Will: Men, Women and Rape* (New York: Simon & Schuster, 1975)

Burke, David, *The Spy Who Came in From the Co-Op: Melita Norwood and the Ending of Cold War Espionage* (Woodbridge: Boydell Press, 2008)

Burney, Fanny, *Camilla* (1796)

Cameron, Deborah and Elizabeth Frazer, *The Lust to Kill: A Feminist Investigation of Sexual Murder* (New York: New York University Press, 1987)

Carson, Rachel, *Silent Spring* (New York: Houghton Mifflin, 1962)

Carlile, Richard, *Every Woman's Book* (1826)

Ceplair, Larry (ed.), *The Public Years of Sarah and Angelina Grimké: Selected Writings 1835–1839* (New York: Columbia University Press, 1989).

Childs, J. Rives, *Casanova: A New Perspective* (London: Constable, 1988)

Clark, Alice, *Working Life of Women in the Seventeenth Century* (London: G. Routledge, 1919)

Clayton, Tim and Phil Craig, *Diana: Story of a Princess* (London: Atria Books, 2003)

Cole, Jean Hascall, *Women Pilots of World War II* (Salt Lake City: University of Utah Press, 1992)

Coote, Anna and Beatrix Campbell, *Sweet Freedom: The Struggle for Women's Liberation* (London: Picador, 1982)

Dallas, Gregor, *At the Heart of a Tiger: Clemenceau and His World 1841–1929* (London: Macmillan, 1993)

Dally, Ann, *Inventing Motherhood: The Consequences of an Ideal* (London: HarperCollins, 1982)

Daniels, Kay and Mary Murnane, *Uphill all the Way: A Documentary History of Women in Australia* (St Lucia: University of Queensland Press, 1980)

Darwin, Charles, *On the Origin of Species* (1859)

———, *The Descent of Man, and Selection in Relation to Sex* (1871)

Davies, Caitlin, *Bad Girls: A History of Rebels and Renegades* (London: John Murray, 2018)

de Beauvoir, Simone (trans. H. M. Parshley), *The Second Sex* (New York: Alfred A. Knopf, 1953)

de Riencourt, Amaury, *Woman and Power in History* (Bath: Honeyglen, 1983)

de Sade, Marquis (Donatien Alphonse François de Sade), *Juliette* (1798)

de Shazer, Marie-Laure, *Chinese Joan of Arc: Qiu Jin – China's First Feminist* (n.p.: de Shazer Publishing, 2016)

Demery, Monique Brinson, *Finding the Dragon Lady: The Mystery of Vietnam's Madame Nhu* (Philadelphia: PublicAffairs, 2013)

Diderot, Denis (ed.), *Encyclopédie, ou dictionnaire raisonné des sciences, des arts et des métiers* (1751–66)

Dixie, Lady Florence, *Gloriana; or, The Revolution of 1900* (1890)

Dooley, Margaret Anne, *Frances Burney: The Life in the Works* (Cambridge: Cambridge University Press, 1988)

Drabble, Margaret, *Jerusalem the Golden* (London: Weidenfeld & Nicolson, 1967)

Dworkin, Andrea, *Pornography: Men Possessing Women* (New York: Perigee Books, 1981)

Edwards, Anne, *Shirley Temple: American Princess* (New York: William Morrow & Co., 1988)

Edwardes, Michael, *Red Year: The Indian Rebellion of 1857* (London: Cardinal, 1975)

Eig, Jonathan, *The Birth of the Pill: How Four Crusaders Reinvented Sex and Launched a Revolution* (New York: W. W. Norton, 2014)

Eliot, George, *Adam Bede* (1859)

———, *Middlemarch* (1871–2)

———, *Daniel Deronda* (1876)

Ellis, Henry Havelock, *Studies in the Psychology of Sex* (London: University Press, 1900)

Ettinger, Elżbieta, *Rosa Luxemburg: A Life* (London: Rivers Oram Press/Pandora Press: 1986)

Evans, Mary (ed.), *The Woman Question: Readings on the Subordination of Women* (London: Fontana, 1982)

Faderman, Lillian, *Surpassing the Love of Men: Romantic Friendship and Love between Women from the Renaissance to the Present* (London: Women's Press, 1981)

Faure, Bernard, *Unmasking Buddhism* (Chichester: Wiley-Blackwell, 2009)

Fawcett, M. G., *Women's Suffrage: A Short History of a Great Movement* (London: T. C. and E. C. Jack, 1911)

Fine, Cordelia, *Testosterone Rex: Unmaking the Myths of our Gendered Minds* (London: Icon Books, 2017)

Figes, Eva, *Patriarchal Attitudes: Women in Society* (London: Macmillan, 1970)

Firestone, Shulamith, *The Dialectic of Sex: The Case for Feminist Revolution* (New York: William Morrow, 1970)

Fisk, Robert, 'The Honour Killing Files', *Independent*, 7–10 September 2010

Fleury, A.-J., *Mémoires de la Comédie Française 1757–1789* (1847)

Fogarty, Anne, *Wife Dressing: the Fine Art of being a Well-Dressed Wife* (New York: Julian Messner, Inc., 1959)

Fradin, Dennis Brindell and Judith Bloom Fradin, *Ida B. Wells: Mother of the Civil Rights Movement* (New York: Clarion Books, 2001)

Fraser, Antonia, *The Weaker Vessel: Woman's Lot in Seventeenth Century England* (London: Weidenfeld & Nicolson, 1984)

Friedan, Betty, *The Feminine Mystique* (New York: W. W. Norton, 1963)

———, *It Changed My Life: Writings on the Women's Movement* (New York: Random House, 1976)

Friedrich, Paul, *The Meaning of Aphrodite* (Chicago: University of Chicago Press, 1978)

Fullbrook, Kate and Edward Fullbrook, *Simone de Beauvoir and Jean-Paul Sartre: The Remaking of a Twentieth- Century Legend* (New York: Basic Books, 1994)

Gardiner, Jill, *From the Closet to the Screen: Women at the Gateways Club 1945–85* (London: Rivers Oram Press/Pandora Press: 2003)

Garimara, Doris Pilkington, *Follow the Rabbit-Proof Fence* (St Lucia: University of Queensland Press, 1996)

Garman, Brian K., *Race of Singers: Whitman's Working-Class Hero from Guthrie to Springsteen* (Chapel Hill: University of North Carolina Press, 2000)

Gesell, Laurence E., *Saddle the Wild Wind: The Saga of Squirrel Tooth Alice and Texas Billy Thompson* (Chandler: Coast Aire, 2001)

Gilman, Charlotte Perkins, *The Yellow Wallpaper* (1892)

Gordon, Lyndall, *Outsiders: Five Women Writers Who Changed the World* (London: Virago Press, 2017)

Gordon-Reed, Annette, *The Hemingses of Monticello: An American Family* (New York: W. W. Norton, 2008)

Gracie, Carrie, *Equal: A Story of Women, Men & Money* (London: Virago Press, 2019)

Graham, Katharine, *Personal History* (London: Weidenfeld & Nicolson, 1997)

Greer, Germaine, *The Female Eunuch* (London: MacGibbon & Kee, 1970)
———, *The Whole Woman* (London: Doubleday, 1999)

Gregory, Mollie, *Women Who Run the Show: How a Brilliant and Creative New Generation of Women Stormed Hollywood* (New York: St Martin's Press, 2002)

Grey, Stephen, 'They Call This Religion', *Sunday Times*, 22 February 1998

Griffith, Elisabeth, *In Her Own Right: The Life of Elizabeth Cady Stanton* (New York: Oxford University Press, 1984)

Grimké, Angelina and Grimké, Sarah (eds), *American Slavery as It Is: Testimony of a Thousand Witnesses* (1839)

Haggard, H. Rider, *King Solomon's Mines* (1885)

Hall, Radclyffe, *The Well of Loneliness* (London: Jonathan Cape, 1928)

Hanisch, Carol, 'The Personal is Political', in *Notes from the Second Year: Women's Liberation* (1970)

Hardy, Thomas, *Tess of the d'Urbervilles* (1891)

Hastings, Max, *The Korean War* (London: Michael Joseph, 1987)

Hemings, Madison, 'The Memoirs of Madison Hemings', *Pike County Republican*, 13 March 1873

Hemingway, Ernest, *For Whom the Bell Tolls* (New York: Charles Scribner's Sons, 1940)

Hensel, *The Mendelssohn Family 1729–1847* (1884)

Herbermann, Nanda (trans. Hester Baer; ed. Hester Baer and Elizabeth R. Baer), *The Blessed Abyss: Inmate #6582 in Ravensbrück Concentration Camp for Women* (Detroit: Wayne State University Press, 2000)

Hersh, Seymour, *The Dark Side of Camelot* (New York: Little, Brown, 1997)

Hibbert, Christopher, *The French Revolution* (London: Allen Lane, 1980)

Hirsi Ali, Ayaan (trans. Jane Brown), *The Caged Virgin: An Emancipation Proclamation for Women and Islam* (New York: Simon & Schuster, 2006)

Hoffman, Merle, *Intimate Wars: The Life and Times of the Woman Who Brought Abortion from the Back Alley to the Boardroom* (New York: Feminist Press, 2012)

Hooker, Claire, *Irresistible Forces: Australian Women in Science* (Melbourne: Melbourne University Publishing, 2004)

Horley, Sandra, *The Charm Syndrome: Why Charming Men Can Make Dangerous Lovers* (London: Pan Macmillan, 1991). Reissued as *Power and Control: Why Charming Men Can Make Dangerous Lovers* (London: Vermilion, 2002)

Hughes, Robert, *The Fatal Shore: The Epic of Australia's Founding* (New York: Alfred A. Knopf, 1986)

Jacobs, Harriet, *Incidents in the Life of a Slave Girl* (1861)

James, E. L., *Fifty Shades of Grey* (London: Vintage, 2011)

———, *Fifty Shades Darker* (London: Vintage, 2012)

———, *Fifty Shades Freed* (London: Vintage, 2012)

———, *Grey: Fifty Shades of Grey as told by Christian* (London: Vintage, 2015)

Jeffreys, Sheila, *The Spinster and Her Enemies: Feminism and Sexuality 1880–1930* (London: Pandora Press, 1985)

Jong, Erica, *Fear of Flying* (New York: Holt Rinehart Wilnston, 1973)

Jukes, Adam, *Why Men Hate Women* (London: Free Association Books, 1993)

Junor, Beth, *Greenham Common Women's Peace Camp: A History of Non-Violent Resistance 1984–1995* (London: Working Press, 1995)

Karskens, Grace, *The Colony: A History of Early Sydney (Crows Nest: Allen & Unwin, 2010)*

————, 'Barangaroo and the Eora Fisherwomen', *The Dictionary of Sydney*, https://dictionaryofsydney.org/entry/barangaroo_and_the_eora_fisherwomen

Kasper, Shirl, *Annie Oakley* (Norman: University of Oklahoma Press, 2000).

Kaye, M. M. (ed.), *The Golden Calm: an English Lady's Life in Moghul Delhi. Reminisces by Emily, Lady Clive Bayley, and by her Father Sir Thomas Metcalfe* (Exeter: Webb & Bower, 1980)

Kelly, Ian, *Casanova: Actor, Lover, Priest, Spy* (London: Hodder & Stoughton, 2008)

Kelly, Liz, *Surviving Sexual Violence* (Cambridge: Polity Press, 1988)

Kennedy, Helena, *Eve Was Framed: Women and British Justice* (London: Chatto & Windus, 1992)

Keuls, Eva C., *The Reign of the Phallus: Sexual Politics in Ancient Athens* (Berkeley: University of California Press, 1993)

Kraemer, Sebastian, 'The Origins of Fatherhood: An Ancient Family Process', *Family Process*, 30:4 (December 1991)

Kraft-Ebbing, Richard von, *Psychopathia Sexualis: eine Klinisch-Forensische Studie*, 12 vols (1886–93)

Kriwaczek, Paul, *Babylon: Mesopotamia and the Birth of Civilization* (New York: Thomas Dunne, 2012)

Krupskaya, Nadezhda (trans. Bernard Isaacs), *Reminiscences of Lenin* (New York: International Publishers, 1970)

Latson, Jennifer, 'While Birth Control Pioneer Margaret Sanger Kept Getting Arrested', *Time*, 16 October 2015

Lee, Martin A. and Bruce Shlain, *Acid Dreams: The CIA, LSD, and the Sixties Rebellion* (New York: Grove Press, 1985)

Leghorn, Lisa and Parker, Katherine, 'Shouldering the High Cost of Development' in *Women's Worth: Sexual Economics and the World of Women* (London: Routledge & Kegan Paul, 1981)

Lefebure, Molly, *The Bondage of Love: A Life of Mrs Samuel Taylor* Coleridge (London: Gollancz, 1986)

Lerner, Gerda, *The Grimké Sisters from South Carolina: Pioneers for Women's Rights and Abolition* (Chapel Hill: University of North Carolina Press, 1967)

————, *The Majority Finds Its Past: Placing Women in History* (New York: Oxford University Press, 1979)

————, *The Creation of Patriarchy: Women and History Volume One* (New York: Oxford University Press, 1986)

Lerner, Max, *The Unfinished Country: A Book of American Symbols* (New York: Simon & Schuster, 1959)

Levy, Darline Gay and Harriet B. Applewhite, 'Women and Militant Citizenship in Revolutionary Paris', in Sara E. Melzer and Leslie W. Rabine (eds), *Rebel Daughters: Women and the French Revolution* (Oxford: Oxford University Press, 1992)

Lewis, Dulcie, *Casting Off the Corsets: A Brief History of Underwear* (Newbury: Countryside Books, 2011)

Lewis, Michael, 'Has anyone seen the president?', Bloomberg, 9 February 2018, https://www.bloomberg.com/opinion/articles/2018-02-09/has-anyone-seen-the-president

Liswood, Laura, *Women World Leaders* (London and San Francisco: Pandora, 1995)

Lloyd-Roberts, Sue, *The War on Women: And the Brave Ones who Fight Back* (London: Simon & Schuster, 2016)

Lowery, Donna A., *Women Vietnam Veterans: Our Untold Stories* (Bloomington: AuthorHouse, 2015)

MacArthur, Brian (ed.), *The Penguin Book of Twentieth-Century Protest* (London: Penguin, 1998)

Macfarlane, Helen, 'Democracy – Remarks on the Times apropos of certain passages in no. 1 of Thomas Carlyle's "latter day" pamphlet', *Democratic Review* (April–June 1850)

Malleson, George, *History of the Indian Mutiny*, 6 vols (1897–8)

Mander-Jones, Phyllis (ed.), *Manuscripts in the British Isles Relating to Australia, New Zealand, and the Pacific* (Canberra: Australian National University Press, 1972)

Markdale, Jean, *The Great Goddess: Reverence of the Divine Feminine from the Paleolithic to the Present* (Rochester, VT: Inner Traditions, 1999)

Marx, Karl and Friedrich Engels, *The Communist Manifesto*, trans. Helen Macfarlane in *The Red Republican*, June–November 1850

Mayer, Catherine, *Attack of the 50ft. Women: How Gender Equality Can Save the World!* (London: HQ, 2017)

Mayor, Adrienne, *The Amazons: Lives and Legends of Warrior Women across the Ancient World* (Princeton: Princeton University Press, 2014)

McCarthy, Mary, *The Group* (New York: New American Library, 1963)

McCorvey, Norma, *I am Roe: My Life, Roe v. Wade, and Freedom of Choice* (New York: HarperCollins, 1994)

McGowan, Christopher, *The Dragon Seekers: How an Extraordinary*

Circle of Fossilists Discovered the Dinosaurs and Paved the Way for Darwin (London: Little, Brown, 2002)

McIntosh, Elizabeth P., *Sisterhood of Spies: The Women of the OSS* (New York: Dell, 1998)

McNamara, Robert S. with Brian VanDeMark, *In Retrospect: The Tragedy and Lessons of Vietnam* (New York: Times Books, 1995)

McNeal, Robert H., *Bride of the Revolution: Krupskaya and Lenin* (Ann Arbor: University of Michigan Press, 1972)

Mead, Margaret, *Male and Female* (New York: Dell, 1949)

Meador, Betty De Shong and John Maier, John, *Princess, Priestess, Poet: The Sumerian Temple Hymns of Enheduanna* (Austin: University of Texas Press, 2010)

Melzer, Sara E. and Leslie W. Rabine (eds) *Rebel Daughters: Women and the French Revolution (New York: Oxford University Press, 1992)*

Messaoudi, Khalida (trans. Anne C. Vila), *Unbowed: An Algerian Woman Confronts Islamic Fundamentalism. Interviews with Elisabeth Schemla* (Philadelphia: University of Pennsylvania Press, 1998)

Midgley, Clare, *Women Against Slavery: The British Campaigns 1780–1870* (London: Routledge, 1992)

Mignet, François-Auguste-Marie-Alexis, *History of the French Revolution, 1789–1814* (1885)

Miles, Rosalind, *Women and Power* (London: Macdonald, 1985)

———, *Who Cooked The Last Supper? The Women's History of the World* (New York: Three Rivers Press, 1988)

Millett, Kate, *Sexual Politics* (New York: Doubleday, 1970)

Mitchell, Juliet, *Woman's Estate* (London: Penguin, 1971)

Moore, Charles, *Margaret Thatcher: The Authorized Biography. Volume One: Not for Turning* (London: Allen Lane, 2013)

———, *Margaret Thatcher: The Authorized Biography. Volume Two: Everything She Wants* (London: Allen Lane, 2015)

———, *Margaret Thatcher: The Authorized Biography. Volume Three: Herself Alone* (London: Allen Lane, 2019)

Moorehead, Caroline, *A Train in Winter: A Story of Resistance, Friendship and Survival in Auschwitz* (London: Chatto & Windus, 2011)

Morgan, Elaine, *The Descent of Woman* (London: Souvenir Press, 1972)

Morgan, Robin (ed.), *Sisterhood is Powerful: An Anthology of Writings from the Women's Liberation Movement* (New York: Random House, 1970)

Morrissey, Helena, *A Good Time to be a Girl: Don't Lean In, Change the System* (London: William Collins, 2018)

Mousset, Sophie (trans. Joy Poirel), *Women's Rights and the*

French Revolution: A Biography of Olympe de Gouges (London: Routledge, 2003)

Muhsen, Zana with Andrew Crofts, Sold: One Woman's True Account of Modern Slavery (London: Sphere, 1991)

Mungello, D. E., Drowning Girls in China: Female Infanticide since 1650 (Lanham: Rowman & Littlefield, 2008)

Nafisi, Azar, Things I've Been Silent About: Memories of a Prodigal Daughter (New York: Random House, 2008)

Neustatter, Angela, Hyenas in Petticoats: A Look at Twenty Years of Feminism (London: Virgin Books, 1989)

Newman, Louise Michele (ed.), Men's Ideas/Women's Realities: Popular Science, 1870–1915 (New York: Pergamon, 1985)

Nicholson, Virginia, Perfect Wives in Ideal Homes: the Story of Women in the Fifties (London: Viking, 2015)

Nietzsche, Friedrich, Die fröhliche Wissenschaft (1882)

Nixon, Richard, 'Cuba, Castro and John F. Kennedy', Reader's Digest (November 1964)

Oakley, Ann, Subject Women (New York: Random House, 1981)
———, Taking It Like a Woman (London: Jonathan Cape, 1984)

Ogilvie, Marilyn Bailey, Women in Science: A Biographical Dictionary with Annotated Bibliography (Boston: MIT Press, 1986)

Olson, Lynne, Freedom's Daughters: The Unsung Heroines of the Civil Rights Movement from 1830 to 1970 (New York: Scribner, 2001)

Orbach, Susie, Fat is a Feminist Issue: The Anti-Diet Guide to Permanent Weight Loss (New York: Paddington Press, 1978)

Paine, Thomas, The Rights of Man. Being an Answer to Mr Burke's Attack on the French Revolution, 2 parts (1791 and 1792)

Parks, Rosa, Quiet Strength: The Faith, The Hope, The Heart of a Woman Who Changed a Nation (Grand Rapids: Zondervan, 1994)

Paton, Diana, 'Enslaved Women and Slavery before and after 1807', Institute of Historical Research series on slavery, 2007, https://www.history.ac.uk/ihr/Focus/Slavery/articles/paton.html

Pizzey, Erin, Wild Child: An Autobiography (self-published, 1995)

Porter, Cathy, Alexandra Kollontai: A Biography (London: Virago Press, 1980)

Purvis, June, Emmeline Pankhurst: A Biography (London: Routledge, 2002)

Rauschenbusch-Clough, Emma, *A Study of Mary Wollstonecraft and the Rights of Woman* (PhD thesis, University of Berne, 1894; London and Bombay: Longmans, Green, and Co., 1898)

Raeburn, Antonia, *The Militant Suffragettes* (London: Michael Joseph, 1973)

Rappaport, Helen, *No Place for Ladies: The Untold Story of Women in the Crimean War* (London: Aurum, 2007)

Raven, Susan and Alison Weir, *Women in History: Thirty-Five Centuries of Feminine Achievement* (London: Weidenfeld & Nicolson, 1981)

Réage, Pauline (Anne Desclos), *Histoire d'O* (Paris: Jean-Jacques Pauvert, 1954)

Reitsch, Hanna, *Fliegen, mein Leben* (Stuttgart: Deutsche Verlags-Anstalt, 1951)

Roberts, Yvonne, *Mad About Women: Can There Ever Be Fair Play Between the Sexes?* (London: Virago Press, 1992)

Rock, Dr John, *The Time Has Come: A Catholic Doctor's Proposals to End the Battle over Birth Control* (New York: Alfred A. Knopf, 1963)

Roosevelt, Eleanor, *The Autobiography of Eleanor Roosevelt* (New York: Harper & Brothers, 1961)

Rose, Phyllis (ed.), *The Penguin Book of Women's Lives* (London: Penguin, 1994)

Rousseau, Jean-Jacques, *Émile: On Education* (1762)

Rowbotham, Sheila, *Women, Resistance and Revolution: A History of Women and Revolution in the Modern World* (New York: Pantheon, 1972)
———, *Hidden from History: 300 Years of Women's Oppression and the Fight Against It* (London: Pluto Press, 1973)

Rowe, Marsha and Rosie Boycott (eds), *Spare Rib Reader: 100 Issues of Women's Liberation* (London: Penguin, 1982)

Rowold, Katharina, *The Educated Woman: Minds, Bodies and Women's Higher Education in Britain, Germany and Spain, 1865–1914* (London: Routledge, 2010)

Roy, Arundhati, *War Talk* (Boston: South End Press, 2003)

Rudé, George, *The Crowd in the French Revolution* (Oxford: Clarendon Press, 1959)

Rule, Jane, *Lesbian Images* (Garden City: Doubleday, 1975)

Ryan, Jan, *Chinese Women and the Global Village: An Australian Site* (St Lucia: University of Queensland Press, 2003)

Saini, Angela, *Inferior: How Science Got Women Wrong and the New Research That's Re-writing the Story* (London: Fourth Estate, 2017)

Sackville-West, Vita, *All Passion Spent* (London: Hogarth Press, 1931)

Sandberg, Sheryl with Nell Scovell, *Lean In: Women, Work, and the Will to Lead* (New York: Alfred A. Knopf, 2013)

Sanger, Margaret, *What Every Mother Should Know: Or, How Six Little Children Were Taught the Truth* (New York: Rabelais Press, 1914)

——, *The Case for Birth Control: A Supplementary Brief and Statement of Facts* (New York: Modern Art Print Co., 1917)

Sanghera, Jasvinder, *Shame* (London: Hodder & Stoughton, 2007)

Sasson, Jean P., *Princess: A True Story of Life Behind the Veil in Saudi Arabia* (Chicago: Windsor-Brooke, 2001)

Scanlon, Jennifer, *Bad Girls Go Everywhere: The Life of Helen Gurley Brown* (New York: Oxford University Press, 2009)

Schlafly, Phyllis, *A Choice Not an Echo: Updated and Expanded 50th Anniversary Edition* (Washington DC: Regnery, 2014)

——, Ed Martin and Brett M. Decker, *The Conservative Case for Trump* (Washington DC: Regnery, 2016)

Schanke, Robert, *That Furious Lesbian: The Story of Mercedes de Acosta* (Carbondale: Southern Illinois University Press, 2003)

Seacole, Mary, *Wonderful Adventures of Mrs Seacole in Many Lands* (1857)

Sen, Mala, *India's Bandit Queen: The True Story of Phoolan Devi* (London: Harvill Press, 1991)

Shaw, George Bernard, *Man and Superman* (London: Archibald and Constable & Co., 1903)

Sherr, Lynn, *Failure is Impossible: Susan B. Anthony in Her Own Words* (New York: Times Books, 1995)

Shirer, William, *The Rise and Fall of the Third Reich* (Lincoln, NE: University of Nebraska Press, 1987)

Simpson, N. F., *One Way Pendulum: A Farce in a New Dimension* (London: Faber, 1959)

Sirleaf, Ellen Johnson, *This Child Will Be Great: Memoir of a Remarkable Life by Africa's First Woman President* (New York: HarperCollins, 2009)

Sklar, K. K., *Women's Rights Emerges within the Antislavery Movement: A Brief History with Documents, 1830–1870* (Boston and New York: Bedford/St Martin's, 2000)

Smith, Joan, *Misogynies: Reflections on Myths and Malice* (London: Faber and Faber, 1989)

Snell, Henry, *Men, Movements, and Myself* (London: J. M. Dent and Sons, 1936)

Somerville, Mary Fairfax, *Personal Recollections from Early Life to Old Age, of Mary Somerville, with Selections from Her Personal Correspondence* (1873)

Sobel, Dava, *The Glass Universe: The Hidden History of the Women who Took the Measure of the Stars* (London: 4th Estate, 2016)

Spencer, Stephanie, *Gender, Work and Education in Britain in the 1950s* (Basingstoke: Palgrave Macmillan, 2005)

Spender, Dale, *There's Always Been a Women's Movement This Century* (London: Pandora Press, 1983)

Sproles, Karyn Z., *Desiring Women: The Partnership of Virginia Woolf and Vita Sackville-West* (Toronto: University of Toronto Press, 2006)

Stedman, John Gabriel, *Narrative, of a Five Years' Expedition, Against the Revolted Negroes of Surinam, in Guiana, on the Wild Coast of South America; from the year 1772, to 1777* (1796)

Steinem, Gloria, *Outrageous Acts and Everyday Rebellions* (New York: Holt, 1983)

Stopes, Marie, *Married Love or Love in Marriage* (New York: The Critic and Guide Company, 1918)

Stowe, Harriet Beecher, *Uncle Tom's Cabin, or, Life Among the Lowly* (1852)

Strachey, Ray, *The Cause: A Short History of the Women's Movement in Great Britain* (London: G. Bell and Sons, 1928)

Summers, Anne, *Damned Whores and God's Police: The Colonization of Women in Australia* (London: Pelican, 1975)

Summers, Anthony, *Goddess: The Secret Lives of Marilyn Monroe* (London: Victor Gollancz, 1985)

Taylor, Sandra C., *Vietnamese Women at War: Fighting for Ho Chi Minh and the Revolution* (Lawrence: University Press of Kansas, 1999)

Teakle, Josephine, 'The Works of Mary Birkett Card, 1774–1817, Originally Collected by her Son Nathaniel Card in 1834: An Edited Transcription with an Introduction to her Life and Works in two volumes' (University of Gloucestershire PhD thesis, 2004), http://eprints.glos.ac.uk/3107/

Tench, Watkin, *A Complete Account of the Settlement at Port Jackson* (1793)

Terrill, Ross, *The White-Boned Demon: A Biography of Madame Mao Zedong* (London: Heinemann, 1984)

Thackeray, William Makepeace, *Vanity Fair* (1848)

Theweleit, Klaus (trans. Stephen Conway, Erica Carter and Chris Turner), *Male Fantasies*, 2 vols (Cambridge: Polity Press, 1987 and 1989)

Thompson, E. P., *The Making of the English Working Class* (London: Victor Gollancz, 1963)

Thompson, William, and Anna Wheeler, *An Appeal of one Half of the*

Human Race, Women, against the Pretensions of the other Half, Men, to Retain them in Political and thence in Civil and Domestic Slavery: in reply to a paragraph of Mr Mill's celebrated 'Article on Government' (1825)

Tuttle, Lisa, *The Encyclopedia of Feminism* (Harlow: Longman, 1986)

Trager, James, *The Women's Chronology: A Year-by-Year Record, from Prehistory to the Present* (London: Aurum, 1994)

Tolstoy, Leo, *War and Peace* (1869)

Tomalin, Claire, *The Life and Death of Mary Wollstonecraft* (London: Weidenfeld & Nicolson, 1974)

Uglow, Jennifer S. (ed.) with Frances Hinton (asst ed.), *The Macmillan Dictionary of Women's Biography* (London: Macmillan, 1982)

Ulrich, Laurel Thatcher, *Well-Behaved Women Seldom Make History* (New York: Alfred A. Knopf, 2007)

Vidal, Mary Theresa, *Tales for the Bush* (1845)

Votes for Women (suffragette newspaper, 1907–18)

Walker, Lenore E., *The Battered Woman* (New York: Harper & Row, 1979)

Wells, Ida B. (ed. Alfreda M. Duster), *Crusade for Justice: The Autobiography of Ida B. Wells* (Chicago: University of Chicago Press, 1970)

West, Mae, *Goodness Had Nothing to Do With It: The Autobiography of Mae West* (Englewood Cliffs: Prentice-Hall, 1959)

Winstone, H. V. F., *Gertrude Bell* (London: Jonathan Cape, 1978)

Wolf, Naomi, *Fire With Fire: The New Female Power and How it Will Change the 21st Century* (New York: Random House, 1993)

Wolkstein, Diane and Samuel Noah Kramer, *Inanna: Queen of Heaven and Earth – Her Stories and Hymns from Sumer* (London: HarperCollins, 1983)

Wollstonecraft, Mary, *A Vindication of the Rights of Men* (1790)

———, *A Vindication of the Rights of Woman: With Strictures on Political and Moral Subjects* (1792)

———, *An Historical and Moral View of the Origin and Progress of the French Revolution; and the Effect it has produced in Europe* (1794)

Woolf, Virginia, *A Room of One's Own* (London: Hogarth Press, 1929)

Yousafzai, Malala with Christina Lamb, *I am Malala: The Girl Who Stood Up for Education and was Shot by the Taliban* (London: Orion, 2013)

INDEX OF NAMES

PICTURE CREDITS